W9-DBT-475

3613
M4125
1974

Theodore Lownik Library
Illinois Benedictine College
LISLE, IL 60532

61.3
612s
976

Social Work Practice

Second Edition

The Changing Landscape

CAROL H. MEYER

SOCIAL WORK
PRACTICE

Second Edition

SOCIAL WORK PRACTICE

Second Edition

118274

Carol H. Meyer

Theodore Lownik Library
Illinois Benedictine College
Lisle, Illinois 60532

THE FREE PRESS
A Division of Macmillan Publishing Co., Inc.
NEW YORK

Collier Macmillan Publishers
LONDON

361.3   M612
M612s   1976
1976

Copyright © 1970 by Carol H. Meyer
Copyright © 1976 by The Free Press
        A Division of Macmillan Publishing Co., Inc.

All rights reserved. No part of this book may be reproduced
or transmitted in any form or by any means, electronic or
mechanical, including photocopying, recording, or by any
information storage and retrieval system, without permission
in writing from the Publisher.

The Free Press
A Division of Macmillan Publishing Co., Inc.
866 Third Avenue, New York, N.Y. 10022

Collier Macmillan Canada, Ltd.

Library of Congress Catalog Card Number: 75–20949

Printed in the United States of America

printing number

1   2   3   4   5   6   7   8   9   10

Library of Congress Cataloging in Publication Data

Meyer, Carol H
   Social work practice.

   Bibliography: p.
   Includes index.
   1. Social service. I. Title.
HV40.M516 1976   361.3   75–20949
ISBN 0-02-921140-9
ISBN 0-02-921160-3 pbk.

Contents

Preface   vii

Acknowledgments   xvii

PART I

Introduction   1

Chapter 1   Dilemmas and Directions   4

PART II

Introduction   39

Chapter 2   The Way People Live: The Context of
              Social Work Practice   42

Chapter 3   Policy and Program: The Contours of
            Social Work Practice   89

Chapter 4   Frameworks and Knowledge: The
            Content of Social Work Practice   119

PART III

Introduction   165

Chapter 5   Social Work Intervention: Its Design and
            Processes   169

Chapter 6   The Differential Uses of Social Work
            Manpower   204

References   252

Index   261

Preface

THE FIRST EDITION of this book was published in 1970, and it seemed time to rewrite it. The changes in society, in knowledge, in ideas, and in perceptions reflected in the passage of these years might have taken place in a generation in a time when life moved more slowly. This rate of change (Toffler, 1970), to say nothing of its substance, is something in itself to be contemplated, especially as we have become so accustomed to it. Yet rapid changes in life style and in human expectations take their toll. As the world shifts in its contours, the character of people and the institutions they create shift accordingly; it is a condition of survival to make this adaptation. Thus we all must run to keep in place, adjust our thinking to the pressures of abrupt new awareness, balance the old against the new, and finally succeed in coping with the present reality while maintaining a clear sense of who we are. These are some of the considerations that went into the decision to rewrite this book.

What is different or more crystallized today? What data do

we examine to assess change? Has anything remained the same? Are there indicators that instruct us about the near future? How shall we ready ourselves in social work roles for the inevitable complexities that must derive from this society (Kuhn, 1962)?

In the world scene there are some newly defined issues that have lately captured the public's attention. Concerns such as overpopulation, the diminishing world food supply, international crises in finance and energy, the expansion of nuclear weapons on the world scene, and ecological imbalance in the environment are some of the issues that are now part of our social and economic vocabulary. The political lexicon has also expanded, to include the end of Vietnamization, the crisis in the Middle East, Soviet–American détente, the development of Third World countries, and of course the emergence of China as a world power. These occurrences, and their latent and manifest effects, are viewed not only as significant indices of the rapid changes that have occurred in the last seven years but also as backdrop for our narrower look at the social welfare scene which will be our major interest in this book. Even the most immediate social work activity reflects the impact of some large human event, for social work as an important institution of society depends for its survival upon its continuing relevance to the social, economic, and political scene.

In the United States social change has not been as rapid in its pace forward as it has been swift in its regression in the last seven years. The brief period of student activism and popular demands for civil rights seemed to be over as quickly as it began. The rediscovery of poverty evoked a scurry of programs and policies, but not a serious diminishment of the condition of poverty itself, or any signs of redistribution of the national income. The need for a national comprehensive health care policy has been well documented, but at this writing no such policy has become a reality. The state of public education remains uncertain except insofar as the line between inner city and suburban school systems has been more firmly drawn. The past seven years have been marked by scant attention to housing, public transportation, or beautification of cities. Inflation and recession have overtaken halting efforts at reducing hunger and unemployment, and there is a scandalous lack of planning in the social and economic arena. This social standstill, as we shall see as this book unfolds, contributes directly to the shape of social work practice in this decade.

The character of American society seems to have shifted too (Kahn, 1973, pp. 3–26). In so brief a time the intense idealism of the 1960s deteriorated into a preoccupation with a Watergate morality. The active popular movements of students, blacks, women, and other groups seeking rights, free expression, and participation in decisions affecting their lives have the air of being caught in a slow motion film; they are there, but their actions are restrained and they give the impression of never quite reaching the goal toward which they stretch. The counterculture has been absorbed by the larger society to appear in art, movies, theater, and life style. Despite the fact that people do not seem to be quite as buttoned down as they were in the 1950s, they are surprisingly silent in the face of the total assault upon them and their social institutions in the Nixon–Ford period. This conservative or self-protective pall that hovers over America has particular implications for the way in which social workers view their purposes. Social workers are not immune to the cautious times in which they live.

Obviously, social welfare programs will reflect the political and social climate; they are often good indicators of the extent to which the people's voice is heard. Yet if concerned citizens are protesting or if some enlightened people are speaking, then no one is listening. It is as if we were all waiting. But for what, or for whom? This hiatus in the progressive development of social welfare is a radical change from the hyperactivity of the late 1960s, when there was talk of total institutional change. This expectation caused a crisis within the profession of social work. Professional social workers were viewed as part of the establishment that was maintaining the status quo, and those who wanted institutional change sought to invent new kinds of social workers who would assist in turning social welfare programs around. Social casework, which was the oldest social work methodology, was associated in the minds of its critics with efforts to adjust clients to their unhappy status. Thus new methodologies were devised that would address the noxious institutional influences instead. A great deal of anger was generated among professionals within social work, and depending upon one's political or social point of view, the "new" or the "old" social work was defended or attacked within the profession and by social scientists, politicians, those in other helping disciplines, and lay people. It was in this milieu that the first edition of this book was written.

It may have been foolhardy. It was written reactively so as to salvage what was possible of the traditional social casework method, but also to demonstrate that the method was essentially applicable to the current turbulent society. It reached back to the philosophic beginnings, and it attempted to design new conceptions that would be utilitarian in the modern scene. The subtitle of the book was *A Response to the Urban Crisis*, because that is how the turbulence was being defined then.

Why write a new book at all, or more precisely, why write a revised edition of this book that was reflective of its time? In truth, in rapidly changing times a book about those times may be outdated by the time it is published and distributed. Its time has passed, and in the slow-moving social welfare scene of the mid-seventies what is there to say? Two reasons underlie the decision to do this book over, and with a new subtitle. The first reason has to do with The Free Press, the publishers who questioned professors who used the book in schools of social work. These professors were asked if they thought there was any purpose in a revision. Most of them said yes, although they differed as to what a new book should be like. The second reason has to do with the author herself, who has found it almost unbearable to read that first edition since its publication, because it seemed obvious that everything could have been said differently and better. The opportunity to do it all over again was irresistible. Here was the chance to rethink rather than react; here was the chance to see how the issues all came together; here was the chance to see if the mountains were molehills or if the new ideas about practice were indeed worth developing further. The most interesting and comforting aspect of this second opportunity is that as one scans the intervening years in social work practice, it is clear that there was a lot of activity, that the crisis of the mid-sixties propelled social workers in record numbers toward self-examination and creative thinking, and that the knowledge and methodology used by social workers have remained open and available to change even yet.

The decision to rewrite once made, we reviewed the careful comments of the professors who knew the book and what their students needed. Their comments and criticisms were decisive in molding the content of this book, but it will come as no surprise that their requirements for a new book were contradictory. It should be worthwhile, as a substantive matter, to mention some of the contradictions, for they say something important about the field of social work and its present directions.

An important question raised was whether or not a book such as this ought to be used in graduate or undergraduate programs. Associated with this was the question of its use as a basic social work textbook. The matter of a continuum in social work education and the differential use of social work personnel in practice continues to be problematical. As in the first edition of this book, the final chapter will address this matter fully. The level on which a book is written undoubtedly is crucial in the decision as to where it will be used in various types of social work education and training. It has always seemed to this author, particularly after almost two decades of teaching in graduate schools and in agency staff development programs, that intellectual preparation for social work practice should be on the highest possible level, no matter the setting in which it occurs or the stage of learner involved. Despite the fact that an undergraduate social work major will not have the same academic background as a graduate student in social work and thus will not be able to bring as much knowledge and trained skill to an idea, the idea itself must be expressed as clearly and as fully as possible. Noting that there is a world of background knowledge from which people select according to their interests and capacities, there should be no holding back of special thoughts in a book about social work practice under the assumption that the reader is not ready for them. The reader will grasp up to and even beyond his level if he is asked to have his mind stretched in a good cause. There can be no primers in a field as complicated as social work, certainly not when undergraduates and graduates have to confront equally difficult problems. The question of whether or not this or any book is to be used by graduates or undergraduates appears to be a side issue; the real question is how and in what roles these differentially educated practitioners will perform in accordance with their professional preparation. Not only is the book not geared to a particular level of student in social work, but to complicate it more, it is available to the author's colleagues at large. It is a statement of what this writer believes to be the necessary shape and direction of social work practice in the current scene, and therefore it is written in a critical vein, where simple and complex are the wrong criteria to use.

As for the question of this being a basic text, that would be an unsuitable use of this or any book in social work. There is no grand theory of social work practice, nor even middle-range theories that are universally accepted. The value of paperback books is that students particularly can select in the marketplace of ideas those approaches to practice that are most appealing, most logical, most subject to empirical investigation, most socially oriented, or even most introspectively oriented. The yardsticks used in this selection are not always rational, but they are subject to value systems held by the reader. Sometimes a school, an academic department, a favorite teacher, or a colleague will influence the student in his selection, but until there is a standardized approach to social work practice, the use of a single basic text can only lead toward intellectual closure, which is the fatal disease of a profession.

Another significant question raised by the professor commentators was whether or not this book should be written for social policy or social work practice courses. There is a measure of irony in this polarization, especially because the way practice is carried out in social work, as in any profession, is reflective of the policies that inform the practice. The process and content of social work practice are defined by the policies and programs which are their aegis. Therefore it is hoped that this book will be viewed as a social work approach to the knowledge and application of practice and policy. More to the point, it is hoped that we will be seeing less separation between these two aspects of social welfare as their interrelationship becomes more apparent. The bringing together of these two areas is the crux of this book, and will be discussed explicitly in Chapter 3. In School Bulletinese, we might refer to the process of bringing together policy and practice as cross-referencing of courses, until the day comes when these courses are joined in their purposes and core knowledge.

A third important question raised by the professors in commenting about the requirements of a new book had to do with whether it should be an updated philosophical treatment of the purpose of social work practice, or a more deliberate effort to develop skills for students as a "how to" book. This is a plaguing question, because it is so obvious that the purpose of gaining knowledge in a profession is to use it; the purpose of all professions is skillful action. Yet we can pose two issues that continue to constrain us from writing a manual of action or a skills-oriented book. The first issue has to do with unfinished business in social work, unfinished philosophical business which still requires that we explore the boundaries and purposes of our practice. The second issue has to do with the still-to-be-agreed-upon way in which the field intends to coordinate and interrelate its multiple areas of knowledge. Without a map that will shape this knowledge to the purpose and function of social work, application of skills will be a scattershot affair. A superficial listing of the kinds of knowledge presently necessary in social work may make its own point. The practitioner must know about people in a variety of roles: as family members, group members, members of communities large and small, client, patient, or consumer recipients of services, coparticipants in social action, workers, students, tenants, and dwellers in the urban, suburban, or rural scene. Individuals have personality structures, developmental needs and tasks, proclivities to relate to others, cultures, behaviors, values, and problems. Environments are variously defined, and social institutions and service agencies contain characteristics of their own that must be understood. There is yet more to be known about categories of age groups and their special needs, about socially defined problems of deviance, and about personally defined problems of unhappiness in one's life. The list is as long and as broad as the viewer's knowledge and experience allow him to comprehend it. The most immediate skill, it would appear, is the ability to put it all together, to recognize the relationships of different components in every case, to strain out the extraneous, and to be sure that the latent factors are not lost just because they are quiet.

It is true that interventive skills do not just happen after this task of knowledge mastery and integration is accomplished, but knowing what we are about and for what purposes is good insurance for purposeful, skillful action. The purposes are yet to be ground out of the practice prism, and this book will once again address the relationship between the aims and methods of practice. Furthermore, in the intervening years there have been several excellent books and articles that have presented carefully drawn skill repertoires (Goldstein, 1973; Whittaker, 1974; Pincus & Minahan, 1973). This book remains back a conceptual step.

A final critical theme related to the previous issue raised by the professors had to do with the necessity some of them saw for students to have something concrete, a "handle" with which to work. Of course concreteness develops on the job as a social worker experiences direct practice with clients. There are practice principles and practice behaviors to be learned, and some would teach these in the classroom, while others would teach them in the field itself. This book is not about those principles, but is more in keeping with the contrary theme raised by other professor commentators. Those thought it would be best to pose a thoughtful challenge to students to think out for themselves what to do in totally new situations. Some commentators spoke of the need for a model, while others appreciated the necessity for students to construct their own model. There were additional contrasting comments in this vein, arguments for more and less identification of problems, and more and less direction on what to do about them. It appears that problems with which social workers work never seem to stand still long enough for us to apply categorical solutions. Yet there are some prescriptive approaches available, and we continue to await empirical results from creative research. The book attempts to address the concerns of these comments, for they appear to reflect, even in their contradictory demands, the state of flux in which the field of social work continues.

When all is said and done, this is a new book and hardly a revision at all. It is probably an example of the way people and institutions like social work continue to adapt in a rapidly changing world; they grow and change and work out new accommodations. Under the right conditions, they sometimes change their very environments, and thus they never make peace with the way things are.

Acknowledgments

A TEACHER and friend once said that it never helps to cram for a comprehensive examination because one has prepared for it all of one's life.

So with a book it is not possible to identify the contributing person or the precipitating moment. Family, friends, teachers, colleagues, students, clients—all have made their mark, and over a very long period of time.

I am responsible for my own thought and expression, but those people have been the source and unfailing critics of my thinking. I hope this book affirms my tie to them.

Part I

Introduction

IT IS REASONABLE to ask, "What is social work?"—but it is not possible to offer a single and definitive answer. It is many things to people, depending upon the perspective from which they view it. It is an institutionalized expression of society's interest in meeting common human needs, but as we shall see, the dilemmas and questions that arise from this simple definition have plagued social philosophers, social scientists, social workers, and politicians for at least 100 years. It is the practice arm of social welfare programs, the organized activity that delivers the services devised through social policy to the citizen–consumer–client–patient. It is a profession that, with society, defines its boundaries of functioning. The profession claims its own expertise in knowledge and skill and provides for the education, training, and accrediting of its own members, but society at large, public and private auspices, and consumers also have their own expectations for the profession. Also, it is a lay activity in which community members participate as board members, taxpayers, con-

1

sumers, and overseers. Further, it is an expression of human values requiring respect for individual rights and acceptance of individual differences, support of personal freedom, and expectation of social justice. It is based upon a particular kind of knowledge drawn from social and behavioral sciences and integrated into a framework to serve social work practice aims. It is, in addition, an array of specialized skills that have evolved from a variety of methodological approaches to practice.

Although social work can be defined in any of these ways, it is unique among professions because it comprises all of these elements at once. In other words, it is not an academic pursuit where knowledge is all; it is an *activity* supported by specialized, necessary knowledge. It is not merely an expression of humane values; it must pass the test of effectiveness as well. It is not a "do your own thing" practice; it is subject to severe criteria of professional accountability. It is not an isolated set of skills; it is a practice guided always by certain knowledge, values and purposes.

One of the most important qualities of social work is that it, perhaps more than any field of practice, is systematically related to the social scene. It is a reflection of the forces in society. When those forces are forward-looking, so is social work. Of course when those social forces turn inward and become reactionary, social work as one of society's institutions tends also to follow that course. Social work may devise and influence social programs; it may lead people toward rational social policy, or it may help its clientele to confront irrational systems, but it remains a function of society at large. It has no laboratory in which it can control its practice without reference to surrounding conditions. It is this characteristic of social work more than any other that often engenders discontent, and properly so, among practitioners. Social workers continually see the harsh impact of poverty upon a struggling family, and then wonder about the validity of helping family members get along better together when money would be the best prescription. Because the political, social, and economic context of social work practice is often more powerful in its effect upon clients than the explicit skill of the worker, it is essential that this context be confronted and understood. Only then will social work practice assume meaning and purpose for client and for worker.

The withdrawal and retreat of social workers from the complex organizational and social forces that confront them at every turn often occurs from feelings of helplessness and lack of comprehension. The more we can understand about how and why clients are so vulnerable and social workers so constrained from being totally effective, the more clearly we can think about cases and perform creatively and skillfully within the limitations of reality, always reserving our critical attitudes toward social injustice in that reality.

We seek perspective on the dilemmas in which we are enmeshed, for there is no substitute in any professional practice for a sophisticated, clear-thinking truth seeker. We suffer enough delusions in our uncertain world for us not to share in any self-created ones.

Chapter 1

Dilemmas and Directions

EACH SEASON brings its own set of problems and paradoxes, and though the headings change somewhat, the essential issues remain the same. The social welfare sector in America is viewed residually (Wilensky & Lebeaux, 1958, p. 138), so that programs that might enhance the lives of people, and in some instances make it possible for them to survive, are provided begrudgingly if at all. They are devised to be a last resort when individual resources have been expended; they are not constructed as a response to changing family life and the increasing distance between the individual and resources in an urbanized, technical, and bureaucratically organized society. Despite the fact that increasing amounts of public money are spent in social welfare programs, including health, mental health, family and child welfare, services to the aged, and correctional and school services, need has overtaken expenditures. More and different needs are being defined every day by citizens and by professional experts, and there are greater expectations for services. Yet the quality of life has diminished for all economic classes, and the least advantaged groups in society remain in their downward spiral. Enter the social worker.

Following is one way of exploring the issues just described, but it should be kept in mind that there are countless ways of doing this. In keeping with our interest in describing the difficult context of social work practice, some central dilemmas will be discussed as:

1. The ambiguity of society's mandate
2. The halting development of social services: from charity to welfare to developmental services
3. The profession: its constraints and opportunities in specialization

The exploration of these dilemmas will serve as the critical backdrop for the discussion of practice. It is healthy for the mind in the spirit of inquiry to proceed from challenge rather than from positioned answers.

1. The Ambiguity of Society's Mandate

The concept of "common human needs" provided the title of a fine little book Charlotte Towle wrote over 30 years ago (1945). It was intended to instruct public assistance workers. The history of that little book is reflective of the status of social work activity, for in the fifties, during the Senator Joseph McCarthy "era," it was viewed as a subversive document and was removed from the shelves of the public agencies. The National Association of Social Workers published the book again under its own aegis, updating the case illustrations but leaving the central material relevant to the common human needs of which Professor Towle wrote so many years before. The needs changed relatively little, but an irony now appears. The provision of services never kept pace with the social definition of need, and one might suppose that the book could be reprinted in another thirty years citing the same needs, still unmet.

What are common human needs in a complex, urbanized society? Food, clothing, and shelter have remained the essentials since the age of primitive man, and these remain as unmet needs among the vast poor population in America. Qualitatively, food and shelter, or nutrition and housing, have become serious deficiencies among the population at large, as have many other amenities like public transportation, parks, and "green space" in cities, "green belts" around them, safe water supplies, sufficient energy to fuel our mechanized lives, and income that bears some relationship to the cost of survival in an urban world dependent upon money exchange for goods and services. Few would argue that these are the common human needs of the physical environment, and yet there is a steady deterioration in the quality of our lives that causes not a little astonishment in the face of the resources available in this country. Unfortunately, social work ordinarily has little political input into this aspect of life, but it surely enters the scene where discontent and outrage are the people's response. The day probably is not far off when social workers will have something important to contribute to the planning of cities and the distribution of income. For now, it is vital to face the ambiguity that despite society's expressed interest in meeting common human needs, particularly as expressed in the social environment, increasingly they remain unmet.

There are equally important physical–social–psychological common human needs that are noted by government, voluntary organizations, and citizen–consumers. These have to do with the need for physical and mental health care, and services for the aged population, children, youth, families, and special groups of people like delinquents, criminals, and other folk who are marked as deviant in our society. Specialized needs have created specialized services, but a great distance remains between affirmation and meeting of these needs.

Statistics and simple observation inform us that there is hardly an individual, family, group, or community that is untouched by the impersonal technological society in which we live. The following demographic data are cited here to offer the reader an idea of the scope of social arrangements, functioning, and dysfunctioning in the physical–psychological–social (or health and welfare) sectors of American life. There is no attempt to relate cause to effect, to account for all needs or problems in mankind, or to develop a statistical analysis. The intent is to make note of the way people are known to live, to alert us to the raw numbers and percentages so as to judge the impact of social work practice on the citizenry, and to suggest one way—perhaps the model way—of studying a problem. It always helps to know the data.

How many people were there in the United States as of January 1, 1975? There were 213,203,059 and a low net gain of 1.6 million per year continued. There were about 80 million persons under 21. How does this number break down into different family arrangements? According to the Bureau of the Census, in 1973 there were 54,373,000 families, and 95.4% of these were nonfarm families. Families headed by women make up 9.6% of all white families, 35% of all black families, and 17% of women of Spanish origin. The Census Bureau said in 1975 that 14% of all American children under age 18 are being raised by their mothers (a jump of 8% since 1960), and working mothers with children under 6 number 29.9%.

Marital status seems to be changing, in that 1973 saw the divorce rate as the highest recorded, 4.9%. According to the U.S. Public Health Service, the rate of out-of-wedlock births continues to rise; the 1970 rate nationally was 10%.

There are indices of socioeconomic failure in the 6.9 per 100 families on Aid to Families with Dependent Children (AFDC), in 21.5 per 100,000 admissions to mental hospitals, and in 20.2 per 1,000 infant mortality (Kogan & Jenkins, 1974). In 1973 the total crime index per 100,000 was 4,116.4

whereas in 1960 it was 2,126.2, according to the Federal Bureau of Investigation. In 1973 the Drug Enforcement Administration numbered known active addicts at 98,988. As for poverty itself, in 1973, before the current excessive inflation–recession economic situation was so apparent, the Bureau of the Census cited 23 million people, 15.1 million white and 7.8 million black and other minorities, as having incomes below the poverty level. More to the point, these numbers reflected 8.4% of the white and 29.6% of the black and other minority groups. The Office of Economic Opportunity stated in 1969 that children under 16 comprised 38% of the poor, and 41% of such poor children were in families headed by a woman. In 1973, the U.S. Department of Health, Education, and Welfare (HEW) reported 3,172,829 families and 11,154,542 individuals on welfare.

All of these statistics are subject to error, but they present a general epidemiological picture of the nature of the society with which social workers are engaged. Some statistics are underreported by people who have avoided the census taker, who are able to gain supports where reporting systems are not in use, or who distort data for self-protective purposes. Some government or voluntary agencies might distort statistics in order to raise more funds, gain more staff, or give evidence of success. Finally, the statistical sources are not all the same, and different years and populations may be counted, or different questions may be asked at different times.

Despite all of these limitations, the few data we have presented do indicate that we live in a nonrural country, that families—that is, two-parent families—are not as stable as they once were, that increasing numbers of single-parent families are in need of child care arrangements where the mother works, that crime, addiction, mental illness, and infant mortality remain as serious social problems, and that poverty and discrimination are undoubtedly the most significant social problems of all.

Social work services, caseloads, and practices greatly need to relate to these data in both quantity and function. Yet American social work is part of a society that assumes a laissez-faire stance as far as social services are concerned. There is no comprehensive mandate in government policy to deal with the problems in living that the foregoing data suggest are inevitable. Thus social work practices are catch-as-catch-can, and take shape according to unplanned agendas. Sometimes a particular agency, state administration, individual social worker, or community group will identify a particular clientele or problem area to attend to. This unplanned approach can develop interesting programs and can proliferate inventive approaches, but always there is the nagging thought that some people and some problems are being overlooked by oversight, because there is no real mandate. This leaves social work practice in a vulnerable position; it can address many problems and still not be accountable by mandate for even the most pressing ones. Yet the data are compelling .

The evidence suggests rather strongly that where it was once feasible for families, neighborhoods, towns, and small voluntary organizations to "care for their own," urbanization and the radical changes in the structure of the family as the center of human intimacy have created the need for social supports on a vast scale. As we shall see later, the need is for developmental services, services that will be available to people as they struggle to cope with a world increasingly given to nonhumane dimensions. Yet the structure of services in America reflects still a commitment to Social Darwinism and the fallacious assumption that everyone can achieve the physical–social and psychological supports necessary for that survival, if only he would find a job. Thus services are generally structured piecemeal, specialized groups are selected for attention, and when these groups are looked down upon anyway, services assume a residual cast and other groups are excluded from eligibility. Still the general social dysfunction remains, there is halting recognition of the evidence, and society at large does not insist upon developmental services to support people in their life tasks.

Perhaps, because people hold on to their old, familiar, and, according to the evidence, distorted views of the way society is, new and harsh changes may seem to belong to other peoples' reality. The "others" who suffer discontents are then viewed as deviants, misfits, ethnic minorities, the poor, restless youth, and so on—people who could not make it for some reason. Historically, in the Social Darwinian tradition, this reason has been identified as a flaw in character or an unfortunate accident of birth, and such a view has inhibited the growth of universal services, which would be a statement that this kind of technical society creates isolation and loss of intimate supports for all people and that thus the burden of responsibility for the easement of life should be society's. When a service such as day care, for instance, is recognized as a requirement in a family where there is a working mother, organized society, looking through its reversed telescope, unfortunately assumes that only the poorest women work (or should work) and day care is provided mainly in order to keep those women off public assistance (Rothman, 1973). Consequently, day care programs are given only the slimmest, most niggardly support, and families are discouraged from using them. Yet as we have noted from the statistical evidence of working women in this country, it is apparent that they now are part of the fabric of American life, and it is hardly credible that day care services are still viewed as un-American, antifamily, and only necessary for welfare mothers in order to keep them off relief.

As long as the new reality is not confronted, the service will be tainted as a residual, backhanded social gesture, and women—rich, middle class, and poor—will not know how to care for their children while they work. The ambiguous way in which social welfare is provided in this matter undoubtedly has to do with economic reasons to keep women out of the labor force in an era of rising unemployment. It has also to do with misunderstanding of the way in which family life is moving in this decade, with the notion that withholding of day care programs will somehow reorient families back to the hearth. Moreover, as with all socially oriented programs, day care as a nonmarketable item is low on the list of priorities for government spending.

The day care example illustrates a serious problem that preoccupies all social workers—practitioners, students, administrators, and teachers. Social services are becoming a necessity of life in the postindustrialized society, yet they are provided and structured in such ways that they severely limit the consumer's access to them; thus there is less impact felt from whatever the social worker might do to help in a case. The scope of need for services of this kind is very wide, and the field of social work is only beginning to match its interventions, once more narrowly conceived, to the breadth of need.

Social work has developed some specializations in social planning (Kahn, 1969) and organization of constituencies (Brager & Specht, 1973) intended to permeate government and other planning organizations. Of course this is the main route to formal participation in changing the structure and scope of services and identifying need from the social welfare perspective. Professional associations in and out of the social work field have entered into active political lobbying in the search for access to sources of power that actually do define needs and promote services. And there are men and women who seek changes in structures through more radical action, so as to urge on social institutions from the outside. Since there is so much to be done to meet common human needs, every bit of activity helps.

The contradiction between intent and action is most often felt by the social work practitioner, who is the one to confront the person in need, the one who is aware of how skimpy is the coverage, how shallow are the resources, and how recalcitrant are the bureaucracies. The practitioner, who must accept the blows and help in spite of all, is the one who carries the professional burden of the ambiguity of society's message. The continuing characterization of social welfare and social services as residual inevitably creates a scapegoat class among the recipients of those services and also among social workers who are associated with them. How different it is in medicine, the prestigious profession, where every citizen–consumer views himself as a potential patient, vulnerable to disease. This perception would never allow medicine or doctors to fall into disrepute for the unreal reasons social workers are tarnished.

There seem to be two options available to social workers under these conditions of criticism. The first is a long-range goal that should engage the profession with forward-looking thinkers in government and voluntary organizations. This is to seek always to devise developmental services to account for social change and the universal need of all individuals to rely on extrafamily social supports as a commonplace matter. Thus as day care, homemaker services, convalescent care, services for all age groups, and so on become available as a matter of social necessity, recipients of service will not be thought of as sick, alien, dysfunctional, or nonproductive. Then social workers will not have to feel downtrodden for being associated with services viewed as downtrodden. The second alternative has its own attractions, as can be testified to by generations of social workers who have participated happily in the role of semialienation, swimming upstream and countering social criticism as a measure of their value. Like artists whose creativity flourishes outside the established state of affairs (L. Rapoport, 1968) and like social critics, whose task it is to remain apart from the average concern, there is much to be said for social workers who will never be satisfied with the way things are and will continue to thrive in the role that serves clients best, without having to be approved of by powerful elements in society.

Meanwhile, need continues to be defined and redefined, colored by political considerations as much as by rational criteria. Services are continually invented in large- and small-scale fashion, often by young practitioners; and patchwork quilt though it is, an amalgam of social services does exist to sustain people who are caught in the most complicated personal–social situations from which they cannot possibly disentangle themselves alone. This is the arena in which social work practitioners work, still unsung but increasingly with the knowledge and skills to intervene effectively.

SUMMARY

We have noted that social work has an ambiguous and uncertain mandate. The need for social supports has gone beyond the narrow definitions of a residual framework and requires developmental service provision. Presently, social workers are frustrated—helping here and there but never enough, in their eyes or in the eyes of the public. Because of the way services are provided, programs are not comprehensive in coverage or in kind. Thus the practice dilemma remains which way to go. Which model should social workers prepare to practice in? They observe the need for developmental provision of services; but the present structure of service remains essentially residual, and that is where practice takes place. This is society's dilemma, in which social workers must play a part because of their social mandate.

2. The Halting Development of Social Services: *From Charity to Welfare to Developmental Services* (Klein, 1968; Lubove, 1965; Mencher, 1967; Woodroofe, 1962)

Social work in America evolved from voluntary agencies that came from the Elizabethan poor law matrix and the Judeo–Christian roots of charity. Humanitarian impulses and those religious concerns that were associated with saving the soul of the giver motivated the provision of voluntary social services in the eighteenth and nineteenth centuries. Sectarianism was integral to the idea of voluntarism, because when groups of private citizens joined in an organized effort to cope with family and child welfare problems especially, their common purpose was to care for their own. It is a primitive and fundamental characteristic of all ethnically bound people that they will seek ways of continuing their clan. As religious groups evolved separately and in different eras in this country, voluntarism, sectarianism, and separatism were characteristic of the first welfare efforts.

One current example of a lag between voluntarism and the welfare of the general public can be seen in the field of child welfare, although one might use any of the social work fields of practice to describe the route taken in the twentieth century from charity to welfare. On the east coast, where the American settlement brought along the English model of voluntary services, child welfare organizations developed in response to the worsening conditions brought about by industrialization. The influence of Protestant, Catholic, and Jewish voluntary social agencies in eastern states is well known, as each took care of their own groups to the extent that their own charitably inclined communities could afford to provide quality services. The influence upon social welfare of these sectarian agencies was so vast that when public facilities developed as a more realistic response to the universal condition of children in industralized families, these organizations remained in positions to authoritatively influence the programs of public agencies as well as their own. The tripartite division of voluntary agencies served their function for almost a century, and might have continued to do so but for the incursion of certain midtwentieth-century realities.

The urban crisis occurred, or at least became apparent to the public at large. This meant that black and other minority people were intent upon being counted as having need for services, and the extent of need expanded beyond any voluntary agency's capacity to cope with it. As occurred when other ethnic groups developed their sectarian agencies, the line of development in the modern scene might have been the addition of a black nonsectarian type of voluntary agency to provide social services to its own people. However, blacks were not themselves well enough organized or sufficiently endowed financially to make such a direction of effort feasible. Typically, then, the public agency through its child welfare services became the primary social agency for black families.

Racial characteristics became a differentiating factor that outweighed the religious factors. Thus therapeutic institutional facilities might be uncrowded by children of one religious (white) group and yet be unavailable to the black child who needed them, and the black child would be confined to an overcrowded public children's shelter. Or adoption agencies would seek adoptable babies for their clientele, and black adoptable babies would remain in congregate care. This anachronistic situation has been mitigated somewhat by the rise of public social welfare services, but in the voluntary agency era, social work practice flourished, developed its methods, carried out the defined programs, and became professionalized mainly in the voluntary sector.

The development of public welfare agencies in this country was spurred by the Depression and the New Deal of the Roosevelt era and was designed to cope with the effects of the social failures of industrialism. Once again in American history it became evident that unemployment and poverty were not caused by personal failure, because the entire world was suffering from economic want. Not only were voluntary agencies no longer able to afford the mounting costs of economic provision for their client groups, but also during this period it became apparent that economic security was a public responsibility because it was recognized that the society had failed (Schlesinger, 1958, chap. 16). The welfare of the public became a political issue, and the charitable age began to diminish, although it never completely disappeared.

The changing role of government in the social and economic affairs of citizens gradually influenced the public to consider that social and economic failure was a concomitant of the kind of society in which people lived and not the result of personal failure. In the ensuing forty years, from the 1930s to the 1970s, the welfare concept became enlarged to include mental health services, family and child welfare programs, medicare programs, research into the diseases of modern civilization, and social insurance against naturally expected risks of living in an industrialized world. Thus, whereas public welfare originally was concerned primarily with economic welfare, the term has evolved into something that might be called services for the public's welfare—a final assumption by government of provision of service and care, economic supports, and research into basic causes of physical, mental, and social pathologies.

But the role of professional social work practice in public agencies has been minimal, particularly when compared with its presence in voluntary agencies. Thus, while this country turned in the direction of assuming public responsibilty for the welfare of its citizens, professional social workers were barely represented in public welfare agencies. We have noted that practice methodology was devised in the voluntary agency system (Meyer, May 1973); thus the employment temptations have not been as compelling in public service agencies for professionally trained social workers.

The 1960s found the public welfare agencies in a serious squeeze between bureaucratic suffocation and extreme public pressure for the services they were mandated by law to provide. The poverty programs of the Kennedy and Johnson administrations were, in a large sense, a response to this impasse and so evolved a new organizational era, of which the *locally devised, federally supported project* was the hallmark. In the effort to bypass what appeared to be the hopeless paralysis of established voluntary and public agencies and in order to meet the increasingly vocal demand of black, Hispanic, and Mexican–American people in the cities who were not receiving their rightful services or the income maintenance that was held out to them, poverty projects that reached directly from the local communities to the federally supported Office of Economic Opportunity (OEO) became a common device for funding of services. The inclusion of the provision for maximum feasible participation of the poor in their own community projects enhanced the popularity of this form of public support of social services, for in some ways it was an ideal opportunity for people to cope directly with their own affairs.

The matter of community control is not a modern urban phenomenon, but its form differs markedly from the older town meeting. Sometimes popular demand itself—the very fact that community people are demanding their rights to a decent income and social services—is misunderstood to be a crisis, but the crisis may be rather in the halting process of government in providing people with their needs and their rights. The sense of community, whether expressed through demands in local community-controlled schools or through community-of-interest groups' pushing for escalated public assistance allowances, more flexible clinic hours, or more accessible social workers, may indeed become the very safety valve that will provide for all citizens in urban America the personal affiliation necessary to compensate for the sense of urban isolation.

But the thrust of the sixties was surely diminished with the incoming Nixon administration. The well-known threat by John Erlichman, the President's assistant, that "now social workers would be looking for honest work" of course reflected the administration's attitude toward social welfare as well. The introduction of revenue sharing with states and the decreasing federal mandate for public welfare expenditures, the complete halt in imaginative planning, the negation of day care programs, and so on speak to the total hiatus of governmental interest in social welfare programs. Ironically, this occurred at the threshold of discovery of how developmental programs might be devised.

Developmental social services are those that recognize changes in family forms, patterns of child care and socialization, relationships of the aging to the community, modes of health care, and other social responses to the urbanized, postindustrial, technological society. Developmental social services are devised on an institutional rather than a residual level, as a social effort to cope with everyone's personal reality. In one sense they may be viewed as preventive rather than therapeutic, or fashioned after a "life model" rather than a "disease model." They assume, for example, that women of all classes will continue to work outside of their homes, so child care will be a necessary service as part of the development of family life. They assume that as people live longer in this mobile society where family ties are becoming increasingly fragile, varied facilities for care of the aged will also be a necessary service, to take the form of everything from meals on wheels to total institutional care. They assume that medical progress will place a greater burden upon community facilities for care of the mentally and physically ill, so a range of services will have to be devised to allow for patients to thrive outside of medical facilities.

Developmental services provide for the strategic location of social supports at the interface between the citizen and the community. Eligibility for these services is gained through status, such as age, parental role, or functional requirement. This kind of eligibility for services is defined by the recognized need, not by the person's personal character; one has only to be a working mother, an aged person, an ex-patient, a child, a young person, or a person with a predefined handicap, etc.

Eligibility for developmental services differs markedly from our historical experience with the concept of eligibility.

The charity movement associated need with good moral character, a deserving attitude, and ambition to strive. The welfare movement associated need with less eligibility, with proof of destitution, and also with some of the features of good moral character as seen in the charity movement. Social insurances, the closest organizational form to developmental services, were associated with past employee contributions to the programs. As we shall explore later, the therapeutic movement in social work associated need with some personal features of motivation, conflict, ego capacity, intelligence, verbal ability, and the like. The social aim of provision of developmental services is far from being accomplished, for while it might seem to be a rational social goal, our present society continues with its other agendas, and the road to social provision remains strewn with the same familiar ambiguities.

SUMMARY

Historically, social work practice found its milieu in voluntary settings. As public agencies have developed in the last forty years, professional social work has had a limited practice role, and in the 1960s war on poverty no role at all. The dilemma to be confronted here is whether or not professional social workers will be able to define a practice role in developmental services, even were they to evolve in the near future.

3. The Profession: Its Constraints and Opportunities in Specialization

Since Abraham Flexner in 1915 asked the question "Is social work a profession?" (Flexner, 1915), many social workers have sought to demonstrate that it is, while others have restrained themselves from a professional commitment or haven't cared. The drive toward professionalism is under-

standable in a technical society where status does indeed
come from the symbols and trappings of expertise, if not its
substantive content; it becomes a matter of self-preservation
for practitioners in all fields of public service to draw their
own circles within which no outsider may enter. Social
workers particularly, who have traditionally worked in host
agencies where the primary services are medicine, psychiatry,
law, and institutional care, have felt the need to define themselves as professionals. The whole society is becoming more
specialized in the services it provides, and social workers are
only as human as every one else.

The critical issues about the state of social work practice
do not derive essentially from the drive toward professionalism, but rather from the preoccupation with it. The hallmark of professionalism is the guarantee of service and protection to the public (Greenwood, 1957), and we would
surely not quarrel with this aim. A second characteristic of
professionalism is the presence of specialized knowledge, a
theory of practice and of the object of practice that is exclusive to the particular professional pursuit. Again, we ac-
claim the presence of such knowledge, for it enriches the
practice of social work and thus the services provided to
people. It matters little that social work is essentially a
borrower of knowledge from social and behavioral sciences.
It puts together this borrowed knowledge in very particular
ways for very particular uses. The way in which social work
utilizes basic knowledge of human behavior and social systems
is what gives social work its stamp.

The question of social work expertise and special knowledge is a complicated one. Many professions have carved out
pieces of life to which they address their skills, even though
the boundaries of their expertise may at times have seemed
blurred. For example, whatever the likenesses between the
doctor and the nurse, the physicist and the biologist or
chemist, or the lawyer and the diplomat, there is seldom
question about the basic identity of the professional practi-

tioner in question. He has the reputation of at least having knowledge about very particular aspects of life and what to do about them. What is the knowledge arena in which the social work practitioner functions?

It is said that the boundaries of social work practice could encompass all of society, the whole individual, the range of conditions from health to pathology, and a very large repertoire of skills addressed to improved individual coping, institutional change, and social policy and planning, and the list grows longer as social workers become part of new social inventions. In effect, it would seem that there are hardly any boundaries to the knowledge that is necessary for social workers to have just in order to get through a working day. Whereas other professional specialists become expert by narrowing their knowledge parameters, social workers must expand beyond measure to broaden horizons of knowledge. Furthermore, the difference between "hard" and "soft" knowledge is more real than apparent when one compares the biologist's laboratory with the social worker's community or agency as the focus of his action.

Social workers deal with unknown and perhaps unknowable complexities in human life; the causes of human stress are multiple and their etiology cannot always be discovered. The kind, scope, and depth of knowledge sought for and needed in social work practice make imperative the borrowing we have mentioned and differentiate the social worker from other professional practitioners. In a way the clergyman could be perceived similarly. He is accountable to society for values that belong to everyone, concerned as he is with the total human condition as well as for interpretation of metaphysical spheres. But unlike the social worker, the clergyman is not asked to prove that his methods work, nor is he expected to solve the unknowns like the afterlife which are related to his area of competence.

Specialization in social work was inevitable, for it would be impossible for a single practitioner to become expert in the extensive range of problems and the methods devised to resolve them. At present, social work is organized or departmentalized in several ways, some of which intersect and overlap others.

Fields of practice as a concept has actually grown up with the entire field of social work (Bartlett, 1961; Kahn, 1965; National Association of Social Workers, 1962; Studt, 1966). Thus previously social workers identified such services and methods as family services, child welfare, psychiatric social work, medical social work, corrections, and school social work. These defined practices derived specifically from the settings in which social work traditionally had been carried on. In an effort to move away from the mark of apprenticeship and to provide for generic education and practice which would not be colored entirely by the specific setting, the concept of fields of practice made provision for the practitioner to become expert in a larger arena than a particular agency; he could move within his general field as a specialist in child welfare, family welfare, etc.

This approach to the concept of fields of practice gave social work trouble, however, because it was unnecessarily restrictive in an era when nonspecified settings and fields were opening up new vistas of service—for example, community psychiatry, labor unions, civil rights organizations, housing complexes, and as yet unspecified social utilities and developmental services. Social work could not expand its scope by continually adding on new kinds of settings; sooner or later the definitions of where practice was to occur had to be reconceptualized. Another reason for the restrictions involved in the early concept of fields of practice was that the single-purpose agency or the single-function field had become dysfunctional for our times. The mobility of the population, the view of the systemic interrelatedness of all aspects of people's lives, and the multiplicity of causation for all psycho-social problems made it difficult to perceive the psycho-social situation as divisible into fields that were once convenient for organizational purposes but not necessarily for the people being served.

It is common that when a client goes into a single-function agency, he tends to define his problem, or it is defined for him, in accordance with the function of that agency. Thus if he has a marital problem and his child somehow gets caught in the middle of his struggle with his wife, a man who goes to a child welfare agency may erroneously view placement of his child as a solution to his situation. The traditional division into fields of practice may have contributed to the critical state of social work practice, because the concept did not follow the natural life style of people in trouble, and it forced upon its clientele a mold that was originally best suited to a practice that was attempting to professionalize itself.

The current use of the field-of-practice concept goes beyond the specifics of setting and the method associated with the setting. Generally the fields are called family and child welfare, health, mental health, corrections, and schools. Depending upon how legislation, funding, and community and special professional interests further divide up the fields, one may construe aging, addictions, alcoholism, housing, etc., as specific fields. The modern feature of this classification is that these fields connote true specializations in knowledge of problems, people, organizational structure, legislation, policies, programs, and practices that are significant to the particular field. While the benefits of specialization may accrue, the profession will have to be alert not to repeat its history, not to allow itself to be locked into discrete and isolated areas of expertise without continued awareness of the commonness binding all fields of practice.

Another kind of specialization that grew from the unformed matrix of social work practice had to do with methodology. Thus, where fields of practice would remain a constant factor, casework, group work, community organization, administration, staff development, and research were the variables that described the social work method specialities. We will deal differently here with the first three methods, because it is evident that the last three would be applicable to all fields of practice or all arenas in which social work practice is carried on.

The defined practice methods of *social casework, group work,* and *community organization* all evolved unevenly. Considering the range of times covered by the development of each of the methods, it would be a major historical achievement to draw clarifying comparisons among them. Each took its own route through history, having been concerned with its particular unit of attention and influenced by its own reference groups, favorite knowledges, and specific subcultures. It is not the aim of this book to trace the histories of the separate methods, nor to evaluate the impact upon human life of one or all of them. We shall come upon the scene only in the present, when the concerns and sometimes the techniques of the three methodologies *appear* to have converged (Meyer, in Kahn, 1973).

The lack of agreement in the field of social work as to viewing the three methods in a unified way has created much confusion for all concerned—students, clients, practitioners—who see so much that they hold in common, but must call to each other over such vast historical and theoretical distances. It would seem that a holistic view of man in society would not rely on disparate views of him as an individual, in a group, or as a member of a number of communities. Despite the fact that all three methods share similar professional values and certain areas of knowledge and that all three constitute the practice of social work (Bartlett, 1970), presently there still are real and imagined jurisdictional disputes that make it difficult to combine the methods into one significant practice.

Of course the higher the level of abstraction, the closer one can get to agreement, but we must be careful to avoid the Scylla of reductionism while staying out of the way of the Charybdis of separatism. It would be as wrong to prematurely melt down into one mold the three different methods as it would be to maintain their different directions for the sake of the territorial imperative alone. Nor is it simply a matter of going back to the drawing board, because the three methods have by now become institutionalized and therefore have certain latent as well as overt functions for their practitioners.

There have been efforts in recent years to bring together the three methods in social work education (Briar, 1968), where students are taught from the beginning that they are "generic" practitioners, and they utilize knowledge and skills that indeed suggest that this long-sought-for integration has been accomplished. Other educational efforts have addressed each method separately and have attempted to broaden the repertoire of skills and techniques. Thus, instead of approaching the problem from the point of view of a basic integration of casework, group work, and community organization, the second view has suggested that techniques could be borrowed and utilized easily within the expanded primary method with which the student or practitioner is identified.

It is obvious that the nature of the social problem being addressed should determine the kind of method used, but it is still a present fact that each method in social work views work with individuals, groups, and communities from its particular perspective. There are many good historical reasons for the compartmentalization of the three methods, some having to do with the political and economic developments of the eras in which each speciality became connected with organized social work, for each approach was intended to serve a particular function for society. These functions have changed as society has changed. Also, the expansion of knowledge has made it impossible for professional practitioners in all fields and methods to become experts in everything attended to by the particular profession of each. The world is very complicated, and no one can know everything.

The search for methods of practice preoccupies theoreticians, for it is always hoped that a literal image will finally instruct the social worker about what to do. Model building usually rests upon empirical testing of probable occurrences, or at least upon accumulated experiences set forth in an orderly and objective way. Thus a model of how a thing should work, given certain inputs, is erected piece by piece for the practitioner to copy and achieve the predicted results claimed by the model. Models are used in the physical sciences and in economics, where it is assumed that certain variables can be controlled or are relatively stable. The ultimate model can be seen in a planetarium, where the planets are located and revolve with mathematical certainty around the sun. The trajectory of a spaceship can be plotted with total accuracy because spatial laws are dependable. In medicine, given the normal skeletal structure and placement of vital organs, working from a model it is possible to predict the outcome of specified medical procedures. When mathematics and physics are the sciences involved, models are a requirement for further research and practice.

In the social and behavioral sciences, and most particularly in an applied field like social work, we are short on certainty and dependable outcomes. Prediction is possible when the most narrow expectations are conceived, but as variables are added, only the foolhardy will predict with certainty. For example, one might expect a bright child to succeed in school, but when we complicate his situation and describe his disturbed mother, his unemployed and enraged father, and his overcrowded school and impatient teacher, then the prediction about his success must be qualified. As a result of the ever-changing variables with which social workers are confronted in each case, and simply because social phenomena will just not stand still long enough to be counted or controlled, there are no real models in social work. This does not leave the practitioner without any image of how to practice, however, because the field is full of approaches to practice that provide action principles based upon a wide range of theories (Meyer, in Smith College Bulletin, 1973).

Practice approaches in social work are based upon the recognition that things are not going well for people in their environment. Depending upon the approach in use, breakdown is located within the person's psychic structure, in his psycho-social development, in his relationships with family or group members viewed as breakdown in communication or conflict in goals, or among people who are particularly vulnerable to the impact of social and economic forces in the environment. In social work's history there has been a continuing emphasis on person-in-situation, or psycho-social, pressures in an effort to practice from a holistic perspective. Some approaches emphasize the bio-psycho-social strains within individuals, while other approaches concentrate on the difficulties created by the environment. Depending on the approach to practice, either person or environment could be the object of change. However, newer approaches seeking to avoid this polarity consider the person–situation as an ecological unit, and seek to right their mutual maladaptations (Germain, 1973).

Different action processes are applied to each of these approaches, as the following chart should help to clarify:

Methodology

Processes	I Person	II Family	III Group	IV Community	The Environment
Intra-psychic	X				Social institutions Laws, politics Social policies and programs
Inter-actional		X	X	X	Economic class Cultural, racial, ethnic factors
Trans-actional	X	X	X	X	School, jobs, housing Environs Life style

In view of the fact that each of the above possible configurations has particular theories and skills, as well as traditions, adherents, and a professional literature associated with them, they have long enjoyed the status of *method* specializations in social work (Perlman, 1966). There is no agreement in the field as to which approach is most acceptable, so they proliferate, sometimes complementarily, sometimes in competition with each other. Recent efforts at combining methods are salutory because they mitigate the tendency to specialize in work with clients in only one role. The blurring of role categories is more consonant with the way people actually live their lives as individuals and as members of families, groups, and communities. Helpful though these methods and processes have been to people, it is unfortunate when they assume primacy as the lens through which the field looks at social work clients, problems, and practice.

There are limitations of this perspective, because when a professional practice is equated with a methodology, no matter its dimensions, the processes rather than client need tend to define who is seen, for what problems, and toward what ends. This determination, as we shall see, may rule people out of service, may prejudge the kind of service needed, or may use method and skill inappropriately as ends rather than as means toward other objectives.

Professional practice is defined by its responsiveness to society's expression of need for particular services that a profession is able to provide. Professionals in social work practice, including its major methods of casework, group work, and community organization, have accumulated techniques to cope with certain specified requirements of society. The underlying social work values they hold in common are quite up to date, in that they explicitly observe the dignity of the individual man and his right to self-determination and self-fulfillment. Traditional principles used in social work have worn well in this new participatory society, for manipulating social resources on behalf of the client and serving as advocate are important among these principles. Social work, perhaps more than any other field of endeavor, has served at the expressed behest of organized society through its social agencies and social services in hospitals, clinics, courts, schools, and institutions. It is a field that has had a great deal of experience in putting into practice society's prevalent values.

Yet despite its apparent utilitarian functions, as a field it is in an uncertain state due in large measure to its integral connections with the unplanned society in which we live; as social programs have developed haltingly in the United States, so has social work. At present the world in turmoil provides mixed messages to social work practice, which responds in kind. Its aims need to be rearticulated periodically in order to remain in touch with the world itself. As for the profession's interests, it would seem essential that practitioners of all persuasions come to agreement about the major aims of social work and their particular place among its wide range of activities.

SUMMARY

Efforts to specialize in methods, settings, and practices with particular kinds of people seem to have contributed to the narrowing scope of social work practice.

There are indications that specialization in fields of practice, where social workers would be experts in all aspects of one field such as health, family and children's services, or corrections, will be the direction of the future practitioner. This then will locate practice knowledge and skills in the context of a range of organizations and service programs. Comprehension of relevant legislation, manpower allocation and utilization, and multiplicity of client problems will produce well-rounded social work competence. The resultant direction in practice will be toward an inevitable broadening of the social worker's repertoire of methods and skills and a greater inclination toward inter-disciplinary work.

Ambiguous Professional Goals

Out of zeal, social workers sometimes have made promises they could not keep, as when they said they could improve the condition of the poor through rehabilitative services, when what was actually needed by the poor was money or opportunity for employment. This is probably one of the most vulnerable aspects of the long history of social work practice. The Social Darwinian concept that held the individual responsible for the economic condition of his life was the framework within which social work practice addressed the problem of poverty. Social workers were not alone in holding this view; it was the prevalent view of an early industrial society that found derivatives of Social Darwinism functional as a way to cope with poverty without affecting the economic system.

The richest period of development of social casework methods occurred during the time that practitioners were attempting to strengthen the poor to cope with their lives. This direction of practice was undoubtedly a contributory factor to the restraint of government in addressing itself to the condition of poverty that was being created by the inequities of society and not by the characterological weaknesses of the person who was poor. In effect, the more successful the rehabilitative measures were in individual cases, the more it could be demonstrated that the person was capable of overcoming his poverty, and thus was basically responsible for having been poor, unemployed, and ill-housed.

In the past decade it was hoped that the civil rights thrust and a great deal of intellectual ferment might have contributed to the potential demise of Social Darwinism. It is becoming clearer to society at last that the solution to poverty is a more equitable distribution of money; the solution to unemployment is jobs; the solution to illiteracy is education;

and the solution to discrimination is equal opportunity. In no area of society's failure to provide for all citizens decent standards of living and working are social work practice and social services still expected to be effective or worthwhile. As an institution of society, social work has reflected the best and the worst movements of thought in that society; it can do no more. Perhaps in the present time, social work will be freed of its previously unclear commitment to cure or treat conditions of life that are not within its capacities to improve.

On another level, in those areas of social pathology that are not strictly subject to political or economic change, social work has been associated with problems of juvenile delinquency, illegitimacy, child abuse, family breakdown, mental illness, and the anomic effects of social and economic failure. It would be safe to say that the limited solutions forthcoming from the years of social work attention to these problems have been limited, and criticism of practice deficiencies in the arena of social work expertise is certainly no mere quibble. These failures may be ascribed partly to a severe lack of basic knowledge of causation and partly to systemic features of all the problems mentioned, where the multiple causes have reached into all aspects of living and thus cannot be channeled by social work any more than by law, medicine, or education alone. It is somewhat paradoxical that in medicine the doctor is not held responsible for the diseases he does not yet understand, and the lawyer is not identified with increases in crime, yet social workers are often held accountable for psycho-social pathology that they do not yet understand or that are not amenable to any known methods. Nevertheless, it is obvious that there is need for massive efforts in basic social research in the field of social work. Typically, in the last decade when research became a popular tool in social work, it has been addressed to evaluation of methods and services and not primarily to basic causation of problems (Beck, 1962; H. Meyer et al., 1965;

Mullen & Dumpson, 1972; State Communities Aid Association, 1968).

On a third level, as we noted earlier, the fact of social work's association with the deprived people in our society may have also contributed to the criticism of the field and have affected its goals. It is well known that lawyers do not like to have social work "bleeding hearts" on their juries, that the "do-goodism" of social workers is an epithet, and that the negative feelings of some citizens about minority groups, the poor, the sick, the disabled, and the delinquent citizens in this country will be displaced onto social workers because they are in a field that is attempting to give service to deprived people. The person in trouble, be he client, tenant, patient, probationer, parolee, or other consumer of social welfare services, is generally the very person who is in difficulty with the society that provides the service or who is unable for psycho-social reasons to cope by himself in society. Thus social workers function in social agencies that are only tolerated by the larger society, in behalf of individuals who are viewed as not having made it, or as disadvantaged and thereby threatening to the normal order of life.

The unpopularity of the cause of social work has been both its major value and the chief reason for its disparagement. No other profession can make this claim. The irony appears when social workers themselves succumb to this kind of criticism and find it to be of greater value to their self-esteem literally to leave the field of unpopular case problems and turn to those that will make them feel less downtrodden themselves.

Finally, there is an organizational level on which social work has been associated with the agency, which might itself be the perpetrator of the social problem. Thus the goals of the agency are viewed, often correctly, as the goals of practice. For example, public housing may erect a functional but unappealing housing complex, set up strict rules of behavior for tenants, and devise stringent eligibility practices. When a social worker is hired to give social services to the tenants or to make the project community present fewer difficulties to the management, the social worker is asked to undo the effects of the management's self-imposed restrictions. He must help the tenants overcome the effects of the ugliness of the project, help them obey the rigid rules or plead for their revision, and ease the eligibility system by readying tenants to enter or by referring those who are excluded.

The alternatives available to the practitioner in this typical situation of organizational self-defeat are very limited. He might refuse to work in the project; he might organize the tenants to rebel against discriminatory practices; he might select advocacy procedures; or he might do the best he can to help the tenants cope with a dysfunctional housing system, while chipping away at its policies. As the practitioner pursues any of these courses of action, he will be subject to criticism by the housing management, the tenant, or the militant social reformer.

Another example of the organizational bind in which the well-meaning practitioner is often caught can be found in public assistance agencies. Legislation, budgetary limitations, and public attitudes combine to promote a dysfunctional program of income maintenance. Budgets are unmanageable, eligibility rules are exclusive, administrative policies are restrictive, and the total atmosphere reflects a philosophy of less eligibility. Moreover, outside of the agency itself, inequities in society having to do with unfair income distribution, lack of job opportunities, and discrimination against already disadvantaged people create the necessity for public assistance as a residual and palliative social program. The social work practitioner, then, in a public department of social services associated with such public assistance programs, is expected to help clients adjust to the fundamental inequities in society as well as to the poor law provisions of the agency. Thus the social worker becomes part of the inequitable system and subject to criticism, even while he attempts to ameliorate the effect of the system upon the people being served.

We have commented in this section about the plight of the social work practitioner who is associated with the ills of society and the dysfunctional systems created by society to cope with its problems. The social worker is in a position of being damned if he does and damned if he doesn't. It is in the nature of his work to be in such a position. His necessary association with the social work agency establishment and his lack of technical solutions to the problems the agencies seek to resolve will always subject him to criticism.

The fact is that social work is a compensatory field of practice, as are many professional helping fields. Were the society going well, were people happy and comfortable, were there no illness and poverty and delinquency and social breakdown, there would be no need for social workers. Will the fine day ever come when they will be out of a job? It would appear unlikely that we are on the threshold of a utopian society; it would be fruitless to pursue the end of perfectability. The present imperfect urbanized society will probably continue to create its own limitations, and social workers—or some helping people—will continue to be called upon to help mitigate the severe psycho-social problems of society. These are the elements of the dilemmas of the profession.

Cause and Function

In 1929 Porter R. Lee challenged social work to keep in balance cause and function (Lee, 1929), and the field has yet to maintain this balance. Social work has both cause or ideals, and function or technical capacity, complementarily and integrally.

In the first quarter of this century, when the transition from a rural to an industrialized society was in process, the inevitable social ills of child labor, outdoor poor relief, the explicit translation of the Elizabethan poor law, and exploitation of the worker and the poor were paramount concerns to early social workers. In this "cause" phase of social work, charismatic and highly individualistic social reformers literally stormed the barricades to bring to public and official attention the harrowing scope of social injustice. By the 1940s, when the Depression had led to enormous organizational reforms, the old charitable, benevolent voices that sought social change were themselves transformed into administrative channels, and the unique expressiveness of the reformer was obscured by the constraints placed upon him by the official chair he occupied. However, today we still hear the cry "Where is the social reformer of yesterday?"

Of course he is gone, or more explicitly he has taken the leadership of a vast social welfare bureaucracy. Once in a while he serves as a representative of professional social work to plead a just social cause to the Congress, but, again, in a depersonalized role as an interpreter of issues and not as a personal leader. Occasionally we find the social reformer of our day as magazine writer or panelist on radio and television shows, and through these media he must compete with the uncounted other demands upon the eyes, ears, and passions of the multimedia-ed public. Finally, we see the social reformer in politics, not often elected, but often provided with a platform on the dais or at the parade.

Whatever mold the social reformer as a personality has had in the past, his personal influence today has decreased, and he has been replaced by institutionalized programs of reform and the ideologies of reform that are expressed most virulently in university settings. Social reform is still vital as a necessary check upon democratic conservatism; it is only that the voices of social reform seem to have become institutionalized.

What of the role of social work practice in social reform —or social change, as we now call it? There are a range of positions that can be taken about this matter. We can view social change roughly on three levels, and they are not often compatible even though proponents of different modes of change might view social problems in the same way. We can assume there would be some agreement that our social institutions, mainly those of the health, education, and welfare complex, are sometimes dysfunctional for this urban and technical age. One mode of change would address the basic institutions themselves, and its adherents would seek to rearrange the structures, roots of power, and perhaps the auspices of these institutions so as to free them from outworn bureaucratic strictures, class affiliations, and political positions. An example might be found in the change of public assistance to social insurance programs to provide for more equitable income maintenance on a massive scale. Perhaps even before this, one might propose more radical measures to redistribute income in the country, but it would be safe to say that the fate of any such proposals for fundamental economic change in this country appropriately rests in the political rather than in the social work practice arena.

Another example would be the whole matter of housing, where social change would occur through urban redevelopment rather than through the piecemeal housing arrangements that have proved to be so inadequate. The level of social change sought here would be basic to the institutions themselves, for it would be understood that those institutions are to a large degree responsible for the troubles people have in getting help from them.

At the other extreme, where the same assumptions may exist about the causes of dysfunctional health, education, and welfare institutions, social change as a concept would not be addressed at all to the institutions themselves, but rather to the individual in an effort to strengthen him to cope with the personal effects of institutional lacks. Proponents of this approach may feel inadequately prepared to cope with fundamental attacks upon society, or may actually hold still to the Social Darwinian belief that it is the individual's lacks that inhibit him from overcoming the institution's shortcomings.

The polarity of these positions about social change reflects the dilemma for every social work practitioner of social conscience, just as the lack of a cure for cancer must affect every general medical practitioner, as every overcrowded school must affect every good teacher, and as every strike of a civil service staff must affect a socially conscious mayor. Indeed, it is very hard to argue that, *given equal alternatives,* social workers ought to refine their practices so that people can be helped to survive the inequities in our society, rather than that they ought to address all of their expertise to a thoroughgoing change or revolution of society itself. Yet the hard fact is that there are no equal alternatives, and that this country is not on the brink of a revolution at this present moment. It seems increasingly unlikely that a total and systemic forward looking change is going to occur in our society now. Moreover, if such a radical movement were to occur, it would undoubtedly be more effectively carried out by the aroused masses of the poor, the black community, and youth than by social workers in their roles as practitioners.

There is yet another option, a middle level of social change, or direct practice, the aims of which may include focus upon both the individual and the institution in an effort to improve the conditions of life in this imperfect society. It seems to us circular reasoning to state that a practice of any kind is irrelevant while the conditions persist that require that practice. Who can deny the presence of inequity in our society? Social work practitioners must affirm it and, as *practitioners,* devote themselves to ways of mitigating the conditions, as well as the effects upon people. The position taken by this book is that the social work practitioner must recognize the issues—both the social problems and the criticisms about social work failures to act—and then take action through practice measures to deal with institutional dysfunction and with the people who need the services of the institutions. Among the consequences of highlighting cause is this joining of technical competence or function so that their balance is maintained.

The constraints on practice are manifold, the problems are immense, and there is only moderate scope to social work practice tools. Yet there is no other profession that is prepared to address the general human needs of people. It is the essential purpose of social work to individualize need and to provide for the growth and development of people in the society with which they transact. The intermediate function of establishing a fit between a person and the source of his functioning, that ecological unit of attention that belongs so uniquely to social work, can be effected through many arrangements and permutations of services and skills in the form of social work practice.

The decision to be a social work practitioner implies a readiness to deal with the immediate problems and concerns of people in their environments. The surrounding dilemmas we have just cited are important to recognize so that the limitations and opportunities in the practice role are clear. People who need help are subject to social, economic, physical, and psychological strains. The practitioner must know all he can about those strains, as well as about the professional dilemmas and ambiguities within which he works. The awareness of these realities will enable the social worker to assume an accountable stance, to practice with a purpose in mind, and to know the difference between rhetoric and competence.

Part II

Introduction

PART II is concerned with the shaping of social work practice; with the variables that house social work methodologies. Just as one cannot tell a book by its cover, one cannot tell a social worker by the skills he uses. The helping professions are seen to have much in common if one views *what their practitioners do as* treatment, rehabilitation, mediation, counseling, and so on. The psychiatrist, clinical psychologist, psychiatric nurse, marital counselor, family therapist, social worker, pastoral counselor, and guidance teacher all function as professionals, all share in a common body of knowledge, all hold value systems that govern their actions; and although each claims special purposes for his work, increasingly the lines between their functioning are blurred, and more often than not it is accidental to whom the client goes for his help.

In order to differentiate social work from the others, we first have to consider its special purposes. A commonly accepted purpose for social work is the improved social functioning of the client, but as valuable an objective as this is, it surely cannot be claimed as unique among other's professional purposes. Another purpose for social work is said to be the easement of the adaptations between client and environment at their interface. Now we begin to move into an arena where no other profession has laid its claim, and thus this may be a unique purpose of social work. A third purpose idiosyncratic to social work has to do with its socially mandated role to individualize people and link them with the social, psychological, health, financial, correctional, and school services and help they need. The harsh fact of the matter is that social workers do not agree as to their professional purposes; therefore it continues to be very difficult to develop general practice modalities, to build a necessary knowledge base through research, and to teach students about what social work is. Without agreement about purpose, practitioners in social work find it difficult to sort out their work from other disciplines, but more seriously, they sidestep the implications of their professional purpose and become preoccupied with methodology as if it were all there was to practice. This emphasis, of course, leads us back to the first problem of having to differentiate from the skills of other helping disciplines.

It is our thesis that because social work is *uniquely* accountable for meeting individualized psycho-socially defined human need in the highly complex postindustrial society, all practice efforts must be associated with and derive from the conditions in which people live, their changing family structures and life styles, and the associations they are forced to make in order to live as well as possible, maintaining a sense of their own uniqueness. In other words, the best test of a social work practice theory is its relevance to the real world. Social change has overtaken traditional "oughts" about the way things should be, and even clinically defined "norms" of behavior have been displaced by new life styles that have been absorbed into the culture at large.

Chapter 2 will discuss the ways in which people live in the mid-seventies in America and the ways in which their changing family lives have created the necessity for an array of services. Social work's special purposes and related individualizing methods have, for good or ill, placed the profession at the fulcrum, the interface, between those services and the citizen–client in need. This is then the *context* of social work practice, the way people live.

Chapter 3 is concerned with the *contours* of practice, or the way problems, services, and clients get defined. The linkage between the client in his life "out there" and his direct contact with the social work practitioner is affected by social policy and the available programs of service. It is social policy that determines how the work of the profession will be classified, or how the pie will be divided so that client need is identified and social work resources are allocated. Social work is not an entreprenurial profession; it is governed by funding, legislators, board members, and, of course, the consumer group itself. It would be impossible to explain practice in social work without examining that dimension.

Chapter 4, the last in this part of the book, addresses the *content* of social work practice. Here we will explore the "map" of social work cases, the framework and structure that uniquely identify a social work problem. Naturally the knowledge base of practice belongs here as the underpinning of its content, and we will identify some substantive matters that will complete the shaping of practice, except for intervention itself, which will be discussed in the third part of the book.

Thus we look at the context, contours, and content of social work practice so as to offer the practitioner a bedrock, a perspective, a purposeful structure from which he can depart to design his interventions and apply his skills in interviewing, in group leadership, in developing resources or modifying institutions through advocacy. The questions of why and for what purposes seem to have priority, and in any case they call upon the most satisfying skill of all, the ability to conceptualize what we do, to measure reality against the abstract, to dream of how things might be, to have a plan ahead of us always, a sense of purpose to make every word and action meaningful as part of the whole.

Chapter 2

The Way People Live: The Context of Social Work Practice

THERE ARE MANY WAYS to determine what people need from social workers. One can locate a service at the crossroads of life, observe the way people live, the strains they are subject to from their environments and their relationships, and the ways they react to these events. Through anticipating from knowledge of people and their environments which populations will be "at risk," one can structure services accordingly so that they will be available when needed. Or through clinical–normative measures, one can formulate theories about the way people should react, given certain variables and based upon selected frameworks of knowledge. Then, when people in some way, as signaled by their behavior or expressions of discontent, fail to meet these theoretical criteria, one can offer help. Finally, one can ask people, through survey methods, what they need and respond accordingly, politics, funding, legislation, and imagination willing. However the assessment is made, it is always most important, in assessing human need, to remember that people live real lives in real social situations. This context, once understood, must color the social worker's comprehension of the problem at hand and, ultimately, the direction of his interventions.

Many illustrations come to mind, and the imaginative reader should be able to discover for himself some implications for practice as he ponders the way people live. For example, we now recognize as an American life style the changing forms and influences of the family in our society, and the accommodations to these that young people have found necessary to make. Nuclear families increasingly live apart from their families of orientation, and particularly in urban living it is difficult for extended families to live contiguously. This is due to unplanned housing development, urban renewal that often desecrates natural neighborhood ties, and small living quarters in cities. Further, social mobility and transience play havoc with permanent friends and neighbors, and small nuclear families must go it alone, especially once they begin to move out of ghettos, where overcrowding ironically provides better for continuance of extended family ties. Kinship ties are differently maintained in different ethnic groups, but in this open society there are many alternatives outside of family life for personal gratification.

Knowing as we do that adolescents in their striving toward identity seek from their parents the freedom to come and go and supports from their peer groups to reaffirm their identity (Lidz, 1968, pp. 298–360), it is inevitable that they will need to escape at times from the closeness of their own families. In simpler times and possibly still in rural areas, a young person could flee to a grandparent's house nearby, or to a long-time neighbor, for solace. These resources are not so available anymore, and yet the bio-psycho-social need of the adolescent remains the same. In quieter times, the young girl or boy who did "run away" certainly was not exposed to or tempted by the wonders of drugs, sex without restraint, and the complex enticements in this society. Thus there are some issues of safety involved today for the urban Huck Finn; there are not only physical and social issues but also subtle psychological issues. Sometimes young adolescents are not able to absorb the shocks of freedom, and there are very few havens that have evolved spontaneously.

This social vacuum, one effect of the evident life style of runaway youth in the present society, is where the social worker might enter. This is the time to invent crash pads for young people, a place to go when expectable tensions mount. A practitioner located at the crash pad or at the access point where the service could be offered would have his individualizing work cut out for him. Through use of his repertoire of methods, tensions could be eased, the young person could better handle his crisis, his parents could be helped to accept this transitional state, and other young people in the crash pad would be an ideal group to work together with on what it means to grow up.

This "case" of social work practice in the real world could not occur without our understanding that housing patterns, changing family structures, youth identity crises, frantic parents, and the search of youth for their peers are all interactive phenomena that serve as the context for services and practice. Moreover, the "case" is a picture of reality; it is not presented as an example of pathology found in the clinic. The social worker gets his clues for action from the way things are, and his knowledge (of housing patterns, family structure and functioning, identity crises, feelings, attitudes and behaviors of the family members involved, group processes, and how agencies like the crash pad can be made most functional and well-serving) guides him to anticipate dysfunction, to make judgments about points of intervention, and to evaluate outcomes.

In the context of the following pages we should be able to identify other types of "cases" that derive from the way people live. It will become clear that the dimensions of practice are complex and, most important, that skills are only meaningful when they serve specific purposes. It would seem to be apparent that simple skills, when viewed outside the context—and, as we shall see later, the contours and content of practice—of social work, are rootless and, perhaps more seriously, aimless. The reader may have already begun to get the impression that the "case" just described could not be conceived of or approached in the same way, for the same purposes, by any of the other helping disciplines. It seems so distinctly the assignment of social work.

The Interdependent Urbanized Environment

Whether one lives in a city, a suburb, or a rural area in America, he has to depend on a money income and essential provisions such as energy, transportation, housing, food, and clothing. Also education, health care, and a range of social services for young children, youth, families, and the aging increasingly are accepted as necessary to the progress and survival of society. Even in the poorest enclaves in the country where geography supports social isolation, as in Appalachia, or in areas where income level is so low that goods must be bartered for want of money exchange, there is federal, state, or local public support for at least a minimum of money or services such as electricity, social security, maternal care, or child welfare. Our world has become so complex that despite the continuing American dream that people can do everything for themselves, it is no longer possible for a single American family or any economic class to be independent of some socially organized, government-supported system of social utilities and social services.

Nor is it simple anymore to think differentially about rural, suburban, and urban life. The quality of life differs, of course, according to the style of living, the area of the country, the density of the population, and the general surround, but some differences are becoming less sharp. For example, the highway has connected cities, towns, and villages to create megalopolises; it is often hard to discern where the city stops and the countryside begins, especially as highway shopping centers have become the new "downtowns." The rise in suburban living has created the commutation phenomenon; when jobs are in the city, it is not possible to tell a city person from a suburban person except on weekends. The proliferation of state universities has attracted rural as well as metropolitan youths, making for a blend of interests among young people and consequently a less rigid distinction between city and country folk. Then there is the ever-present television, which may be the second great leveler of us all. All boundaries—not only geographic but cultural, ethnic, age, grade level, political, and class—are diminished if not erased by television.

When we tote up the effects of television, mass transit, social mobility, transience, and universal reliance upon resources outside of the intimate family circle, it is evident that this kind of society has created an interdependent population. Alienation, egocentricity, withdrawal, social isolation, and elitism continue to exist of course, but there is no escaping the reality that Social Darwinism is and always has been a fallacious idea. All people in such a society as ours are influenced by social change and the need for services; some enjoy a better quality of life than others, but no one is without the constraints of the postindustrial society. There is no hiding place from crime or addictions, from mental illness, from generation gaps and miscommunication, from child neglect, from the needs of the aged, from racial tensions, from overcrowding, or from breakdown in services. There is no flight to suburbs that will not find social problems taking root there. It seems that these are not features of an urban crisis after all; they seem to be the state of the urbanized world everywhere, affecting everyone. If social workers were to accept the challenge to engage in these problems on a vast scale, there would be no ambiguity then about their mandate.

The Special Case of Cities

As we have just noted, social work is not solely an urban type of practice; but as a social institution that is responsive to human problems, it has proliferated along with the service structures most often found in *quantity* in the cities, because that is where social problems are first noticed and are perhaps most interlocking with nonserving environments. A brief focus on urban living as an important context for social work practice must include concern with people of all classes and ethnic, racial and religious affiliations, for the city is where the greatest mixtures of people are able to live in a contiguous series of communities. But the urban poor have the greatest need for social services.

Slum living in the city means more than being poor. In every civilization poverty has carried its particular burdens, so that as a condition of life it has been harrowing for the eighteenth-century Londoner and the twentieth-century Mississippian. There never was any glory in being poor, despite the romantic and religious teachings to the contrary, and being poor has had historically a debilitating effect upon the individual. His poverty has kept him hungry and deprived of all other basic necessities of life, but more, it has chained him to the leavings of the society at large—all of the institutional hand-me-downs finally belong to the poor.

And slum living is more than even that; it is a living and breathing daily reminder to the individual that in an affluent society he is deprived and denigrated. In a mobile society, he is trapped within his neighborhood. In a materialistic society, he is without any of its concrete rewards. In an increasingly educated society that is tooling up for the post-cybernetic age, he is illiterate. In a society that strives for superior medical care, he is the sickest both mentally and physically. In a society that reaches the moon, he must cling to his out-moded fire escape.

The slum is poverty, but more than that, it is everything that is old-fashioned in a modern society; it is a massive expression of cultural lag that is knowingly supported by the total society that lives outside of it. Moreover, the environmental ills that affect all people who live in the city affect the slum dweller more intimately, because he cannot ever find alternate modes of living or afford compensatory mechanisms to deal with them.

The plight of the middle-class city resident is well known: he must pay too large a proportion of his income for his rent, and he can seldom find sufficient room or a satisfactory arrangement of space, light, air, convenience, and safety. He is not restricted in area as is the slum or ghetto dweller, but often he is wrongly viewed as if he were as free to take the city's offerings as the high-income city dweller. He does not share the restrictions or the squalor of the poor resident, but neither does he find the kind of accommodation in housing that makes for a pleasurable life. He suffers along with every other city resident from air pollution, outdated public transportation facilities, jammed traffic, an ear-piercing decibel count in the streets, overcrowding in schools, hospitals, clinics, social agencies, department stores, and supermarkets. His troubles, when compared to the troubles of the poor, are not as fundamental, in that he can afford to cope better with the inherent problems of urban life, but in truth every city dweller shares in its strains.

The modern city is a place where people are born or are required to live for many reasons. To the degree that people live there in order to seek freedom and pursue their interests of whatever kind, the price they must pay for these opportunities is costly when it is measured in terms of human health and personal dignity. Why, then, do so many people live in the cities, and what is to be their fate?

Why People Live in Cities

The city has always welcomed men in search of services (Yarmolinsky, 1968, p. 1268). As the demand for services outgrew the possibility of their provision in smaller units, cities have served as the clearinghouse for experts in everything. It has been said that "in the city every occupation, including mendicancy and prostitution, tends to become a profession" (Martindale, 1968, p. 53). It is well known that most of the technical innovations presently available came into being within the last fifty years; thus the burgeoning of knowledge has made it imperative for specialization to occur. For example, on one city block there may be a repairman for radios, television sets, kitchen appliances, and electrical wiring. There is no longer a general electrician, any more than there is a general doctor who could possibly know everything necessary in medicine.

Massive populations who have come to cities in the last fifty years have in themselves created the demand for services simply in order to be able to exist together. So, for example, cities provide a range of services from police to transportation and sanitation—services that derive from conglomerate living. Moreover, as our society has perfected its production of goods through mechanical means, services have become a major employment outlet for increasing numbers of people. In other words, people join together to make the most economic use of each other's services, and then services become the end product as providing them becomes utilitarian for people. The vast increase in range and complexity of services in this century has characterized urban living both advantageously and, where services contradict rather than complement each other, disadvantageously. In all cases, however, the availability of services affects the popularity of individual cities.

> The urban environment . . . is a medium for transmitting the form and content of contemporary society, a territory to be explored, and a setting for the testing of identity [Carr & Lynch, 1968, p. 1279].

We shall have more to say later about the changing role of the family in society, but here it should be noted that as the influence of family declines, a nation's culture and tradition are made explicit through the larger social environment. Although urban life might be considered as the root of our present social evils, it is also the source of a rich variety of experience, offering to all citizens many more stimuli than families ever could provide. Perhaps this phenomenon helps to explain why young people so often choose to find their interests outside of their family life. The city not only provides cultural experiences through its theaters, movie houses, concert halls, and museums; it also arranges for every possible kind of entertainment, social exchange, and above all difference and alternatives, so that city dwellers need merely look for and find opportunities to pursue their natural style of life. It is this individualized landscape that draws people together, making the crowded urban environment a highly personal experience.

The ready accessibility of all the familiar social, educational, and physical experiences in the city offers to people a diverse way of life, but it carries with it the looming potential of getting lost and overwhelmed. As with the service possibilities, so the stimuli of the city and the opportunities to pursue one's individual identity may create tension when one does not know exactly what one's identity is, nor where to look for it.

Cities have grown in America since the Civil War, and the urban way of life has become typical for 96 million people in this country. Actually, 53% of the population occupy only 0.7% of the nation's land, all concentrated in but 213 urban areas (Davis, 1965, pp. 3–24). Furthermore, of the 213 million people in America, 70% live in urban centers and half of this number are under 30 (*Pocket data book,* 1967, p. 5). The process of urbanization has been going on for 5,000 years, but only in the last fifty years have migrations and technological change occurred at such a pace that the urban way of life has become for many a problem way of life. The great attraction of ethnic and racial diversity has turned into a nightmare of interpersonal conflict. The opportunity for individual freedom has turned into a roller coaster for turned-on youth. The availability of cultural pursuits and entertainment has turned into a massive traffic jam in the streets and at the ticket windows. The presence of educational advantages has turned into a political struggle for the minds of the young. The hope for almost unlimited employment opportunities built upon service systems has turned into an organizational potpourri, so that people cannot get work even though their labor is necessary for the city to thrive. Equally important, the services themselves do not reach the citizen at large. It seems that our laissez-faire attitudes have countermanded the obvious necessity for planning in all areas of urban living, and the result has been the near chaos that was recently called the urban crisis. In order to draw implications for social work practice in this urban situation, we must look more closely at some of the problems before us.

Problems of Power Relationships

The increasing numbers of blacks, Puerto Rican, Mexican, American Indian, and other people who have moved to urban communities have enhanced the inevitable strife that occurs when the haves and have-nots confront each other. Cities have always been the first resting place for foreign immigrants, at least in coastal areas, and there has always been the strain accompanying the confrontation of new peoples with the older citizens. The strain comes from economic dependency and differences in living habits and cultures alien to the existing one. However, in the early part of this century there were differences that mitigated the power conflicts that are now occurring in the last half of the century.

In the first place, the European and the Asian immigrant brought with them the cultures they had had in their own countries. Thus they belonged to each other and had allegiances with the past that helped them to thrive in a new country and to find an identity. Second, the major foreign immigrations occurred before World War I and before the end of the industrial and the beginning of the technical era. In 1890 a mere one-fifth of the urban population was foreign born. There were job opportunities in factories, for example, that were commensurate with potential skills of the immigrant people, and they organized through unions and other associations to protect their labor. Third, except for Oriental people who have been a minority in this country, most of the immigrants from abroad were Caucasian. Thus, except for habits of living and language, which could be changed in only one generation, they could find their way into the major society through integration. Despite the burdens they carried and the discrimination they met, sooner or later they could become part of all that was going on in their new world.

The situation is presently quite different, inasmuch as the ethnic minorities who have replaced the Europeans in cities are for the most part of all different colors, which makes their integration into the mainstream of society difficult when that society is one that protects the apparent purity of its race. In the first place, nonwhite people are excluded through a range of discriminatory measures because of their color, and in the second place, the factor of color makes nonwhite people visible, and thus they cannot avoid the separatism forced upon them by the white community at large. It is now more than a case of haves versus have-nots, because the deprivation suffered by nonwhites is so pervasive that there is not even hope for sufficient opportunity toward which they can strive. As the National Advisory Commission on Civil Disorders (1968, p. 125) states:

> Negroes could point to the doctrine of white supremacy, its widespread acceptance, its persistence after emancipation and its influence on the definition of the place of Negroes in American life. They could point to their long fight for full citizenship, when they had active opposition from most of the white population and little or no support from the government.

The lack of federal planning and responsibility for programs that would equalize the income and employment opportunities throughout the country has made it imperative for poor blacks, Puerto Ricans, Mexican–Americans, and American Indians to migrate from mainly rural areas north to the urban centers in the country. They have come in large numbers and have gained a little economic security in exchange for tremendous social losses.

> I want to talk about the experiences of a misplaced generation, of a misplaced people in an extremely complex, confused society. This is a story of their searching, their dreams, their sorrows, their small and futile rebellions, and their endless battle to establish their own place in America's greatest metropolis . . . and in America itself.

So did Claude Brown (1966, p. vii) describe eloquently the plight of the southern black who came to New York City. And what did they bring, and what did they find?

Black migrants have come from southern rural areas where their reliance on the land that no longer provided a living kept them connected with the slave milieu that is a mere 100 years past. Due to the formula of public assistance payments where individual states determine their own budgets, wealthy states like New York, for example, could hold out a better living grant than could poor states like Mississippi, and this difference contributed to the migration north. Also, in the early half of this century, going north was thought to be a step forward to employment opportunities that provided for more mobility than farming. The north has been "where the action is" and has drawn young people to it to find that action. So they came, as did the Puerto Ricans from rural areas and poor cities, and the Indians from despicable reservations, and Mexican–Americans from useless productivity.

They brought with them their lives and their families, but little else. How could they have been prepared for the crowds, the dirt, the temptations of drugs, the complicated requirements of sanitation facilities, indoor plumbing, and the terrible distance between work and home? How could they have known about the rules imposed upon all city people, the reliance upon organizations, the socially distant professional behavior of people in schools, hospitals, and social agencies, and the cruelty of strangeness? How could they have been prepared for unemployment, underemployment, continuing poverty in spite of the promise of some new kind of comfort in the city?

After the long-sought-for and significant Civil Rights Bill was passed in the Congress in 1964, and the Supreme Court decision upholding it in 1974, it became evident that black people were not going to gain with any speed the rights of access to good schools, housing, employment, medical care, or social services; integration of black and white people in a society of equal opportunities came to be only a dream. The major crisis of cities in the 1960s evolved at the point that black leadership began to assert Black Power, which probably was the only possible course of action for a long-time-oppressed people who could wait no longer for their civil rights. While Black Power was interpreted to mean a range of things from extreme nationalism and separatism to community control of schools, it was seen increasingly as a force that was necessary for black people to find identity as individuals in an alien white society. Whereas European migrants carried with them this vital sense of identity and created their own power subsystems in this country, it cannot be forgotten that black people were physically prevented from achieving such a sense of community, by 250 years of slavery and an ensuing 100 years of being second-class citizens.

The economic decline in the 1970s has had a serious if not disastrous effect upon the social advance of all minority people in America. Politically the black community has increasingly assumed a new visibility and real power base in its elected officials, mayors, and congressmen, and in improved representation in most social institutions, professions, and labor unions. Yet the community control of and participation in local educational, health, and social service programs remain scattered and unplanned, perhaps accounting for a continued sense of alienation of client–consumer from the institution that is set up to serve him.

Facing the Fact of Money

One of the most important results of the transition from a rural to an urban way of life is the increased reliance of individuals upon money income. Living in the city means that one cannot grow one's own food, wear simple clothes, or go without shoes; nor can a family build its own house on a corner of land and take care of its maintenance. Moreover, due to the increasing complexity of technology and the requisite division of labor, it has become necessary for all people to rely upon a wide range of services that cost money. Living in the city requires a mode of dress, social behavior, and expenses that were hitherto not necessary to life on the farm or even in the small town. "Within the city life has been transformed from a struggle for a livelihood with nature into an interhuman struggle for gain" (Martindale, 1968, p. 34).

There are only limited ways in which people may get money, which is the rock-bottom necessity for living in the city. They may earn it entirely through work or through subsidization of their work, they may enter the social insurance scheme of the nation and be insured against the natural risks of industrial life, and/or they may subscribe to the residual public assistance programs for income supplementation. Whatever the mode of income maintenance, people must have that income.

There is a series of issues having to do with the values placed upon work in this country. Sooner or later America will have to contemplate questions having to do with guaranteed employment and with government's serving as the employer of first or last resort. We will need to cope creatively with automation, the shorter work week, and our inability to know how to use leisure time. We will need to accept the fact that everyone cannot work, particularly the very old, some mothers of young children, the severely emotionally or physically disabled, and the technologically unemployable person. Is the day very far off when Puritan values held in America about work will have to give way to acceptance that the necessity for money income in an urban society may be overriding and that income may have to derive from sources other than work?

Whatever the choices among various guaranteed income schemes like family allowances, negative income tax, or demogrants, since income is vital to urban living, there must be public provision for families to have income so that they can survive. We must emphasize the requirement of money in our discussion of urban living, because we know that it is impossible to exist in the city without it, not only because food, clothing, and shelter cannot be attained through any other means known but also because the urban scene is typically defined by distances that have to be traveled via transportation that costs money. There is a negligible amount of recreation that is free, and the rent must be paid. In short, in order to benefit from the very services the city is expected to supply, one must engage in financial transactions. Therefore, the amount of money one has more than any other factor defines the way one will accommodate to urban living and assigns one to an economic class.

These economic class differences, of course, are fundamental to the problems before us. A decreasing number of individuals who live in cities can afford all or most of the comforts of life, and yet they too suffer from the outrageous environment, i.e., air pollution, crowds, faulty transportation systems, unpleasant architecture, and loss of connections with each other and with the society around them. Moreover, they too feel the impact of social upheaval, transfer of power, and faltering institutions; they too react with fears of revolt, crime, and drug use. The poor black, Puerto Rican, Mexican, and Indian people feel all this strain and more, because they do not have the money to cope with its effects and are too often hungry. In our culture, work has the highest priority not only as the means to earn an income and for nation building but also because of its long-felt ethical value in character building. Yet unemployment figures may rise to 10% at the same time that the unemployed are considered to be second-class citizens.

When people do go to work, there are insufficient facilities for the care of their children. When people get sick, they must wait a very long time at clinics, and they do not universally receive the best available treatment. When they go to school, they do not get the best education, and parents have come to feel that children are not being educated for the real world in specific cultural terms. Unions, politicians, professionals, civil servants, all representing the range of establishments, seem to be at war with the people they are there to serve. The machine seems to have broken down; is there any way to fix it?

Redefinitions: Psycho-social to Ecological
Thinking

There is a long tradition in sociology, urban planning, economics, and architecture of defining the urban environment in geographic or spatial terms, when in fact the city is more than a series of types of environment. Cities are defined geographically as inner cities, megalopolises, linkages of cities, and slums and so forth, and yet these terms do not help us to understand them from a social work practice perspective. It is equally hard to describe cities as a collection of neighborhoods, when urban redevelopment and other causes of mobility contradict the neighborhood concept. The modern city is more than a marketplace and less than a community; it is more than a conglomerate of individuals and small groups and less than a collection of social systems; it is more than a local, politically autonomous environment, and it is less than an expression of a grand national scheme.

It seems hopeless to assign spatial definitions, and no comprehensive definition would meet the requirements of all the urban specialists and particular interest groups. "In a large city there are a multitude of overlapping jurisdictions of influence" (Tunnard, 1968, p. 10). This explanation would clarify the functions and structures of theaters, jobs, neighborhoods, and social institutions that may be far across town and yet serve a particular individual or group of individuals. In any event, it has been noted that "the American city has always been a place where things ought to be better than they are." There is observable evidence that there is no geographic conception of the city possible, except perhaps for the slums, which are "place-defined communities." Thus it would be more cogent to define cities in terms of "life space" and address social service programs accordingly.

People tend to cluster about their functional interests,

sometimes around buildings that house specialized industries, political and legal centers, barrios where tropical foods are sold, or black ghettos where people feel equal to each other. The interest in maintaining geographic organization as the pivotal concept in cities has been described by Yarmolinsky as an expression of "the convenience of the serving agency over the person being served. . . . Clinics are in hospitals; parks and playgrounds are in other people's neighborhoods" (1968, p. 1267). As organizations tend to be grouped away from the people whom they should serve, it has become necessary in recent years to erect "outreach" and "satellite" structures in order to countermand that tendency.

In viewing the boundaries within a city that tend to define the life style of the inhabitants, it is important to reiterate that lower-class people are always more reliant than other income groups upon public and sometimes voluntary service organizations. One must therefore be more alert to the locations of these services. Lyle Fitch has said:

> Middle and higher-income people are highly mobile; their roots tend to be in professional, cultural, and other interests rather than in the geographical neighborhoods where they happen to be living at the moment. Manifestations of trouble tend to be concentrated in central cities; the middle class can, and frequently does, escape by moving to the suburbs where its members spend much of their civic energy building fortifications against incursions by the poor [1968, p. 1146].

In a sense, the poor in the city are land-locked; they are forced to live on terms that are defined for them by politics, public welfare, hospitals, schools, business, and all the other social and economic institutions that they do not necessarily build for themselves. It would seem evident that social work practitioners need to be located exactly in those varied institutions where people go. Whereas the middle class may define its "neighborhoods" in accordance with its economic ability and special interests, the poor man's "neighborhood" seems to be defined by the presence of services.

Participation as a Reality

Development is whatever increases the individual's involvement in self-motivated choice and action, whatever increases his power to formulate and execute personal intentions, whether delighting in the moment or planning a course of life [Carr & Lynch, 1968, p. 1278].

Assuming that the development of the individual is a fundamental social aim in our present world, this statement provides the rationale and possibly the major guideline for participation of people in the programs of their lives. The complexity of human life in the city tends to freeze people in defensive molds, probably so that they can better cope with the continuing contextual contrasts around them. It would seem that society's present efforts to raise the influence of the individual partially reflect the growing feeling of threat of the emerging Orwellian man of 1984. If technological change is to make it decreasingly possible or necessary for man to control his environment and the things around him, then society will need to compensate through opening avenues for man, at the very least, to control his personal and social destiny.

Where are the opportunities that might be made available to him? Except for his ballot and participation in occasional mass protests it is unlikely that the individual can affect the large national decisions that control his life, such as those of the nation's involvement in wars, in space races, in tax policies, and in government welfare programs. Also it would be hopeless to strive for the individual man's control over electrical power failures, television programming, or the proportions of steel to concrete in a skyscraper. But what can man control in relevant ways? What, in fact, is his business in particular? What affects him personally and is therefore in the arena of his competence? What aspects of his destiny must he participate in to maintain his integrity as a person with individuality?

The traditional American expressions of man's legal right to his own decisions have concerned such intimate matters as his choices of friends, lovers, and marriage partners, the number of children he wants to have, and how he will conduct his life inside his home. His affectional decisions may not always be under his conscious control, but they will be his by nature, and he will be able to express them as long as they do not conflict with the law. For example, he may beat his wife as long as she does not go to court to sue him for cruelty, or he may neglect his children as long as the terms of his neglect are not defined in the statutes. Furthermore, during the minority of his children, a parent may make certain decisions about their conduct, their discipline, their schooling, their social lives, their decisions to marry, and so forth, to the degree that his relationship with his children makes it possible.

Thus internal, family, and affectional choices are typically expected to belong entirely to the individual, within certain broadly prescribed legal and behavioral requirements. This is understood in a democratic society, that the public through government, police, listening device, or any investigative arm is not permitted constitutionally to invade the privacy of an individual's home, although we often note breaches in enforcement of these rights. To a large extent most individuals in our society do enjoy or at the least expect these rights of personal freedom, and they are not ordinarily contested.

But what of the individual's rights to participation in his own destiny when he steps out of the confines of his home and his relationships expand to include the outer society and its social institutions? In the courts, his rights are prescribed by law and judicial interpretation that are subject to higher court review. There is innate provision built into the law for the individual to participate in his own behalf. Even though there are instances when the legal process breaks down, the intent of the legal system in this country is nevertheless to provide participatory opportunities for every individual equally. Social security as an institution of society also defines clearly the ground rules for a person's participation in the program; as long as he is eligible through status for a particular form of social security, he may receive it with equity. To the extent that social institutions are governed by legal statutes or universal policies that are objectively determined by the Congress or by the computer, the individual's rights as a citizen are theoretically almost as safe as they are in his home. When these rights are abused in the face of legal and constitutional protection, it becomes a political matter to challenge governmental control.

Difficulties seem to arise when professional expertise is in question, when decisions are made arbitrarily by specialists. Let us presume that experts in social work, medicine, teaching, housing administration, police work, school, and university administration do indeed know more about their specialities than the individual consumer of their services. When politicians, who may or may not know more about some issues, take stands, they are subject to reelection, and thus must listen to a certain extent to their constituents. In politics as in the law, the individual benefits by some measures of political control over many of the inhibitions of his life. It is not always so when it comes to professional expertise. We know that when we go to an automobile mechanic or we bring in a plumber or electrician, he is the expert and we must abide by his decision to act upon his perception of what the trouble is. If something goes wrong, we have certain limited options of our own: we will not use him again, we can hold up his payment, or we can complain to his organization or to the Better Business Bureau or to a local authority. Nevertheless we are in a real sense at his mercy, as long as we do not have his technical competence. This kind of technical competence really belongs under the heading of things over which none of us can have direct control, because technology has surpassed our capacity to cope with all of its ramifications. We can only control the decision to use a particular technician, and then we may try to make him accountable to us.

When it comes to professional competence, the individual is faced with the same lack of knowledge of the art, science, or craft of the professional person involved. As he will increasingly require professional services in this complex world, he has no choice but to seek them. Actually, there are unlimited opportunities for a person's participation in professional service, but often they are overlooked. To a large extent this occurs because of professionalism and status requirements among experts. Often the oversight may be unintentional and may be due to overwork or organizational restraints, or it may occur because participation of the client–consumer may cause trouble, take time, or be threatening to the feeling of competence held by the professional. Then again, the oversight may be due to deliberate attitudes that the individual being served is uninformed simply because he is a layman—consumer, client, or patient.

> Life is increasingly composed of impersonal components that displace personal colorations leading the individual to summon the utmost in uniqueness and particularization to preserve the personal core of the self [Martindale, 1968, p. 34].

Where is it more appropriate for the individual to achieve this uniqueness than in the areas of his life where his very individuality is at stake?

A surgical patient needs to know what is going to happen to him and why; a parent of a school child needs to have a say in the kind of education his child is getting; a university student needs to exercise some control in the aims and conditions of his education; a community of tenants ought to arrive at a mutual decision about the rules under which they can best live together; and a client of a social worker must have free access to the rationale underlying actions taken in his behalf. We are not saying that expertise is unimportant: the teacher can teach better than the parent, the doctor has more knowledge than the patient, and the social worker understands more than his client about the meanings of the psycho-social situation in which the client exists and the ways to ease strain. But as the client, patient, parent, or student is the object of the service, he must have his chance to object, to choose, to withdraw, and to modify the actions that are happening to him. Policies and rules ought to enable the process or the service to work; policies and rules themselves are not services, and consumers should have the most to say about these.

Individualization as a Social Invention

If the future could bring a resolution to our present social conditions, we might imagine that all communities would be well designed with adequate housing and planned green areas, that rapid transportation would be clean and efficient and that private cars would not be necessary in the cities, that political institutions would be responsive to the people's real needs, that all social institutions would function expeditiously, that social utilities would be available for all people, that social insurances, health care, and education would reach the theoretical horizons already established, and that individuals would have sufficient money to live comfortable lives in a more equitable society. Admittedly this is a future that is beyond our present dreams; in fact urban dysfunction exists because of failures to meet our requirements in all of the areas just mentioned. Nevertheless, if we can permit ourselves to dream and if we can truly imagine such a millennium, there would remain an inherent restraint in urbanized life that would not be cared for no matter how progressive our social and economic schemes. The fact of modern life that characterizes it and no past living condition is the inevitable claim of the crowded, organized, institutionalized community against the freedom and fulfillment of the individual. The necessity to draw this urbanized society to human scale remains and will remain, because social advances will require increasing institutionalization of services and with it may appear tendencies to overlook individualization.

The increasing institutionalization of life has been written about by novelists and social scientists and is of course observable to everyone who has had to cope with the network of services in the city. One hears comments like "The source of most information in the city is the telephone yellow pages." Cities by their very nature require "legal control, based on rules which are deliberate, explicit and have a special machinery for enforcement which becomes more prominent; the mores and the folkways less" (Wilensky & Lebeaux, 1958, p. 119). The individual must be reduced in his personal influence over his life, and yet ironically, due precisely to this fact he must strive himself, alone, to remain an individual doing the work of his own life and giving expression to his own feelings. Thus the urban environment must cope with a mass society, and the individual is left to fend for himself against great odds, just exactly when he needs his individuality the most.

Ultimately, we confront the problem of selecting out of the total social system those particular provisions that will meet the needs of a particular individual. "The more complex the resulting system, the greater the need for specialized human intervention to guide people through it" (Yarmolinsky, 1968, p. 1272). This has been said another way, that people "need a guide through a civilized jungle, and planning and coordination of specialized services" (Wilensky &

Lebeaux, 1958, p. 14). The urban condition requires vast specialization, and at present there is no specialist in the liaison function that will connect individuals with services; there is no accepted individualizer of the urbanized environment. It is this function that we are suggesting is the natural function of the social work practitioner.

We shall look more closely at the rising influence of public social institutions and the waning impact of family life, religion, and voluntary associations. The urban society in America seems to be replacing preindustrial, puritan, Victorian, rural modes of life. So we observe values changing, sexual roles being rearranged, inhibitions diminishing, planning turning to attention to the moment, authority being challenged, the rise of unofficial power groups, and cynicism about the industrial–military establishment. In this latter third of the twentieth century people in cities in particular are expressing their concerns as constituents, and the social niceties of even one generation ago are changed. The family, the church, the school, the university, the social agency, the hospital—none of these once revered institutions are any longer autonomous in their particular functions. Their authority is being challenged, and yet increasingly do people rely upon their services.

Social work is but one of the social institutions that is being challenged, especially so because it among all of the others has represented a prior way of life. Its past affiliation with charity pales in this day of public responsibility to guarantee a decent standard of living; its past attention to intrapsychic conflict seems odd in this day of free life styles and open alternatives; its private organizations seem outdistanced by the increasing public control of institutions. Yet its basic values regarding the dignity of individuals, its particular expert history in helping the individual and society to get along together better, and its social aims would seem to make social work particularly qualified to carry out the task of individualization in the urbanized society.

The Rise and Fall of Social Institutions

A major paradox of modern life seems to be that while traditional social institutions like the family and the church and formal organizations like government, schools, hospitals, and social agencies are losing their public support and functional effectiveness, at the same time people are required to rely more heavily upon these extrafamily services that must be available in the community. Institutionalized human services, although increasingly necessary for survival in the urban world, have become almost like a bitter pill that consumers must swallow. Although it is probably not necessary to belabor the point which has become common knowledge, it always helps our discussion of the extent to which change has forced upon us the requirement of services to recall the evidence of the change in family structure and function. We will take pains not to identify these changes as family breakdown, because the prevalence of change would suggest not a social aberration, but a different life style. One cannot characterize a social phenomenon that is so widespread as pathological; it is probably more accurate to characterize it as a shift in the structure and function of social institutions.

Changes in the Role of the Family

The rate of marriages in this country increases, but so does the rate of divorce. The birth rate continues to decline, but the rate of illegitimate births increases. Both factors suggest that one-parent families are going to have to rely increasingly upon extrafamilial social supports. There is a steady increase in the number of mothers of children under 18 who work and must find outside child-caring arrangements. Education begins at increasingly earlier ages and ends at later ages, indicating not only that the period of adolescent dependency is prolonged but also that children and youths increasingly are subject to extrafamilial influences in their lives. The life expectancy for Americans has increased markedly, suggesting that health and welfare services for the aged will become highly significant and remain so as long as the aged do not continue living with their adult families.

The facts that the population in America is increasing in numbers if not proportionately and that people are living longer even though the birth rate is declining suggest that the crowded world is going to demand *quantity* health and social services. Furthermore, considering that nuclear families separate more quickly from their extended families and that the time of child rearing within the family itself has lessened, educative and socialization functions are increasingly being assumed by extrafamilial and public institutions. Almost as soon as the child is able to function without his mother, he comes to rely on extrafamilial resources; family structures, like cellular structures, proliferate into separate units very quickly in America. Babies are increasingly born in hospitals after their mothers have had clinical prenatal care. Infants are cared for by child rearers who may not be their own mothers, in group day care or family day care facilities, by baby sitters, and in other makeshift arrangements. Toddlers attend Headstart, nursery school, or prekindergarten classes, and children do not leave school until they are beyond the age of late adolescence. When children and youths are not in school, they attend organized recreational programs and, particularly in the urban environment, create their own leisure time activities in the streets. Young adults marry earlier and have babies earlier than they used to; thus they leave their primary families to begin the fast-moving cycle again. Less and less do we find members of families depending upon each other for physical sustenance, social control, or the transmission of culture. These prior functions are carried out by extrafamilial institutions.

Of course the advent of Women's Liberation, zero population growth, pro-abortion groups, and new experiments in different styles of family living as well as the letting down of extramarital sexual restraints are reflections of the changes that have already occurred. Whatever the form of the modern family, its function has changed from primarily economic division of labor into child-rearing and work roles. Intimacy and affectional needs can be filled extralegally, and statistics bear evidence of the fact that married couples have less chance of remaining married.

When we look at statistical indices of psycho-social change in our modern society, it becomes even more apparent that individuals have come to require organized social institutions. Obviously the family cannot now, and rarely could previously, provide the specialized care that is required when one of its members is sick or disturbed or in trouble with the law. It is commonplace to accept the fact of public or institutional care for people who suffer from psycho-social pathological conditions. As population increases and urban tensions do not recede, the statistics of individual breakdown seem harrowing.

Addictions, crime, delinquency, dependency and neglect, dropping out of school, physical illnesses, mental illnesses, and retardation, are the major pathologies that have to be addressed in the modern society. Thus we find that courts, prisons, hospitals, clinics, and family and child welfare agencies have become the modern caretakers for those people who are in trouble. Physicians, psychiatrists, social workers, nurses, therapists, and remedialists of all kinds have become the technicians of society, and their services are absolutely necessary in light of the statistics of psycho-social breakdown that command attention. The family as an institution does not have the necessary skills or resources to cope with breakdown of its individual members; help has become a public responsibility.

Returning to the population at large that does not experience the psycho-social problems we have just mentioned, it is important to recall the extent to which *all* people rely upon extrafamilial organizations and institutions for their survival in the urban world. Presently, as stated in Chapter 1, these human services are conceptualized as residual or institutional services and developmental services. Out of our interest in finding the place for individualizing services in society, we have constructed a scheme that will describe the emerging developmental services in transaction with age groups. There is a systematic relationship between the individual and the social institutions with which he intersects at any stage of his life. We can observe this intersection through a developmental lens in accordance with the natural development of the individual, or we can view it through a residual lens when the individual presents maladaptive modes of functioning. It is possible, through such a systemic view of individuals in transaction with their environment, to note the areas in which normal anticipatory crises of age, role transition, and development will occur, as well as to note where pathological crises might erupt.

We have claimed that living in this complex, technological society itself is a major stress event in which all citizens, but especially the poor and minority groups with less resources, suffer the anomic and isolated deprivation of collective living in an unplanned and unresponsive environment. As long as society is organizationally unresponsive, pathological responses on the part of individuals may actually be accommodations to the present life style of the country. Unless universal and developmental services are available at all points of intersection, it may be a nightmarish inevitability that residual and problem-focused human services will become institutional necessities for all citizens.

Where Individuals and Institutions Intersect

A transactional picture of the individual facing age-specific tasks (Erikson, 1959, chap. 2) that require need-meeting social institutions must follow from the *prior assumption* that certain universal and primary physical, mental, economic, and social needs must be met for people of every age and condition of life. Thus we would begin with the requirements for food, clothing, shelter, health care, sufficient money, education, employment opportunities, provision for social insurance, and leisure time pursuits. These are recognized to be so fundamental in a humane society that it might seem unnecessary to even make a comment upon them. Of course the requirement of all individuals for love and intimacy and human relationships is probably the must fundamental need of all, but even such instinctive requirements tend to rely for their appropriate expression upon a bedrock of the other needs we have mentioned that have to be met.

Assuming the obvious necessity for social provision in some form or another for these basic requisites of life, we can view pictorially the transactions that can and often do occur among individuals and health, education, and welfare services. The intention here is to illustrate the typical and normal transactions that occur for all people in society, and it will then become clearer what the role of social work practice might be if it were to pursue a goal of *locating services where people are at the time that the services are needed.*

The accompanying chart, being suggestive of a way to view individuals as they intersect with natural life crises and service provisions, has not included all the unseen and possible need-meeting structures that are presently and potentially available in our society. In order that the reader's imagination may roam of its own accord, we will cite as well the following *locations* where all individuals go at some time in their lives, usually when they experience stress and strain, but increasingly because in the urbanized world, extra-familial resources have become a significant nurturant for people.

Normal Individual Transactions

Individual Developmental Age-Specific Tasks and Needs*	Expectable Transitional Crises and Typical Problems	Available Institutions Providing Social Services
I. Infancy, 0–3 *Tasks:* Basic trust vs. mistrust; autonomy vs. shame and doubt *Needs:* Mothering, care, learning, verbal and conceptual skills	Role transition for parents, working mothers, absent fathers *Typical problems:* Inadequate parenting Unwanted children Neglect and abuse Marital conflict Physical handicaps Mental retardation	Income maintenance programs Prenatal care centers for medical care, advice, and parent education Hospitals, clinics Well-baby stations Family services Child welfare services Homemakers Home helps Day care Protection Placement (foster care, adoption)
II. Preschool, 3–6 *Tasks:* Initiative vs. guilt *Needs:* Learning, socialization, play	Child's separation from home Changing tasks of child rearing *Typical problems:* Inadequate socialization Lack of supervision Behavioral reactions	Nursery school care Group care services And see above as appropriate

III. Grade school, 6–13
Tasks:
Industry vs. inferiority
Needs:
Intellectual and social stimulation

Expanding world and increasing stimuli to be coped with
Typical problems:
Social and learning failures

School guidance services
Recreational services
Developmental group services
And see above as appropriate

IV. High school, 13–18
Tasks:
Identity vs. identity diffusion
Needs:
Achievement, partial separation from parents

The time for decisions about sexual identity, work, and the future
Typical problems:
Identity crises
Alienation
Addictions
Delinquency
School maladjustment

Youth services, hot lines, crash pads, etc.
Vocational counseling
Correctional services
Addiction services
And see above as appropriate

V. Young adult, 18–21
Tasks:
Intimacy vs. isolation
Needs:
Opportunities for self-fulfillment in adult roles

Leaving home
Marriage
Working
Typical problems:
Unwed parenthood
School–work maladaptation
Marital conflict
Addictions
Crime

Marital conflict legal aid services
Probation services
And see above as appropriate

Individual Developmental Age-Specific Tasks and Needs*	Expectable Transitional Crises and Typical Problems	Available Adjustment Social Services
VI. Mature adult, 21–65 *Tasks:* Generativity vs. stagnation *Needs:* Expanding opportunities for self-development in life roles	Household management and child care (refer as in a cycle to category I) *Typical problems:* Family breakdown, divorce Financial need or mismanagement Parent–child conflict Work, career failure Disability, personality disorganization Death of family and friends	Family court services Medical and mental health services And see above as appropriate
VII. Aged adult, 65 and over *Tasks:* Integrity vs. despair *Needs:* Living arrangements, physical care, continuing opportunities for self-development in roles of aged	Physical and mental depletion Loss of friends and separation from family Retirement Death of spouse and friends *Typical problems:* Sickness Loneliness Social isolation Economic deprivation	Meals on wheels Centers for the aged Income maintenance programs Foster grandparent programs Foster family care Institutional care And see above as appropriate

* It is evident that each stage is cumulative. People do not develop in discrete stages; there is overlapping and always residue from previous stages. Thus "And see above" (in the third column) indicates that available services are applicable at all stages, whereas some are more prominent at certain times.

74

The Location of Services

We have already mentioned hospitals, clinics, and schools, as well as family and child welfare agencies and recreational centers. Outside of family and kinship groups, churches, and fraternal orders, there is a world of social structures that is literally integral to the individual's natural life space as he conducts his life. As a matter of fact, hospitals and social agencies are most closely related to physical, social, and emotional breakdowns in human life; what of the structures that are related to health? Schools, neighborhood organizations, associations of professionals, civil servants, and laborers, housing complexes, commercial establishments, parks and playgrounds, and cultural institutions are but a few of the locations where people *are* as they make their usual excursions through life. And yet the thrust of professional attention has been in those structures where people end up because these normal institutions of life somehow failed to meet their needs. Thus institutions for the sick, the mentally ill, the penal offender, the neglected child, and the neglected aged person appear to have overtaken those that are appropriately in the mainstream of life.

We have seen that social institutions have gradually become specialized in provision of services and meeting of needs of individuals in all stages of their lives and in all roles they enact. The family no longer is the locus of production, socialization, religious training, education, or authority, and it remains "structurally dependent on external systems, making it impossible for the family to exist as an entirely self-sufficent unit" (Leichter & Mitchell, 1967, p. 27). Yet there is a primary function still left to families that, as far as can be seen presently, cannot be transferred satisfactorily to the society at large. "The family is emotionally intimate, and its historical duration for the individual is often greater than other groups; it is expected, in our society, to be the locus of emotional expression and emotional support for adults as well as for children" (*ibid.*, 1967, p. 284).

This being true, there are streams in the organization of society that seek to protect the integrity of family life, if its primary purpose rests only in its provision of intimacy, affection, and generativity. It is important to note both the necessity and the limitations of family life so as not to exaggerate either aspect. Family life functions have changed in the urbanized society; family life may not have broken down as much as it may have taken on a highly specialized burden of providing an arena for affection and intimacy. This requirement for all individuals must surely be of major concern to social institutions that seek to promote individuality for all people.

The postindustrial or technological era which we now confront is characterized by urban living and its inherent complexities and isolation. We see social institutions serving individuals in most aspects of their lives, many of them supportive of family life and others substituting for family life. As we have discussed, none of us is any longer capable of coping with our specialized needs in society. As our chart has shown, from cradle to grave we intersect with society in informal and formal ways, and the transactions that occur thereby are systemic as individuals and institutions affect each other through feedback mechanisms.

Developmental services follow the present natural life style of the individual; they need not be confined to the pathologies with which we are familiar. Theoretically the entrance of social organizations in the lives of individuals will contribute to prevention of later breakdown of functioning of both the individual and society. Transactional relationships mean that the process of reform is not linear or one-directional; the existence of developmental services not only will provide necessary services for individuals but also will be a barometer of need in the community as individuals in a sense "inform" society of social breakdown and unmet need.

Developmental services, then, are becoming the hallmark of the technological, urban society, and necessarily they will be highly bureaucratized agencies.

The question will confront us as to how these agencies can be drawn to the human scale and made accessible and responsive to individualized need. One way we have mentioned earlier is through decentralization of services, making them, wherever possible, local and based in neighborhoods and defined communities. Thus a day care service might be in a neighborhood where families live, and a family service might be located in a downtown business area, accessible to working men and women. Further assuming that the strains of modern life are such that family problems are almost universal, family and child welfare services and family life education would, in this view, be a developmental service.

Social institutions which are essential to the conduct of urban life must be humanized. Individualizing social work services could facilitate the adaptation of urban life to the individual, so that he does not become overwhelmed by its impersonality.

It is our thesis that the urbanized society in large and small cities and in megalopolises will increasingly need to provide institutional supports for all individual citizens. Some members of society are more able to cope with strain and crisis than others, either because they are more capable in some way or because they have easier lives and more money and resources to cope with life; nevertheless, it seems apparent that urban strain is not to be confined to a particular class of people, nor to any ethnic group alone. Urban living, the condition of life for increasing millions of people in this country, is impartial; it has an impact upon everyone.

A second thesis, presented early in the book, is that social work practice has gradually been failing in its primary mission, which has been to provide individualized social services as they are needed. This failure may be attributed to overspecialization, to technical concentrations without significant meaning, to preoccupations with professional status, to undiscriminating borrowing from other disciplines, particularly medicine for its practice models and psycho-analysis for its practice theory, with politics as the practice model in the case of community organization. One of the binds in which social workers find themselves is that the work they do best, the individualizing work in social wel-fare, is often thought by others to be done perhaps even as well or better by volunteers, neighbors, family members, the clergy, the family doctor, the bartender, the public health nurse, the teacher, any professional something else, or a well-meaning friendly person. If this is the actual image held of the social worker, then somewhere social work has not made explicit to the public what its expertise is. Here we are not talking about a mere public relations matter, but about the content and quality of the social worker's practice itself.

So we are faced with the picture of community need on the one hand and a potentially relevant practice on the other hand. Our concern is to try to bring these two forces to-gether. The communities of today present the highways and byways in the modern world, and it can well be the social work practitioner who will place himself at the crossroads (Reynolds, 1934), the points of intersection where individuals meet society. Perhaps it is not possible to identify as pro-fessional those actions that are undertaken to promote in-dividuality in a society. Perhaps, as in less urbanized condi-tions, we might yearn for a more intimate role of the family, the neighborhood, or the church, or for the friendly general practitioner or the town sage as the person who will best listen to our troubles and tell us where to go to make use of the community's resources. Undoubtedly, it would be pleasant to have back that world, but it is quite gone—if in-deed it ever existed in the idealized form. It is gone along with the sense of homogeneous community, quiet streets, clean air, absolute respect for authority, well-behaved youth, obedient Negroes, kitchen-bound wives and mothers, one-family houses in the city, and horsedrawn carts. The do-it-yourself motif may be a reaction against the overspecialization of society, but if professionalized and humanized help is available and can be demonstrated to be better than do-it-yourself or lay services, social work practice may help to fill the need felt in all of urban society.

The Limitations of Institutional Services

The provision of human services by the public or private sector of a community may be an indicator of social responsibility or of social control, depending upon who is providing the services and toward what end. For example, services for delinquents, narcotic addicts, or unmarried mothers take on a different coloration when their fundamental aim is to control the outbreak of the problem rather than to actually give helpful attention to the person who suffers the problem. We have observed the necessity in the modern society for human services to be provided outside of the family, in the community and through social institutions. Yet we cannot be assured that the public's institutions will prove to be lenient in their standards for human behavior, in their observation of individual privacy, or in providing really free alternatives for action. The intimacy of family life appropriately provides for secrets, for tantrums, for illogicalities and for halting steps toward development; its best purpose is to support uniqueness. Can we be assured that public or socially sanctioned voluntary agencies will truly provide for human differences and give people the freedom to be, or not to be? We have made our comment upon the inevitability of extrafamilial developmental and universal institutional services, and now we must work at its implications. For if we do not build in individualizing protections, then we will run the risk of becoming an Orwellian society holding out a predefined mold of human being.

It is around the humanizing of services, the protection of the maximum amount of individuality in public provision of services, that our narrative of the problems of urbanized life revolves. We have spoken earlier of the sense of isolation and anomie, really the feeling of powerlessness, that seems to characterize our lives in the urban and technical society. We vote in elections and sometimes we work through political or social organizations hoping to promote interests we hold in common with others. More and more in our society we find less response from centralized government and bureaucratic service agencies; our problems and our sense of loss seem too diffuse to communicate and too vast for officials to cope with. Paul Ylvisaker has said, "Thanks to the Negro, we have developed a fourth branch of American government . . . the March" (1967, p. 682). Perhaps this form of demonstration of need was heard more than any other individual outcry, short-lived though it was. Is the sense of powerlessness to find its expression in violence, or will it be possible to meet it through the primary involvement of people in the institutions that are necessary for their survival in the urban world?

Richard Goodwin, who has made some observations on the current "large and serious revolutionary movement" in this era, states:

> There is a serious discontent not only with what we as a Nation are doing but with who is doing it. There is a challenge to the "power structure" itself, which means simply the methods, institutions, and people by which decisions affecting the public are made [1969, p. 38].

The political rallying cries heard earlier in this century had to do with substantive promises of a chicken in every pot or a car in every garage, or the feeding of one-third of the nation. There was an understanding of the need for greater beneficence on the part of agencies of government or private enterprise which has presently given way to a popular search for participation in the very decisions involved in the allocation of goods and services. This is not to say that goods and services are not essential to people and most particularly to the poor—but rather that the movement seems to be directed toward changing the process of provision. According to Goodwin, it is the sense of powerlessness in this regard that is felt by all classes and is the "source of the public's unhappiness."

It is perhaps a presumption and an oversimplification to compare people's present frustration at being "given to" without a chance to be involved in the terms of the giving with the old experience the poor had when social workers gave them Christmas baskets. Although this may have been a kind action and even a life-saving service for a family, in the end it may have been a source of anger to the family that was forced by circumstances into the compromising position of grateful recipient. Despite the fact that most goods and services today are not given through charity, but are paid for in some fashion by the recipient and are not intended to be of the let-them-eat-cake variety, the role of passive recipient must be an uncomfortable one. The human services that are presently accepted as an important responsibility for government to provide for its citizens are increasingly those services that once were provided by the family. This public, institutionalized, and specialized provision of basic human, individualizing services has become an absolute requisite of modern living, and the protections of individuality and participation in important decisions are no longer present as they were when families were able to care for themselves and to take the primary role in the rearing of children and the transmission of culture.

The loss of intimacy that has accompanied the decline in influence of the family is matched by the anonymity and detachment of the technological age, making the need for meaningful participation in the events of one's personal life even more important. The worker in a factory has no opportunity to develop a significant investment in his own work when he must deal with a mere fragment of the product being made. He may never know what value his skill serves, and he may never see the end product he has helped to create. The loss of connectedness is apparent in the case of the office worker, too, who has become the backbone of the organization world that could not run without computers, automatic typewriters, and Xerox machines. However, as the buttons are pushed, the most skilled and highly trained office worker may never know the meanings of the input or the output. If all IBM cards look alike, what is the difference if one set counts stock transactions and the other heartbeats?

The salesman, the designer, the manager, the technician—all develop generic skills having less and less need for reference to the particular purposes of the skills they perform. The day does not seem too far distant when professionals too will be relying upon machinery and electronic translation that will determine more effectively than the patient, the client, or the student the nature of services needed. Our civilization is faced with the need to return to all people who are caught up in technological progress some access to individuality and participation in the ordinary processes of life.

The observation was made over and over again during the middle years of the 1960s, the years of social outbreak, that *at least* black and student movements had causes to pursue; the activity of protest has meaning in and of itself, quite apart from the object of the protest. This notion is reminiscent of the heightened expression of human values during the Depression years and during the London blitz, when people were kinder to each other under the threat of a common problem. We know of the camaraderie and the excitement felt by those who march together, sit in, or form communes. Yet it would be an irrational society that sought a continuing state of protest, demonstration, and rebellion —or war or depression—so that its citizens could experience a sense of meaningfulness and unity through participation in "doing their own thing." The task before us is somehow to humanize the necessarily organized world so that people do not have to suffer the sense of remoteness and isolation from control of their own lives.

A people suffering from institutions that can't respond, problems that are virtually left untouched, and the myriad uncertainties of their own private and public existence must inevitably rise in protest [Goodwin, 1969, p. 44].

So our traditional primary social institutions like the family and the church, and the structures of another age, like homogenous neighborhoods, one-room school houses, character-building youth organizations, and town meetings, have declined in their influence. In their stead have risen bureaucratic monoliths, bigger and presumably better health, welfare, and education establishments, and increasing codification of the way in which their services will be provided to the people. As professional expertise improves, knowledge, skill, and technique in the health, education, and welfare areas of urban life achieve fantastic heights. But it may be, ironically, that those achievements could hasten the decline of personal control. For social distance is increasing rapidly between the efficient bureaucracy and the individual who must rely on it. The medical staff that is competent and self-confident is less likely to take the patient into the decision-making processes that concern the patient. Thus efficiency may in itself tend to isolate the patient from participation in his own life's decisions. We are not only concerned about the inefficiencies of bureaucratic organizations; in fact when they break down they are more likely to hear from their consumers than when they are operating on a high level of efficiency.

The dilemma is indeed one of institutional affluence, where a plethora of services, and most particularly good and expert services, could separate and isolate further the individual who is forced by the urban condition to rely upon institutions that are outside his control and jurisdiction. How can this distance be reduced so that humanization in urban terms will evolve as the hallmark of a democratic society?

Each person who seeks the solution to this most crucial problem of institutional affluence perceives the answer in his own terms of reference. Clearly it is a problem that must be attacked on all fronts at once; all approaches are locked together systematically; all rely upon each other for their potential effectiveness.

Promotion of Participation

We have assumed that all people in this society need to have, and not only to feel, a sense of participation in the forces and institutions that affect and control their lives. There is no simple prescription for this in a crowded, unplanned, and competitive urbanized environment, where the sources of goods and services are so remote from the citizen who must partake of them. So that we can see the total system of human services, those that provide for health, education, and welfare, it might help to break up the spectrum and view the components of the system separately. Here we are addressing the ways in which the service systems might be better able to provide for participation and involvement of the individual.

1. The primary function of *institutionalized human services*, of course, is improvement of the quality of life through the provision of adequate financial resources, housing, recreation, education, health care, transportation, and access to the advantages of the community and the beautification of the environment. If the general quality of our lives

could be enhanced, we would, of course, have less reliance upon residual service structures, and people undoubtedly would feel less unhappy about their lives.

2. *Planning* would need to provide the physical possibility for the smallest possible units of health, education, welfare, housing, and recreational facilities. Housing projects, if only somewhat smaller, would reduce the span of management and provide for a degree of face-to-face contact for tenants. Hospitals that had outreach health and clinical facilities spread through communities would be able to utilize the centralized facility for patient care and research rather than for general family care. Schools dispersed throughout neighborhoods would give parents and teachers their opportunity to communicate and would provide for full community participation. Welfare offices and social agencies, if decentralized, would become part of the fabric of community life, as would all other requisite social institutions, and would be more capable of providing services in accordance with the natural life style of the particular community groups they would serve. And should there not be within easy access in every community a library, park, day care center, theater, and meeting hall? Although it may all sound unreal to even suggest such guidelines for community planning, it would be completely unreal to consider other humanizing aspects of modern life without reference to the physical planning that is interrelated.

3. *Bureaucratic organizations* must decentralize so that their services will be closer to the people, more visible and accessible. Once they are localized, they will of course come under greater influence of their constituency, whose members might serve in all instances as local policy makers, bridges between the agency and the people in the community, collectors of data, translators of needs, and, increasingly, working participants in programs.

4. *Individualizing services* will be required to help people negotiate the complex service systems, to bring institutions

and citizens together in their common task of provision for
survival, and to provide direct help to every person who
wants and/or needs it. The nature of these services, the
terms of their availability, their aims, and their methods
ought to reflect the highest degree of community participation. These individualizing services, more than buildings,
organizations, and policies, are close to the individual's own
interest and would provide for his particular expression of
himself. Just as a community board might participate with
the administrators of the local hospital in determining the
most convenient clinic hours, it would be possible for the
community board to bring to the attention of the hospital
the prevalence of a health problem showing itself in the
neighborhood. Would it not be even more appropriate for
this process to be invoked with social agencies as increasing
numbers of recipients of service take their places on boards
and advisory committees?

The *terms of service* are community issues and actually
have little bearing upon the professional's expertise. Who
is to be served, under what eligibility rules, for what purposes, and under what conditions are the terms that would
best be decided by the people who would receive the
services. This feedback process is being demanded by
organized groups in the black, the poor, and the student
communities, and although it might appear to be a threat
to the professional doctor, lawyer, teacher, and social worker,
who have all enjoyed rather total autonomy in assessing
terms of service, this participating process can only support
the professional services themselves. People have begun to
recognize their need for participation in the remote institutions, and they will not wait too long before they insist
upon it.

The implicit threat to professionals is of course similar
to the threat of popular demand upon governments. Will
the people "take over"? Will vested interests be exposed
and exchanged? Will favored professional techniques and

stances be challenged and found wanting? The risks are very real, but the alternatives are limited.

In the first place, the primary purpose of professionalism is to serve the public, and the public of today wants and needs to have something to say about the services it requires. Second, participation in the terms of service could enhance the use of the services by the public. Consumer feedback to the institution of information, of unmet need, of timing and coverage of services would engage people more purposefully in the processes of help. This kind of engagement can only improve the quality of help: in more instances cases can be found before too much damage has occurred, clients can be helped into care by their neighbors, professional experts can be known by their patients, people in the community can be called upon to provide supports for those who are in difficulty, the lines of communication between person and organization will be open, and resentments will be less likely to build. And a third reason for providing for this kind of participation in the terms of service has to do with the increasing complexity of causation of physical, psychological, and social problems; the multidimensional threads of causation and the unknown directions of social change seem no longer to be within the boundaries of any profession's capacity to understand or to solve. It would seem, then, that the only way to remain in touch with the strains of social phenomena is to seek the feedback from the constituency that reflects those strains.

Thus we reach for a new form of institutional services in the urbanized context. Perhaps this will happen before "the fire next time," so that, unlike a Phoenix rising from the ashes, there will be a sophisticated, modern institutionalized response to the stifling, remote and debilitating urban condition.

We come, then, to the role of social work practice that must derive from such a view of the urban scene in the modern age. There will be, undoubtedly, an increasing role for the practitioner. Participation by the public in the terms of service will create demands for relevant and expert professional practice, for an effective practice that can be identified as different from that which one's neighbor or psychiatrist or community leader can provide.

Now that we have viewed the intricate context of social work practice, the next step on the way toward shaping practice is to observe the way social work screens in clients and their problems, the way in which practice is given its contours.

Chapter 3

Policy and Program: The Contours of Social Work Practice

WE HAVE EXPLORED the state of the field of social work, the environmental context in which people live and from which their physical–psychological–social needs derive, and the halting, unplanned response of social institutions to the rapidly changing life style. What has it all to do with the daily practice of social work? As suggested earlier, the very existence of social work practice is an *institutionalized* response to common human needs, needs that evolve from the late-twentieth-century living. The laboratory for social work practice is life itself, the unplanned, disordered, often unhappy and anomic life that people lead in their struggle to achieve love and intimacy, pride in their work, and sufficient economic and physical resources to lead healthy and fulfilled lives.

How these needs and requirements of life are defined, who

89

defines them, what services are to be organized to meet the
need, and how these services are to be delivered are some
of the concerns of social policy. By definition social work
practice must have continuing reference to these policy
considerations, and in its turn social policy would be only
an abstraction without its action arms and legs of social
service programs and their delivery through social work
practice. This connection, when made explicit, exercises
some constraints upon practice even as it poses challenges
and opportunities to create new services and to expand practice boundaries.

Social Policy: Too Little, Too late, Too Uncertain

Policies that govern services and practice in social work, as
in medicine, are made by public legislation, by voluntary
board and administrative decision, and occasionally there
is participation from professional staff and even the client
group that is in the consumer role. These policies give direction to the services performed, but they must be supported
by funds and there must be adequate staff available to carry
out the agreed-upon services; thus the mere existence of
policy is a guarantee neither of its application in the first
place nor of its quality in the second place. Furthermore, the
United States is notoriously policy-shy in the area of social
legislation; in social as in economic matters it favors a
laissez-faire, let-the-family-do-it approach to the intrusion of
specific mandates to guide family behavior or to support
family life. Therefore, although we have commented upon
uncounted ways in which the postindustrial society has
overwhelmed the family's ability to nurture, socialize, and
care for its own members, there is still lacking a "family
policy" as such in this country.

What does this mean? It means that there still is no public responsibility for seeing to it that families do not become poorer by virtue of having children, or even that families have access to the means by which they might choose not to have children. There is no recognition that new family life styles exist and that working mothers comprise most of the population of mothers of children under 18, so there is no national policy to provide group or family day care services as a response to the need of this high proportion of American families. There is no social policy addressed to the special needs of youths who separate from their families earlier in their lives than ever before, nor is there a grasp of the impact of cities on family life, making it increasingly difficult for families to cope with familiar tasks that presently need shoring up with social services. The management of the situation of the aged population is scattershot, the approach to mentally ill people is uncertain, the programs for people in prison are antediluvian, and even health care policy is being thought of from the point of view of medical insurance and corporate economics instead of from that of human need. All in all, the lack of coherent policies that relate to the health and welfare of individuals remains as one of the most serious injustices in our society. The lack of social policy is in itself an expression of national policy; the Pentagon suffers no lack of attention or budget, nor does any major corporation in danger of failure.

Finally, the limitations of social policy are noted in the lack of agreement about the purposes of some policies, if not their contradictions. The ethic of self-reliance in America, the myth of Horatio Alger, and the ringing 1972 inaugural pronouncement of Richard Nixon when he was elected by the largest majority ever in the United States, "Ask not what your government can do for you; ask what you can do for yourself," are all echoes of Social Darwinism and the capitalist ethic. Historical, international, social, and economic evidence to the contrary, people in America are led by government and other powerful forces, including their children's text-books and their Sunday sermons, to believe that it is strength of character and will power that make it possible to cope with the strains of today's society.

We have touched briefly on the edges of these strains—poverty, ill health, depersonalization, loss of family supports—and none of these is the result of loss of will power; each of them has its own set of socioeconomic causes and palliatives. The maladaptive results of people having to go it alone in a society that provides the least in services and care can be found in problems of starvation, child neglect and abuse, crime, delinquency, school dropouts, addictions, psychosis, depression, and family conflict. The contradictions in the purposes of social policy come into play when programs are invented to stave off the maladaptations people make in their efforts to cope with strain; it is then that society cringes at the thought of "too much freedom," "too much welfare," "too much mollycoddling," and the resultant policies straddle the purposes of providing services to protect society from people who are in need and of serving people in need be-cause as citizens they have the right to services.

Obviously the services, were they introduced earlier, would mitigate some of the excesses in behavior that society com-plains about. But as they are provided on the basis of residual need, that which remains when people cannot go it alone, then of course they must be focused on pathological events and unhappy behavior. Through circular reasoning people come to despise the very services that they need. By the time they are provided, the services are geared to social control rather than to self-determination, to therapeutic methodology rather than to developmental easements. There is no escape for the poor, and there is only avoidance by other economic classes. Thus the image of social services remains as negative, and even those who need them look upon them with fear or disdain.

The Role of Social Work in Policy Matters

The practice of social work is entirely interwoven with these issues in social policy formulation. Social services are the tools of the social worker, and the structure of those services determines precisely what he will do in his practice. How problems are defined and what services are to be allocated, when, and to whom are the policy–practice questions that undergird all social work activity. In order to understand fully the implications of the connection between policy and practice, one has to agree about the basic assumptions, or ground rules. We are governed in our discussion by a variety of sources: the National Association of Social Workers (NASW) Code of Ethics, the professional literature, social legislation, research and theoretical justification, popular expectations of social work, and practice wisdom. Taken together, they teach the goals of social work practice from which methodology should evolve (not the other way around).

As noted before, it is well understood now that in the history of social work method development, methodology for a time became an end in itself. Particular clients were sought who would best be able to use a method, problems were defined in such a way as to suit the aims of the method, and services were organized so as to promote the continuance of the method. While this process did indeed enhance the skills and develop the technical repertoire of some methods, it also tended to rule out of service as ineligible those clients with problems and objectives for service that were unsuitable. Further, the development of methodology required extensive investigation and selective application, and thus the time of service was often unlimited, so that skills were sharpened by advanced practitioners and decreasing numbers of clients were provided with the method itself. Finally, service delivery that did not require the high level of skills, and was in fact irrelevant to the aims of the method, was given less importance in the total scheme of practice, and inevitably the bulk of clients in need of the total range of services were excluded and left to the attention of lesser trained social workers.

In view of this history of practice in social work, it seems important to mention the following assumptions or principles of action to guide the policy-oriented practitioner of this age. We will consider four principles: accountability, epidemiology (knowing the range and extent of problems), autonomy of thought and action, and accurate perception.

1. Social Workers are *accountable* for those people defined as being in need of social services, be they called clients, patients, citizen-consumers, populations-at-risk, group members, or members of status or age groups. This means that wherever a social worker practices, in whatever field or setting, once the client group is defined (by whatever name), eligibility is determined only by membership in that group and not by any other criteria. Thus social workers do not use eligibility determinants like a *crochety* old man, a *hostile* mother on public assistance, an *ungrateful* delinquent, a *runaway* foster child, a *resistant* family member, an *angry* relative of a mental patient, an *uncooperative* medical patient, a *child-abusing* parent, a young man who *won't work,* etc. Once the service is defined for a classification of client, accountability demands that even the most difficult client be given equal access and attention. Under the imperative of accountability, a person who requests a service like public assistance or day care or a treatment residence for her child should not have to pass a test of motivation for personality change in order to obtain the service (Mayer & Timms, 1970). If a methodological model does not fit the client, then a different, more applicable model ought to be used.

But there is an even more significant implication of this assumption, which is that once need is defined by or on behalf of a particular group, there will be an inevitable *quantitative* impact upon service. Those practitioners who work in public agencies will be familiar with the meaning of open intake, for it not only permits the entrance of all kinds of clients into the helping system; it also allows for large numbers of clients who at times might overwhelm the system itself if there is insufficient or inadequately prepared staff. Currently there are proportionately few professionally trained social workers in public agencies, and therefore the bulk of individualizing services are being provided by the least trained practitioners. The reasons for the lack of graduate social workers in public agencies are complex, but they probably have something to do with the still-present preoccupation in the field with the development of methodology. If one is more concerned with improving one's "skills" than in providing services, then one avoids the setting that is overwhelmed by clients and their needs.

Voluntary agencies, those that are not part of the federal, state, county, or municipal systems of government, would seem to be subject to considerations of accountability as well. Private or religious agencies generally receive their funding from the public in the form of contributions, and to some extent from government funds. While individual voluntary agencies cannot be held as accountable for coverage as can public agencies, they can provide coverage through organizing networks of services or through assuming specialized tasks not undertaken by public agencies. The issue of public and voluntary service structures begs the question of accountability, for indeed health and welfare services are not market items, and the continued existence of voluntary agencies relies upon their ability to provide their services to those people who are in their geographic, status, or problem definition "catchment areas." No social service agency is really immune from the requirements of accountability, once the terms of its coverage are defined.

The use of accountability as a significant assumption in

modern social work practice is not a haphazard choice. Considering the complexities of the world in which we all live and the fact that social provision in services to the aged, children, and sick people, for example, is burgeoning in response to identified need, there is going to be an overwhelming demand for social work services. Social work practitioners who are educated and experienced in carrying less than a dozen cases are going to have to retool to meet the professional demand that will be made uniquely of social work. Those who have viewed skill development narrowly will have to reconsider and observe that refined skills are also necessary and appropriate when applied to a broader base of client problems. We might have to review the kinds of skills we use so as to assure their relevance to the kind of social need that exists and their adaptability to the principle of accountability.

Accountability also implies responsibility for the well-being of the client group assigned by government or private auspices to the social work profession. Logic suggests that preventive service brought into play earlier in the process of the development of problems rather than later would be the most appropriate aim of intervention. Yet most of the methodologies in social work have been devised from therapeutic and not preventive models of treatment, and the prevention goal seems to be continually in search of a method (C. H. Meyer, 1974). Finally, there is an aspect of accountability that borders on other assumptions but has its place in the philosophy as well as the methodological concerns of practice, and that is parsimony or economy of effort, the least done for the greatest outcome. In view of the spread of services, the increasing numbers of people we expect to be wanting and needing those services, and the not unlimited numbers of social workers who will be available to provide these services, parsimony seems to be a requisite.

There are vast implications to be drawn from this concept, such as briefer worker-client contacts (Reid & Shyne,

1969), attention directed toward client functioning and environmental modification rather than efforts at personality change, increasing use of dyad, triad, family, and group objects of help as well as enlargement of the unit of attention (person-in-situation) in order to address balance and fit and adaptation (Germain, 1973). These shifts in practice goals, while appearing to be accommodations to the demands of accountability, will be discussed in Chapter 5 as being most reflective of the modern life style and new knowledge.

Accountability as the most fundamental charge to social workers means a charge to get the job done that is assigned. Serious consideration of this charge would have us review fragmented agency services, ping-pong referrals, arbitrary weighting of some services over others, the development of some professionally desirable practices over others, unplanned allocation of services, and the promotion of specialized practice models that are not fitted into a plan of total coverage. While the idea of accountability is not new to the profession, the pressure for it is such that where social workers do not fill service needs, agencies and other auspices are engaging other helping personnel to fill the vacuum. A commitment to accountability, as we shall see, will have a considerable effect upon the practice goals of social workers.

2. *Epidemiology,* or knowing the range and extent of problems, is as essential to the repertoire of the social worker as it is to the doctor in the clinic. How else but through knowledge of the presence and dimensions of a problem would a social worker know how to develop appropriate programs? Practitioners in this field are notoriously casebound, so that when they are asked to describe a social phenomenon, they present a single case illustration. Some graduate students were surprised when, as an assignment, they studied the characteristics of the caseloads carried in their agencies. They found startling data, such as that the modal sex-age in a child guidance clinic in a ghetto was 10-year-old boys; they thought it would be 14-year-olds. They

were uncomfortable about their prior diagnostic judgments when they realized that most of the out-of-wedlock mothers they were seeing were 12 and 13 and not 17 or 18 years old.

Both of these findings indicated something new in the way of the program structure. Continued schooling for the girls did not have to await specific, diagnostically determined need in each case; here was a statistic that dramatized immediately the need for agency action on a large scale to provide the necessary continuing education for 12- and 13-year-old children whose education had been interrupted by their pregnancies. The situation of the 10-year-old boys was found to be similar among agencies; the age of troubled children has decreased. These were boys who were in difficulty in school and on the streets, and, as it turned out when they were recognized for the large group they were, children with no recreational or after-school opportunities. The program implications all but called out for attention; earlier each child had been viewed in isolation, as if only he suffered the pathological results of ghetto living. In both of these examples, neglect of epidemiological data distorted the reality of the children's lives, and without passing judgment here on whether or not the psychotherapeutic activity that was pursued was of greater priority, it is evident that developmental service possibilities were overlooked.

Knowledge of the range and extent of problems would also provide for the social worker a perspective on what is "out there" to be done and therefore how to assign priorities for his work. For example, if a social worker is given a caseload without reference to its representativeness of problems not touched by his agency, he will be given only half of the knowledge he requires to do an accountable job. Twenty-five cases, fifty cases—what do they represent? Are there twenty-five or fifty more families in the neighborhood or catchment area with similar problems? Are there a thousand?

In the first case, perhaps the twenty-five or fifty cases can be absorbed through using more parsimonious treatment methods or changing individual contacts to group meetings. In the second case, there will need to be a meeting of community residents and agencies to determine the nature of the 1,000 problems and what is to be done by whom. To assume that the worker's caseload is all he has to think about is to deprive him of being an important part of the social welfare structure and to delude him into thinking that he has time enough to do alone everything that is needed and that he has done his part in coverage. As long as there are not enough graduate social workers particularly to assume this kind of coverage, then society will come to share the social worker's delusion until it becomes apparent that an awful number of people are not receiving services.

Understandably, when need is so pervasive, the practitioner seeks ways to defend himself from too much awareness of the realities "out there." However, it is our assumption that the reason for social workers' avoidance of problems that are theirs to account for is that they are trained to not see and to not count; they are expected to keep their noses to the grindstone and to do their work well with their clients and to not notice what the agency chooses not to notice. It is not within the work ethic of the social work practitioner to demand to know, despite the fact that student after student begins his professional career with that objective in mind. The response to knowledge of the scope of need does not have to be guilt and retreat. An action-oriented professional might confront such a reality and devise ways of inventively providing services.

3. *Autonomy of thought and action* on the part of the practitioner follows from the necessity to know the range and extent of problems and to be accountable for the social service needs of people. In the next chapter we will discuss the kinds of knowledge necessary for practice itself; here we refer to the expectation that the practitioner use his intellect creatively and independently, as he derives skills from the knowl-

edge available. It might seem like an empty gesture to comment upon autonomy, as one ought to assume that this is one of the chief characteristics of any professional. Yet social work has a long professional history of internal controls, career-long supervision, process recording for administrative purposes, bureaucratic rigidity, and, in some instances, worker passivity. It has been thought that it might be impossible for social workers to perform autonomously in their work because of the way in which their activities are bound by the social agency structures in which (by definition) they work. It is true that worker autonomy is subject to administrative policies, the structure of services, and the vagaries of bureaucratic flimflam. Yet the alternative would be an entrepreneurial or private kind of practice which would lead us even further away from the goal of accountability.

There are two essential difficulties with viewing this kind of practice as a solution to the constraints of social agency practice. First, it is impossible for a professional field characterized by private practitioners paid by fees to assume accountability for all of the people it is to serve. The fields of medicine and law are examples. Second, it is technically impossible for an individual practitioner to command the multidiscipline and multipurpose services, in quality or quantity, that are required to meet our modern view of human need. Thus the practitioner in private practice usually defines himself along methodological dimensions and pursues the identical route social casework has pursued through recent history.

Therefore, for good or ill, the practice of social work is linked with social agencies, just as the practice of some medical specialities like surgery is linked with hospitals, and teachers with schools; they are, by definition, structurally and functionally connected. But the question of autonomy still remains; a profession of "agency employees" is not a profession at all. That a professional (a doctor, teacher, social worker) is employed by an institution need not diminish the freedom to think straight and practice with craftsman-ship—unless a profession so induces its young recruits to behave. When social workers are not engaged in under-standing and working with the whole scheme of social work problems, including the policy framework for practice, they naturally tend to do what they are given to do. This is especially true when the job involves a dozen or more cases; social workers always have enough to do. In fact, no one is ever busier than a social worker with a large caseload.

Without full awareness of the ways in which social policies as reflected in agency policies and practices *define* those busy jobs being done, the practitioner soon becomes task-oriented and afflicted by tunnel vision—this is the scourge of accountability. The development of professional account-ability begins with social work education. (Chapter 6 will deal with some of the differences in the degree of autonomy among different academic levels of social work graduates.) It is with the orientation to context, purpose, and account-ability of social work that the practitioner begins to locate himself in a very large scheme of service provision. Very early in that process is when the student must be encouraged, and be offered the teaching models, to ask questions such as these: Who decides that is a problem? Why is the service set up that way? Who is left out? What is the cost and who pays it? What are alternative ways of designing services? What sources of knowledge can be used to support social work intervention? What practices apply in these situations but not in those?

These are critical questions that should be raised in the spirit of inquiry, and the new social worker quickly learns that some answers are still forthcoming, that all answers change depending upon different circumstances, and indeed that often there are no answers at all to some difficult ques-tions in society. The practitioner who assumes this intel-lectual stance in his professional behavior is prepared to carry it on in his career in social agency practice. Being knowledgeable, critical, and effective in his work, he brings professional autonomy even into large bureaucratic agencies.

Of course, some people are more courageous or aggressive than others, but intellectual clarity, adherence to principles, and respect for craftsmanship in designing programs and in carrying them out are not qualities that rely upon advocates primarily—that is, unless advocacy is the considered intervention in a particular situation. The ability to recognize each case as an exemplar, to lift ideas to the level of concepts and working principles, to have wisdom about the background issues when an action is taken or a law is passed—these are qualities of the mind not of the feet or the loud voice. The expressed aim of all professions is expertise in a specialized field, and no less do social workers seek that aim. The fact that social workers function in social agencies changes this goal not a bit.

As social policy and agency structures become more reconciled with practices and skills as part of the total approach to social work, it will become evident that policies and structures themselves are *part* of the cases and the problems being served. Sometimes the policies are so obstructive, narrow, or negligent, as in certain intake restrictions, that cases cannot be served without first attempting modification of those very policies. At other times policies can be designed in the best interests of all concerned, and then a change of visiting hours in the hospital, a group meeting for intake, or a coffee pot in the waiting room may affect deeply the direction the case will take while it is under care and ever after.

Thus, increasing familiarity with the dimensions and scope and content of social policy and the impact of agency structure and services will expand the boundary of knowledge and activity for the professional social worker. As meaning, purpose, and rationale are understood, the practitioner matures in his expert's role; as he grows, he develops security and acts autonomously. This is the reasoning that has led us to assert that autonomy is intricately connected with accountability and the process of epidemiology. The presence of this mind set will prepare the worker for his grasp of specific issues in the policy–practice framework of social work.

4. To call for *accurate perception* of social problems and related social services is another way of saying that it is important to view human need through the right end of the telescope. Given the proper professional mind set, a sense of accountability, an awareness of the scope and range of problems, and the autonomy to think and act in response to real concerns, the social worker will be freed from only methodological constrictions. He will recognize need as it is expressed in life around him, from empirical evidence, from continually asking questions of the potential client group he seeks to serve, and from theoretical investigation. He will not then constrict his practice to only what he deduces from clinical observation. To the degree that a professional in any field gains his knowledge, skills, experience, and thus his *perceptions* from the breakdown of forces, he will have a distorted, residual view of the problem at hand. Then, as the tail wags the dog, services will be geared to problems defined through clinical lenses rather than through other contexts of life.

The school teacher who views his students all as having reading problems will have to construct a classroom environment with remedial devices and special assignments, requiring time he doesn't really have, so as to offer tutorial attention that will both wear him out and give the children a sense of failure in a tense, competitive, and difficult learning atmosphere. Contrast this picture with a classroom where a teacher assumes a normal readiness among pupils to read and thus can make reading a pleasure rather than a chore. Of course some children will have reading problems, but the classroom will be geared to growth and development of all the children and remedial work will be a sideline rather than a characteristic of the school day.

In the second example, if reading problems appear to take over as modal in the classroom, given what we know about normal child development, age-specific cognitive readiness, and the expectation that children want and need to learn for their own sakes in order to be able to master their environments, it would have to be assumed that the failure of reading is due to causes outside of the children themselves —in the school atmosphere, in their home conditions, in the need for eyeglasses or breakfast. In other words, it is to be expected in the normal run of things that children seek to learn to read as part of their normal development in this culture. A classroom atmosphere should support that, while still providing for special help where children fail for lack of cognitive ability or for other idiosyncratic reasons.

The first classroom, viewed through a residual lens, implies a whole set of semi-therapeutic–rehabilitative conditions. The second classroom, seen developmentally, addresses the reading task as a life task; where there is failure, special attention to improved mastery is not the same as viewing the teaching of reading as a therapeutic problem.

In medicine, where a developmental approach to health care would seem to be harder to demonstrate, there are many examples of prevention where service is structured so as to avoid clinically defined breakdown. The doctor who seeks to keep his patients healthy devises with his patient a regimen of regular visits and adequate diet appropriate to his age, weight, and general physical picture, and trouble is anticipated where possible. When clinical symptoms appear, they are viewed appropriately as conditions of disease, but patients who are well are hardly viewed as a mass of yet-to-be-developed symptoms. There is time enough for that if disease occurs. The public health model in medicine is well known, where a clean water supply is considered the first appropriate measure to prevent certain diseases. Also, in dentistry, it is now understood that fluoride in the water can prevent tooth decay and painful visits to the clinic. Young lawyers have begun the practice of instructing certain client groups about their legal rights before it might seem necessary to go to litigation. Thus a welfare mother would have access to this information as a practical matter to aid her in her claim for assistance; she might then never have to become a legal client with a claim.

It would appear that social work, the profession most intimately connected with people's life tasks, unique styles of life, and the social institutions which support or obstruct their adaptations, would be most interested in accurate perception of the way things are in reality, before they are screened through the artifacts of pathological labels. Recalling that life in the urbanized society is the context of practice and that policies give practice its contour, we will consider contrasting approaches to a series of social work problems. Since policies always govern practices, it is not the presence or absence, but the direction or attitude of these policies that will concern us. We will be able to see that practice differs markedly in accordance with context and with which contour is followed.

1. The Problem of the Unmarried Mother

Theoretical explanations of out-of-wedlock pregnancies range from those that assume a psychoanalytic point of view (Young, 1954) to those that take a socioeconomic posture (Vincent, 1961), with cultural, ethnic, and other sociological explanations in between (Roberts, 1966). In order to see how practice is defined by policy that derives from theory, a particular view of the world, epidemiology, practice wisdom, or any other context, we will select the two opposite theoretical extremes as illustrations.

A. *The unmarried mother in search of the resolution of the oedipal conflict* is the most traditional conception of this problem. In its outline, the girl unconsciously seeking to have sexual relations with her father finds a "faceless man" who will be a stand-in for the father. As with married girls, the ultimate oedipal resolution is to have a baby; but in the case of the unmarried mother, the baby's father is barely disguised as a substitute for the young mother's own father, and the resultant guilt pushes the young mother to offer the baby to her own mother, almost as if she hadn't had the baby herself, but did so through identification with her own mother. The unconscious need served, the unmarried mother has no "real" connection with the "faceless man" or even the baby, who is, after all, merely a symbol of her oedipal acting out, or perhaps even of herself. It is as if the girl has lived on two levels, one a fantasy and one a reality.

Traditional social agency services and social work practices have been structured to serve the theory. For example, helping the unmarried mother to overcome her denial of reality, that is, that she is pregnant with a real baby, is a primary objective of casework treatment. This entails helping her face the fact of her pregnancy sufficiently to go for prenatal care and to plan for the baby. Assuming that the baby is the product of unconscious acting-out behavior and is therefore not a wanted child as a responsibility, plans need to be made to care for the baby either through involving the girl's own mother or through adoption. The baby's father, the "faceless man," is often not brought into the treatment plan because he is as symbolic in the pregnancy as is the baby. The young mother may be offered shelter care if she is very young or inexperienced or afraid of her parents' wrath, and from the beginning an effort is made to help the girl understand the reasons for her pregnancy, which are unconscious, according to the theory.

This being a treatment objective, the motivation for treatment must be high, intelligence adequate, and verbal ability good, for the level of treatment must be insight development, or resolution of unconscious conflict will not occur. The therapeutic objective here demands highly skilled psychotherapeutic staff—social workers, psychiatrists, or psychologists, and no staff less qualified than by graduate education. The assumption of adoption of the symbolic baby places the agency's services in the sectarian mode and inevitably rules out of eligibility babies of different religions. The depth of treatment required demands a lengthy time span and a small caseload because of the necessity to divide the day into fifty-minute segments. The theory, then, conditions the agency's policies, which in their turn determine the kinds of services and practices to be conducted by the staff.

Once again recalling the context of practice and the concepts of accountability and epidemiology, how well does this approach to practice in social work meet the criteria of service? The accompanying illustration indicates that between the starting point of identification of the population-at-risk and the conclusion where resolution occurs, there is excessive attrition. The least number of unmarried mothers are served by the highest skilled staff using methology rather than service as the primary interventive variable.

Census of unmarried mothers	Number of unmarried mothers of a specific religion	Number of unmarried mothers with appropriate motivation, intelligence, verbal skills	Availability of skilled psychotherapeutic staff	Adoption and resolution of conflict

B. The opposite conception is that of *the unmarried mother as a young woman reflecting current sexual mores* who is in need of prenatal care, help in planning for her baby and her postpartum experience, and possible help with family relationships, work or school, and child care (Shlakman, 1966). Here we view the same client, whose problem is defined quite differently and therefore demands a different kind of service structure and practice approach. The theoretical context here is that sexual mores have changed radically, making it possible for teen-agers to have free access to sexual intercourse and thus to the greater risks of pregnancy. Economic and psychological variables intrude in the process, especially having to do with knowledge and availability of contraceptive devices, pills, etc., the presence of strong family relationships, the life models in the young girl's community, competing interests in school, work, and recreation and leisure time interests, and the stimulation of overwhelming alternatives.

Of course, the true neurotic girl who seeks to live out her oedipal fantasy and the psychotic girl whose ego is not capable of sorting out real from fancied experiences will be among this group of unmarried mothers. The wide range of possibilities in this formulation requires a wide service structure so as to effectively meet the specific, individualized need of each pregnant girl. A single model as described for the first type of unmarried mother would never do for those clients who could not fit into that type. The policy governing the service structure and the practice mode would have to take into account the broadest view of need in these cases, and the chart depicting accountability would have a totally different configuration. Adoption services, for example, would not necessarily have to be joined to services for unmarried mothers, because it would not be assumed that every unmarried mother was acting out an unconscious fantasy, thus making the baby only a symbol who might best be adopted for its own welfare. If (sectarian) adoption services were maintained separately as a specialized program, it would not be essential to place sectarian strictures on the services to unmarried mothers because the baby (always a religious symbol) would not necessarily be in contention.

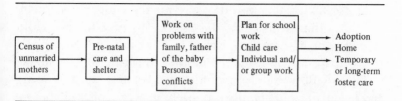

It should be noted that there is no narrowing of the service structure, no loss of eligibility, no loss of account-ability, and that there is a recognition of the reality of numbers. These are services universally and *characteristically* needed by all young unmarried mothers; the way in which they are offered is differential, but by policy they would be available as needed. No unmarried mother with any psychological, intellectual, economic, ethnic, verbal, physical, or motivational quality would *by design* not have access to these services. What is known about the specific needs of this group of clients will define the nature of the service, but the service net will be larger than with the first approach, and, as we shall note in Chapter 6, there will be opportunities for varied levels and kinds of human service staff to function in this scheme, whereas they would be too unskilled to be of use in the first scheme. Recalling what we have said about quantity of services as part of society's expectation of social workers, the decision to approach services to unmarried mothers in this way is reflective of the real world's events and a commitment to accountability.

2. The Problem of Child Placement

A child in foster care placement suffers deeply from the separation from his mother, his friends, and the familiarity of his neighborhood and school. We assume here, perhaps too readily for a typical example of child placement, that all means possible were used to prevent the placement. That is, a job for the mother and day care for the child, or adequate public assistance to allow the mother to care for the child at home, or homemaker service as a socially and financially inexpensive way to assist the mother in caring for her home, or outpatient medical or psychiatric care, or a better housing arrangement and family counseling were offered before placement was even considered. The availability and use of these preventive services of course are subject to social policy considerations, and under any rational scheme of practice that serves the cause of the least possible separation of children from their parents, it would be unthinkable for the social worker not to exhaust all preventive services before placement was offered. The invention of these preventive services, the decisions made as to their availability, the bringing together of the services with the person in need of them—these are some policy considerations that must be translated into practice actions by the social work practitioner.

Returning to the "case" itself, where it is now assumed that despite all preventive efforts the child must be separated from his mother and placed in the home of strangers, there are further interventive choices possible that could be illusive to the practitioner who is exclusively methodologically oriented. For example, the practice repertoire may be defined narrowly insofar as the unit of attention (the child) and the aim of practice (managing the separation) are concerned. Typically, a child welfare worker sees his task as that of helping the child "work through" his feelings about separation, and this treatment choice has its own multiple permutations.

A worker whose yardstick of practice competence is intrapsychic change would utilize the therapeutic relationship with the child literally to work through older, perhaps repressed, fears having to do with rejection, and by use of the transference would attempt to help the child perceive his current reality differently as a result of loosening him from his primary neurotic preoccupation. On the other hand, a worker using crisis intervention as a model of treatment (Parad, 1965) would help the child "do his grief work," according to the clear steps prescribed by the model. Further, the model expects that in the process of coming to terms with the crisis, in this case separation, the client's defenses are overwhelmed, and the very imbalance of the functioning ego would allow the client to recognize certain maladaptive patterns in his total functioning and therefore might with help be able to make some more radical changes in his perceptions and behavior. Thus our child client might through the crisis intervention experience achieve a more productive level of behavior as a result of his coming to terms with his separation anxiety.

Before moving on to other interventive possibilities, it would be worthwhile to ponder the implications of these and other therapeutic approaches to the problem of child separation. There are some difficulties to be found in the *exclusive* use of therapeutic approaches; some of the restraints have a long history of criticism, while others derive from quite new considerations having to do with new knowledge and the advent of developmental services.

Historically, as we have noted earlier, the selection of an intrapsychic treatment modality depends upon the motivation, capacity, and opportunity of the client to use introspective help, and in some circular fashion, perhaps as a wish-fulfilling prophecy, practitioners tend to seek out those particularly qualified to use the therapeutic model in question. What then of the child who is recalcitrant in these matters? What of the child who defines his problem differently and claims institutional or parental negligence as the cause of his problems? Furthermore, knowledge especially in the field of communications and general systems theory instructs us that the parent–child and foster parent–child relationships are reciprocal to say the least. In fact, when seen through a systems lens, the behavior of a natural parent reaching out for contacts with the child, for example, can easily be understood as contributory to possible defensive behavior on the part of the foster parent. Thus the child in placement as part of that particular triad can hardly be understood and treated without reference to his multiparent influences. So therapeutic attention to the child's necessity for grief work through confrontation of what has happened to him would be only a partial help if the foster parent had some need to keep hidden the truth about the child's parents, for example, or to keep suppressed the child's expression of homesickness.

The advent of developmental services raises even more pressing questions about the exclusive child-centered therapeutic mode of practice. Recalling that family structure is changing, that there are increasing numbers of single-parent families, and that in a postindustrial society it is essential for families to have a money income, it becomes evident that "something has to give" as far as institutional provision of services is concerned. There is presently little hope that the United States will have a family allowance program that pays the full cost of child rearing. Thus, especially in the case of lower- and middle-class families, the alternatives are limited but self-evident: reliance on public assistance or employment *and* the use of day care services.

The isolation of families with two parents from their own families of orientation further indicates the necessity of immeasurable supports such as homemaker or home help services, Visiting Nurse Association (VNA), etc. In effect, the demands of urbanized life upon young families are placing increasing strain upon child care. Further, society is gradually assuming greater responsibility for socialization and education of children at earlier ages, which is another indication of the gradual shift of responsibility of child care from family to other social institutions. These factors indicate that child welfare services will be expanding and that child placement might become a totally different modality than it is today.

Returning to the hypothetical case example, keeping in mind the considerations just mentioned, we would be most interested in fitting the child's placement experience to his own life style so as to allow for a minimum of disruption, particularly as we expect that placement might indeed become an increasingly common social provision. Children might experience temporary placements as child care, and if such were to be the case, their original parental ties would have to be sustained.

What other interventive possibilities are available to the social work practitioner functioning under the umbrella of a developmental social policy? Placement of the child in the neighborhood where he lives would, in a simple act, reduce the *real* loss of ties suffered by the child. The encouragement of parental visiting of the child and the temporary, possibly weekend returns of the child to his home (Loewe & Hanrahan, 1975) would make less necessary the "working through" of separation. There are cases where parental unfitness is an issue in placement, but in such cases priority should be given to surrender and planning for permanent substitute child care. Then, separation is inevitable and has to be given therapeutic attention. But in most cases, permanent separation would not be necessary with appropriate supportive and supplemental services.

The judgments used to decide the child's placement experience are based upon law as well as clinical considerations having to do with parenting capacity and whether or not the child can thrive better in a foster home. The decision as to placement and its purpose should be made at the time of placement itself, and where it is to be temporary or foster care, interventive efforts to improve the natural parent–child situation should begin then. Assuming that placement is determined as temporary, common sense would obligate the practitioner to maintain ties between the parent and child. Where legal and clinical considerations lean toward permanent separation, the practice task is totally different, in that the child should be able to expect permanent care by subsidized foster or adoptive parents, and the shape of the case will change.

Where temporary care is the purpose of placement, the ecology of the case will change and all interventive efforts would be directed toward engaging or reengaging the child in his familiar world. Obviously, there are implications for selection of foster parents who could sustain a true foster relationship of this kind. A less ambiguous placement status would allow for a less ambiguous foster parent role, and the conception of foster parents as child welfare team members might clarify their roles and expectations. Under developmental service structures there would be no question as to who the child's mother really was. Temporary child care would not demand of child, natural mother, or foster mother any greater role exchange than is experienced in day care, group care, or school.

It is noted, then, that the way in which child placement is defined by policy determines the way in which practice will occur. Whether the problem is separation, identity loss, or role confusion, these common problems of the child in placement can be treated in clinical terms or mitigated by a shift in policy.

3. The Problem of the Mentally Ill

This can be illustrated by the case of a patient who is about to be discharged from a mental hospital. Again, had prevention been a reality rather than a figment, the patient's contact with his own family, community, and way of life might not have been severed, and the task of helping him return to the community would not be so drastic. Nevertheless, multiple interventive choices are available, as in the child welfare case example. The therapeutic model would address the patient's anxiety, fear of new experiences, resurgence of old rejections, etc. While these considerations always attend the discharge of a patient from a long hospitalization (or placement), is it not more parsimonious to arrange as a matter of policy to maintain connections of the patient with his family, job skills, school work, etc.? In other words, the preparation of the patient for return to his community as a matter of policy must begin at the first contact with the patient. This act of maintaining connections would greatly influence the practice model being used.

4. The Problem of the Aged

In the case of the aged, one can view most clearly that policy discussions are the key not only to human welfare but also to the practice modes that address the aged and their problems. In this as in every field of practice, the wider the choice of life plans, the closer we come to providing true individualizing alternatives. For example, if a community provides an old age home as the single alternative to aged people's remaining in their own or their adult children's homes, then the social work practice task to help an aged person adjust to an unwanted plan is quite limited and painful for all concerned. The added presence of alternate services, such as meals on wheels, volunteer visitors, community health and recreation centers, and opportunities for aged people to serve as volunteers themselves would allow for a real choice as to desired living plans—to remain at home or to live under group care. The community's or agency's policy regarding its service provisions is crucial not only to the aged person's options but also to the social worker's intervention planning.

A skillful interview with an aged client assumes purpose and significance when it is possible for action to flow from it; it has limitations when the client has no alternatives. More often than practitioners are aware of, the main practice task is the development of a new service. It is at this juncture of program development that policy and practice come together. It is for this reason that it is so important for social workers to understand the context of their practice, to know how people live and what this kind of world requires for survival.

Accurate perception of a case in its psycho-social dimentions means that a practitioner has to view his skill as bringing together the policy and practice concerns that are relevant to the kind of case with which he is working. The examples just cited can be further illustrated in cases of the penal offender, the physically ill, and people with special handicaps and disabilities. Each field of practice defines its clientele in a number of ways, and defines a practice model to suit that conception. A view of clients as sick requires a therapeutic or remedial practice model, but a view of clients as reflective of the way life is requires extra individualizing dimensions through inventions of programs consonant with life style. One must always assume that clients or patients who are alienated or are physically removed from their families and communities will need to retain their ties, because they will be going home some day, or at the least will need to keep alive their image of belongingness.

The clientele of social workers are people in their particular environments, and it is the mandate to social workers to discern a means of easing lives. Consciousness of the ways in which policies and practices define social problems is a primary step toward a proper methodology, for it is evident to clients and social workers that the failure of social institutions and the overwhelming presence of systemic social problems are offering a very serious social reality with which all people have to contend. In the field of social work there are countervailing forces working all the time against the best efforts of practitioners who are seeking meaningful interactions with clients and alleviation of social problems.

Looking into any arena of practice one recognizes the pattern. In a family court, the social worker assigned a big caseload has to rank his clients in accordance with some system of his own as he selects among them those who will be most responsive to his help, or who are most in danger, or whom the judge has tapped for special attention. In order to meet the requirements of the court, of his clients, and of his own limited time, the social worker ordinarily concentrates on the most helpable, motivated, appealing, or challenging, depending upon many factors. The fact is that every family cannot receive the same amount of attention, and the attention or treatment itself may not be adequate to the complexity of the problem. Usually intervention on a program level will make the caseload more manageable. For example, using self-help groups like the Fortune Society, organizing a specialized employment service for probationers, engaging family members in prison-related activities all would tap some aspect of concern in the client's life. Such programs would expand the scope of intervention available to a single social worker, and at the same time would be reflective on the client's own real world. The task ahead seems to be to provide through new program designs for individualized attention to all on the caseload, keeping in mind the principles of accountability, epidemiology, autonomy, and accurate perception.

The intent of introducing policy and program considerations as dynamics in social work intervention is of course to illustrate the efficacy, parsimony, and social utility of manipulating service arrangements so that people can be enabled to live their own lives with autonomy and fulfillment *without* having to experience psycho-social breakdown first. *Flexible services* allow for true individualization in case problems, whereas rigid organization of services leads to funneling of the client into a predetermined category so that he will fit into the existing unitary pattern. *Involvement of client groups,* community organizations, consumer groups, etc., in defining the nature of their need allows for a more responsive service system that will closely reflect the concerns of the people involved. *Professional accountability* for the social problem being confronted allows for a wider access to service, hard knowledge of the extent of the problem, and broad-ranging social worker roles, and makes it possible to include new kinds of manpower in the service network.

The knowledge required for this policy–practice perspective would be different from that which has been required by social workers functioning as traditional case-workers or group workers, and the interventions that would flow from this perspective also would change to accommodate the newly formulated unit of attention. The next chapter of this book will be concerned with this knowledge, the bedrock on which social work practice performs its interventions.

Chapter 4

Frameworks and Knowledge: The Content of Social Work Practice

Social work practice is based upon knowledge as well as upon values and skills.

As with the notation of accountability as a basic assumption in social work practice, it would appear to be patently obvious that knowledge is fundamental to all professional activities. However, this is a more complicated issue than it seems, because of several related phenomena. One fact is that in the current period the profession of social work has not agreed upon the kinds of knowledge it requires in order to do its job.

It may be that this lack of coherence has a great deal to do with uncertain commitments as to the purposes and

Theodore Lownik Library
Illinois Benedictine College
Lisle, Illinois 60532

levels of accountability of social work practice. A clinically inclined practitioner may rely totally upon a theory of personality for his knowledge base, and which theory often depends upon some arbitrary factor such as the section of the country in which he lives, the school of social work he went to, or even his own life experiences. A social action–minded practitioner may deny the relevance of personality theory in favor of knowledge about how bureaucracies work and how they might be changed. A committed family therapist may be totally concerned with communication theory and other knowledge that explains the transactions of family behavior. A social worker with groups who is essentially concerned with the enhancement of group members' relatedness would address structural, functional, and group-developmental theories that serve his practice. So with all practitioners who have been educated and who practice in a specialized mode, leaving the knowledge parameters of general practice to catch-as-catch-can.

A second fact is that the state of knowledge itself is uncertain and research in social work is still haphazard. The promise of empirical findings through social work research has not been fulfilled (Kadushin, 1959), and when sound research does appear, the uncertain commitments in social work lead practitioners to use selective inattention; if the findings fit what we are doing anyway, we will use them, but if they do not, we will ignore them. There is not a strong undercurrent of demand in social work for research evidence.

Thirdly, we are in a period of civilization when the failures of all social institutions from the family and church to government services have so affected people that there is a kind of anti-intellectual stance apparent, and individuals have to come to "do their own thing" in order to seek fulfillment on their own terms as long as social supports appear to be so uncertain. The evidence of this phenomenon is in encounter groups, wild therapy, consciousness-raising groups of all kinds, and self-fulfilling action groups. The young social work practitioner is not immune from the same influences as other people are under, and where practice is governed by individual inclination, one can expect no reliance on formal knowledge.

Knowledge significant to social work practice. As we have said, the choice of knowledge depends upon the purposes to be served by social work practice. It is not yet certain that methodological specializations such as casework, group work, family treatment and community organization are diminishing in favor of the more appropriate specializations of social work in fields of practice associated with age groups and characteristic problems, i.e., family and child welfare, corrections, mental health, general health, school social work, the field of the aging, and addictions. But the influence of specialized methodology is still so forceful that it seems to be more realistic for now to present the purview of a framework of practice and continue to hope that the field moves inexorably toward a commitment to some accountable practice model and develops specialized knowledge in specific fields and problems. It is hoped that the model of the true expert in social work will be the practitioner who knows his field—the specific bio–psycho–social characteristics of the population to be served, relevant legislation, research, and organizational aspects involved in the appropriate spectrum of services. In this book we are addressing the knowledge underlying practice qua practice, for all expert knowledge finally comes down to the doing of something or the carrying out of service programs.

As we have noted, the conception of the purposes of practice determines the boundaries of the unit of attention and method parameters. In our view, the purpose of social work practice is to enhance the (mutual) adaptation of person(s) in the real environment so that the individual in his own terms and as a member of family, group, and community will find the best possible way of life through growth and development and survival of his person, his relationships, and his own life style. To this end, the individual has to be seen in an ecological or systemic relationship with his environment comprised of social networks, physical or concrete surround, and idea systems expressed in culture, the arts, politics, etc. The intent of practice in social work is to enable the person to carry out his essential life tasks as defined by considerations of his age, the socioeconomic condition of his life, cultural, ethnic, and racial affiliations, and his particular problems or maladaptations. Concurrently, the intent of practice is to seek out, develop, manage, and change environmental factors to create the optimum conditions for the individual to develop his capacities and interests (Germain, 1973).

What kinds of knowledge are needed by the practitioner in order to carry out these purposes of practice (Kamerman et al., 1973)? A framework or a map that will locate all of the relevant components is the first essential, and we will address this in terms of general systems theory with its transactional processes. Then, to have a way of viewing the person in transaction with his environment requires a sound background knowledge in modern ego psychology (Erikson, 1959; Hartmann, 1958; R. W. White, 1963). Also, one must have sufficient social science knowledge of the social, economic, and cultural forces that serve as the condition of life for various groups of people. Finally, a social worker needs expert knowledge of social policy, law, and agency structures and the substantive data about people and their problems, populations-at-risk, and special characteristics of the field in which he is practicing.

The Unit of Attention

The "what" to which social work pays attention undoubtedly will color the "how" of its practice and the requisite knowledge. A convenient term for this object of practice is the unit of attention. The choice of the unit of attention rests in several considerations, such as the consensus of the community and social work's own definitions about the particular aspects of life that are to be the social worker's turf. Although it must be granted that such decisions are seldom made rationally and that sometimes a public health nurse or a mental health worker may vie with a social worker for the opportunity of working with a particular client group or providing a special kind of program, in the marketplace where professional practices are pondered, tested, and traded a general agreement usually evolves, at least about the broad boundaries of all professional practices. A state may license; a profession may set up internal guidelines; a community may demand certain services. However territorial imperatives become structured, health, education, and welfare services eventually are allocated along some generally agreed-upon lines. The basic factors that ought to determine the unit of attention for any practice are the knowledge, skill, and ability to do something about the object it addresses—to be effective in providing its assigned services.

In the field of social work, where the boundaries of practice are potentially as broad as in social welfare and as narrow as in psychotherapy, it is more difficult than in most professions to define the unit of attention. A definition derives from observed needs in the community, values held by the profession, the history of its past actions, and, to a large extent, the base of knowledge and skills that would hold out the promise of effective service. However the definition is arrived at, it will ultimately express the purposes of social work practice; thus it is important to look carefully at the implications of various approaches to the unit of attention.

One way to define the unit of attention is to create problem classifications such as delinquency, child abuse, unmarried mothers, school drop-outs, interpersonal conflict, and effects of mental illness. But as fruitful as it would be to have a functional classification system of psycho-social problems (Finestone, 1960), the fact is that there is no universally accepted scheme yet in present use, and as all problems need to be subject to interdisciplinary services, such categorization would not really specify the units of attention that could be addressed by social work practice. Furthermore, definition by problem category would tend to confine practice to pathology and social breakdown and not to health or prevention.

Historically the unit of attention in social work has derived from modes of practice; thus social casework traditionally has focused its methods upon individuals and families, group work upon formal and informal groups, community organization upon community groups and processes. As we have noted, this division of labor increasingly has become untenable for a number of reasons. People actually live out many roles, sometimes all at the same time, as individuals in their families, groups, and a variety of communities—as citizens of the world. It is no more useful, probably less so, in social work to individualize in accordance with a methodological speciality than it is in medicine to view an individual as a set of limbs, a collection of organs, or a network of nerves. In assessing the individual and his condition of life, particularly the person who lives in a mobile urban society where the social context is ever changing, it has become quite impossible to address a single social status such as the individual qua individual or the individual in his family, groups, or community and expect to encompass the reality of the total and systemic experience of that person.

A third way of conceptualizing the unit of attention is to address categories of people in a variety of statuses. In this approach one would not need, as in the first approach, to presume the presence of problem or pathology, nor would the object of attention need, as in the second approach, to be forced into a preexisting practice mold that is defined by social work methodology and not necessarily responsive to the requirements of the people to be served. Typical of the statuses that would be the units of attention are ethnic groups, children, youth, working mothers, the aged.

These statuses are not related to problem categories per se; they are reflective of the special strains imposed by the nature of our society. The mere fact of having any of these statuses may be a "problem" to someone, particularly, for example, if one is black, poor, and a working mother, but none of those statuses indicates individual breakdown, even though its "problem" characteristics are evident in light of the conditions created by society at large that provide so little in the way of social supports for people of these statuses. Yet defining the unit of attention so that emphasis in service is provided for a particular group of citizens selected out from the mass has certain drawbacks. The question of universalizing the unit of attention in social work versus specifying certain groups to be given a high priority for service presents us with a major dilemma.

To *universalize* means, as Richard Titmuss says (1968), to recognize that "diswelfare" occurs to all people. As we have noted, our modern urbanized society is in a state of near-revolutionary change and all of the inhabitants of cities and megalopolises—which increasingly is almost everybody in this country—are subject to the strains of this crisis. Moreover, the problems of environment, social isolation, and impersonal bureaucratic institutions affect all citizens in one way or another, and it does not appear that social planning on a national basis will evolve quickly enough to mitigate the effects of these problems. To universalize means to assume the right to services as opposed to demonstration of need; it means that services would be made available before the articulation of problems, and service would thus become part of the fabric of society available to all in the same sense as other facilities.

We noted earlier that this view of service delivery is

called *developmental services*. There are significant problems with universalizing services or devising a unit of attention that would encompass all versus some people. Some people do not have equal access even to universalized opportunities, nor do they enjoy the use of their own private resources that would compensate for "diswelfare." If the unit of attention in social work practice were addressed to all people, the avoidance of priority approaches could lead to lack of services for those people who need them the most. This is one of the horns of the dilemma.

On the other hand, there are also issues to consider in formulating the unit of attention around *selective* statuses, where special attention is given to some people because of their greater need and their greater reliance upon public or extrafamily social institutions. Titmuss has brought out real concerns about choosing this approach. In selecting out of the whole those particularly deprived groups who would require priority attention, there would need to be some form of means test to define eligibility.

Where then would one draw the line? Assuming the poor are to be the primary concern of social work practice, it would be an arbitrary designation to assert that those families with income under $4,000 would be eligible, and those with income above ineligible. The need to draw some kind of line could force people into functional molds that would not necessarily suit their style or even accurately describe them. Another example might be mentally ill people; here again one would need to determine eligibility boundaries that would inevitably become rigid in order to maintain the focus of selectivity.

Despite the fact that this approach to defining the unit of attention would provide for priority attention to certain statuses of people in special need, it would be impossible, as Titmuss points out, to avoid the stigma of the status, the meaning of which could interfere with voluntary use and public support of services. This dilemma has confronted social work practice throughout its recent history and may account for some of the criticisms it has suffered. Practice is damned for focusing upon services to poor people and not solving the problem of poverty, and it is damned for universalizing its attention and thus avoiding primary attention in its practice to poor people.

There seems to be only one way out of this double-bind situation, and that is to define the unit of attention in social work practice broadly enough to include all people who would make use of social work services, making the definition flexible enough to account for all categories of need and open enough to respond to continually changing expressions of need. After all, a theory of practice cannot be tied to a single status of people, such as blacks or the poor, because times will change and need will be different; the problems of deprivation will look different in other times, and the people who suffer from deprivation may be other minority groups or groups with newly defined problems.

Titmuss has summed up this approach as follows:

> In all the main spheres of need, some structure of universalism is an essential pre-requisite to selective positive discrimination; it provides a general system of values and a sense of community; socially approved agencies for clients, patients and consumers, and also for the recruitment, training and deployment of staff at all levels; it sees welfare, not as a burden, but as complementary and as an instrument of change and, finally, it allows positive discriminatory services to be provided as rights for categories of people and for classes of need in terms of priority social areas and other impersonal classifications [1968, p. 135].

Once a position is taken that social work practice should include in its unit of attention all people, with provision for selective attention to those in greater need, the burden upon differentiation through a diagnostic or distinguishing process of assessment becomes even greater if social work practice is not to become a total abstraction that would be *about* the people to be served, rather than *with* them.

In order to specify the unit of attention in individualizing social work practice, we will continue to call it a *case,* the unique, differentiating unit that separates a person from all others (Cannon, 1954). It is important to note that we are not referring to any particular kind of case here, but merely to the conceptualizing of the unit of attention. In other words, although use of the case formulation is familiar to social caseworkers, in the present context we would also differentiate as cases those groups and communities that are addressed in individualizing terms by all social work practitioners.

Although the notion of the case historically has been the unit of attention for all professional practices, its meanings have changed considerably as evolving values, skills, and knowledge changed the perspectives of the case. In social casework the boundaries of the case have expanded; there has been a move from attention to intrapsychic conflict to attention to interactional functioning, from the person *in* his family seen in family-centered terms (Scherz, 1953) to the person *and* his family seen in transactional terms (Minuchin, 1974; Spiegel & Kluckhorn, 1954). In other words, use of the case as the unit of attention does not condition the practitioner to became psychoanalytic, or medical, or legal. The concept of the case is a movable one; its boundaries will change with the times. In order to place it in modern dress, we must identify the new *knowledge components* that are relevant to understanding a case, adapt *the process of individualizing* the case to the present social context, and adjust our conception of *aims of practice* with the case that will be consonant with the state of knowledge, the availability of skilled personnel, and the policy-induced contours of practice.

Terms and Ideas in a Changing Field

So many developments in social work practice have occurred in the last few years that it is necessary to provide a kind of lexicon so that the reader can differentiate among terms and can determine for himself which ideas are immediately useful and which are in the early stages of evolving. In the following pages terms are used and ideas discussed with as much precision as possible, but they are not defined in any one place. For the sake of clarity and for the purpose of having a road map, some of the essential ones are mentioned here.

General systems theory (GST) *as a perspective* is rather fully developed later on. It refers to the *frameworks* of knowledge, the *relationships* of variables to each other, the *processes* that explain the way systems function. It is not a theory of objects themselves, it offers no predictable judgments, and it provides no model of intervention. It merely provides for a way to draw the actors (animate and inanimate, psychological and social) together into a unit of attention for the practitioner to see the interventive possibilities.

The ecological systems, or eco/systems, perspective, drawn from GST and the science of ecology, is concerned with "the adaptive fit of organisms and their environments and with the means by which they achieve a dynamic equilibrium and mutuality" (Germain, 1973, p. 326). Even though general systems theory and ecology derive from different theoretical bases (while both drawing on the science of biology), together, in the eco/systems concept, they provide a helpful perspective for viewing the interconnectedness of variables in cases, with special attention to the interrelatedness of persons-in-environment. This construct of person-in-environment has been, and remains, the central concern of social work practice, but a shift in perspective from a linear to a systemic shape has engendered some changes in the purposes and processes of practice.

As social work practice theory has evolved to encompass—or recapture—the mutuality of individuals and their specific environments interacting with each other, the eco/systems perspective has been useful in capturing the transacting elements in the configuration of cases. The perspective requires, as the earlier psycho-social construct did not, that the practitioner include in his case assessment and interventions environmental variables significant to each individual in the case.

PRACTICE MODELS

A change in perspective carries with it the inevitability of a change in practice model, or metaphor which practitioners follow or think about as the "image" upon which they base the work they are doing. When the traditional linear perspective of practice was psycho-social, there were ambiguities in purpose, knowledge, and values that led caseworkers to concentrate upon the psychological half of the equation, leaving the social part to the whim of the individual practitioner, agency, or theoretician. This concentration on the psychological aspect led practitioners to seek causation of problems within the person, so that people in states of trouble, conflict, maladaptation, disturbance, etc., were viewed as "sick" or "responsible" or inadequate to meet the demands of society. This perspective was syntonic with the *medical model* and *disease metaphor* of practice. The implications of this perspective and this model of practice are familiar to clinicians. The search for causation of the problem and treatment for cure generally remained confined to the person. Thus psychotherapeutic measures were devised as logical interventions. What has been needed has been a theoretical rationale to connect the person and his environment and to focus upon the transactions and adaptations between them.

Once one utilizes an *eco/systems perspective* and transactions among persons and environments are the salient constructs, then a medical model and disease metaphor are obviously impossible to use. We are now talking about relationships of variables and the *consequences* of their transactions; we are not talking about how things become the way they are and what *caused* them. When we contemplate the person in his milieu, we are dealing with mutuality of one to the other, of adaptations going *both ways,* of assessing imbalance and righting it, of devising an appropriate "fit" between the person and his environment, of interventions in the environment as well as with individual coping mechanisms. Thus we are far beyond disease and medicine; we are following life and its processes. And as the eco/systems theorists (biologists) say, life is the metaphor or model for practitioners to pursue.

THE MODEL OF LIFE VIS-À-VIS THE LIFE MODEL

The matter of a "life model" is still undeveloped theoretically, and there are different interpretations of the concept. According to Germain, who has developed the model for social work purposes, "The approach is patterned after the behavior of well-adapted or socially competent people of varying life styles in solving problems, dealing with discomfort, stress or crisis, and managing symptomatology without decompensation or regression" (1973, p. 327). This model relies heavily upon concepts of autonomous ego functions.

Ego psychologists like Hartmann (1958), Erikson (1959), and White (1963) have written about such functions of the ego that seek adaptation in the environment, as opposed to those ego functions viewed primarily as defensive and at the most mediating of the environment. The autonomous ego drives to have an effect upon the environment and seeks out growth-inducing experiences in the environment. The notion of an "action ego" changes the person from passive recipient to active doer on his own behalf.

The *model of life* is a more modest form of the "life model," which this author considers to be still at an incomplete level of development in social work practice. In other words, in the following chapters we are not assuming that there is a life model of practice that is as yet as well developed as was the prior medical disease model. While having gone beyond pursuit of the medical disease model, for reasons mentioned earlier, we have to recognize that a *practice* life model does not yet exist. This is probably because we have not yet devised dependable or predictable approaches to reinforcement of adaptations between the person and his social and physical environment. However, *life* exists, and if we sharpen our observations, recast our perspective, and advance through research on an empirical base, we may yet devise a valid life model of practice. The life context of practice referred to in this book is a compromise solution to our current situation. The eco/systems perspective *requires* a life model of practice; until we have developed the components of this model, we can learn a great deal from the way people manage their lives in a world that is full of stress.

An example comes to mind that relates crisis intervention in situations of *mourning* to models of the way different cultures cope with mourning *in life* itself (as opposed to the clinical context). Every culture provides for rituals and steps that will enable mourners to cope with loss. What else are Irish wakes but opportunities for families to face the reality of death, to have affectional supports, to review the past, and to prepare for the future? Crisis intervention, as a model of social work practice, contains all of the steps that are present in normal life rituals. Are there other "models" in life that will offer helpful clues to social workers in the way people care for their children, manage separation, marriage, conflict, and drinking, etc.?

However the life model is developed, it will have a profound effect upon the interventions used by social workers, the knowledge base, the way services are organized, and the way help itself is defined.

The Boundaries of the Case

The lens through which one would look at a case should be fashioned by the social context of that case. In the urban situation, where people are wedged together in all degrees of congestion and where they must be reliant upon each other and upon services in order to survive, the view of the case would need to be through a broad lens, so as to encompass all of the essential elements.

In social casework practice there is a tradition of viewing cases in a *linear* perspective; problems are traced directly to causal factors, as though with a pencil from A to B. Thus one might view a case of a child's problem behavior as caused by a disturbed parent, a case of schizophrenia as caused by intrapsychic disturbance, a case of reading failure as caused by some breakdown between school teacher and child. The perceptual *boundary* of the case is defined within or by the primary actors, narrowly conceived along a *line* of vision. In another context, reading a page is a function of linear dimension, as is listing factors sequentially in a social work case. Not only is a linear perspective a narrow one as far as case boundaries are concerned; it also promotes an isolating and self-contained view of case phenomena.

A linear view of man carries with it a certain nostalgia for self-reliance, individuality, and privacy. Who would not wish to return to the era in this country when people could determine the boundaries of their own existence, shape their own opportunities, and pursue obtainable goals? Of course the frontier myth was applicable only to certain people, but Social Darwinism kept the myth alive. It was thought that one could control his life and survive through being fittest, but even though the field of attainment was more open before the twentieth century, in fact most people did not have access to equal opportunities or they were not born equal. It does not seem possible today to approach a case as if it were independent of the circumstances of life surrounding it. There is no person of any class in the modern world who can manage his own life without reliance upon others or upon formal organizations. Thus, to view the case through a linear lens, as if man were a self-sufficient being who could be understood in a straight line, as it were, is a kind of hopeless confrontation of reality.

Our lens would shed greater light upon our understanding of the case if it had an *interactional* prism, with which it would illuminate the actions of individuals upon each other. Granting our assumption that people in the urban society are locked together, willingly or not, in their sometimes opposing efforts at survival, the view of a case would need to make provision for perceiving the many sides of the interactional processes and the actors in the scene. This broader lens would suit our purposes better than the first kind, for it would bring into focus a case of at least dual components, reflecting the interdependence of individuals in their multiple roles. Thus such a lens would not define a case as being a man, a woman, and a child, or even a family unit, but rather a man as husband, father, or wage earner in *relationship* to a woman as wife, mother, wage earner, or homemaker, and also to children serving their function in the family as sons and daughters, as students, and as members of peer groups. The interactional threads binding all of these individuals to each other would be observed and lend themselves to description.

In recent years theory of behavior has been enhanced by conceptualizations of certain interactional processes, such the double bind (Bateson et al., 1956), complementarity (C. H. Meyer, 1959), schism and skew (Lidz et al., 1957), and pseudomutuality (Wynne et al., 1958). So the interactional lens encompasses individuals in their many social roles that define their relationships in family, work, school, play, and all other social activities; moreover, viewing a case through this lens makes it possible to identify the processes that connect people, thereby opening opportunities for more precise intervention when relationships falter.

An interactional lens, however, is still too narrow in its scope when it is focused on individuals in their varied roles and relationships, for our perception of the urban condition suggests that there are other "actors" affecting all human experience, "actors" who may not even be in the relationship sphere of the individual in question but yet affect his life, "actors" that take the form of organizations and social networks which have become intimately connected in the life style of every individual in modern society.

In order to grasp the meanings of these multiple elements in every case, one needs to change to a *transactional* lens so as to comprehend the influences that literally cross over the individual, affect him, and are affected by him. The notion of transaction suggests multidimensional interactions all in interplay with each other. A transactional view of the case does not mean a mere addition of components, but rather a reconceptualization of them, so as to be able to view a *system* of interweaving forces, all having reciprocity and feedback with each other. Before we look into a scheme for dealing with these multiple threads in every case, we should take note of the widened parameters of the case that are suggested by this transactional view. The boundaries of a case will contain all of the variables that are subject to social work intervention. That is why it is so important to know how to draw the boundaries correctly.

The case boundaries would include the individual in his several social roles, interacting with those with whom he has intimate relationships, usually his family, but *in addition* the boundaries would include the dynamic environment of which he is a part. This would, differentially, include his extended family and diffuse relationships, his place of work, the schools his children attend, the neighborhood in which he lives, and the social, political, and commercial institutions that intersect his life. Moreover, the case boundaries would encompass his affiliations to culture, ethnicity, and class and his specific value orientations. In the event that the individual has formal connections with a social agency, the agency itself would be a component of the dynamic, affective environment and thus also be viewed as "an object or instrument of change, rather than a given" (Germain, 1968). Clearly, the breadth and complexity of the case viewed through a transactional lens is going to require the use of vast amounts of knowledge, which must also be put together in some convenient way for the practitioner's use. The unit of attention in social work *is the case,* but it has very wide boundaries that have to be comprehended. First we need to find an organizing approach for the requisite multiple theories, then we need to identify the primary knowledge areas, and finally we need to place the whole individualizing process in a context of intervention. We must see how it would work in practice.

"The Case" as a System

General systems theory, despite its mechanistic language, makes possible an organized view of the individual in his multiple interactions; it provides a convenient form for viewing the parts of things in an interrelated way so as to avoid fragmentation and disparateness. Menninger has commented on the part–whole question by differentiating the molecular point of view which assumes an entity to be invaded, from an atomistic or holistic point of view, where one sees "the totality of a living organism . . . not as the product of addition of parts, but as a unit within which parts may evolve *only by a deliberate and temporary shift of focus on the part of the observer*" (Menninger et al., 1963, p. 90). Keeping in mind that general systems theory is actually a theory about systems—a *framework,* and not in itself a substantive theory—it can be applied to many subjects, ranging from space trips to the moon to inventory measures used in industry to the social work case. Boulding says of general systems theory that it is:

. . . the skeleton of science in the sense that it aims to provide a framework or structure of systems on which to hang the flesh and blood of particular disciplines and particular subject matters in an orderly and coherent corpus of knowledge. It is also, however, something of a skeleton in a cupboard—the cupboard in this case being the unwillingness of science to admit the very low level of its successes in systematization, and its tendency to shut the door on problems and subject matters which do not fit easily into simple mechanical schemes [1968, p. 3].

The theory has so many attractive possibilities as a scheme for organizing knowledge and as a framework for action that one must be careful to avoid overdetermining its value and thus ironically creating a closed system of the theory itself. An example of this can be found in *reductionism,* the result of forcing one system of ideas into a mold that would fit another system that is, in fact, unlike it. The danger in this is that neither set of systems maintains its own integrity, especially when one is a theory of apples and the other a theory of oranges. Reductionism could obstruct us from advancing our view of the transactions of the individual in his sphere of society. An example given by Reinhard Bendix (1963, p. 61) suggests that:

If the symbols of a culture are taken as a clue to the characteristic personality types of its participants, then we underestimate the incongruity between institutions, culture patterns and the psychological habitus of a people, and we ignore an important part of social change [1963, p. 61].

The accepted traditional social casework view of the *person-in-situation* illustrates the problem of separatism between social and psychological sciences. This concept requires the connective *in* or *and,* because the person and the (social) situation have different theoretical components and are actually measured by completely different yardsticks. The sciences of psychology and sociology are conceived on different levels of abstraction and point toward different levels of intervention, and the state of knowledge is such that to compress both kinds of knowledge into one would either psychologize society or sociologize personality. Thus, while keeping both sets of knowledge systems separate and intact, our task is to intertwine the useful person-in-situation concept in such a way that the hyphen is no longer needed. Through a systems conceptualization, we might be able to view person-in-situation as a transactional or *field* construct rather than view it, as we have been accustomed to do, in linear or interactional terms. If it were possible (and of course it is not) to capture the essence of all possible theories about everything related to human behavior, sociocultural factors, social organizations, social planning, and method itself, it would be more than ever necessary to apply a systemic approach to the use of all that knowledge.

A conceptual umbrella is necessary to sustain a transactional view of a case, for without the reworking of the *organization* of ideas, one would be left with a lot of unparallel and disconnected meanings about concurrent happenings in every case. It would not take long for a practitioner to develop an affection for a favored theory; this has proved so in social work practice for fifty years as the pendulum has swung between inner and outer emphasis, even though the underlying concept has remained the person-in-situation. In a systemic view there is no inner or outer, but rather an operational field in which all elements intersect and affect each other. John Spiegel (1956) comments on this problem of the common arrangement of data in linear form, which makes it almost mandatory to assign a hierarchy among levels of data. A familiar illustration might be the description of a case as one where a working mother who was clinically diagnosed as a hysterical personality had no plans for the day care of her children, and the caseworker, while noting all of these components in the case, might seize upon the clinical manifestations and overlook the social problem of the need for day care. Spiegel writes:

> One handicap of linear hierarchy is that by focusing at one level then everything else becomes environment. We focus at points of interaction and neglect those interactions taking place in the extended field over time [1956, p. 17].

If we view our little case illustration transactionally, with the process going in all directions and reverberating back again, having modified all of the components, the case becomes one of a working mother with clinical manifestations of hysteria whose children need day care which may not be available in the terms of her need, because her relatives are not available to care for the children, because of the neglected neighborhood in which she lives, or because of the child care system in the city which allocates services along nonfunctional lines. Furthermore, the mother's need to work might stem from her lack of money, which would potentially connect her with the welfare system, with her husband's lack of support, which could involve the family court system, with her wish to get into the working world, which would connect her with the employment situation, or with her deep psychological push to avoid intimate relationships with her husband, which might lead her toward the social agency or mental health systems in the community. Whatever the assessment of the case, the parameters for intervention are broader than the mother and her child, and causation may be identified in any or all parts of the field of the case.

As the family's situation has implications for the delivery systems in the community, so indeed does the set of service systems reflect back and affect the structure and function and adaptation of the family. As Spiegel would say, these are all field phenomena; they are not hierarchical or linear, nor do they necessarily derive from each other. They intersect at various points in the existence of all the factors—the mother, her children, her husband, relatives, the institutions involved—and the balance of forces. Viewing a case in these terms makes it difficult to determine where one set of conditions begins and another leaves off, for they are in circular motion with each other; all depend upon the others for functional survival. When seen in this transactional state, they make the case for the social work practitioner who might intervene at any salient juncture and make a difference in the lives of the individuals involved (Atherton et al., 1971). The vast opportunities for intervention in such a broad-scale view of the case will have significant impact upon changing social work practices and the use of nonprofessional manpower.

General systems theory is in a stage of rapid development. Its characteristics are changing as more becomes known about it, as new fields become interested and theoreticians try to make new applications of it. The reader is referred to source and derivative materials here for a comprehensive understanding of the theory itself (Von Bertalanffy, 1966, 1967; Katz & Kahn, 1966; Hartman, 1970; Jainchill, 1969; Rizzo et al., 1969), for in the context of this book our purpose is merely to provide tools of conceptualization for social work practice and thus to show how systems theory can be helpful.

It would be a long detour to present a thorough exposition of systems theory in these pages. We continue to refer here to the social work case as a system and not to social work methods, which, of course, have their own systems characteristics. Also, it is important to note that we are not discussing theories of "social systems." It is common today to read about social workers "working with systems," or clients "interacting with systems." This is not the idea we are addressing here. Rather, we are interested in identifying the transactional processes explained in general systems theory (GST) so that we can devise a construct, map, or framework for understanding how it is that when one event occurs, a series of other events are set off in reverberating fashion. We seek to recognize the *relationship* among variables, not their defined characteristics. The systemic transactional connections between the person and his environment are our interest. To pursue the person *and* system notion is to return us to the old, plaguing dichotomous thinking of person and situation. We seek instead to erase the "and."

We will illustrate some of the systems concepts with another kind of case example, because the level of abstraction is still quite high in this theory, and examining the concepts through a typical case should make them more meaningful.

A three-year-old black boy is admitted to a general hospital in a ghetto area of the city for severe and extensive burns from lye. He sustained the burns as a result of coming between his parents when they were having a fight, and the mother threw the first available weapon at the husband. The weapon was a bowl of lye that was on the kitchen table.

The child must remain in the hospital for several months, during which he has to undergo skin transplants and a series of other complicated medical and surgical procedures. Thus in the language of the hospital he is a patient of pediatric, medical, and surgical services, and probably of several other categories of care, like a burn clinic, an orthopedic clinic, a skin clinic, an eye clinic, and a urology clinic. Moreover, he is known and visited regularly by a social worker, a psychiatrist, a psychologist, the whole range of doctors in all specialities and of all ranks, nurse's aides, attendants, housekeepers, and volunteers.

His family consists of his mother, aged 19, his father, aged 22, and a baby sister aged 1½. The mother's parents and brothers live in the south, and she has no present contact with them. The father has a mother who lives in a neighboring community and is the sole wage earner for her three children; her older children have left home either to be married or to go into the army.

The little patient's own family lives in substandard housing, an old slum railroad apartment divided into three rooms that all open into each other. Toilet and kitchen facilities are limited, the house is dirty, and the rent is too high for either the value of the apartment or the income of the family.

The mother dropped out of high school in her junior year when she became pregnant at 16 with her first child, and the birth of the second child continued to keep her confined to her home. She wanted to return to high school but never quite knew how to arrange it, and she had no skills to do any kind of part-time work that was worthwhile to her. Her vocational aim is to be an office worker, and while she is intelligent, she has no skills that would make this possible. The father is a high school graduate, having worked to support his family at an auto repair shop. He became interested in advancing to a mechanic's status and took advantage of an OEO program to get involved in job training. At the time of the fight, when the child was burned, the father had just received a certificate that would qualify him for a better job in a large automobile service station.

The history of the marriage indicated a rather good relationship between the couple; they had a romantic attachment and had interests in common in their social outlets and in the children. The major source of irritation had been the mother's inability to go back to school or to work; she felt herself to be too young to be confined to her house all day, and she expressed her resentment to her husband and to the children in many ways.

While little is known of the family backgrounds of the boy's parents, it is understood that they grew up in stable families, although neither of them had fathers at home. The wife's father died when she was very young, and the husband couldn't remember ever having had a father living at home. Her background was southern and rural, and his was northern and urban. Neither of them had been particularly militant about political issues until the death of Dr. King, at which time they both became interested in a local movement to support Black Power in the ghetto and in the community at large. One of the wife's discontents was that her husband was out in the workaday world and could make contacts in the movement, and she was unable to do so as easily. Both parents appeared to be well-functioning, although the wife seemed to have a depressive quality about her. The husband had a more devil-may-care attitude and did not worry as much as his wife. Their fight was actually no more intense than any other argument they had, except for the crucial fact that she threw the lye in the heat of argument. Generally, they did not do violence to each other, but the lye was there and she threw it.

It is assumed in systems theory that systems are either *closed* or *open*. For a system to be closed means that components are self-contained and not dependent upon their surroundings for survival. For a system to be open means that, as in the case of all living organisms, there is an *exchange* of energy between one system and another, between the element and its environment. As ecologists inform us, there are no examples of closed systems in life, as plants, animals, and minerals all take something from their environment, utilize it for their own growth, and then return some substance that has been modified by the exchange back into the environment. When social organizations, personalities, and relationships are viewed as systems, they can be described by the characteristics of open systems, for they must be mutually dependent upon each other for "survival." Yet it is not uncommon in viewing social systems that we find some that tend to be closed and end in a state of disintegration or entropy. When social systems are conceptualized as closed, they are not following a life model and, in a sense, are doomed as far as continuation is concerned.

We all know of theories that are closed insofar as being responsive to new knowledge is concerned; in such cases the theory, although a perfect entity, becomes dysfunctional in light of the new knowledge, and it finally is put to rest. The theory that the earth was flat could not survive in the face of evidence that the earth was round, and since the absolutism of the flat theory did not provide for the new information of vanishing horizons, it finally achieved a state of entropy. We know of small societies, where the sexes were kept separate and children were not born to replenish the society, that achieved a state of entropy as the elders died. Because they did not let in new influences, they could not generate a continuing society and thus became extinct. The matter of boundaries is important for our understanding of closed and open systems. Where the parameters of one system—whether broad or narrow—are too rigid and locked against intrusion from another system, the entity will not be viable.

Recalling our case illustration, there are several psycho-social events operating all at once, and as we said that general systems theory provides a tool for conceptualizing and is itself not a substantive theory, we will do no damage to the boundaries of any of the operational theories by viewing the case systematically.

We see at once a set of *personalities* that in this case are relevantly the boy in the hospital, his parents, and his baby sister. We view them as interacting and bound together through the common strands of their *family system,* and their reliance upon each other keeps open the access of boy to family and that of family to boy. They would appear closed if we were to look at the child, for example, in a linear way, assuming that he was only a conglomerate of instincts and attitudes that had no bearing upon his family, or no responsiveness to their influences. Further, we see a *hospital system* and its many subsystems in the specializations repre-sented by the many personnel we have mentioned. A con-tinuing exchange of energy or influence among hospital, child, and family would characterize an open physical–psycho–social system, although we often find some examples of efforts at closure creeping into hospital organizations.

Of course when closure occurs, it affects the interactional consequences. For example, the matter of visiting hours can be used to confine the hospital's activities and stiffen its systemic boundaries, or visiting hours can be used as an opening wedge for the family and hospital systems to inter-change with each other and keep both systems open. Another example of openness or closedness of communications be-tween the family and hospital systems is often found in the kind of medical information that is provided by the staff to the family or patient. Where the patient is kept out of the planning for his care and treatment, the hospital maintains closed boundaries which can affect the patient's improvement. Furthermore, where the hospital is not responsive to the patient's complaints about his care, there is less hope that appropriate changes will take place in the hospital system at large. We see that one system relies upon another for sustenance, and only as its boundaries remain permeable can we expect that system to stay alive and open.

As far as the parents are concerned, one might take a psychogenic or developmental view of them as having suffered familial and economic disadvantages themselves which could explain their marital conflict. On the other hand, one could also view them as responsive to the environment and in this case find that the husband's recent affiliation with a job training program had secured his vocational future at the same time as the wife was feeling the pressure of rearing two small children in the face of her career disappointments. The notion that "energy" or causation can be identified in environmental systems, as well as within personality systems, is well provided for in a systems framework.

In the *feedback process,* where energy is imported into the system, the theory accounts for the effect upon the system of the new source of energy, where the existing status of the system becomes transformed through the transactions of the person–family–environment systems. In our case example we could identify the change of self-image experienced by the father when he sees the possibility of becoming a mechanic. Recalling that this is a black family that is apparently conscious of its black identity, its members' asscociation with community organizations would undoubtedly contribute to a change of self-image from them all, creating hope for a better standard of living and possibly playing a part in the wife's sense of impatience about not being able to work.

The resultant marital conflict or the fight that resulted in the little boy's being burned by the lye might also be understood as a reverberation of similar factors. According to the narrative of the case, although we do not know exactly what triggered the fight, we can now assume that the marital tensions were partially responsive to the changes in the husband's vocational status and the rising sense of expectations the couple were experiencing. One could cite the use of the lye in systems terms by commenting upon the poverty subculture in the ghetto, where lye is a requirement to cope with insects and rodents and, as a reflection of that way of life, lye that is available in a bowl on the kitchen table becomes the poor man's weapon in domestic violence.

The feedback process operates not only within systems but also *among them in cyclical fashion.* In other words, after the lye-throwing incident, the private fight between the marital partners has become a public matter because the child has been burned, and the hospital has had to become involved in the family's activities and relationships. This provides the potential for "reworking" the interpersonal relationships and "returning" them improved, as it were, to the family system. The very fact of the publication of their fight makes possible the intervention of social service or psychiatric care or the provision of day care services, so that the wife might also go to work, or whatever treatment action that is seen to be relevant to the case assessment might be taken.

Where a state of tension occurs within the system, the only way in which this tension can be expressed and thus subside is through environmental reciprocation and reinforcement. Using our case again, we note the family's participation in community processes which in turn contribute to the family's improved sense of dignity as black people in a hostile environment. Frustration occurs when the family's improved sense of dignity propels it into wanting greater participation in the benefits of society at large; that is, unless the world responds relevantly with money and housing, the tension will build and create even greater frustration and discontent if it is not relieved in the system at large.

A dynamic balance is achieved when the system is in a

steady state—when it is in motion but retains its original characteristics. In our case illustration we can assume that the marital relationship has proved to be workable for the couple, although it has been set off balance at a time of marital crisis that seems to have been precipitated by the new job opportunity. If the complementarity between the marital partners is to be sustained, either it will occur by itself and they will "right themselves" through their own natural style of functional adaptations or they will require some kind of professional help. In order to maintain their complementarity, or previous homeostatic balance, intervention will have to take into consideration the couple's tolerance for each other's job advancement, for example.

Another example in this case of the homeostatic principle that would govern intervention or explain the case might be seen in the absence of the boy from the family while he is in the hospital. As he is an integral part of the family and serves a significant function, exemplified by his coming between his parents during their fight, his confinement to the hospital will require that his parents make some accommodation, alone or with help, to right their family balance. Assessment of ensuing imbalance would have implications for the hospital's flexibility in providing for family visiting, etc.

Assuming that the parents in our case would want to be more compatible about the question of their job competition as well as to live better in the society, the paths to these goals are multiple. In systems terms, *equifinality* operates as a principle—the assumption that there are many ways to achieve a single aim. Depending upon the assessment, the kind of family situation this is, and the kinds of systems with which it interacts, a range of approaches to these parents' accomplishment of their aims for themselves are possible theoretically. Beginning from "the inside out," the parents could undergo psychoanalysis and attempt to resolve their basic personality maladaptations; they could have marital counseling through a family agency; the wife could be helped to return to high school, so that she could go to work; or day care services could be made available, so that she could go to work or return to community action activities.

As far as the child in the hospital is concerned, he could be treated medically only, or he could participate in ward activities to counteract the onset of "hospitalism"; visiting hours could be expanded to make possible his father's visiting around his working hours and his mother's visiting whenever she felt able to do so; a social worker could be available to see his parents when they visited; and the total range of hospital personnel could be engaged to provide for him a milieu with a health-promoting atmosphere.

One or all of these interventive modes would derive from the systems framework. A simple picture follows of the systemic relationships between the family in our case example and the social systems in their transactional field:

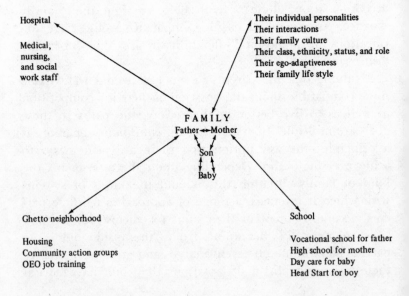

Hospital

Medical,
nursing,
and social
work staff

Their individual personalities
Their interactions
Their family culture
Their class, ethnicity, status, and role
Their ego-adaptiveness
Their family life style

FAMILY
Father ←→ Mother
Son
Baby

Ghetto neighborhood

Housing
Community action groups
OEO job training

School

Vocational school for father
High school for mother
Day care for baby
Head Start for boy

We have said that these are the relevant and transacting processes in the case. Assuming their concurrent influences upon each other, intervention, wherever it occurs, will have a feedback effect upon other parts of the system. "The case" has become a system of related factors; the assessment has expanded to include the systems related to the individual; interventive tasks can be located in any part of the case, for these will effect other parts. The individual or the institution becomes "the client," because appropriate attention to either theoretically will enhance or at least affect the functioning of the other. The social context in which this family lives is expressed in its way of life, just as the contours of hospital policy are expressed in the potential social worker activities.

Changing Areas of Knowledge

We have noted that a systemic view of "the case" may help to place a boundary around the unit of attention, and that the social work case in point has boundaries that are larger than the person. Clearly, the knowledge areas necessary for a practitioner are vast; they extend to whatever is salient for a particular individual situation. Thus a person who is an addict–client will require of his social worker that he have *substantive knowledge* (about drug addiction in this case), and the same can be said of unmarried mothers, neglected children, marital partners in conflict, mentally and physically ill people, etc.

But weighty though these intellectual demands are, and difficult as it may be to keep up with the ever-changing substantive knowledge about people in varying conditions of life, there is yet more that needs to be known by a social worker in order that he practice wisely. In the diagnostic or assessment process, the conceptualization of a case in systemic terms requires a *knowledge repertoire of individual, group, organizational, and community processes,* all of which occur simultaneously over time in many cases. Furthermore, as the case boundary is as broad as the individual's life style warrants, a practitioner has to have a working knowledge of *social policy*, both in order to know its impact upon the case and in order to use his professional efforts to affect it and keep it relevant to changing conditions. This is why it is limiting to stay within the confines of social casework, group work, or community organization, for the boundaries of a "case" are social work field boundaries, and they call upon all methods in social work (Bartlett, 1970).

Historically, social work has drawn upon theories of dynamic psychology and psychoanalysis, in particular, for its knowledge of personality development and behavior. In different eras sociology, anthropology, political science, economics, law, and medicine have served as theoretical resources for social work. As society has pressed its demands for different social arrangements, as research has turned up new connections, so knowledge itself has changed. There is an inevitable lag in all professions when it comes to keeping up with new knowledge, partly because in the period when the professional student is in school he tends to be taught the content that derives from an earlier period. Unless professional education succeeds in teaching students how to keep their minds open, the next generation of students will, of course, perpetuate the lag by remaining wedded to older and perhaps outdated knowledge. In professional education, a corrective for this lag rests in a freeing pedagogical method; in professional practice, it rests in devising a sufficiently *open methodological system* that new knowledge contributes to new practice approaches. Only to the degree that new knowledge can find its way into a professional practice, to be acted upon and applied relevantly, will that practice remain appropriate in the ever-changing society.

What kind of theory of behavior is essential for the social worker to practice?

1. Assuming that social work practice must attend to

what is happening in life, in the streets and where people are, a theory of behavior would need to be one that explains how most people develop and cope with their lives—in other words, a theory of "normal" or developmental behavior.

2. Assuming that social strain and limitations in the environment make it difficult for many people to develop their potential fully, so that they fail to cope successfully with their lives, the behavioral theory would need to explain as well the continuum from health to illness, from ability to cope to failure to cope with life.

3. Assuming that the function of social work is to help individuals in their many roles make an adaptation to their lives and find a sense of fulfillment, the behavioral theory would need to identify external as well as internal mechanisms of adaptation and mastery, so that they become recognizable.

4. Assuming that social work practice is to be addressed to effective balance between individuals and the social institutions they inhabit and not to basic personality change, the theory of behavior must have an equilibrating component that will explain the balance of inner and outer forces between the person and his environment. Whatever the theory, it cannot be merely descriptive, static, or closed as a system; it has to be made applicable to the natural life style of individuals, which changes over time and across subcultures. An appropriate behavioral theory is that which is open to new knowledge as it occurs and applicable to varieties of behaviors, and is also within the boundaries of professional expertise, so that it can be known well. Briefly, a useful theory should be relevant to the practice that makes use of it.

There are, of course, uncounted theories of how and why people behave as they do, if we assume that human behavior is more than the existential encounter. The theories range from religious ideas about spirituality to scientific behavioristic notions that would computerize actions for understanding and control. In between these extremes are the range of theories that are based upon the basic social structure of the family and the development of children in this structure. Although there are variations upon the Freudian theory of human behavior, the idea that people are what they are because of what has happened to them in their growing up is the common twentieth-century conception of human behavior. Freud's discovery of the vast repressed area of the unconscious has colored the discoveries of social and behavioral scientists in this century. There are many levels on which one can use this theory, and in social work practice it has been a pivotal theory that has explained personality development.

Unquestionably, one might argue for or against this theory or any number of orthodox or eclectic uses of it, but the fact remains that a characteristic of any professional practice is that one needs *some* theory from which to depart. This differs from the academic pursuit, where one may ponder the contributions of any and all theories in order to develop a theory of theories or even to merely enjoy reveling in the likenesses and differences of various theories. Such knowledge, in academic pursuits, can become an end in itself; but a practice requires theoretical tools, so that the practitioner of whatever discipline will bring a frame of reference to the situation he addresses. In order to act in a disciplined and professional way, we must finally select a theory or a set of compatible theories, so that we can get on with our work.

The thesis in this book is that Freudian-based theory that has found new expression in the modern ego theory of Hartmann, Erikson, and White, attempts to explain *developmental* determinants and personality structure. It is a useful theory that has had acceptance and demonstrable success in many situations over the last thirty or forty years (Hamilton, 1958). Again it has to be said that there are other theories of human behavior that would explain individual actions and that would be useful for practitioners who would presume to help others. However, because we need to get on with our work, we will not attempt here to discuss the host of theories, but rather will try to assess the uses of *this* theory in social work practice in the modern urban era.

It has often been said that the trouble with social casework is that it is "too Freudian," and it is hard to know what that means. If one uses theory correctly, be it Freudian, Rankian, Watsonian, or Skinnerian, it is hardly possible to be "too" anything, because it is essential to know as much as possible about the content of the theoretical formulation being used. Perhaps the "too Freudian" accusation derives from the fact that, in truth, early social caseworkers stayed too close to the Freudian theoretical model of *treatment*, rather than to Freudian explanations of human behavior. The practitioner must have a theory of human behavior so as to understand behavioral phenomena. However, what he *does* with it, how he transposes it into social work methodology, is a social work, and not a personality theorist, matter.

The issue about Freudian theory and psychoanalytic treatment is very complicated, because the theory has been simultaneously defined, further refined, and practiced. Therefore it has been exceedingly difficult to separate knowledge from application. In other words, as social casework theoreticians and practitioners sought to learn about Freudian theory, they had to learn from psychoanalysts, who were practicing within their discipline and thereby discovering theoretical constructs. It is our view that the fusion between evolving psychoanalytic theory and practice had its adverse effect upon social casework practice because the line between the two was not drawn sharply enough.

There are many unfortunate illustrations of this sad occurrence. For example, in schools of social work where practicing psychoanalysts have taught courses in human growth and behavior, they have demonstrated aspects of theory through illustrations of their own practice, and a generation of social workers has confused the theory with the practice. Another example can be found in the case-worker's predilection to know all, once having understood the concept of the unconscious. This route has led to thera-peutic disasters, in that the unconscious has often represented the "all," and in the early days social work practitioners did attempt to bypass necessary ego defenses and search beyond them for root causes of behavior and for unconscious idea-tion.

A further example can be found in the current day when practitioners seek that one-to-one, transference tinged con-frontation between social worker and client, as if this were the preferred and only method of resolving human problems. Out of this preoccupation with the professional's expert knowledge of psychic processes and the object–client who appeared always in transference terms evolved the appearance of a practice in social work that indeed looked as if it were a modified form of psychoanalytic practice requiring a maximum of social distance between worker and client.

Freudian theory of personality has undegone many changes as people like Erikson (1959), Hartmann (1958), Menninger (Menninger, et al., 1963), and R. W. White (1963, 1973) have contributed to the expanding knowledge of ego psychology. It is this development that has provided for external expres-sion of internal psychic processes and has, therefore, enhanced the possibility of a conceptual connection between the person and his environment. It has facilitated the entrance of nonpsy-choanalytic practitioners, like social workers, into the arena of personality, for with the rediscovery of ego functioning (Stamm, 1959), it has become possible to address behavior without the use of psychoanalytic techniques of probing into the hidden parts of personality. As we shall see in later chapters, this possibility has significant implications for ex-tensive social work intervention and differential uses of manpower.

An approach to viewing the personality as functioning along

a broad range of balance to imbalance has contributed to the current idea that treatment might relevantly be called *help* and not necessarily *therapy* (Schwartz & Schwartz, 1964), and that the signs of dysfunction are more appropriately diagnosed or assessed through viewing the individual in his own terms of reference, in his own life style, and not according to diagnostic labels; the clinic has moved outdoors. The person as a self-balancing system interacts reciprocally with the situational systems that are salient for him (Rabkin, 1970). Ideally a society should provide through its established institutions the necessary supports and services that would reinforce the individual's capacity to cope with his life and functioning in that society.

The person-in-situation configuration always has been the unit of attention in social casework, but the problem was that there was no total explanation of the entire concept. To the extent that personality theory presented a coherent whole, there was a natural tendency to explain the two sides of the configuration through the use of psychological knowledge. In order to understand the social situation, which, of course, has no base in personality theory, one has to draw upon fragmented theories in social science, like theories of social role, social class, cultures, groups, communities, family structures, reference groups, and social problems. An ecological/systems perspective has provided the framework for reconceptualizing knowledge in reciprocal terms. As Devereaux wrote:

> The real objective is not to determine whether the phenomenon is ultimately a psychological or a socio-cultural one, but to analyze the dovetailing, interplay, and reinforcement of all factors [1963, p. 25].

As personality and social theories are measured by different yardsticks and are articulated in different languages on different levels of abstraction, we are still far from the state of unifying all knowledge of the person-in-situation under one theoretical awning.

Assuming that people seek in their own cultures and reference groups for modes of personal expression, it then becomes incumbent upon us to have specific knowledge of those sociocultural forces. Further assuming that people function in accordance with particular, socially defined roles, the concept of social role becomes an essential part of the practitioner's knowledge repertoire. Finally, assuming that people intersect at all times with organizations that are the hallmark of urbanized society, knowledge of organizational theory and the way bureaucracy functions would need to share intellectual space with knowledge of the person. Thus, according to Herman Stein's suggestion (1958, pp. 227–228), social science at large provides for *substantive* knowledge about the nature of a particular society, ethnic group, or social class subculture—facts about the social structure of specific communities, about the significance of distributions of various kinds of social data, and about specific behaviors under specific conditions. Social science also contributes *theoretical concepts* about the relationship between culture and personality, implications of bureaucratic cultures, and theories of social role, reference groups, and family structures.

We have said that all people live in a social context—albeit in individual ways—in their own specific life styles. Knowledge of the elements that comprise the individual's social situation may not be found all in the same place, and it may not be as immediately applicable as knowledge of personality, but as people are organismically related to their social milieu, there can be no conceptualization of feedback without the relevant knowledge of that milieu. It is as if only one child were on a seesaw: while the board is over to one side, it is impossible to assess the balance of the total mechanism. Thus we see that the broadened parameters of the "case" create an intellectual challenge to the social work practitioner. The psycho-social situation that must be assessed in order to know what to do to help requires a systemic, organizing framework so as to make practice a possibility. Only in academic study can knowledge be an end in itself; the knowledge to which we have referred has its specific and particular uses for each individual client.

Modern Notions of the Ego and the Life Model

According to biological and ethological theorists from whom ecological theorists (Germain, 1973) in the behavioral sciences and the professions draw their knowledge, man comes into the world innately equipped for adaptation (Du Bos, 1972), and requires particular environmental conditions to achieve his adaptive tasks all through his life cycle. Various ego psychologists have approached the potential action or adaptive possibilities of man through their particular perspectives (Bandler, 1963). For example, Hartmann (1958) has assumed an innate (conflict-free) ego with autonomous functions which are adaptable to the average expectable environment. Through alloplastic measures that enable us to modify our environments, autoplastic measures where we modify our own behaviors, or changing or moving away from environments, Hartmann postulates we are to maintain an adaptive capacity to our unique worlds. White (1963) posits an innate feeling of "effectance" and "competence" which pushes us toward having an effect upon our environments, always seeking out growth-inducing experiences. Thus one can understand the phenomenon of curiosity for its own sake, and the sense of accomplishment that comes with mastery of a problem. Erikson (1959) has described ego development through phase-specific task resolution in interaction with physical, social, cultural, and institutional environments, as well as cogwheeling of generations by which each creates growth-producing environments for the other.

These modern ego theorists have gone beyond viewing ego functions as only defensive of unconscious impulses and as devices to cope with anxiety. They have posed other ego functions having to do with autonomous drives not identical with psychosexual conflict, either being innate or evolving out of normal accomplishment of developmental tasks. From these theorists have come such concepts as cognition, language, memory, coping, mastery, social competence, learning, exploring, and other ego functions that serve as adaptative links to environments. All of these theoretically are available in all humans for dealing with their environments (Brewster-Smith, 1968; Coelho et al., 1974; Bowlby, 1969, 1973; Gladwin, 1967).

In life itself, we know there is conflict, trouble, maladaptation, social failure, mismatching of people in marriages, illness, crisis, inequity, strain on family life, and death. One might organize these problems in different ways —as developmental crises, role-transitional crises, and environmental stresses, for example. In every stage of life, in every status and role, people are confronted with imperfections in others, in themselves, and in society. Average expectable environments are not as expectable as they once were (Wallerstein, 1973), and thus people are called upon to draw out an ever-larger repertoire of coping mechanisms in order to tolerate and find an accommodation with changing life styles, multiple family forms, emergency situations, rapid change, bombardment by external stimuli ranging from television to rock music, and the extreme mobility in every aspect of society. The rhythms of life are increasing, and literature, art, theater, and music are showing us the real truth when they remove visual and aural boundaries and allow us to figuratively or literally join the artist in his medium; even the stage has removed the proscenium that once permitted a clear distinction between reality and the play. This kind of world requires a facile ego, and ironically, the very fluidity of the boundaries in all environments may provide for a greater mutual adaptation between a person and his particular environment.

Some concrete illustrations of the permeability of environments and the concomitant opportunities for ego growth and adaptation come to mind (Seabury, 1971). Modern schools usually have movable desk chairs—a real step forward in the school environment from rows of soldier-like, nailed-down desk chairs. What does the flexible arrangement do for the growth and development of school children? It allows children to mix with others, to change their friends, to adapt to their ear and eye capabilities, to accommodate to their daily moods and interests, to have a taste of what the real world will be like with its multiple demands and competing stimuli. In other words, the flexible seating (an environmental idea) provides children greater opportunities to explore their school universe, to grow at their own pace, to utilize special skills, to rehearse in the protected environment their activities in the real environment.

Modern life is characterized by mobility, particularly in industrialized countries like the United States, where skilled workmen and executives often move with their jobs. Also, in this country where city neighborhoods may give way to urban development projects or highways, or where people move to suburbs when they can afford it, mobility is an important phenomenon. In our culture young people move out as do the aged, and family structures change as a result. Moving from one place to another involves more than physical relocation, although that creates its own demands upon an individual's or a family's coping capacities. New environments create their own pull for the curious and the learning person, and the necessity to rearrange a family life style, while often viewed as a crisis (R. Rapoport, 1963), is equally often an opportunity for growth. A new look at marital and child–parent relationships, a new plan for child care, for transportation, for time of meals, for recreation, school, work, and socializing with others—these demand of families an active role in their own transition. Ego theorists would say that the purposeful activity itself, the process

through which the adaptation to the new surround is accomplished, is growth-inducing.

It may be possible now to think about generalizing from
these examples to situations where people must make role,
status, and location transitions of a somewhat different kind.
Foster children, hospitalized patients, penal offenders, and
institutionalized children are examples of populations who
must cope with tasks of ingress and egress, for these are built
into their status. Social workers can learn from modern ego
psychology, joined with an increasingly sophisticated understanding of how environments can be bent, to enable
successful mastery of the transition and increased growth as
a direct result of that mastery. In all of these examples, to
speak of "bending" the environment so as to provide an
opportunity for the person to master the task of role transition, would be to indicate that the foster child, penal
offender, institutionalized child, or hospitalized patient
should be offered experiences to ready him for the new
environment.

In accordance with the age, cultural ideas, and particular
social situation of the person, the *environment* has to be
considered as the field construct described earlier in the
systems framework. Life space is a psychological–environmental construct; it is composed of people in the client's
social network, the helping disciplines themselves, the policies
of institutions and organizations, and the concrete structures
that define a person's life. Thus environment is subject to
influence and to change in the service of the client's growth
and development. The environment has to be *masterable*
in order to provide for mastery. The key to developing
growth-inducing environments lies in the understanding
that environments are the components of the client's life
space.

The enterprising reader will begin to think about the
creative ways in which environments can be bent to make
them comprehensible. Changed visiting hours in institutions?

Minibus transportation for parents from city to out-of-town institutions? Regular visiting arrangements between natural parents and foster parents? Opportunities for job training in prisons? Meaningful work experiences for youthful offenders? Changing of agency manuals to mean what they say? Explicit conditions of eligibility provided to clients? Permitting animals in housing projects? Provisions for privacy in living spaces? Provisions for neighborhood child care services? Museum trips for children? Outings for groups of mothers who have never left their neighborhoods? Home help services? Adult education classes? Prenatal instruction? Expanded library facilities?

These are all environmental opportunities waiting to be bent in the service of the client who is waiting to utilize his innate ego capacities in the service of his own growth and autonomy. The pejorative connotations of "concrete services" must give way to the notion of "an ego trip." The implications to be drawn from this "reorientation" are vast, because old, favored notions about exclusive reliance on the professional relationship, therapeutic techniques, and seeking of causation and cure, inevitably must be modified. When the individual's own psychologically and culturally determined life style becomes the unit of attention, the aim of practice would be to right the impaired balance; the issue would not be a problem to be solved, but rather a previous balance to be restored or an improved balance to be established. "The therapeutic model has led to a search for primacy of problems underlying the presenting request or even unrelated to it" (Germain, 1968). The assumption of norms of behavior has heretofore governed the helping process, and has encouraged practitioners to seek the deepest causation for variance from the norm and ultimately to find a way to "cure" the perceived "illness" or problem. According to Schwartz & Schwartz (1964), there has to be a distinction between treatment as a clinical procedure and help that would follow the life process.

Returning to our conception of the case as a system of interacting and reciprocal forces, a practitioner might address any or all of the significant elements that are dysfunctional for the individual client and would seek in that field of influence the adjustment of those factors that are proving disruptive. Where the aim of this search is to establish a state of balance, then primary attention would have to be given to the nature of the present imbalance, the precipitating stress, the individual coping mechanisms to be enhanced, and the forces in the environment that can be mobilized to reinforce the individual's urge toward a self-righting balance in his specific situation. The field of study, as we have mentioned, would comprise the individual and all of those people and institutions that affect and are affected by him, including the social worker himself and the service organization. This field or unit of attention directs the practitioner to an immediacy of task definition and certainly expands both the parameters of the case and the nature of the job to be done.

The individualizing process remains a useful tool for assessment of the case; it is the *case* that has extended its boundaries. The chief purpose of assessment still is to know what is relevant to do; it is the range of the intervention possibilities that has become enlarged. As the modern social work practitioner confronts the scene, with which he himself is systemically related, he will view the individual client as pivotal in a transactional field. Through "transactional sectioning" the practitioner will be able to select tasks of intervention, because in each salient "section" there will be a cross section of the whole. This is not the same as partializing, where only a piece of the person's situation is addressed at the source, because in systemic thinking the person-in-situation is an organismic whole where all parts reverberate in each other.

The social work practitioner will need to be expert in his comprehension of the nature of human beings living in a complex urbanized environment, and his particular expertise will be found in his knowledge of how the person and the situation reinforce each other or, more likely, fail to do so. In our view of the unit of attention being the individual in his life style we have left behind the concept of clinically defined disease, and we may even have put aside the require- ment of becoming a client in order to be helped by a social worker. Bringing together what we have observed earlier about the nature of the society, the rising influence of public social institutions, and the broader conceptions of the individualizing process, we can now turn to discussion of the modes of social work practice intervention that could be reflective of all these changing elements.

Part III

Introduction

WE HAVE TAKEN some pains in the foregoing chapters of this book to set the scene for the discussion of methodology in social work practice. By this time it should be evident that we do not see method as an entity, standing by itself without reference to what is going on in the world. *It must be reflective of the milieu in which it is practiced,* in our case the social environment. Thus it must account for the extremely fluid roles being enacted by citizens, for heightened tensions, for pressures that derive from discontents, and for participation of people in the terms of service that affect their intimate lives. *The aims of social work practice are probably more important to identify than its techniques,* because techniques used for obscure or irrelevant aims can serve no social purpose and sooner or later those techniques come in danger of being ends in themselves.

We might suggest again that the primary aim of social work practice is to enable people to command their own lives and destinies to the greatest extent possible in light of the isolating, technological, specialized, and hopelessly complex world in which we live in the last half of the twentieth century. In view of the fact that public institutions have gradually encroached upon personal functions and that publicly defined goods and services have compensated for each individual's inability to provide them for himself, an important part of commanding one's own life and destiny is the opportunity to be connected with those goods and services that are provided increasingly through impersonal organizations. Thus the aims of social work practice have to include ways of connecting people with goods and services, possibly by arranging pathways, promoting accessible organizations, advocating, and strengthening individuals to cope with the confusing array of urban structures and diffuse relationships that are symptomatic of the modern world.

Once social work practice is placed in a relevant social context, *its methods and techniques will only take on meaning when they are viewed within a recognizable framework.* In social work that framework is constructed of components of *knowledge* about individual, group, and organizational behavior, community structures, social institutions, social policy and sociocultural determinants, and the *skills* necessary to work with people who reflect all of these aspects of life.

In addition to knowledge and skills, social work practice rests upon a set of *values* that guide its working principles and define the ways in which knowledge is used. These values have been described as traditional humanistic, Judeo-Christian values that include acceptance of people as individuals in their own right, respect for their differences and their integrity, and promotion of the social good. Without a framework surrounding practice activities, the methods and techniques used in social work would look like the work of individualizing that goes on in all human encounters. Neighbors talk with each other; ministers counsel their congregations; politicians listen to their constituencies; doctors sympathize with their patients while they care for their bodies; psychoanalysts treat people for their personal problems; and teachers, nurses, lawyers, psychologists, and bartenders, along with all others in special social and professional roles, individualize their clients and their friends and relatives directly to be of help, or indirectly in the course of another, more primary activity.

Thus the explicit framework that defines social work practice is important to keep in mind, for the primary work of social work is individualizing, which is also the process that occurs formally and informally on all occasions, among all people. It is a continual challenge in discussing the purposes of social work to avoid underestimating and generalizing it as a process that everybody can use with the same effectiveness or overestimating it as a singular solution to the strains of urban living. In truth, it is a practice that has grown through history as an organizational expression of society's interest in providing help to people. Through time the concept of help has changed, as has the notion of what people are to be the objects of help and what is to be the controlling agent of help.

The practice of social work seems to have surpassed its original purposes, and it is time to look at its present-day functions which may yet prove to be more necessary and effective than its functions were in previous eras of our history. As we consider social work practice in new ways, we are not concerned with the generalist *versus* the specialist. Specialization is viewed as occurring in the particular field of practice selected by the social worker. General practice concepts and processes are the thrust of *all* social work practice.

Before we examine the process of individualization that would have relevance for social work practice in the modern world, a word needs to be said about the *role of expertise,* for we have pointed out in earlier chapters some of the changes occurring in our society that are posing challenges to the once assumed clarity of the professional's functions.

Knowledge of what is best for a client is no longer as sure as it once seemed, partly because the world is too complex to be thoroughly known by any professional discipline. The authority of knowledge is increasingly challenged by thinking young people and newly liberated minority groups in society who have viewed its structures afresh—and with alarm. A practice like social work, for example, also has had to confront squarely its limitations in solving basic economic problems or creating basic social change, and thus the usefulness of its expert knowledge may be suspect. Finally, the need for people to participate in the terms of service will inevitably impinge upon the arena of expertise that has been held up as one significant aspect of professional practice. We cannot discuss the expertness of social work practice in the process of individualization without taking these issues into consideration.

The following two chapters are addressed to intervention itself. Chapter 5 discusses its design and processes, and Chapter 6 discusses the practice roles carried differentially by those at the many levels of social work manpower. In our view, the design and processes cannot be thought of separately from the matter of roles, or who will carry out different tasks in the total design.

Chapter 5

Social Work Intervention:
Its Design and Processes

A PRIMARY CHARACTERISTIC of an individualizing process is
the differentiation of people one from the other, a singling
out from the mass. According to the unit of attention that
a practitioner addresses, whether it be a person, a family, a
group, or a community, individualizing terms have to be
applied. Therefore a person must be known by his identifying bio-psycho-social characteristics, his role and status in
his immediate society, his interactions with those meaningful
people around him, his modes of adaptation and of coping
with his world, his strengths, and his problems. His uniqueness may differentiate him as a black person from all other
blacks even though his most significant reference group
may be the black ghetto in which he lives. He may be poor,
but he will survive in his state of poverty in his own life
style, accommodating, angry, aspiring, or complacent. He

may be mentally ill, delinquent, addicted to narcotics, or even well adjusted in the society, stable, and earning an income; whatever his condition of life, we will know him as an individual only through understanding his very particular needs, feelings, desires, physical and mental characteristics, and style of life.

When a family, a group, or a community is similarly individualized, it is known through its uniqueness, despite all that it holds in common with other like groups of people. This differentiation process is familiar to social caseworkers as *psycho-social diagnosis,* the "knowing through" or, in Gordon Hamilton's terms, "understanding of the need or problem the client presents" (1951). The first definition of psycho-social diagnosis was stated by Mary Richmond as "an exact a definition as possible of the social situation and personality of a given client" (1917). According to Menninger, "diagnosis is not a label, but understanding for specific help" (Menninger et al., 1963, p. 171).

On the face of it, it would seem that diagnosis as a synonym for differentiation, designation, or distinguishing one from a class of objects should be a perfectly acceptable concept to serve an individualizing process as practiced in social work. Yet it is one of the greatest areas of contention within the field of social work itself, and perhaps even about the field from nonsocial workers. It is important to ponder this phenomenon, that a utilitarian concept has somehow gone astray. Is it a utilitarian concept? What features seem not to sit well in the modern social scene? Are there perhaps misunderstandings about its meanings, or misapplications of its primary purposes? Diagnosis, like any other practice concept, is a creature of its times. As a movable and responsive notion, it should undergo transformations in every era and reflect the sociocultural, economic, and psychological determinants of the day. If it does not, then its usefulness is at an end; if there is a core of usefulness to the concept as it moves through history, then in each changing period it must be reexamined and reevaluated in current terms.

We will look again at the diagnostic process itself and think about what can be retained and what might have to be changed. The *what,* or *object,* of diagnosis has always changed through time, even if the how of it has remained the same. The *uses* to be made of it in treatment or in expanded forms of help have also changed in response to the changing scene, even though the purposes of the diagnostic process as a guide to treatment have remained the same. Assuming that diagnosis is an essential component of the individualizing process that must distinguish among people and be the precursor of any kind of treatment, help, or service that is geared to the individual's requirement, we can explore its changing subject matter, the object it must address in these times, and its changing uses. We continue to perceive diagnosis as an important concept which needs only to be placed in the proper contexts of modern urban society and new knowledge.

Misconceptions about Diagnosis

Despite the life-long efforts of Gordon Hamilton to demonstrate the contrary, diagnosis has a medical connotation. Useful as the concept may have been as a term of psycho-social assessment of the case, it is defined in the dictionary and thus by the public as "determination of a diseased condition; identification of a disease by investigation of its symptoms and history" (*Oxford International Dictionary,* 1955). Perhaps it is the medical connotation that has given so much trouble through the years, for the dictionary definition unfortunately does confine the meaning to disease, symptoms, and history. When taken literally, instead of in the context of the theoretical translation made by Hamilton, the dictionary definition does indeed place severe limitations upon the modern practitioner. According to Hamilton:

> Essentially, diagnosis is the worker's professional opinion as to the nature of the need or the problem which the client presents. It is not a "secret labeling of the client," it is not an uncontrolled adventure into the mysteries of life; it is a realistic, thoughtful, frank and "scientific" attempt to understand the client's present need, which is always a person-in-situation formulation, including interpersonal relationships [1951, p. 214].

The medical term directs the social worker to pathology or psycho-social breakdown after the fact, as it were. Even Hamilton's concentration upon *what is the matter* presumes a problem status in the case. When we consider the possibilities of broader boundaries of practice and ideas about earlier intervention in the status of a case, we find that exclusive concentration upon pathology, problem, and "what is the matter" might prove to be excessively confining.

Another problem with the medical definition is that it leads one to seek *symptoms,* which of course serve as clues for the doctor or the psychoanalyst about the nature of the disease entity. The practice of social work is not analogous here for several reasons. In the first instance, the view of a psycho-social case includes social factors interacting with personal ones, and in the example of a malfunctioning poor family living in deplorable slum housing conditions in a ghetto area of the city, it would be almost impossible to identify symptomatology unless one were to oversimplify the concept by stating that the society was diseased and poor housing was one of its symptoms. Although such a designation might give us a clue to the problem at hand, it would not lend itself to a classificatory scheme or direct us to a treatment measure that was feasible for practice.

Second, the identification of medical symptoms is usually the end result of tedious clinical study; the eruption of a symptom has meaning only if it is known to belong to a category of like behaviors that have been observed clinically over time. As the parameters of each social work case are so broad, including the person and all aspects of his life in society, the conceptual net would have to be large enough to catch all the fragments of the case in order to place them in a classification system that would provide for comparison of other, equally large case components.

Also, classical symptomatology has become an outworn term for modern medicine, particularly for those specialities like public health, general practice, and psychoanalysis in the present era. As Menninger says so well in his view of *The Vital Balance,* symptoms are economic devices employed by the ego "in the maintenance of organismic equilibrium and integrity . . . though being helpful in this regard, they add to the total difficulties of adjustment" (Menninger et al., 1963, p. 71). Thus symptoms are not to be seen as signals alone, but rather as part of the state of being in which the individual finds himself; symptoms seen in ego terms need not necessarily be considered expressions of disease, but, in Menninger's view, are adaptive mechanisms and part of the total life situation of the person. This view of the symptom might lead us away from the medical model of diagnosis, because it need no longer be seen as an expression of disease, but rather as a function of ego adaptation and coping capacity.

The third part of the definition of diagnosis that has proved to be confining to social work practice is the requirement for *history.* Presuming a diseased condition, in medical diagnosis it would follow that it would be essential to understand whether the symptoms—the way in which the disease is known—were of long or short duration, so as to determine whether the disease state was chronic or acute. Also history would tell the doctor a great deal about the patient's characteristic ways of living and coping with his disease, and this knowledge would give the doctor some predictive help. Where the social worker has pursued history as the primary source of understanding of his client, he has taken a proper course in light of the medical model he has followed. Although social casework might be criticized for borrowing this diagnostic model, it ought to be praised for its integrity in borrowing it *in toto,* for piecemeal borrowing would have made the system theoretically inconsistent. As long as a practice is addressed to disease, the expression of symptoms is the primary way to identify the pathological state, and history would then be the chief tool for understanding the meaning of the symptoms in the total economy of the person's past and present physical and mental adjustment.

There is no question that knowledge of the history of a person's development would enrich the understanding of his life. Literature is peopled with biographies and autobiographies which explain historical events better than political analysis could ever do. Humanity is ever curious about how people got that way and what made them do what they did; this curiosity is undoubtedly one of the most salutary expressions of our humanity, for we seek to know our brothers and to comprehend them totally. The life history belongs as well to lovers who want to know each other, to children who need to know from their parents and grandparents about how it used to be and what their roots were, and to all professionals who can only understand the presenting complaint or condition of their clients when they can see the threads of their actions developing in the past. There is no endeavor that is not clarified through the knowing of history.

Obviously, as far as professional practice is concerned, limits have to be set upon the kind of history that is sought and the time back to which data must be traced. These limits are usually defined by the nature of the service being provided. Thus a school teacher would need to know a child's school record; a lawyer, the previous relevant behavior of his client; a doctor, the course of his patient's disease or state of health. In professional circles, different from the intimate associations where people know each other's past in order to become closely related to them, psychoanalysis is probably the prototype of history-taking in depth. This is because the treatment method is in itself a redrawing of the patient's history, his childhood viewed through mature eyes with the aim of releasing him from its grip upon his present life. It is this model of history-taking that was followed by social casework in those early days of learning about psychoanalytic theory.

In the history of social casework there have been efforts to displace this theoretical model in favor of one that would be more present-centered. Other models, albeit not diagnostic ones, were sought in *functionalism* (Taft, 1944) and in *problem solving* (Perlman, 1957), which emphasized the helping process itself, out of which, it was expected, would come sufficient understanding to offer help without reliance upon past history. It seems that the diagnostic emphasis upon pathology, symptoms, and history has become an anathema to those who would bring social work practice into the modern scene. In some quarters it would seem that, as if in reaction to the medical mode, some other practitioners in social work would seek no theoretical model at all, but would simply follow the client's own path without intruding upon him any degree of professionalized knowledge, for fear of intruding upon his pursuit of his own life.

Notwithstanding the criticisms of diagnosis, and the confusion of the process of *knowing* or *individualizing* a person with medical and particularly psychoanalytic diagnostic and treatment methods, it is our thesis that respect for individualization *requires* knowing the person, the group, or the community. Although we would also depart from the medical model, we will attempt to translate the concept of diagnosis, as a useful differentiating construct, into a present-day social work framework. We will call it assessment.

Assessment as the Key to Intervention: The Map of a Case

The ecological/systems view of "cases"—that is individuals, families, groups, communities—requires that the social work practitioner explore the relationships or transactions exchanged between the person(s) and the impinging environment that is composed of physical, social, cultural, and all other forces external to the person(s). The interface between person and environment is fluid, in that it is impossible to totally separate out internal from external cause and effect. The feelings a child may have who fails in school can hardly be viewed discretely from the teacher's attitudes toward him. The child and teacher are locked into a transactional relationship, where each contributes to the other's reactions. The interface, the conceptual locus of their "meeting," is the territory where the social worker enters and participates with them in improving their transactions or their social functioning (Gordon, 1969).

In the example of a group of mental patients in a hospital ward, the interface may be between their development and the hospital's rules, where some mutual adaptation may need to occur. In a sense, there is no psychological side to any case that does not include some external or environmental influence. The transactions go both ways, and where many actors and several environments are involved, the transactions go in all directions. For this reason among others, it is vitally important to understand that an ecological–general systems (or eco/systems) approach to social work practice does not mean the same thing as dealing with a person or an organization as a system. It means that the *processes* of general systems theory are utilized—the notions of reciprocity, feedback, etc.—not that each aspect of the case is a separate social system. Of course one can apply a social systems theory to the components of social work, but it is an eco/systems transactional approach that is used here.

The unit of attention in social work includes the person(s)-in-situation, or -environment, and within that unit there are adaptive exchanges existing all the time. The conception of *knowing a case* is so broad as to make "diagnosis" a dysfunctional term. A term such as *assessment* implies the necessity for individualizing and knowing a case as the basis of intervention, but it has no commitment to disease, to symptomatology, to clinical–normative judgments, or to prescribed goals or outcomes. The assessment of the unit of attention is in itself a process, the beginning of intervention. It can be concretized as the making of a true *map* of a situation, a map that should be drawn with the client himself. As an assurance of the contract, a mutual definition between social worker and client of the situation confronting them, the drawing of a map could elicit a joint understanding of the salient and relevant features of the client's story. This process would mitigate a practitioner's proclivity to hold "hidden agendas" in his work with clients, and to have "closet treatment plans" even though he intends to begin where the client is.

Following is an example of a case carried in two ways. The first presentation illustrates a diagnostically based treatment plan, and the second presentation illustrates an eco/systems approach to assessment and intervention. The case was carried first on the basis of a medical disease model, second on the basis of an eco/systems life model of practice.

The setting of this case was a child guidance clinic, where the presenting problem was that a 13-year-old girl suddenly refused to go to school and showed other evidence of regressive behavior. The mother brought the child to the clinic at the suggestion of the school, and she herself was worn out and baffled by the problem.

It was soon discerned that the father of the 13-year-old girl had made a sexual advance to her, and she had reacted by almost complete withdrawal from friends, school, and social activities. The mother had little sense of her own worth, was almost totally confined in her interests to her home and church, and according to family custom kept her own ideas and feelings to herself.

PRESENTATION I

After history-taking interviews with mother and child, separately, a clinical conference was held and the psycho-social diagnosis made that the child was traumatized by the sexual experience and that she needed to work through her feelings about the experience and about her father. It was thought that this could be done best with the social worker, who would utilize the transference to help the child sort out her oedipal fantasies and to help her accept the reality of her own status as a growing 13-year-old. The mother was not included in the treatment plan, and no time limit was placed upon the treatment.

This plan did not work out well because the mother and father were concerned about what was going on in the clinic, and as they began to "interfere," the child found it too guilt-provoking to participate fully in treatment. Also, she was not excessively verbal or introspective by nature, and no progress was noted.

Consultation was sought by the social worker.

PRESENTATION II

The case was reworked and recontracted. The mother was brought back to the clinic (the father of course refused to come), and the mother and daughter and social worker reconsidered the problem as it affected their lives. They constructed a map, literally drawing the case for themselves, and in the process of developing a schematic perspective, each person in the interview made a particular contribution so as to develop the story of the problems at home.

The map looked like this:

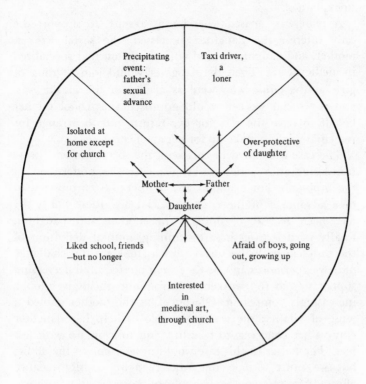

It was determined through this assessment that the daughter, apart from her father's sexual advance, was over-protected and that her fears of boys and sex were quite generalized to fears of going places, of new relationships, and of growing up. The family was religious and the mother went to church services as her main activity outside of the home, but she was too shy to socialize even at church. The daughter became interested through her art class and through the church in medieval art. A mutual assessment was made that the daughter's withdrawal and social–psychological regression were not unlike her parents' general social isolation, albeit theirs was on a more mature level in that they carried out their age-specific, family, and work roles and tasks. The sexual advance occurred once and remained unexplained.

A plan was devised whereby, as a start, to support the only interest the daughter expressed, the social worker, mother, and daughter would visit a museum that specialized in medieval art. Then the daughter would join a group of girls at the clinic who were as fearful of life as she was, and the social worker would approach the school on her behalf to pave the way for her return and to arrange for remedial work to make up for her absences.

The case continued in this vein, the social worker always translating into action tasks whatever she understood of the problems. For example, the mother was encouraged to take advantage of the church's social activities, which she had been fearful of doing. The mother and daughter, totally participating in a continuing, mutual definition of the problem with the social worker, took up the challenge of new experiences and, as time went on, required decreasing supports from the worker as they found themselves to be increasingly competent. Of course, as the mother gained a sense of vitality, she was more able to help her daughter express her concerns, to face life, and to grow up with less fear. The father in this case would never come to the clinic, but we must assume that the changing family balance affected him too, and probably fortuitously, for the improvement in well-being of mother and daughter could not have gone on had he obstructed them.

What is the difference between these two presentations? In the first one, the diagnosis was confined to the symptomatology and the problem was perceived as intrapsychic. The plan for the daughter to grow up through the transference assumed that the primary influence in treatment, if not her life, was to be the professional relationship. The diagnosis itself was made in the clinical conference, offering neither mother nor daughter the opportunity to use cognitive or reality-testing ego capacities in sorting out their problems. The case was limited in its design to the one-to-one verbal encounter, avoiding the daughter's life-space and family, and other social networks as the source of her psycho-social nutriment and the context of her development.

The second presentation illustrates the involvement of the mother and daughter in the definition of their problems, and the opportunities offered for them to make choices about how to improve their situation. The unit of attention, as seen in the map that was drawn, suited their view of the situation as far as they were willing and able to go with it. The worker, operating on the theory of ego mastery, competence, and effectance, assumed that "growing up" experiences and tasks provided in many forms would allow the daughter to mature with less fear. Recognition of the systemic relationship of the daughter with her mother and father and the necessity for them to find self-fulfilling outlets made the case a family case rather than an intrapsychic case. Translation of attitudes and feelings into tasks and actions opened up interventive possibilities beyond the impact of the therapeutic relationship.

One can conclude from this discussion that when we exchange the idea of sick and well for that of imbalance and balance, or maladaptive and adaptive fit, the client's life space itself can be molded to become the source of his well-being, even as it once was the source of his difficulty. The key to intervention is the appropriate, mutually defined assessment (Gottleib & Stanley, 1967), for without a proper understanding of what the case is about, intervention would be haphazard and even potentially dangerous. The social worker's accountability in practice rests on his expert "reading" of the interacting and multiple variables, or the "map" of a case. The plan or design for intervention will flow from that comprehension, so it has to be seen as the vital first step in the interventive process.

A reconceptualization of practice, or a modernization of the concept of diagnosis, as is being attempted here, is of course subject to criticism from many quarters. Particularly, the traditional clinically oriented practitioner undoubtedly will feel that time-tested procedures are being bypassed. "Clinical social workers" who utilize a medical disease perspective might raise serious questions out of their experience and expertise in clinical casework and in psychotherapy. Yet, in light of the arguments set forth in this book, a different conceptualization of cases (and therefore practice) is essential.

As an exercise, let us view some common "clinically defined" case problems and translate them into an eco/systems context to see what is lost and gained in so doing.

1. School Phobia

Assuming that the fear of going to school has roots in unresolved oedipal ties and that it takes form in the actual refusal of the child to leave home, there are different interventive options available, depending upon one's perspective in such a case. The clinically oriented practitioner might want to "work through" the fears with the child, while the eco/systems—oriented practitioner would want to engage the mother and the school in easing the child's steps toward separation, and at the same time would want to help the mother seek new outlets for her own fulfillment so as to be more able to let the child leave her. Perhaps the father and siblings also are placing conscious or unconscious demands upon the school child, and if so, their own fulfillment has to be found elsewhere. Further, the eco/systems worker would seek out all realistic and threatening sources of the child's fears of attending school, never settling for a singular psychic cause–effect relationship as between a sexualized fear and its expression in school avoidance.

2. Depression

Assuming that feelings of emotional deprivation, often traced to the oral period, can affect people at vulnerable times of their lives, the clinically oriented practitioner might psychologically "feed" the person through an intensively supportive psychotherapeutic relationship, perhaps aided by chemotherapy. A social worker using an eco/systems perspective would help the person seek out in his life space *some* source of gratification, no matter how small, to begin with. With the support of the worker, the client could slowly begin to master even infinitesimal life tasks, building a sense of competence through the activity itself. Simultaneously, the worker would attend to the environmental supports—would seek some *one* in the social network, some improvement in the physical quality of life, some environmental response that would reinforce the client's own sense of his worth.

3. "Acting-Out Behavior"

Assuming that this is a reflection of faulty ego capacity, where impulses are not subject to appropriate ego functions such as judgment, perception, reality testing, and object-relatedness, people with this clinical label, especially adolescents, are difficult to treat in any therapeutic perspective. The clinically oriented practitioner with patience and courage might pursue such a client with the offer of treatment as the best alternative to trouble with school, parents, the law, etc. In cases where it is necessary to restructure ego functions, the use of a therapeutic relationship as the primary tool makes for a long and tedious process. The eco/systems perspective orients a practitioner to the dynamic use of environment as the ultimate stage for the client's "acting out." It is from his real (object) relationships that he will learn judgments, reality testing, perception, etc. Use of peer groups in such cases would provide a sounding board and ego reinforcement for the client.

An eco/systems practitioner, in drawing with the client a map for assessment, would be found to recognize the family's or the school's role in the problem behavior, were it double-bind messages, overprotection, excessive discipline, permissiveness, or whatever. The case activities would lead the practitioner through the client's life-space supports and countersupports. Interventions would be located *wherever* they seemed salient; they would not be designed primarily to tap intrapsychic causation. The eco/systems perspective broadens one's view of the unit of attention, and it follows that interventions would open up a vast and as yet unknown repertoire of practice behaviors.

These are but three examples of the way in which case problems can be reconceptualized without loss of the individual "in the system." Interventive possibilities are open to individualized designs, and the multiple levels of potential help provide for a variety of modalities (individual, family, group, community, organizational) and thus for a mixed repertoire of helping personnel. Once he has achieved this kind of interventive possibility, the social work practitioner is able to approach the social mandate of accountability. But it all rests upon a reconceptualization of cases, their boundaries, and the supporting knowledge base.

STRATEGY AND TASK

A specific example of this approach is found in a study of social work practice in a prison. Studt (1963) reports an approach to help of prisoners that cross-cuts all methods in social work. Her use of the concept of task and strategy planning has a strong bearing on the case we are trying to present in this book.

We have set up certain requirements of help that derive from the modern social scene. Among these are that the person to be helped must participate fully in the process, because this is an age where little else is left to individuals except the mastery of their own life goals, and this has to be protected, at the very least, by social work practitioners. Studt recognizes the problem when she asks whose goal determines how various tasks will be related to each other. Is the agency to assume that its social mandate defines goals of action? Or is the worker to rely on his professional expertise, his values, and knowledge to take the lead in focusing the goals for the client?

Studt suggests that "the worker achieves his professional goals through the client's presentation of his." In other words, the social worker and client will have common goals, with different tasks allocated for reaching those goals. In Studt's view, the worker must provide the conditions necessary for the client to carry out his tasks; the worker functions through indirect actions, while the client does what he must do as a primary responsibility in direct activities. It is evident that only the individual himself can accomplish the tasks required of his life stage and particular situation. "This distinguishes between imposing professional values as experts, with the client as recipient of services, and real self-determination." As demonstrated by Studt, this conceptualization of practice involves professional help in accordance with the client's natural life style and unique commitments, as opposed to prior assumptions underlying interventions of the professional expert to change the client's life.

The practice model that Studt suggests is "making a situational analysis and planning appropriate intervention strategies, establishing and guiding over time in each case a set of working relationships among task-related persons . . . regardless of method." The description of this model takes in many of the characteristics of the model we have been attempting to devise in this book. In Studt's article to which we have been referring (1968) as in the work of Cumming & Cumming (1962), Schwartz & Schwartz (1964), and William Caudhill (1958), in psychiatric hospitals—she proposes a model of organizational behavior that would give expression to her practice model. She speaks of "people working together instead of employing experts to do something," and she comments upon the need for social workers to have a responsible role in the agency which will give them the freedom of movement to create practice situations that will affect the client's conditions. She sees a pooling of functions and their flexible use to support the work of the clients in managing their own tasks.

This is surely a difficult model to fit into the typical hierarchical one usually found in bureaucratic structures. Such a model would require a total relaxation of statuses to provide for different kinds of intervention called for by the immediate situation. It would require a downward and outward delegation of authority, so that client need, rather than agency manual and administrative decision, would determine the plan of action. It would require a design for free flow between and among personnel, client, and administration, so that participation and feedback would be built into the structure. In other words, a modern view of social work practice would make it necessary to change the traditional view of organizations to make it possible to provide a meaningful social work service.

We have made some comments upon the changing social scene in the urbanized community and the necessity for participation of clients as citizens in their own self-help. The professional expertise rests in precise assessment of the person-in-situation and in knowing how, where, and under what conditions to allocate personnel and facilitate a plan of action. But none of these can occur while the practitioner and the client are bound by archaic agency structures.

In the first place, Studt does not confine her model to traditional modes, but relaxes it to apply to a transactional situation; she wants to locate the problem, the issue at hand, and to provide all of the exigencies necessary to deal with it. The problem defined as person-in-situation may be composed of individual people, dyads, triads, a group, or an institution in its spatial boundaries, all of which might be potentially obstructive or enabling in an individual case of psycho-social dysfunction. This is an organizational strategy, and as we have tried to show, individuals interact with organizations at all steps in their lives. One can hardly assess the person separately from the situation; thus, as the process has come to include large parameters to study, these are the components that need to be treated or helped.

In examining the task and situational strategy approach, we must inevitably deal with organizational factors that form the other half of the person-in-situation configuration. For the social work practitioner as "agency in action" will be carrying out functions that the agency is set up to provide, and both worker and agency, like all aspects of social institutions and city structures, become connected with the individual's behavior.

Other Models of Social Work Practice

In the search for relevance, mental health and social work literature have described theoretical developments and practice experiments that all seem to be reaching for similar aims. Such interventive modes as group treatment, family treatment, and milieu therapy reflect the movement toward systemic thinking, for the broader the unit of attention, the more are systemic variables included in the case boundaries. Furthermore, when the unit of attention includes those people and situations which are in the individual's transactional field, the focus on the here and now and on righting the balance of forces in the case becomes paramount. The greater the number of variables attended to in the case, the greater the chances of effective intervention.

In citing group, family, and milieu treatment as alternative modalities to direct work with individuals in social work intervention, we are assuming that practitioners are becoming versatile in working with a variety of units of attention. While the techniques of working with individuals depend upon the *locus* and size as well as the purpose or function of the group, family, or milieu involved in the case situation, the principles and aims of practice are not too dissimilar. In varied modalities, as in fields of practice, social work practitioners carry along the same basic knowledge and reach toward the same purposes of improved social functioning. A systems perspective that provides for proper assessment of transactions among the salient components of the *unit of attention* applies in the case of the person-in-situation, the family, the group, and the institutional milieu.

We have said that the chief aim of the social work practitioner is to individualize, to sort out "the case" from the mass. As the parameters of the case become enlarged to include variables in the individual's transactional field, proper assessment will enable the practitioner to determine where in the total field intervention is needed in order to restore balance or equilibration between the person and his significant social situation. This mode of practice would appear to be well suited to this society, for it is congested and at the same time isolating; people suffer from its restraints even while they seek reinforcement from its institutions.

The social work practitioner, if located at those sites where people go in the normal course of their lives, could fulfill the need of humanizing or individualizing the urban environment. All people need to be touched by another person while they move through the increasingly bureaucratized urban environment. Most people need help in negotiating that environment, in learning about its resources and how to use them. Some people need help in advocating for their rights to services. The urban strain is demanding, and there is no single cure for all of its ills; it is a meaningful aim to contribute as a social work practitioner to the easement of that strain and to the enhanced coping of the individual in his struggle to survive anonymity.

The interventive design in a particular case situation

should be related in some way to the specific environment in which the person is psychologically or physically located. That is his immediate ecological space, and ordinarily that is where the maladaptation or lack of fit occurs. The salient life-space problem might be expressed among peers or family members, at work, in hospitals and courts and schools, or in sites that have not yet been thought of. Developmental social work practice will seek its own level.

Availability of Social Workers at the "Crossroads": Implications for Intervention

We have attempted to make a transition from viewing people in need of social work intervention as sick to viewing them as being in some state of maladaptive fit with their environments. We have said that urban life creates situational disorders just by virtue of its existence, and that its effects upon citizens are more or less undiscriminating. We cannot overlook the fact of differences in the capacities of individuals to cope with social strain, for we know, from our individualizing stance, that the particular balance of influences and interactions makes every person-in-situation different from every other. To individualize is not to address a person in dysfunctional terms; therefore a recipient of social work services could be called client, claimant, patient, customer, consumer, student, constituent, or citizen. The contract for service is what is crucial in each social work encounter, not the particular role in which the person sees himself.

Assuming that potential consumers of social work services are "out there" and are as yet untouched and unknown, the matter of location of social workers is a crucial one, for availability at the "crossroads of life" is essential if the practitioner is to meet the citizen. The clinic must move outdoors; the old notion of the "little red school house and little white clinic" (M. A. White, 1965) must be reevaluated, the definition of problem must be broadened to some non-prejudicial notion like imbalance, and the social distance of the social work practitioner must be reduced. Furthermore, we know where the stress points are in the urban scene, and it is at those places that practitioners will have to be prevalent in order to provide the greatest degree of preventive intervention.

Earlier, in Chapter 2 (see pp. 72–74), we presented a developmental chart that suggested that social work practice could be conceptualized as being influential at certain intersections—developmental and transitional crisis points—in the lives of all individuals. Let us try here to operationalize that developmental chart, depicting the individual and his transitional interactions with social institutions; let us try to imagine where social work practice will stand in these crisis points.

As a location "in time," we might start with birth, surely the first of the developmental crises for the infant and one of a series for the parents and relatives. In keeping with our commitment to stay with prevention as much as possible, let us envisage a social work program in a prenatal clinic. (In the *next* chapter we will discuss in detail the role of non-professional manpower, for we must be certain not to confuse the presence of social work practice with insistence upon the graduate professional at all points.)

In a prenatal clinic there will be the usual range of concern on the part of the pregnant mothers, going from complete acceptance of the fact of the coming baby and sufficient resources to cope with the new member of the family to severe anxiety on the part of an unwed mother who is immobilized by the forthcoming responsibility. Pregnancy always brings with it a certain degree of normal anxiety. In the urban situation where extended family life is so difficult to pursue, the pregnant mother may not have the support of her own mother's presence, and if she is poor, she has quite a chance of not having the baby's father at home. Her problem will be intertwined with her condition, and to some extent she may have reassurance from the doctor who is attending to her pregnant condition. Yet the matter of planning for the baby, for income while she herself is not working, for care of the older children at home, for future planning about childbirth, for the housing squeeze she may be anticipating, and for the idiosyncratic factors that are marks of her individual case will be in evidence. Moreover, the natural tensions occurring between the mother and the soon-to-be-displaced father and the children at home may be of some burden to the pregnant mother. In some respects, to describe the lot of the pregnant mother waiting in the prenatal clinic is to describe the natural life situation of all pregnant mothers.

Help may range from a kind word, a supportive arm, a telephone call to the welfare department or intervention with the medical personnel, to a long talk to air the tensions the mother is feeling, to a longer talk where she might use reflective processes to wonder about herself and her patterns of behavior. The very presence of the individualizing practitioner, who might in this case at first be a nonprofessional social worker, in itself might serve to prevent the ultimate rejection of the new baby, or the slow torture of marital conflict that could develop. Furthermore, the developmental crisis of pregnancy may in some instances be the very moment when the mother is most accessible to help for a long-standing psycho-social problem that has been bothering her and interfering with her happiness. The point is that the location of the social worker on the scene of the natural life event will in itself make help available and more possible. The reader will note that we have not asked of the mother that she go downtown for an appointment, that she sign up or be highly motivated for treatment, or that she define herself into a typical client role. Shlakman notes that "social welfare services have either been tangential to the population-at-risk, or deterrent in philosophy and practice" (1966, p. 67). It seems obvious that the way to address the person-in-situation unit of attention is right in the real situation, that is, the client's reality, and this way can be used not only as case-finding but as the life-space opportunity for social work intervention.

We might illustrate any of the intersectional points of relationship between the person and the social institution, such as the nursery school when the child attends for the first time and the mother feels she cannot leave him. Or we might follow the child's career through school and its entrances and graduation times, or the parents' employment career, or the daily life processes in which everyone partakes. At each point of transition there may be no *problem,* or there may be; at each point there is the necessity to negotiate the community and the bureaucratic institutions that have come to characterize it. For the helping agencies to succeed at all, efforts have to be made to tailor services to individual needs.

Often social workers in the very settings in which they work do not recognize opportunities for intervention. In waiting rooms of hospitals, courts, and social agencies there are always relatives and friends waiting for their loved ones, or for word from the doctor, or for the particular decision that will affect their own lives. How often do we pass by and not recognize human need in its most anxious state. The presence of a helping person in those "highways and byways" would be not only humane but also preventive of potential psycho-social disequilibrium.

In attempting to locate individualizing services "in space," or at those places where people intersect in the normal course of their lives, we are of course entering the institutional or developmental sphere of social welfare, in contradistinction to the more familiar residual sphere. Prior to exploring a legitimate role for social work practice in locations where "preproblem" circumstances occur, it is important to address some difficult questions. Let us suppose that adequate social insurance programs were to supplant the present public assistance method of providing income maintenance. People would then receive income on the basis of their status relative to a predefined group judged by the Congress to be vulnerable to average expectable and natural risks of life. With the termination of the means test and the eligibility study, where social workers traditionally have determined individual need on a case-by-case basis, and the coming of the universally agreed-upon right of all citizens to an adequate income, we would need to ask *what role social work practice would have in such an objective income maintenance scheme.*

Social insurance means that need is defined in terms of universal risks that are applicable to the total population and not in terms of personal failure or individual problems. Thus, if we were to contemplate the use of social work practice in a social insurance system, we would surely need to reexamine the definitions of practice which presently relate individualizing services to people with defined problems, or we would be guilty of turning the clock back and imposing a residual coloration on an institutional program. If we personalize an appropriately impersonal program, will this attention to the individual damage the concept of universality and objectivity? This is a most difficult problem, for a modern social worker would not want to confuse the insurance concept by defining need on a case-by-case basis when government had advanced to the point of defining economic need through legislation and statute. The problem can be solved by maintaining a separation between the income maintenance program and the social work service and by treating the social insurance office as if it were a "community." And in fact, although the social worker has no role in an objective income maintenance program, the currently existing prototype of social security office is an ideal location for case-finding in a developmental scheme of social work.

The typical social security office presents an atmosphere that is markedly different from that of the public assistance office. The latter is often in a run-down condition; staff is overwhelmed by pressures; clients struggle through the bureaucratic obstacles in order to get their basic needs met; the total morale in the system suffers from cynicism and discrimination against the poor and against the people who work with them; and the atmosphere is permeated with an attitude of scapegoatism. On the other hand, the social security office, because it is a federal agency, is an insurance instead of an assistance program, and is financially and attitudinally further removed from the local citizen–taxpayer, does not suffer from the same characteristics as the public assistance agency. The office is usually pleasant, the furniture modern, the equipment up to date, and the personnel well trained to perform their well-defined task of connecting the claimant with his rightful income. Staff training is mostly directed toward developing attitudes of acceptance and responsiveness (De Schweinitz & De Schweinitz, 1961), because the staff's primary tasks are not substantive. They do not decide who is eligible; they do not have the authority to rule claimants in or out of the social insurance system. Rather, laws, policies, and ultimately machines govern those decisions. Thus, in the British spirit, a worker in social security is primarily a civil servant carrying out the nation's policies that are determined elsewhere. The dissatisfied claimant who has exhausted his benefits must take his concern to the politician, and the office itself becomes merely a corridor through which are exchanged rights and income. It is obvious that quite a different purpose is served in social security and public assistance offices, and as form follows function, there is no individualizing service performed in the social security office. This is why one must be alert to the question about the role of social work practice in a kind of structure that has, up to now, wisely kept itself removed from the stigma of traditional, residual social work practice.

The social security office is a most desirable location for individualized services because it is used by increasing numbers of citizens who typically have not yet articulated problems sufficiently to gain them entrance into the range of possible client systems that might be connected with residual social work agencies. What a fine location in which we might explore the possibilities for early social work intervention!

Who, after all, goes to that office at the present time? According to law, every individual in the social security system who is to receive medicare, the man or woman who has arrived at retirement age, the woman whose husband has just died, the young children in a family whose father has been killed in an industrial accident—and if social insurance programs proliferate as we expect they will, there will be more statuses of people there. For example, family allowances will mean that citizens will become attached to their local social insurance offices as much and as often as they become connected with any other single institution in society. And they will not all be poor or disadvantaged in other ways, or sick or old or addicted or delinquent. They will be people who will represent the total range in society; they will represent all classes, ethnic groups, ages, and degrees of social adaptation. They will be sick and they will be well, and most of them will be average in every regard, because social insurances will define average status in the citizenry.

At present, when people are in contact with the social security office they are enduring some psychological and social crisis, as expressed in their need for economic re-arrangements. At present, referrals to social agencies are usually made by receptionists or claims clerks, but in such instances people must make themselves "cases." They must articulate a problem, find the motivation to pursue a referral, and actually conceptualize their difficulty as a social work problem, thereby permitting themselves to enter a client system. That is the way it is now.

The use of social work practitioners or their nonprofessional designates as individualizers of the social insurance system need not interfere with the objectivity of the program or with the desires of some people to not have help. Availability is probably the key principle, for most people in the urban complex can use help in negotiating their lives, and most particularly do those people need help who are under the strain of crisis events in their lives. As the nature of help is usually characterized by the structure in which it is provided, help in this instance would undoubtedly range from listening to a recently widowed woman who needs to talk about her husband, to actively arranging with her for a different way of living.

The entire spectrum of life is represented in the social security office, and it would seem to be a most likely location to provide evidence of the government's concern with the individualizing of social systems, beginning with its own federal program. As long as the individualizing services are not admixed with the primary income maintenance program or with any other requirements except the claimant's need and desire for help, it can be demonstrated theoretically that the two levels of service can exist without contaminating each other's aims.

Developmental social work practice also could occur whenever social institutions exist to serve people in specialized areas of their lives. In the main, these are health and educational institutions, employment offices, police and fire stations, housing, religious institutions, license bureaus, libraries, day care centers, and social utilities of the kind described by Kahn (1969, p. 189). Furthermore, in the private or commercial sphere, we similarly ought to view union halls and shopping centers as likely locations for the provision of individualizing services, as places where people go in their pursuit of their daily, complicated lives in the city of today (Weiner et al., 1973; Skidmore et al., 1974). Generally people are not at the doors of any clinic or agency until they have articulated a problem or until someone else has noticed one; in order to reach them through early intervention, it would seem obvious that practice would have to be associated with "normal" everyday institutions with which people are involved in the course of their lives.

Certainly we are not proposing that social work services be imposed upon people, but simply that they be available at times of stress. Also we are not saying that social work services would take the place of the primary service being offered in any of the institutions or locations just mentioned. Rather, we are suggesting that bureaucratic structures break down in the area of individualizing when they become too large and too specialized in the function they are established to perform, and that as organizational services have come to replace family and other intimate supports, there is a need for such agencies to provide that intimate function of individualizing, relating, advocating, and helping people to connect appropriately with the service being offered.

In a school the teacher is supposed to teach; that is his primary function, and he must be given the time and opportunity to do that. The presence of a social worker in the school building makes it possible for the teacher, the child, or the parent to make use of his services at the moment of stress. The model we propose is similar to that where a roaming social worker or team of professionals and non-professionals are present in the school and part of the broad educational responsibility of the school system. Assuming that the work of the school is to educate children, all children are known to the schools, and they are potentially the community to which the social worker attends; the school boundaries in the neighborhood thus become the social worker's catchment area. As the social institution which is used by almost all families in the area, the school is a likely place to pick up incipient family troubles that range from lack of solvency to marriage conflicts to parent–child problems. The PTA, for example, is a logical place for a social work service to be addressed to some kind of specific social action, and the halls and the lunchroom are ideal offices for the preventive social work practitioner.

In a hospital, there are many models of social work service, some that are built around medical clinical entities which follow the doctor's practice and some that are more general and exist somewhat outside or on the fringe of medical practice and provide services in their own right. For example, a social work service might be connected with all of the specialized clinics in the hospital. These, after all, are expressions of the expertise developed in several areas of medicine; they do not reflect the way people are in general; people are not fractures or infectious diseases or skins, etc. Yet it is functional to connect individual social workers with those clinics that focus on specialized medical problems, since that is where the out-patients are assigned and sickness generates tensions and psycho-social imbalance best handled by social workers.

Another model of medical social work practice is where the social work service might exist as a generalist organization, available for direct service to all patients and for consultation to all hospital staff when needed. As in the school, the social work practitioner might simply be present in a waiting room and be observant about incipient problems that might or might not be connected with the illness that brought the family to the hospital. In the school education is the purpose that defines the direction of services; similarly, the services of the hospital must be directed toward medicine —but people take their total concerns with them wherever they go. Thus an available social worker with an individualizing function would be located in such a way as to pick up problems before they were articulated in advanced clinical terms.

We might generalize from schools and hospitals to all other social institutions and private commercial establishments, each having its own function and each needing that special individualizing service that could be made available by social work practitioners.

In examining the various kinds of organizational schemes that form the present and potential boundaries for social work practice, it appears that individualizing services need to be defined by the nature of the setting in which they occur. Yet a practitioner might select an area of specialization from the entire range of human activity, which includes health, education, labor, corrections, family and child welfare, housing, etc. Specialized knowledge about the area in which the practitioner chooses to work would be essential for him to become expert in the salient systems of knowledge that described the case.

There are guiding principles for social work services that evolve from the development of ideas in this book. Interestingly, despite the reliance upon organizational readiness and program flexibility, each of these principles could be applied by the individual practitioner. Not exactly a practice model, these principles hold out the expectation that social work practice will attain a stronger relationship to the concrete and aspirational realities of our times:

1. To serve as many people as quickly and parsimoniously as possible
2. To view individuals in their natural life situation as part of a transactional field of person-in-environment
3. To provide for reestablishment of psycho-social balance rather than for "long term" therapeutic efforts at "cure"
4. To intervene directly to strengthen individual coping mechanisms and to reinforce social supports

Practice Skills and the Professional Relationship

The specific skills involved in social work intervention of this or any type potentially are so vast as to defy classification.

Practice behavior must be adapted to specific practice experience; it is the art aspect of social work for each practitioner to use himself creatively and in the particular ways that his own personality allows. Some social workers are calm and quiet and provide their supportiveness through gesture and a few words. Others who are more active and outgoing may take hold of situations with a greater sense of excitement and engagement. Both should be accountable for assessing the need for supportiveness in a case, but each will express it differently. The encounter between social worker and client(s) has to be a purposeful relationship, always leading to some kind of action by and in behalf of the client. This relationship will be colored by the social worker's capacities and self-awareness, as well as by the client's need and total life experience. Whatever nuances the professional relationship reflects, the modern versions of social work practice demand that the relationship be a tool to move the case forward, and that except in special situations it not be an end in itself.

The traditional social work emphasis on the professional relationship has to be reevaluated in light of the model of practice in use. Where a life model is in use and potential interventions are viewed as located everywhere that is relevant in the life space of the client, the professional relationship may actually be the least of the therapeutic efforts in a particular case. This is not to say that each encounter between practitioner and client(s) should not have a professional, objective, client-centered perspective. Rather, it means that the relationship itself may not be always the most significant variable in the interventive system. Once the boundaries of a case have been opened up it is possible to locate intervention at any point in the sequence or map as mutually agreed upon by client(s) and workers. The general systems theory of equifinality says that there are many routes to a single goal. This suggests, for example, that in the case of the 13-year-old girl who was afraid to grow up, the social worker could engage the mother, the clinic group of girls, the school, and the museum visits as supports and enticements to her desire to mature. The professional relationship was used to this end, but it turned out not to be the central means of the child's development.

The reliance on the use of the professional relationship as the primary skill in social work practice is a carry-over of the medical (or psychoanalytic) model of practice. It undoubtedly is the chief tool of the psychotherapist who defines cases as psychological. In social work, the psycho-social unit of attention indicates an eco/systems perspective. This does not mean that the worker attends to the psychology of the person and that all else in the surround is a social system. Neither does it mean that the worker manipulates environmental variables without reference to specific client needs. The eco/systems approach reaches for the transactional exchange between person and environment, or life space; it is neither psychological nor environmental in focus; it focuses on the interface between.

The erasure of the hyphens in person-in-situation (a linear concept) has been a conceptual goal in social work since Mary Richmond's *What Is Social Casework?* was written in 1922 (C. H. Meyer, Purposes, and boundaries, 1973). This goal seems to be within sight as a systemic concept when we view the person in his life space. Once it is achieved, the use of the professional relationship as the primary interventive tool pales beside the vast possibilities in creative design of social policies and programs, promotion of intimate family and social relationships through family and group modalities, bending of environments so that the client can make use of urban choices and rural supports, and encouragement of people and organizations in the community to command their own services and to suit them to their own life style.

These kinds of intervention, along with the array of skills each situation demands, tap the adaptive potential of people and of environments and social networks. They assume that the client knows best about his own needs and wants, and that he is, in the last analysis, the only one able to make changes in and on behalf of himself. The social worker's expertise in knowledge about people and environments is matched by his skills in enabling, allowing for growth, and participating in creating conditions of life that make it possible for people to find fulfillment. The practitioner's careful and conscious use of the relationship is thematic in all of the work he does, but the arena in which he works is larger than the one-to-one encounter.

Developmental services, professional accountability, location at the crossroads of life, and an eco/systems perspective of person-in-situation all come together to suggest a life model of social work practice. Since real life is the context of social work practice, and since society has made necessary the institutionalization of individualizing human services, this seems to be the moment of choice for professional social work to grasp the opportunity to provide those services. As for the alternatives, it seems that social work already has practiced those for over fifty years.

The choice has to do with whether or not social workers are going to view themselves as psychotherapists who, like psychiatrists, psychologists, and others in the "fifth profession," treat people primarily for intrapsychic problems. Readers of this book should recognize that in this author's view, people and their problems in living are also the subject of social work intervention. Despite the shared concern among professions for people in trouble, there is no profession other than social work that encompasses the people to be helped within their social context. It is this focus that is served by our thrust toward developmental services, the concomitant eco/systems perspective, a life model of practice, and a clear sense of social accountability.

The profession of social work is unique in its interconnectedness with social forces, both governmental–organizational and environmental (cultural, ethnic, ideational, eco-logical). Also, it is characterized by interventions focused upon family and group relationships. There is no way in which social workers can continue to straddle professional purposes and maintain a viable profession. Psychotherapy just does not de-scribe the complexities of social work interventions; clinical parameters do not come close to encompassing the spatial and psycho-social boundaries of social work cases; psychoanalytic theory is insufficient as background for explaining the way persons-in-situations transact; and selected client groups who could best utilize psychotherapy do not necessarily reflect the general population for whom social workers have assumed responsibilty.

The tasks of managing caseloads, defining interventive tasks, inventing supporting knowledge, and devising useful research still lie ahead. But once social work purposes are agreed upon—if ever they can be—the creativity of the tasks will offer a new and unambiguous challenge to this genera-tion of social workers.

Clearly, if social workers are to move into the life of the community and be available at the potential developmental stress points where people are, there will have to be a major revamping of the use of social work manpower. Mastery of this difficult issue will probably be the key to the continuing usefulness of social work in this country. Everything we have said about coverage, inclusion of large numbers of people as consumers of social work services, and attention to the broad transactions of individuals in their environment sug-gests that a vast army of individualizing practitioners will be necessary to carry out the mandates of this form of practice. In the next and concluding chapter we will look at the possibilities for differential uses of manpower that would suit the purpose of greater individualization in the urbanized environment.

Chapter 6

The Differential Uses of Social
Work Manpower

IN THE SEVEN YEARS since work on the first edition of this book was begun, the issue of manpower in social work has become as significant as we then anticipated. The idea that modern society will have to rely for its human services upon a proliferation of multiple levels of manpower is being granted as an assumption today, even though the projected organization, aegis, and uses of manpower are still far from clear and agreed upon.

This is a difficult political and economic era in which to discuss manpower issues in social work, because at this writing there is an unbalanced employment market that makes no sense except in light of the uncertain mandate to social work discussed earlier in this book. The manpower issue is actually many issues. First, there is established public need for social services, and a lack of governmental attention to this. Thus in one sense there is a manpower shortage even though there is also unemployment of social workers. Second, there is the issue of varied levels of social service manpower. The educational "continuum" and the differential use of manpower in social work present problems that remain far from solved. Finally, there is the issue of the relationship between the social work practice model and differential use of manpower.

In this chapter we will address all of these manpower issues assuming that the present political climate will change, and that current social worker unemployment is a phase to be short-lived. Legislation in the areas of health, aging, and child welfare services, for example, will create the necessity for social workers to be employed; but even then it will be necessary to confront ways in which the varied kinds of social workers will be utilized. It is a matter of manpower strategy, quite independent of the issue of shortages.

The present economic situation in postindustrial countries has suggested to many scholars of the subject that continued industrial growth does not solve the problem of unemployment, particularly outside the area of jobs requiring highly specialized technical skills. There is a lack of utilization of nonskilled people, youth, older people, part-time workers, and women. Some of this unemployment is due to institutionalized racism, sexism, and ageism, and some undoubtedly is due to sheer lack of job availability and diversity in the industrial arena. Furthermore, ecological concerns, education, machines, computers, and changing work values have begun to challenge people to think about work in areas of society apart from factories and merchandising establishments. The human services in both public and voluntary sectors are rapidly becoming the "work places" for almost two-thirds of the working population.

A sketchy look at some self-help groups alerts us to the vast service potential in Alcoholic Anonymous, Weight Watchers, the Fortune Society, Synanon, the Foster Parents Association, the Organization of Adopted Children, Parents of Retarded Children, Child Abusers Anonymous, and all the unknown or unnamed indigenous groups of parents of school children, people with defined health problems, and groups of disaffected and alienated people. Not only are these groups of people finding mutual aid in their association, but also they are being served by others who are like them. From the manpower point of view, there are human service jobs being carried out in self-help groups, and their numbers are probably vast and are growing.

Then there are semiautonomous groups and organizations that are devoted to the hazards of our society—service efforts that develop in response to need that is not institutionally recognized or at least is not available in terms understood by the people who need them. Hot lines, abortion counseling, rape counseling, encounter groups, runaway pads, and community breakfast programs are some examples of these service efforts. Add to these the institutionalized service programs that are always understaffed and in need of service providers, such as hospitals, courts, schools, child welfare agencies, nursing homes, well baby clinics, day care programs, recreational centers, foster grandparents, retirement counseling, meals on wheels, home helps, friendly visitors to the aged and the homebound, institutions for retarded, delinquent, and dependent children, and so on and on. The service potential for employment is as open-ended as our social vision allows.

It is obvious that service roles would be recognized in the very arena in which social workers have accountability. Health, education, and welfare are after all the aegis of human services, albeit defined with more rigid boundaries than people requiring services might define the field. It is this common turf shared by social work and the human services that offers the simultaneous challenge and opportunity. The medical profession is coming to terms with its own need for paraprofessionals, as is the profession of education. It may be taking professional social work a little longer because of its own developmental process of defining what it is and what it does. But time has run out, and presently social workers must include in definitions of practice the reality that human service manpower is out there, working in larger numbers than ever, and attaining visibility and acceptance by locating itself very close to the people it is serving.

The social work profession, reflected in the National Association of Social Workers (NASW) and the Council on Social Work Education (CSWE), and the social agencies' hiring practices have moved in the direction of official recognition of differentially educated manpower. In 1970 the NASW permitted holders of bachelor's degrees into the association, in 1974 the CSWE began the process of accreditation of undergraduate social work programs (B.S.W.), and increasingly social agencies and social service departments in hospitals have employed A.A., B.A., and B.S.W. graduates. Still, it is not clear how jobs are being defined differentially, and there is presently a debate as to what the educational continuum (A.A., B.S.W., or B.A., M.S.W., D.S.W.) should be like in content and objectives. Added to the lack of consensus in these matters is the political–economic situation which has restricted employment in all fields connected with social work. Thus the matter of differential manpower is somewhat contentious for the professional graduate social worker who feels threatened by job loss. This is a real threat when the value of the undergraduate-trained social worker is perceived in competitive rather than complementary terms.

In light of this uncertain context, it might seem foolhardy to undertake a discussion of a model of manpower utilization. The intraprofessional debate seems to be about matters other than manpower alone. This is appropriate, because as we have noted, one cannot consider differential uses of manpower in social work without *at the same time* defining the purposes of practice, the approach to cases, and the nature of interventions. For example, social workers who view practice essentially as psychotherapy, where worker-client counseling is the primary service and the therapeutic use of the relationship is a goal in treatment, would find only peripheral the use of less educated personnel.

In association with this approach to practice, what after all could an undergraduate social worker do except work on concrete tasks most explicitly defined outside of the practice core in the case? This has been the traditional way in which undergraduate staff have been used in psychotherapeutic casework. Cases defined as having a psychological core, where all else is viewed as social or environmental, can utilize undergraduate workers to arrange for supportive services and necessary resources. However, in such cases the undergraduate worker has no real contact with the person or family, unless someone is considered to be outside the context of the professional relationship. This model of manpower follows the model of practice, in that the psychotherapeutic practice approach assumes environmental inputs to be external to the client's psychological reality and thus cases can be handled only by highly skilled graduate social workers. In this illustration the use of differentially educated social workers is most clear; the determination of tasks is made by the graduate, and the tasks of the others are limited to arranging for concrete services to suit the needs of the case.

Another example is in the use of the ecological/systems approach to practice, where the "map" of the case includes the relevant totality of the client's life as the unit of attention. As the "core" of practice in this approach is not singularly the professional relationship, but rather is governed by the principle of equifinality, cases may reach their conclusions through multiple interventions. From this perspective, it is possible to contemplate a fuller degree of utilization of social work manpower on all levels of educational preparation. A client's management of a life task, such as finding a job, parenting a child, or returning to school after a truancy, might require the careful attention of a social worker helping the client to understand the problems at hand, to take risks, and to master the demands of the situation, while at the same time doing what is possible to reduce ambiguities and arrange for service provision. This model provides for a variety of worker and client tasks, probably classifiable on some scale of simplicity to complexity. There is no "core" theme established a priori as an aspect of the model, although in the assessment of the case one might be discerned. In this conception of practice there is no conceptual separation between the person and the environment, for they are connected through the mutual fit and the transactions between them, and the social worker intervenes at their interface.

Comparing the two models of practice only in the framework of the manpower issue, it would appear that the eco/systems approach allows for greater diversity in the job of the undergraduate social worker, opportunities for direct work with clients, and a perspective on practice that is holistic and not confined to the environmental aspects of the case. It is likely that as undergraduate programs proliferate and become accreditated, large numbers of men and women will find job opportunities in social work services, and if they are educated well, they will seek a comprehensive perspective on case problems and will want to apply their new knowledge and skills as meaningfully as possible.

Accommodations to Lack of Manpower Strategies

Any view of the issue of manpower in a field of practice must depend upon one's perception of the aims and practices of that field. Thus, in social work, were one to assess its purpose as being mainly to treat in hopes of curing clinically diagnosed individuals and families within traditionally structured social agencies, then one would need to count the pool of professional social workers and relate this number to the best estimate one could make of potential clients. Where there was a disparity between supply and demand, one would either attempt to expand the numbers of graduates to meet the need or restrict the numbers of clients to places available in each agency.

This mode of coping with particular kinds of manpower shortages is a familiar one; it accounts, in part, for waiting lists, for restrictive intake policies, for expedient and un-planned short-term treatment schemes, and sometimes for group treatment. Where these policies and practices are used as accommodations to the shortage of graduate staff and not as utilitarian in their own right, they may reflect the effort in the field of social work to get around the professional manpower shortage without changing the fundamental struc-ture of services or aims of practice. Another example of the way in which the field has attempted to deal with the "numbers game" related to the graduate manpower shortage has been to exert strong efforts to increase the numbers of graduate workers through provision of more graduate schools of social work, larger classes, more scholarships, modified programs, and other devices for expanding numbers.

As we saw earlier in this book, the field of social work is in an uncertain state, suffering from its own identity crisis and from diminishment of social resources. It seems that while psycho-social need has been getting out of hand as far as the quantity of demand is concerned, professional graduate social workers, who are limited in numbers, have been increasingly less able to meet the demand. We have noted that the nature of the demand for service will be changing, and if the social work profession restricts its boundaries of service to those clients who seek psycho-therapeutic help, then society may have to invent new hu-man service providers. If such restriction occurs, there will be no shortage of graduate social work manpower, because the defined professional task will be so narrowly conceived that there will be enough graduate social workers to do the job without expansion.

The dilemmas posed by issues of manpower usage possibly have been salutary, because they have literally forced the field to reexamine its practices and purposes. This seems to have been a roundabout way to rethinking social work practice, but it served the immediate purpose of coming to terms with reality. Manpower shortages are not what is wrong with social work practice, but if the pressure of staff needs has opened up the field for review, then it has been a valuable problem. In any case, a manpower strategy must be part of the total reconceptualization of social work practice. The primary question is, is there a shortage of graduate social workers? In accordance with the direction of a developmental approach to social work, the answer is yes, there is. But in the present political atmosphere, where social services are being restricted and professional practice is being downgraded, the answer is no, there is not.

The Extent of the Professional Shortage

The gap between supply of and demand for professional social workers is distributed unevenly among fields of practice, with public welfare agencies accounting for proportionately fewer professionals than other settings. According to a 1965 estimate made by HEW, there were 12,000 professional vacancies in 1965 and 100,000 were projected for 1970 (U.S. Department of Health, Education, and Welfare, 1965). (Since the publication of the HEW study considerable question was raised about these figures even before the current economic downturn. Shortages in manpower usually are politically and economically defined, and evidence of need for social workers is bound to be modified by those considerations.) As social services became integrated into proposed health care facilities, different models of mental patient care, new approaches to neighborhood-based small group homes, and so on, the gap will continue to widen. The deficiency may be even greater than official estimates described it, for many unfilled staff positions go unreported, either because of a sense of hopelessness about funding or recruiting staff or because administrative actions are taken to reduce services or speed them up as an accommodation to the lack of staff; thus the unfilled positions become more or less invisible. A major factor contributing to the professional manpower shortage is that seventy-nine graduate schools of social work enroll approximately 17,000 professional graduates a year (Ripple, 1974, p. 14). About half of this number graduate each year. Clearly it is presently a statistical impossibility for graduate education to keep up with the ever-increasing gap between the supply of and demand for professional social workers. Finally, we must keep in mind that these estimates of shortages apply to current conceptions of social work practice. Were the field to assume the stance about individualizing practice that we are discussing in this book, and were the graduate viewed as the typical practitioner, the gap between supply and demand would be so phenomenal that a solution would indeed be out of sight. It has been granted that we are discussing this subject on two levels: the current status of manpower utilization and the vision of what ought to be or could be—or might have to be, if professional social work is to continue to survive.

Some Causes for the Gap between Availability and Need

Apart from the obvious factors that we have noted as causes for the uncertain manpower strategies, the increasing public need and the proportionately small supply of graduates, there are other reasons that account for the problem. Barker & Briggs (1966) and others have made careful, well-documented statements about the *lack of manpower strategy* in social work that finds expression in at least three ways:

1. Graduate professional workers are *unevenly distributed,* so that fields of practice that are in the greatest need of them are often the ones that have least of them; some fields of practice actually have too many professionals for the scope of the service they offer, while other fields cannot attract and hold professionals. And the competition for them is too often governed by parochial factors rather than by client need.

2. All kinds of social work manpower, professional and nonprofessional, graduate and undergraduate, are *not used differently,* in accordance with particular knowledge and skills. Thus professionals may be underutilized and nonprofessionals may be overutilized. This lack of functional clarity makes for waste of available manpower in a tight employment situation that can ill afford it.

3. *Inefficient practices* also waste valuable graduate manpower when tasks are not reviewed or reconstructed in light of manpower realities and newly defined approaches to "the case." Some examples may be seen in cases that remain in treatment for years, without focus and without end; in cases where social workers do tasks that are best performed by the client himself or an organization in his community; in cases where referral and intake procedures require repetition of the exploratory process; and in cases where immediate intervention in the environment rather than treatment interviews would be not only more appropriate but also more saving of worker effort.

Thus the manpower "shortage," or lack of manpower strategies, can be viewed as a symptom of dysfunctional case and staff practices; it is a problem that is larger than the issue of numbers, and it requires solutions that transcend the issues of increased recruitment for professional education and more equitable deployment of staff among fields of practice. The manpower issue itself has become a rather convenient scapegoat within social work, where it is often heard that "if only we had more staff, money, faculty, space, training supervisors, time, etc.," the job could be done. We will attempt to demonstrate here that the manpower issue is systematically related to the traditional social work scheme of services, and the problem is circular. There is a manpower "shortage" because practice in the field of social work continues to pursue a clinical mode. Furthermore, the lack of a coherent manpower strategy, that is, differential use of levels of personnel, may well be politically and economically determined. Thus the field may be unable to confront squarely an appropriate and rational strategy for reasons quite apart from practice principles.

Some Implications for Practice

One of the most serious effects of the lack of manpower strategies upon even the most sophisticated and refined practice is that it may actually distort the accuracy of a case assessment or the appropriateness of a plan of intervention. This is not simply because undergraduates may make a misassessment, or because the graduate staff is hurried or overworked and therefore may overlook significant factors in the case. The problem is more complicated and has something to do with the residual nature of social work practice. Where a case is defined in clinical normative terms and there is a severe shortage of professional treatment resources (due, in large measure, to the manpower shortage), case planning will often reflect this reality.

As an example of this negative kind of self-fulfilling prophecy, we know the all-too-typical case of the black adolescent boy who has been adjudged delinquent and is in need of a residence of some kind. Although we are not here designating whether the residence ought to be treatment-oriented or health-promoting in its program, the boy in our case example is known to be unable to return to his home and must go somewhere where he will be helped to cope better with his life. Further, assuming that the reasonable alternatives indicated for this boy range from a treatment kind of residence to a carefully selected foster home, a protected boys' residence, or a state school with limited facilities for delinquent boys, can we imagine where he would finally go? Because of limited facilities, the boy might not fit into the programs of any of the prescribed places, either because he is of a minority group, is too old or too young, is too aggressive or too passive, or is too sick or too well psychologically. It is not uncommon that an accurate assessment, which would demand an appropriate resource for him, will sooner or later become masked by the impossibility of getting him to the facility he really needs. So a disturbed boy who needs a certain treatment center will sooner or later be viewed as perhaps not so disturbed, because the only residence available to him is the state school; or, lacking even that resource, review of the case might finally indicate that he is able to go back home after all.

Practitioners all know cases where similar accommodations to professional shortages have had to be made. There are cases where the prescribed treatment arising from an accurate assessment would be hospitalization, group therapy, or individual treatment but, primarily as a result of lack of manpower strategies, none of these treatment resources are available. Often, in such cases, first-aid measures are used as a compromise or as a holding action. Thus the main purposes of accurate assessment and careful planning are bypassed, practitioners become discouraged, agencies become defensive, and the client in question may actually be misled. Unless there is a major reorientation in thinking about manpower strategies, clients will continue to suffer from gaps in services.

There is a second deleterious effect upon the nature of practice itself that derives in part from the lack of manpower strategy, and it appears in this instance that this vacuum serves some latent function for the field. Obviously, where lack of professional graduate staff is a major administrative problem, therapeutic programs will be devised for increasingly smaller groups of clients. Thus intake policies, which depend upon the availability of workers skilled enough to do the job, must accommodate to reality by becoming increasingly exclusive. The potential client group may become only those who are "treatable" or "workable" or those people who are "able to use the services of the agency." However the lines of eligibility are drawn, around treatability or motivation, problem classification, or even ethnic group or class affiliation, the agency's services must be restricted. This will mean not only that increasingly fewer people will be served but also that practice will become increasingly residual.

With limited professional graduate personnel an agency can ill afford to reach out into the community for more cases or place its intake process much further back in the interventive scheme to reach people earlier in the course of psycho-social breakdown. Limited professional graduate manpower may even appear as a justification for restriction of services, and this very restriction itself serves as justification for providing strictly clinically based, therapeutic programs. The ultimate result of this residual direction of social work programs might be that practice would literally paint itself into a corner and finally into oblivion. While society calls out for individualizing services, professional social workers who might be best qualified to provide these services become further and further removed from the scene.

Proposed Solutions

The purpose of this book has been to suggest an approach to social work practice that would be relevant to the current social scene. In the attempt to redefine the boundaries of "the case" and to envision practitioners carrying out early interventive individualizing tasks somewhere in the person's unique transactional field, we have pointed out the necessary changes as to where social workers would need to be located, the aims of help, and how the practice model might be viewed in systemic rather than clinical terms. This effort to reconceptualize the purposes of social work practice comes out of the conviction that the time is overdue and that urban populations are in danger of becoming lost in the bureaucratic maze; our proposal has not been suggested as a way to address manpower issues. Yet a strategy for the use of manpower is an essential part of the proposal of a different model of practice.

Obviously, if the therapeutic model cannot be sustained with manpower arrangements now existing, it would be ludicrous to imagine that a much broader conception of practice would be effective with the same kind of manpower arrangements. The therapeutic model of social casework practice *requires* that a professional worker be the therapeutic agent for every case. We have established that the scope of the case has widened beyond the one-to-one ratio of worker to client, and presently caseworkers in their practice include dyads, triads, families, and groups, where the aim of casework is treatment. It must follow that the best treatment would occur only where the worker was professionally skilled; any use of nonprofessional workers, therefore, would be an *accommodation* to the unfortunate reality that there is a shortage of professionals.

However, were the developmental social work practice model to be followed, a professional graduate worker would not have to be the primary therapeutic agent, mainly because therapy would not necessarily be the primary method in the case. Our systemic view of the case would make provision for a nonprofessional worker to intervene at various intersections, not as a compromise, but as a diagnostically chosen first-choice worker who would be used to carry out that task to which he was the best suited.

Given the assumptions about a systemic model of practice,

the role of the professional graduate practitioner would be one of accountability for, but not necessarily of direct action in, every case in his assignment load. If the graduate worker were located in an emergency service of a large hospital, he might be allocated the responsibility for the entire population of the clinic, or if it were a very crowded clinic, he might share the clients with any number of other professionals, for a proportion of whom each would be responsible. A "caseload" then might number into the hundreds, but there would be unlimited numbers of various kinds of nonprofessional undergraduate personnel available to carry out the bulk of the case-related tasks.

Theoretically, at the point where graduate social workers assume the multiple roles (which are all part of the practice role) of case consultant, diagnostician, case planner, sometimes therapist or advocate, and leader of the social work team, there could be a sufficient supply to actually cover the total "client population" defined by an agency program. We might even see the day when total neighborhoods are thus attended to, when all the residents of a housing project are known, when every person who must go to a hospital is touched in some way by the individualizing social work service. When manpower no longer serves as a restraint upon social work services, it may be possible to move all of practice back into the sphere of early intervention before psychosocial breakdown. But the subject of differential use of manpower is very complicated, and it is important to consider it in detail, so that all of its dimensions are laid bare.

Differential Use of Manpower

There are issues connected with the definition of terms, so it is important to state what is meant here by the manpower terminology used in this chapter. In the first edition of this book it was relatively clear that the term *professional* could be associated with *graduate* social workers, and the term *nonprofessional* with undergraduate social workers. However, this is not too clear a differentiation any longer, since the NASW, as the professional association of social workers, opened up its membership to bachelor-level graduates and since the CSWE begin accrediting bachelor's degree social work programs. In 1973–74, in about 215 approved programs, there were about 30,000 students enrolled and approximately 9,000 graduated (Ripple, 1974, p. 14). These undergraduates will be eligible for NASW membership, and the term *professional* thereby diminishes in specificity.

There have been interesting reactions to this development, full discussion of which is outside the scope of this book. A group of clinical social workers formed in order to demonstrate a qualitative difference in professional expertise. At the time of this writing, a task force of the CSWE (Ripple, 1974) is attempting to redraw professional education levels in hopes of making the B.S.W. the "generalist" and the D.S.W. the "specialist" practitioner, effectively eliminating the role of the M.S.W.

For purposes of discussion here, there is still virtue in descriptively separating professional from nonprofessional social work in light of the proliferation of A.A. programs—in 1970, almost 200 community college programs enrolled about 10,000 students (*ibid.*, p. 9). Generally, where staffing is under discussion, we will address manpower descriptively as graduate and undergraduate, and where relevant, further specify as D.S.W. or M.S.W. on the graduate side, and B.S.W. or A.A. on the undergraduate side. Yet the issue is not confronted through merely assigning descriptive designations. There remain, in this author's view, certain conceptual, philosophical, and practical differences arising out of differential educational preparation for the profession of social work. Apart from the professional appellation, which may be more symbolic, political, or economic in meaning, there are certain attributes that are associated with a professional's competence in knowledge and skill and with his capacity for autonomous practice. Professional graduate education addresses just those qualities, and as yet, the undergraduate B.S.W. programs do not—or cannot—do this while at the same time preparing students in basic languages, social science, natural sciences, and arts and humanities.

This author is in disagreement with the aims of specialization sought by the clinical social workers, but she is in total agreement with their aim of identifying a professional outcome in graduate education. As for the projected plan of the CSWE task force, this author recognizes its investment in expanding B.S.W. programs—but finds it ironical that, with social work practice now on the brink of effectiveness, demanding greater, not less educational preparation and greater, not less professional autonomy, the CSWE would view this as the period in history when the front should be manned by armies of undergraduates with tasks not differentiated from graduate-level work.

The proposal that the next degree would be the terminal D.S.W. "practice" degree suggests that the CSWE anticipates a very small, elite core of social workers at the apex of the manpower pyramid. This model might leave the greatest number of social workers at the middle and at the base of the pyramid; that is where the practice activity will take place, and that is what we are considering in this chapter. As our discussion develops, we will explore ways in which to use undergraduates as essential team members, but our underlying assumption remains that the term *professional* has greater significance in action as a result of graduate education in social work. This may change in the next decade, but at present it would seem that developmental social work requires, above all, the most knowledgeable, accountable, skillful, and autonomous professionals that graduate education can prepare.

Undergraduate social work personnel are called by many titles, and there are always implications that are broader than the titles themselves. The main point, however, is to keep in mind that our discussion will relate to *differential* use of professional and nonprofessional, graduate and undergraduate manpower, for where nonprofessionals or undergraduates are viewed as substituting for or less than professional graduates or as preparing for professional graduate status we will have missed the point entirely. It might bear repeating here that differential use of nonprofessional or undergraduate social workers is not to be construed as an accommodating measure because there are not sufficient graduates or professionals to go around. Moreover, undergraduates and nonprofessionals cannot be expected to perform in the same way as graduate professionals, and as we view the use of various kinds of manpower as a permanent condition of social work practice in society, undergraduates and nonprofessionals will need to have an integral career line that is comparable to that of graduate professionals. This career line should not necessarily lead into the graduate professional line, except through graduate education, but should have its own direction and goals.

As we are using *professional* as the pivotal concept, i.e., professional versus nonprofessional, we need to affirm that which the professional is characterized by. In light of the fact that graduate education is a requisite for professional knowledge and skills, it is important to understand just what it is that the social work graduate student learns in school that cannot be learned on the job or through life experience. To the degree that there is a component of professional knowledge that is currently only available through formal education, the differentiation among personnel will be easier to assess.

The typical curriculum in a graduate school of social work includes study of social and behavioral sciences pointed toward specific understanding of the work, social welfare history and policy, research, fields of social work, and theory and practice in one or all of the major social work methods. The scope of these areas of knowledge is broad enough to understand the person-in-situation field, including the range of life styles and problems most commonly met in practice and included in the social welfare structure. The knowledge base of practice, of course, is the major factor that differentiates a professionally educated social worker from an agency-trained worker. The scope, depth, and focus of the knowledge would differentiate the M.S.W. from the B.S.W., as would the experience and maturity brought to bear on the subject matter. Preparatory field work would reflect this differentiation as well.

The theory of practice itself provides for a broad repertoire of roles and techniques, making the graduate worker mobile as he selects appropriate measures of help in each case situation. That a graduate social worker is not "trained to tasks" or oriented to a single setting, but rather is educated to generalize his practice through many kinds of functions, across the boundaries of social institutions, and with a variety of people—this is the chief differentiating factor between the graduate and the nongraduate worker in social work. The professional hallmark is a broad base of knowledge applied with skill within the structure of a theoretical framework of practice. Professional education contributes to the individualizing process because it provides the practitioner with multiple lenses through which he views cases, thereby increasing the chance that the individual will not be perceived in too narrow a cast. Briefly stated, the current mode and content of professional education for social work actually are suitable to the view of the individual in his transactional field; the professionally educated social worker should have the framework for assessment and range of interventive techniques in individual, family, group, and community work necessary for individualization in the modern society.

Definitions of Undergraduate Social Workers

All terms assigned to a group of people carry implications about their significance. A common name given to those personnel who work in a field of practice but are not actually professionals of the field is *paraprofessional.* Meaning "alongside of," the concept is clear, that a worker of some nonprofessional status works alongside of a professional worker. Although the term is quite dignified and thus has particular usefulness, it may perhaps be too dignified in social work, where the tasks of workers in both statuses have not yet been delineated. In contrast to medicine, where the term paraprofessional actually designates a person who has a specific paramedical function, a paraprofessional in social work seems to lend more social distance to the concept than would be desirable; it is perhaps a bit pretentious for the present status and functions of both the professional and the nonprofessional social worker.

At the other extreme, the title *nonprofessional,* although accurate (if one associates it with undergraduate education), says not too much but too little about the worker. Although it is a purely descriptive term, it nevertheless carries the connotation of a nonsomething. It doesn't specify any kind of task, it is too diffuse in its meaning, and, most serious as an objection, it creates a polarity between professional and nonprofessional statuses. It might even seem to place the worker out of the social work system altogether.

The term *subprofessional,* of course, has an even more negative connotation and would always signify that a worker was less than someone else. This designation would not contribute toward the goal of teamwork and would undoubtedly create more difficulties than a title ought to.

Another common title that has somewhat demeaning implications is *aide.* This signifies an assistant or a helper, and although a professional worker might, indeed, have several kinds of aides, including clerical and administrative aides of one kind or another, the term does not really explain the meaning of the worker who carries out his own integral functions in a case. A term that served as a compromise in recent years was *preprofessional,* but like *aide,* it carried the implication that the professional status was the most valued, and that the preprofessional worker was only waiting until he was able to transfer to the professional status. Whereas in individual instances this may have occurred, the use of the term *preprofessional* merely helped to postpone the day of reckoning; the preprofessional could actually remain in that state permanently. In any case the task he was expected to perform required an affirmative title that actually denoted a status of its own.

Having thus dispensed with the para, non, sub, and pre, terms, as well as with the aide that is assistant to the professional, we need to consider the possible affirmative job titles that come closest to explaining the nature of the person's job and provide for him a career line and a sense of purpose for the job itself, in its own right. Such a term is *social work technician*. This term and *social work assistant* do not seem to be as popular as is the simple term *social worker*. However, for reasons mentioned earlier, it seems important to differentiate graduate from undergraduate preparation. *Social worker* should have a specific meaning, but the politics of the profession being what they are, it appears that the title itself is a contentious issue. The inevitable result of a struggle over a shared title usually turns out to be a licensing procedure introduced to protect the professional's use of the title. This legal action would effectively realign positions in a way that the use of the term *social work technician* might avoid. For purposes of discussion here, undergraduates will be called technicians, for the time being.

Related Disciplines

There are several types of nonprofessional social work personnel who have specific functions in the field of social work but are not ever preceived of as social work technicians; a nonprofessional working in social work might actually be a professional in another field, like a psychiatrist with a specific treatment or consultative role in a case, and not be doing a social work technician's job at all. Other examples of non-professional persons who often are involved collaboratively in a social work case are the homemaker and the foster parent, each of these adjunctive workers having assigned tasks that are significant to the welfare of the individuals in the case but are not defined as social work tasks. Further examples of nonprofessional and nontechnician personnel may be found in institutional or milieu staff; cottage parents and arts and crafts teachers carry out defined functions that are not construed as social work, although they perform within the boundaries of the social work case.

All these kinds of professional and semiprofessional categories hold in common the fact that they each have their own specialized knowledge and functions, their own career lines, and their own reference groups. Although they are often vital to the conduct of case actions and may work under the aegis of a social work agency, they address the system of the case through other means than social work practice.

On the other hand, the social work technician would be viewed as a member of the team that has as its major function the individualization of people in their environments. The technician not only would be integral to the total social work function but also would have his own career line and appropriate tasks assigned to him that could reflect the total social work scheme of intervention. The concept of the team is particularly useful when one views the case in systemic terms for, as we noted earlier, the transactional field that radiates from the individual is full of opportunities for intervention on many levels; there are potentially endless numbers and kinds of vital tasks that need to be carried out in all social work cases, and these tasks, defined by professionals, could be allocated to technical workers. Recalling that the systemic view of the case provides for early intervention in accordance with the client's life style, when we consider the possible tasks, we will be able to account for very wide use indeed of the technical social worker's skills.

Still considering the definitional aspects of the career technician in social work, his educational background theoretically could range from high school drop-out to college graduate. If professional competence is seen to derive from knowledge gained in graduate school, then it will be important to relate the technician's level of education to the tasks he is expected to carry out. Thus a social work team might include a professional who would be responsible for the whole course of intervention in a case and a college graduate who might differ in the kind and quality of tasks he carried out from the high school drop-out worker, who might also be on the team. As the spread of educational level increases, it will be necessary to assign even more carefully tasks that are relevant to the competences of the workers.

A word ought to be said about the *indigenous worker,* whose characteristics are often confused with educational characteristics. Indigenous actually means "native to," and thus an indigenous worker might be a college graduate who lives in a certain neighborhood and is selected for the social work team for exactly that reason. An indigenous worker may be of any educational background, and his special skill will be his intimate connection and knowledge of the client group that is being served. He may play a vital part as a member of the social work team, as a bridge between the team and the neighborhood, as interpreter of needs, or as neighborhood entrepeneur. As we shall try to point out later when we discuss the varied tasks of professionals and technicians, the indigenous worker could be a valuable social work technician, and as such he would have to have a career line to pursue.

We have cited the various kinds of personnel potentially available for social work intervention on a massive scale. However, there are many hard questions that will have to be dealt with before technicians can be drawn into the organization of practice in social work. Can career lines be guaranteed? Can technical tasks be sufficiently gratifying to warrant careers? Can meaningful tasks be defined and teased out of traditional professional functions? Can professionals find sufficient rewards in indirect treatment and the assumption of consultative roles? Can the total social work function be defined?

Approaches to Differential Use of Staff in Social Work

There are some studies of staff utilization in social work (Barker & Briggs, 1966; Breiland, 1964; Epstein, 1962; Heyman, 1962; Schwartz & Sample, 1972; Richan, 1961; Sobey, 1970), but far too few that devise a conceptual scheme and control the input and output so as to assess the relative merits of various kinds of models. Many approaches to the subject describe informal, individual agency experiments that have usually evolved from pressures of the manpower shortage. Although it is understandable that in the frantic race to close the gap between supply of demand for professional manpower, most social agenices work alone at their own expedient accommodations, the fact remains that there can be no accommodating solutions to the problem without fundamental changes in practice itself. Despite the fact that these changes have not been occurring with noticeable rapidity, it might be clarifying to review and evaluate the ways in which the field presently differentiates between professional and technical staff functions in social work.

1. THE CASE AS THE UNIT OF DIFFERENTIATION

This may be the most common factor of differentiation, but it has severe drawbacks as a classificatory scheme, mainly having to do with the utilization of professional knowledge and skills and a corollary overutilization or inappropriate use of technical knowledge and skills. To appropriately assign cases to one or another level of staff, it would be necessary to define the cases as simple or complex, healthy or sick. This would be almost impossible to assess without adequate diagnostic knowledge. Thus a graduate professional practitioner would need to be drawn in some fashion anyway into every case, in order to make that assessment.

Where cases are differentiated according to the degree to which they reflect inner and outer problems, or emotional versus concrete need, this approach tends to dichotomize the case in ways that are antithetical to the conceptualization of social work cases as psycho-social and of individuals as pivotal in their fields of transaction. In a word, it is not possible in a systemic approach to the case to divide the case up into inner and outer need, for there is an intrinsic relationship between the two aspects of the person-in-situation configuration. Of course there are unplanned and arbitrary ways in which cases are assigned, but we are attempting here to take necessary steps beyond those demanded by expediency alone.

2. THE TASK AS THE UNIT OF DIFFERENTIATION

The idea of a fixed, specific unit of work to be exacted from a practitioner has certain attractive possibilities, because if it were possible to predefine such tasks, it would be relatively easy to allocate them appropriately and to train technicians in their use. The difficulty with this approach is that tasks in social work generally go in clusters, and they are not without implications for more complicated work. For example, making a school visit is hardly a defined task, when there are unaccounted variables that are involved in the process. Another problem with the assignment of tasks to technical workers is that they often are the menial or residual tasks that professionals do not want to do in cases, and thus they may be unrewarding for the technician as well.

Finally, when some tasks are too precisely predefined, they tend to be rather concrete, and their value, as well as their drawback, is that they tend to require repetition. This will make for a certain kind of rigidity in the work and ultimately in the process of carrying it out, so that it soon becomes a meaningless and routine gesture in the total conduct of the case. The client would then be ill served, and the technician would soon be bored and disinterested. Tasks can be grouped and allocated with some clarity, but we shall see that they have to be understood as integral to the case planning so as to avoid routinization and meaninglessness.

3. WORKERS' QUALITIES AS THE UNIT OF DIFFERENTIATION

This is a common approach to the problems of allocating the case assignments in social work, but it does not remove the burden of the necessity to devise a manpower strategy. The differentiation is actually made at the time of recruitment and selection of staff, when an assessment is made as to the particular expertise of the graduate or the undergraduate worker. Graduate professionals are assumed to have special qualities in knowledge and skill arrived at through maturity and education, undergraduates and nonprofessionals whose educational preparation is still untested, are more apt to be selected for their personal qualities and experiences. Then, depending upon the needs of the case, that staff member who is "best suited" to carrying out the treatment tasks is assigned to the case. Clearly, this is an approach that requires the least effort in clarifying the job to be done and in rearranging the patterning and functioning of staff. Yet in this arrangement it is still to be determined, through assessment of the case, those functions or tasks that will prove to be the best "fit" between worker and the case.

4. ORGANIZATIONAL FACTORS OR THE UNIT OF SERVICE AS THE DIFFERENTIATING UNIT

In this approach, professional and technical staff are assigned differentially to the *location* in the agency where certain types of problems are expected to appear, and it is assumed *a priori* that those problems will require one or the other level of skill in practice. Thus in some agencies it has been common to assign nonprofessionals to the places where services are to be provided and professionals to the locations where "personal problems" are to be handled. This approach is similar to the case, task, and worker differentiating schemes and carries the same disadvantages. There is always a great deal of functional overlapping when cases or problems of individual clients are divided up for administrative reasons, and more importantly, as the core practice component in social work is the assessing, individualizing assessment of "the case," the *a priori* assumption of level of skill needed tends to sidestep the real issues in the manpower dilemma.

5. THE CLIENT VULNERABILITY, WORKER AUTONOMY SYSTEM OF DIFFERENTIATION (Richan, 1961)

This is a more sophisticated approach to the differential use of staff, because it comprises more than one variable and accounts in some measure for the multidimensional client–worker interaction. The approach is interesting, but it has some of the same drawbacks that we have noted in the other schemes. Particularly in regard to the initial assessment of client vulnerability, a professional worker would need to be involved directly in every case in order to make a proper assignment to the right staff person. Another concern that this approach raises is that the assessment of vulnerability or complexity, by whatever standard, might tend to once again, as in the days of clinical preoccupation, lead toward a hierarchy of client troubles which would inevitably impinge upon worker status and ultimately create a new form of residual service.

As far as the notion of worker autonomy is concerned, this would be a more fruitful direction to pursue were there not such a wide range of worker competences in both the professional and the technical spheres. The field of social work is presently hard put to assess the relative skills of a recent professional graduate who is up to date in knowledge and a graduate who has been practicing for many years without educational refreshment. As for technical staff, as they will not have been "pretested," as it were, in graduate school, and as by their nature they would represent the universe of possibilities as far as personality characteristics and knowledge and skills are concerned, the degree of worker autonomy would be difficult indeed to assess.

6. Episode-of-Service Approach to Differential Use of Staff (Barker & Briggs, 1966)

This approach is the most highly refined, and sophisticated scheme yet devised for differential use of social work personnel. It provides for flexible boundaries in regard to the kinds of service given, groups of cases, and teams of professional and technical workers. In other words, the approach is not tied to narrow considerations that would relate only one worker to one case, or to a definition of a single task. It combines a sequence of tasks or cluster of activities that move along with changes in the case. The maneuverability of the *episode-of-service* approach is its great asset. It is intricately related to the *goal* of the service. The means used by the social worker team to arrive at the goal derive from relating the requirements for reaching that goal to the available skills of the team members, and there are vast arrangements possible to provide for an array of competences, so that infinite kinds of skills could be made available to the client. The differentiating scheme lends itself very well to a reconceptualization of practice and an imaginative use of combinations of professional and technical social work manpower.

The Indigenous Worker

We are almost ready to discuss a model for an appropriate utilization of manpower in a developmental approach to social work practice. But first it is necessary to deal with the special case of the *indigenous worker* and the associated issue of careers in social work for undergraduate or nonprofessional personnel.

There is a growing body of literature citing studies and experiences of the increasing use of community people in social work and mental health services (Barr, 1967; Birnbaum & Jones, 1967; Pearl & Reissman, 1965; Specht et al., 1968). Understandably, there is a tendency to overdraw the values of wide use of indigenous people. In the first place, as we have noted in our earlier discussion about the practice of social work, it is a field that often appears to the public to be based upon the neighborly application of common sense. Naturally, if sensible friendly visiting were all there was to it, and if citizens are becoming fearful of the increasing institutionalization of their personal lives, then there would be a sense of relief in knowing that neighbors or at least people in the same situations as they could be as helpful, if not more so, than an organizational representative like a social worker. This tendency to seek the most informal and parsimonious solution to a problem is as natural as wanting an aspirin to do the work of more complicated medical procedures. As a matter of fact, in accordance with our interest in patterning practice in light of the natural life style of clients, the aim of informality and parsimony or economy of treatment procedures is a very respectable practice goal.

The assumption that indigenous personnel can better perceive the needs and required services of people in the community has been thoroughly explored in at least one examination of the subject. As Barr (1967) evaluated the popular notions of the special advantages in using indigenous personnel, he dealt with several common dictates that were found wanting. For example, in response to the idea that indigenous people are more like other members of the community, Barr pointed out that this is not necessarily so, because in the case of Mobilization for Youth (MFY) it was noted that the people who served as workers were actually more successful and upwardly mobile than their neighbors and that in their aspirations toward middle-class values they tended to be better educated and managed their lives better. One could site similar possibilities in an indigenous group of alcoholics, where the very success of the man who had controlled his addiction and attained a helping role would set him apart from the others in the group.

Barr concludes that it is not possible to generalize about the indigenous person's special knowledge and skill in conceptualizing community needs, but rather that it is important to select community helpers in accordance with their individual personal qualities. Thus a potentially helpful indigenous person would be one who was warm and friendly or especially knowledgeable about the subculture of his neighborhood and not a person who qualified merely by happening to be indigenous to the neighborhood.

Barr cites another common overgeneralization, that of the indigenous person's being a more acceptable model to the client group than the professional social worker. He challenges this idea in light of the fact that the indigenous worker often tends to be harder on his neighbors than a professional person, in his effort to prove that he is not naïve or able to be manipulated. The assumption that the poor worker is perceived as more helpful to the poor client than is the middle-class worker is not always correct, and the perception, if in fact it does exist, is not always accurate. The middle-class or professional worker ought to be more knowledgeable about community resources and how to bring them to the client's need, and his middle-classness need not necessarily be an obstacle, *as long as need is met.*

Barr points out that the one time when the indigenous person is probably more useful as a role model is prior to the client's engagement in the social work service, or at the time of intake, when he does not trust the social worker because he does not trust the system from which the social worker comes. This issue is an important one today, in light of the increasing division of races in the urban scene. Are we prepared to affirm that only a black person can be perceived by other black people as helpful? In the beginning perhaps so, but help is not necessarily defined according to racial lines; the level and content of the help ultimately will determine its value.

A third assumption about the special value of indigenous workers is challenged by Barr when he questions the idea that they have special competence because they "have been there" and know best how to negotiate the system. Barr points out that in the case of MFY such knowledge was actually quite specialized and limited in scope. It is one thing to know how to reach a public assistance worker on the telephone and quite another to know how to cope with the intricacies of a large welfare bureaucracy and confront it on the correct level of abstraction, using the most meaningful language.

Barr affirms the existence of certain qualities of style that are less formal, less distant, and more "directive, partisan, and active," which were characteristic of the MFY indigenous workers. Such style is something that professional social workers might try to emulate in light of their interest in working with groups of clients who are of different class or ethnic affiliations than they. Yet there is more to practice than style and partisanship, for without knowledge of the facts and meanings of a case, no amount of passion and activism can assure the client the kind and quality of service he requires. Barr further agrees with other experts on the subject in his view of the bridging function of indigenous personnel, where they serve as connections between the social organization and the community. The indigenous bridge may connect class with class, race with race, professional with client, and ultimately service with need. The caution presented by Barr is against romanticizing the effectiveness of indigenous workers. Professionals can learn a lot from working with them, and they have unique tasks to perform, but to overstate their qualities and affirm their use as substitutes for the professionals is to beg the question of how to narrow the manpower gap and provide more relevant services to people.

A second major reason that seems to underlie the current pressure to expand the use of indigenous workers is that it is seen as an employment opportunity for unskilled people and therefore a way out of poverty. We have discussed the transition from an industrial to a service employment market, where trade skills have had to give way to managerial and personal qualities. This change in the employment market has contributed to the very serious technical unemployment of people who are already socially and educationally disadvantaged. The fields of social work and mental health services have been the logical sources to which society has looked for mass employment of technically unemployed people. As long as one keeps in mind the fact that employment of the poor through social work services is not identical with the giving of services, one can explore the possibilities without being tyrannized by a fallacious outcome.

We are not saying here that full employment is not one of the most important ways out of poverty, for it most certainly is just that. Rather, we are saying that even if there were infinite jobs to be filled by poor people in social work, the filling of these jobs could not be equated with service of quality. We have just cited some of the reasons for this, in discussing our assumption that there is more requisite knowledge and skills in the practice of social work than can be taught to or applied by indigenous workers who have not been through the educational experience that provides those requirements. To the extent that we keep separate the two goals of excellent social service and full employment, we can explore the potential market in social work services for the employment of poor people.

The employment market for indigenous workers in social work is probably unlimited, as unlimited as is the potential sphere for social work services at large. When we discuss the realignment of staffing patterns and the differential allocation of tasks in our conceptualization of social work practice, we will see that the indigenous worker might necessarily become a significant member of all practice teams. When staff positions are apportioned carefully, when there is a manpower strategy, there will be an important place for indigenous workers.

It is impossible to know at this time if the places potentially available for some poor people will make even a dent on the rate of unemployed people in the cities of this era, but the view of developmental social work services that addresses the client's transactional field will certainly provide for enhanced use of personnel of various kinds more than the clinical model of practice ever could. However, it is not sufficient to open up job possibilities, for whatever purpose, unless there is a clear vision of the career line a person might follow. People need to be promoted, not only in terms of job titles, salary levels, and other signs of real or imagined status but also in terms of the variety and complexity of their jobs. The matter of "new careers" is a crucial issue that has to be confronted before wild employment takes place; the next steps need be foreseen before the first ones are taken.

Issues in Careers for Technicians: Guidelines for the Design of New Careers

In an excellent monograph, Sidney Fine (1967) has differentiated between the worker who holds a job and the trainee who is on a step in a career ladder. The special qualities of a career job rest in the educational atmosphere in which the worker is trained, where mistakes are treated as learning opportunities, where he is given some degree of freedom in carrying out his tasks, and where the tasks are used as the basis of increasing knowledge. Fine also contributes a distinction between the *prescribed* and the *discretionary* content of a job. The former type of content is defined by the supervisor, sets limits on the means by which the work is to be done, and holds out certain expectations for results. The latter content is decided by the person doing the job, and there is the expectation of use of judgment, where the trainee chooses his own alternatives at each stage. The proper combination of these two kinds of job content undoubtedly would clarify the specific work expectations for technical social workers.

The most important point made by Fine is that tasks themselves do not have prescribed or discretionary content. For example, making a school visit and referring a person to a clinic are tasks, but different aspects of the why, when, and how of carrying out those tasks are both discretionary and prescribed. The ideal aim in developing career lines for any type of personnel is to increase as far as possible the discretionary possibilities in all job functions. The hallmark of professionalism is exactly that of wide discretionary powers; the limits of discretion may be narrower for the technician. Some discretion must be possible or the growth of a career will not be realistic. In other words, the career technician must be able to look forward to increasing responsibility both in the scope of his job and in the opportunities to make judgments and select alternative means of carrying out his job.

In order to achieve the goal of developing a manpower strategy, of providing a vast array of individualizing services, and of utilizing professional and technical social work personnel, it is evident that the first decisions that need to be made will have to do with the definition of practice and *the delineation of tasks and functions.* The second set of decisions will have to be about how to *increase worker autonomy* through relating worker skills, knowledge, and experience to the job to be done. Related to this is the necessity to formulate a model of staff patterns that would accommodate the professional and technical social work team concept. Each set of tasks allocated to the technical person will, of course, modify the functioning of the professional person. Needless to say, promotional opportunities, personnel practices, salary levels, and provision of in-service training still will be essential components of any plan to revise the social work system to include responsible use of career technicians with professional social workers.

In determining the kind and content of career lines in social work, we come back to the same need to reexamine the purposes of social work practice. Changes in manpower arrangements, like adaptations in knowledge of human behavior and social science and modifications of practice models, all require revision of the aims of social work. Changes cannot be pasted onto old conceptualizations, for all changes, when viewed systematically, affect and are affected by the content and the purposes of the job to be done. When "the case" is viewed in its transactional field, the work to be done is addressed to that field, and the essential tasks are then allocated across the varied manpower dimensions. Conversely, if we were to make such a statement from a manpower point of view, we could say that the essential manpower issue is such that the field of social work must devise formal arrangements for technical staff to divide the work with professional staff. This will inevitably modify the clinical model of practice, for psychotherapy cannot be carried out by undergraduates and nonprofessionals and the job must somehow be redefined to make use of different job skills.

Beginning with the assumption of the need for individualization in our society, we must confront the issue of spreading the services of organized social work manpower. In order to achieve this aim, it is necessary to reconceptualize "the case" and to find imaginative ways of using differential manpower so as to be effective in intervention in the individual's transactional field. Wherever one starts, the conclusion is the same, because all of social work knowledge, techniques, values, objectives, manpower uses, and practices themselves are components that are systematically related to each other.

Some Approaches to Differential Use of Manpower in Teams

In assuming that the professional–technical social work team is the most flexible model for the differential use of manpower, there are within that model, several ways of allocating the tasks to be done.

1. The Professional as Supervisor of Technicians

This is a common approach, used quite often in social agencies like public child welfare departments where there is a preponderance of nonprofessionals who carry the major direct practice function in the agency. "Saving the professional" for supervision does not necessarily contribute to raising the level of direct practice, because the technician must carry the whole case and thus has an almost unlimited range of discretionary control over his actions and the direction of the case. The responsibility for the diagnostic assessment is his, as well as the responsibility for the range of interventive techniques. Lack of educational qualification in this instance would tend to make the case ill served, for the technician could not, without a framework of knowledge, correctly assess the individual's total psycho-social situation and his need.

Administrative arrangements, manuals, written policies, staff training courses, and supervisory conferences can only define the boundaries of the technician's practice; they cannot substitute for formal professional education. Where the professional is used in this way as supervisor, he tends to oversee staff and not cases. Thus the quality of practice must rely upon the accident of the quality of staff available, and the client can have no assurance of direct expert attention.

2. THE PROFESSIONAL AS CONSULTANT ON CASES

This approach copes better with the issue of providing direct expert attention to the individual client. When the supervisory function is carried out by a senior staff person, it may tend to be more administrative, and thus more capable of being filled by an experienced technical worker who has *come up with the career line*. The professional would be "saved" for the tasks for which he has been educated. We have said that the diagnostic assessment of a case is a high-level task that requires specific knowledge of the psycho-social configuration. The decision about what is out of balance in the case is the pivotal determinant that finally calls all interventive tasks into action.

If there were only one senior surgeon in the only hospital in a city, difficult dilemma though this would be, it might be a more judicious use of his time and his skill to "stand behind" the resident surgeons, making the diagnostic assessments of the brain damage and directing the hands of the resident surgeons who would wield the surgical tools, than to operate himself on only a tiny proportion of the patients in need of surgery. The social worker as consultant would be directly involved in the vital assessment and interventive decisions in all cases, and the technician would carry out the direct interventive or treatment tasks.

3. The Professional as Team Leader

Here the professional would enter into direct practice, carrying out difficult functions in cases and utilizing technicians either as specialists in particular tasks or as the "arms and legs" of the professional in every case. The matter of the *technician as specialist* can be illustrated by imagining a pool of workers, each of them having an area of expertise achieved through education, life experience or staff training. For example, one worker who might be a college graduate could become expert in making referrals to homes for the aged; he would need to know a great deal about the referral process, but perhaps even more about the resources for the care of the aged in his community. As he built his knowledge of the subject, became acquainted with the staffs and programs of the various homes, etc., he soon could enjoy a rather large measure of autonomy or discretionary control over his work. While the technician gains expertise in home finding and in matching client needs with the resources, the professional, in this model, retains control of the assessment and decision-making in the case.

Depending upon the setting or field in which the team is located, technical specializations can be defined in any area of life that is relevant to the clients' potential needs. Thus one might assign an indigenous member of the team to case and problem finding in the neighborhood, an undergraduate technician team member to supervision of children in foster homes or to aged persons who are housebound. The task assignments could be as varied as the kinds of cases there are; the two principles to be observed in this form of staff utilization are that the professional is accountable for every case and that the technical and indigenous workers develop expertise in carrying out a variety of interventive tasks. The opportunities for staff advancement should be apparent, because the undergraduate technician and indigenous worker would be able to achieve increasing levels of expertise in a field of competence, ultimately arriving at the top of the career ladder, where they might supervise other technicians or indigenous workers who are working in the same area of competence. The opportunities for increased discretion in the job are open in this model.

The other kind of team arrangement to which we have referred is the kind where the technician serves as the "arms and legs" of the professional, not as an expert in a pool of experts, but almost as an aide to the professional. In this arrangement, the professional might have one or more technicians assigned to him who would carry out a variety of tasks as called for in each case. Although this approach has the advantage of variety and less chance of routinization of work, it does not offer quite the same opportunity for the technician to rise on a career ladder parallel to the professional. This is because the professional would retain supervisory responsibility for all of the tasks on the case, and the technician would not necessarily achieve competence in a particular pursuit. Competence would have to be assessed through some measures of deepened knowledge and proved experience.

Whichever of these approaches is utilized, the professional as team member would be able to increase his span of work, serving more people and reaching out into the client's entire field of transaction.

A Manpower Utilization Case Example in a Hospital

It is too early in the development of manpower models to assert which kind ought to be utilized in a particular field of practice, but there are unlimited possible arrangements that can be imagined. The following is an example of a plan for the use of professional and technical manpower that reflects all that we have been discussing in this book. Let us imagine a large city hospital located in a ghetto area, where people use the emergency clinic much as middle-class people might use a private doctor's office. Actually, because mechanical aids are becoming essential in medical care, because there is a shortage of doctors, and because medical specialization often requires group medical practice, the use of general clinic resources is increasing in all communities, no matter the level of income. Although middle-class people may still have private doctors, it happens increasingly that doctors ask their patients to go to the nearest clinic so that they can have access to the whole range of medical resources.

Assuming, then, that the local general or emergency clinic will serve as a typical resource for the catchment area peopled with the entire range of medical problems, such a location would be a perfect place to test out the social work practice model which we have been addressing. Where the hospital becomes an institutionalized part of the life of the community, like the local community center or the social security office, we are no longer dealing with a residual conception of service. Social work services would have the opportunity to be located where people are and where they are pursuing their natural life styles and encountering the crises of life with differing degrees of coping capacity.

While the following chart is addressed to the scene of a hospital in the ghetto, it might also be addressed to a variety of like communities such as neighborhoods, tenant's groups, schools, and the host of social utilities and other social institutions. There are several principles to be drawn from this design, among which are two that are particularly significant.

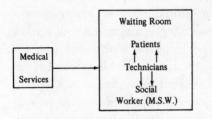

Technicians meet everyone in the waiting room and bring patient data to social worker (M.S.W.) 1,* who makes a diagnostic assessment of need.

There are several dispositional options available to the professional social worker at the clinic:

1. Mark NO CASE MADE.
2. Assign case to social worker (M.S.W.) 2 for interview to clarify situation.
3. Assign case to supervisor of pool of social work associates† for direct action on services requested.

Diagrammatically, this process would look this way:

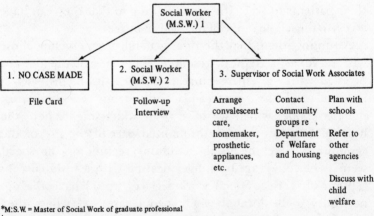

*M.S.W. = Master of Social Work of graduate professional
†Social work associates = undergraduate technicians, indigenous workers, aides, etc.

In the first place, the entire "population" (in the instance of our illustration, every person who attends the clinic) would be accounted for or touched in some way by a social work associate who would be the individualizing arm of the institution in question. This screening action connotes *opportunity* for advocacy, information, and a broad range of help. The choice as to the use of the help would be the person's, for the primary service (in this case medicine) would be available for him whether or not he needed or wanted social work intervention. Second, the primary case decision functions would rest with the professional social worker, related to the technician more or less as head of the team, or at least as consultant on case actions. Of course, this is but one approach that has been tried. Every setting has to define its own manpower arrangements in accordance with its function and client needs.

As the threads of our proposal have become woven together, the whole cloth of social work intervention in the modern urban scene is before us. The "case" will be an individual in his field of transaction. Social work practice intervention is conceived as sufficiently wide-ranging, flexible, and relevant to the needs of people that it can be called into play wherever in the client's field there is imbalance. A variety of social work personnel who would carry out a yet-to-be-defined host of tasks would be available as integral and necessary within the social work interventive scheme. The professional social worker then would apply his knowledge and skills appropriately in assessment, planning, and intervention, and the client–citizen would be met in his own unique milieu. Were such a preventive design put into action, there might be less reliance upon residual social services, and less need for social workers to hold so tightly to the clinical model of practice with its primary aim of cure. An eco/systems view of a problem allows for a differential manpower model such as depicted in the hospital chart.

A Manpower Case Example in a Public Child Welfare Agency: The Case for Staff Development as a Manpower Strategy

There are decreasing numbers of graduate social workers in public child welfare agencies, a result of the loss of training grants in recent years. Yet legislation and need as defined by community standards and as expressed by the client group have increased the range and quantity of service in this field. The boundaries of child welfare today include day care, homemaker services, family counseling, group services, foster family placement, small group homes, treatment residences, shelter facilities, adoption, services for unwed mothers, and, most recently, protective services in cases of child neglect and abuse. This and the family service field are the only two fields in which the primary services are social work; thus it is of some interest to note that at least in child welfare there is little observable interest among graduate social workers in increasing their numbers there.

One could speculate about the causes for this, but in this chapter it is more to the point to cope with its consequences. In one large state there are 1,000 nonprofessional (including B.A. but not B.S.W.) workers and 300 nonprofessional supervisors who work only with cases of child neglect and abuse. The only professional staff in the agency are essentially in administrative or staff development positions. This means that the direct practice and supervision of that practice are carried out by workers who are judged by all elements of the social work profession and the community to be ill equipped (except by experience) for their jobs. This is *not* an atypical staff situation in public child welfare, although many states have been able to attract and maintain some graduate social workers in practice or supervisory roles.

A manpower case like this would test the mettle of any profession to solve, if indeed it is solvable at all. There are some rock-bottom requirements when it comes to social services, particularly when the service has to do with the most damaged and needful families in the community. In this example there is no "differential manpower" issue, because there is no differential manpower, and there ought to be. Even in urban medicine or in wartime, paramedics have doctors to report to, to ask questions of, to seek advice from. America has not developed its medical practice on the model of barefoot doctors. This child welfare example is included here because it is not uncommon, and on a smaller scale in rural areas the issue of professional accountability is exactly the same. A social work service that claims to help people in defined areas of need has to be based upon particular knowledge and utilize identifiable methods. If the existing staff does not possess these, then agency, community, governing boards and agencies, legislators, etc., ought to be engaged in correcting these deficiencies. In other words, the problem redefined might be a political–bureaucratic problem and not a manpower utilization problem at all.

Moving onto the assumption that we might gain a sprinkling of graduate professionals among the supervisory staff, we are confronted with a typical manpower pattern in public child welfare—a few professional social workers out of 300, and no professionals among the direct practitioners. The issue, then, is how to make the professional's knowledge go the furthest. The following chart depicts some options:

I	II	III
PROFESSIONAL SUPERVISOR	PROFESSIONAL CONSULTANT	PROFESSIONAL STAFF TRAINER
with five to seven workers	with three or more nonprofessional supervisors, each of these responsible for five to seven workers	with X number of supervisors in a group, to work on shared problems

It is evident that option III utilizes the professional most widely as far as effect upon practice is concerned.

Staff development should be built into every agency organization plan, even where all staff are highly qualified by virtue of their education. In the case of public child welfare agencies or any setting where there is an insufficiency of knowledge and practice skills available, staff development is an absolute necessity. In large bureaucratic agencies, as this author has written (C. H. Meyer, 1965), it is important to locate training as conceptually close to the practitioner as possible. Training institutes outside of the agency, visiting lecturers, and training limited to orientation and not related to ongoing work tend to be systematically unrelated and nonintegral to the daily practice problems faced by nonprofessional workers. We might say that where a range of social work knowledge and skills are unavailable, qualitative differences come about through closely honed staff development programs that are applied *differentially* according to level of staff education and definition of the work load. In staff development as in differential manpower utilization, we are always governed by the aims of practice—which takes us back once again to confrontation of the implications of the practice model we select.

The "All Things Being Equal" Approach to Differential Use of Social Work Manpower

We looked at the "case" of a large hospital with a mixed staff of graduates, undergraduates, and other technical assistants, heavy caseloads, open and undifferentiated intake, and the aim of providing every patient with the opportunity for social work attention. Then we looked at the "case" of a public child welfare agency with *mandated* functions and a social work staff with limited educational preparation. In such agencies, social workers generally feel overwhelmed by their jobs and gain no status from having complete autonomy, since they are often helpless in instrumentalizing this freedom and translating it into purposeful, successful action.

What of the social work service that is not overwhelmed by numbers of clients and not inhibited by lack of appropriately prepared staff? "All things being equal," with proper staff resources and a developmental view of social work practice, how might manpower and practice issues come together into some kind of "model"?

Using a voluntary family service agency or a child guidance clinic as the example, do any of the issues previously cited remain significant? We must assume that while these agencies may gain a higher proportion of graduate professionals from the social work manpower pool, the pool is not bottomless. Further, we can envision such success in meeting need as defined in the community that intake will increase and that as it does, different kinds of clients will hear about the service and will make new kinds of requests for service. Private funding being in the state it is today, it is likely that public money will continue to subsidize voluntary agencies and that this will mean that the clientele served will have to be representative of the community in which the agency is located. So however narrowly social work has in the past defined itself as available for some but not all clients, social circumstances have presently overtaken that model.

Thus, in our "all things being equal" agency, a different practice approach has to be entertained in order to account for the wide socioeconomic–cultural–ethnic–psychological–intellectual need that is becoming identified. A social work team, perhaps similar in some respects to the Barker & Briggs (1966) episode-of-service model, would be interesting to observe in action.

A family in stress, viewed in an eco/systems perspective, would be in transaction with its kinship group, a school, possibly a day care center, a work place, recreational resources, a resource for an aging parent, and so on. Stress in the marital relationship or in the parent–child relationship usually is reflective of, feeds upon, and is fed upon by this total ecology in a case. The location, definition, and assessment of the problems are the most difficult tasks, and they call upon a graduate social worker's total knowledge repertoire to determine what is out of balance and what can be done to fix the imbalance. The allocation of case-related tasks should derive from a team conference, and according to the Barker & Briggs idea, this conference would deal with who on the team is best equipped to handle different case-related tasks. Should the adolescent son be in a group? Should he have a big brother role model? Should he have tutoring in a subject he has failed? Should he be part of his family's treatment?

Depending upon the assessment, one or all of these actions might be taken, and not all of them would require the services of the graduate professional. In fact, some tasks would underutilize his skills, while they would be perfectly suited to the interests, capacities, and experiences of an undergraduate social worker. There is hardly a case that cannot be viewed in this way. Even redefining a case of depression would make possible action tasks that are often survival mechanisms for people who are deeply depressed.

The functioning of all social work manpower is case-related, and while the first central professional task is to understand or assess the case properly, there are countless interventions to be designed and carried out by the total range of social work manpower. There is no hierarchy intended; practitioners do best what they are educated to understand.

So it all comes together in the practice and the manpower models. As in earlier days, when casework required exclusively professional therapeutic personnel, developmental social work requires a full range of practitioner types, because the interventions cover a range that is beyond the skill of any single type. We have observed that the practice–manpower connection is related and problems and issues in both areas will have to be addressed together. Just as developmental social work may turn out to be what society needs, so its use of an array of differentially educated personnel may turn out to suit the human service potential in this era in our country. It is hard to know if the profession of social work is going to adapt to a new reality, but whether it does or not, people are going to need social services and society will allocate the task of delivery to some group. It has to do so. Our closing note is one of hope that the field of social work will be ready and eager to accept the mandate.

References

ATHERTON, C., S. MITCHELL, & E. SCHEIN. Locating points for intervention. *Social Casework,* March 1971.

BANDLER, B. The concept of ego-supportive psychotherapy. In H. Parad & R. Miller (eds.), *Ego-oriented casework.* New York: Family Service Association of America, 1963.

BARKER, R. L., & T. L. BRIGGS. *Trends in the utilization of social work personnel: An evaluative research of the literature.* New York: National Association of Social Workers, 1966.

BARR, S. Some observations on the practice of indigenous non-professional workers, in *Personnel in anti-poverty programs.* New York: Council on Social Work Education, 1967, pp. 51–61.

BARTLETT, H. *Analyzing social work practice by fields.* New York: National Association of Social Workers, 1961.

BARTLETT, H. *The common base of social work practice.* New York: National Association of Social Workers, 1970.

BATESON, G., D. JACKSON, J. HALEY, & J. WEAKLAND. Toward a theory of schizophrenia. *Behavioral Science,* 1956, *1,* pp. 251–264.

BECK, D. F. *Patterns in use of family agency service*. New York: Family Service Association of America, 1962.

BENDIX, R. Personality reductionism. In N. J. Smelser & W. T. Smelser (eds.), *Personality and social systems*. New York: John Wiley & Sons, 1963.

BIRNBAUM, M. L., & C. H. JONES. Activities of the social work aides. *Social Casework,* special issue on Project Enable, December 1967.

BOULDING, K. E. General systems theory: The skeleton of a science. In W. Buckley (ed.), *Modern systems research for the behavioral scientist*. Chicago: Aldine Publishing Company, 1968.

BOWLBY, J. *Attachment and loss*. New York: Basic Books; vol. 1, *Attachment,* 1969; vol. 2, *Separation,* 1972.

BRAGER, G., & H. SPECHT. *Community organizing*. New York: Columbia University Press, 1973.

BREWSTER-SMITH, M. Competence and socialization. In J. A. Clausen (ed.), *Socialization and society*. Boston: Little, Brown and Company, 1968, pp. 270–320.

BRIAR, S. Flexibility and specialization in social work education. *Social Work Education Reporter,* December 1968.

BRIELAND, D. *Differential use of manpower for foster care in a public child welfare program*. Springfield, Ill.: Department of Child and Family Services, 1964.

BROWN, C. *Manchild in the promised land*. New York: Signet Books, 1966.

CANNON, A. Guiding motives in social work. In C. Kasius (ed.), *New directions in social work*. New York: Harper & Brothers, 1954, pp. 13–31.

CARR, S., & K. LYNCH. Where learning happens. *Daedalus,* The Conscience of the City, Fall 1968.

CAUDHILL, W. *The psychiatric hospital in a small society*. Cambridge, Mass.: Harvard University Press, 1958.

COELHO, G. V., D. A. HAMBURG, & J. E. ADAMS. *Coping and adaptation*. New York: Basic Books, 1974.

CUMMING, E., & J. CUMMING. *Ego and milieu*. New York: Atherton Press, 1962.

DAVIS, K. The urbanization of the human population. In D. Flannagan (ed.), *Cities*. New York: Alfred A. Knopf, 1965.

DE SCHWEINITZ, K., & E. DE SCHWEINITZ. *Interviewing in social security*. Washington: U.S. Department of Health, Education, and Welfare, 1961.

DEVEREAUX, G. Two types of modal personality models. In N. J. Smelser & W. T. Smelser (eds.), *Personality and social systems*. New York: John Wiley & Sons, 1963.

DU BOS, R. *The god within*. New York: Charles Scribner's Sons, 1972.

EPSTEIN, L. Differential use of staff: A method to expand social services. *Social Work*, October 1962.

ERIKSON, E. H. Identity and the life cycle. *Psychological Issues*. New York: International Universities Press, 1959.

FINE, S. *Guidelines for the design of new careers*. Kalamazoo, Mich.: W. E. Upjohn Institute for Employment Research, 1967.

FINESTONE, S. Issues in developing diagnostic classifications for casework. *Casework papers 1960*. New York: National Conference of Social Welfare, 1960, pp. 139–154.

FITCH, L. C. Eight goals for an urbanizing America. *Daedalus*, The Conscience of the City, Fall 1968.

FLEXNER, A. *Is social work a profession?* New York: National Conference of Social Work, 1915.

GERMAIN, C. Social study: Past and future. *Social Casework*, July 1968.

GERMAIN, C. An ecological perspective in casework practice. *Social Casework*, June 1973.

GLADWIN, T. Social competence and clinical practice. *Psychiatry*, February 1967, *30*, 1.

GOLDSTEIN, H. *Social work practice: A unitary approach*. Chapel Hill: University of North Carolina Press, 1973.

GOODWIN, R. N. Reflections: Sources of public unhappiness. *The New Yorker*, Jan. 4, 1969.

GORDON, W. E. Basic constructs for an integrative and generative conception of social work. In G. A. Hearn (ed.), *The general systems approach: Contributions toward an holistic conception of social work.* New York: Council on Social Work Education, 1969, pp. 5–11.

GOTTLEIB, W., & J. H. STANLEY. Mutual goals and goal-setting in casework. *Social Casework,* October 1967.

GREENWOOD, E. Attributes of a profession. *Social Work,* July 1957.

HAMILTON, G. *Theory and practice of social casework,* 2d ed. New York: Columbia University Press, 1951.

HAMILTON, G. A theory of personality: Freud's contribution to social work. In H. J. Parad (ed.), *Ego psychology and dynamic casework.* New York: Family Service Association of America, 1958, pp. 11–37.

HARTMAN, A. To think about the unthinkable. *Social Casework,* October 1970.

HARTMANN, H. *Ego psychology and the problem of adaptation.* New York: International Universities Press, 1958.

HEYMAN, M. Criteria for the allocation of cases according to the level of staff skill. *Social Casework,* July 1961.

JANCHILL, (SISTER) M. P. Systems concepts in casework theory and practice. *Social Casework,* February 1969.

KADUSHIN, A. The knowledge base of social work. In A. J. Kahn (ed.), *Issues in American social work.* New York: Columbia University Press, 1959, pp. 39–80.

KAHN, A. J. Social work fields of practice. *Encyclopedia of social work.* New York: National Association of Social Workers, 1965, pp. 750–754.

KAHN, A. J. *Theory and practice of social planning.* New York: Russell Sage Foundation, 1969.

KAHN, A. J. (ed.). *Shaping the new social work.* New York: Columbia University Press, 1973.

KAMERMAN, S. B., R. DOLGOFF, G. GETZEL, & J. NELSEN. Knowledge for practice: Social science in social work. In A. J. Kahn (ed.), *Shaping the new social work.* New York: Columbia University Press, 1973, pp. 97–147.

KATZ, D., & R. L. KAHN. *The Social Psychology of Organizations.* New York: John Wiley & Sons, 1966.

KLEIN, P. *From philanthropy to social welfare.* San Francisco: Jossey-Bass, 1968.

KOGAN, L., & S. JENKINS. *Indicators of child health and welfare.* New York: Center for Social Research, Graduate Center, The City University of New York; distributed by Columbia University Press, 1974.

KUHN, T. *The structure of scientific revolutions.* Chicago: University of Chicago Press, 1962.

LEE, P. R. Social work: Cause or function? Presidential address, National Conference of Social Work, 1929.

LEICHTER, H. J., & W. E. MITCHELL. *Kinship and casework.* New York: Russell Sage Foundation, 1967.

LIDZ, T. *The person: His development throughout the life cycle.* New York: Basic Books, 1968.

LIDZ, T., A. CORNELISON, S. FLECK, & D. TERRY. The interfamilial environment of the schizophrenic patient: II. Marital schism and mental skew. *American Journal of Psychiatry,* 1957, *114.*

LOEWE, B., & T. E. HANRAHAN. Five-day foster care. *Child Welfare,* January 1975.

LUBOVE, R. *The professional altruist.* Cambridge: Harvard University Press, 1965.

MARTINDALE, D. Prefatory remarks, in M. Weber, *The City.* New York: Free Press, 1968.

MAYER, J., & N. TIMMS. *The client speaks.* New York: Atherton Press, 1970.

MENCHER, S. *Poor law to poverty programs.* Pittsburgh: University of Pittsburgh Press, 1967.

MENNINGER, K., et al. *The vital balance.* New York: Viking Press, 1963.

MEYER, C. H. Quest for a broader base for family diagnosis. *Social Casework,* July 1959.

MEYER, C. H. *Staff development in public welfare agencies.* New York: Columbia University Press, 1965.

MEYER, C. H. Practice models: The new ideology. *Smith College Bulletin,* February 1973.

MEYER, C. H. Purposes and boundaries: Casework fifty years later. *Social Casework,* May 1973.

MEYER, C. H. Social work practice in old and new contexts. In A. J. Kahn (ed.), *Shaping the new social work*. New York: Columbia University Press, 1973, pp. 26–55.

MEYER, C. H. *Preventive intervention: A goal in search of a method*. New York: National Association of Social Workers, 1974.

MEYER, H., et al. *Girls at Vocational High*. New York: Russell Sage Foundation, 1965.

MINUCHIN, S. *Families and family therapy*. Cambridge, Mass.: Harvard University Press, 1974.

MULLEN, E. J. & J. R. DUMPSON. *Evaluation of social intervention*. San Francisco: Jossey-Bass, 1972.

NATIONAL ADVISORY COMMISSION ON CIVIL DISORDERS. *(Report)*. New York: Bantam Books, 1968.

NATIONAL ASSOCIATION OF SOCIAL WORKERS, Commission on Social Work Practice, Sub-Committee on Fields of Practice. Identifying fields of practice in social work. *Social Work*, April 1962.

Oxford International Dictionary, 3d revised ed. London: Oxford University Press, 1955.

PARAD, H. J. *Crisis intervention*. New York: Family Service Association of New York, 1965.

PEARL, A., & F. REISSMAN. *New careers for the poor*. New York: Free Press, 1965.

PERLMAN, H. H. *Social casework: A problem solving process*. Chicago: University of Chicago Press, 1957.

PERLMAN, H. H. Social work methods: A review of the past decade. *Social Work*, vol. 10. Tenth Anniversary Symposium. New York, National Association of Social Workers, 1966.

PINCUS, A., & A. MINAHAN. *Social work practice: Model and method*. Itasca, Ill.: F. E. Peacock Publishers, 1973.

Pocket data book U.S.A. Washington: Government Printing Office, 1967.

RABKIN, R. *Inner and outer space: Introduction to a theory of social psychiatry*. New York: W. W. Norton & Company, 1970.

RAPOPORT, L. Creativity in social work. *Smith College Studies in Social Work*, June 1968.

Rapoport, R. Normal crisis, family structure and mental health. *Family Process,* March 1963, *2,* 1.

Reid, W. J., & A. W. Shyne. *Brief and extended casework.* New York: Columbia University Press, 1969.

Reynolds, B. Between client and community. *Smith College Studies,* 1934.

Richan, W. C. A theoretical scheme for determining roles of professional and non-professional personnel. *Social Work,* October 1961.

Richmond, M. E. *Social diagnosis.* New York: Russell Sage Foundation, 1917.

Richmond, M. E. *What Is Social Case Work?* New York: Russell Sage Foundation, 1922.

Ripple, L. *Report to the task force on structure and quality in social work education.* New York: Council on Social Work Education, August 1974.

Rizzo, N., W. Gray, & T. Kaiser. A general systems approach to problems in growth and development. In W. Gray, N. Rizzo, et al. (eds.), *General systems theory and psychiatry.* Boston: Little, Brown and Company, 1969.

Roberts, R. (ed.). *The unwed mother.* New York: Harper & Row, 1966.

Rothman, Sheila. Other people's children: The day care experience in America. *The Public Interest,* Winter 1973.

Scherz, F. H. What is family-centered casework? *Social Casework,* October 1953.

Schlesinger, A. M., Jr. *The coming of the new deal.* Boston: Houghton Mifflin Company, 1958.

Schwartz, E. E., & W. C. Sample. *The midway office.* New York: National Association of Social Workers, 1972.

Schwartz, M. S., & C. G. Schwartz. *Social approaches to mental patient care.* New York: Columbia University Press, 1964.

Seabury, B. A. Physical space in social work settings. *Social Work,* October 1971.

Shlakman, V. Mothers at risk: Social policy and provision, issues and opportunities. In F. Hazelkorn (ed.), *Mothers-at-risk,* Garden City, N.Y.: Adelphi University, 1966.

SHLAKMAN, V. Unmarried parenthood: An approach to social policy. *Social Casework,* October 1966.

SKIDMORE, R. A., D. BALSAM, & O. JONES. Social work practice in industry. *Social Work,* May 1974.

SOBEY, F. *The non-professional revolution in mental health.* New York: Columbia University Press, 1970.

SPECHT, H., et al. The neighborhood sub-professional worker. *Children,* January–February 1968.

SPIEGEL, J. P. A model for relationships among systems. In R. R. Grinker (ed.), *Toward a unified theory of human behavior.* New York: Basic Books, 1956.

SPIEGEL, J. P., & F. KLUCKHORN. *Integration and conflict in family behavior.* New York: Group for the Advancement of Psychiatry, report 27, August 1954.

STAMM, I. Ego psychology in the emerging theoretical base of casework. In A. J. Kahn (ed.), *Issues in American social work.* New York: Columbia University Press, 1959, pp. 80–109.

STATE COMMUNITIES AID ASSOCIATION. *The multi-problem dilemma.* Metuchen, N.J.: Scarecrow Press, 1968.

STEIN, H. D. Social science in social work practice and education. In H. J. Parad (ed.), *Ego psychology and dynamic casework.* New York: Family Service Association of America, 1958.

STUDT, E. Organizing resources for more effective practice. *Social Work,* vol. 10. Tenth Anniversary Symposium, New York, National Association of Social Workers, 1966, pp. 41–54.

STUDT, E. Social work theory and implications for the practice of methods. *The Council on Social Work Education Reporter,* June 1968.

TAFT, J. *A functional approach to family casework.* Philadelphia: University of Pennsylvania Press, 1944.

TITMUSS, R. *Commitment to welfare.* New York: Random House, 1968.

TOFFLER, A. *Future shock.* New York: Random House, 1970.

TOWLE, C. *Common human needs.* Washington: Government Printing Office, 1945. (Revised, New York: National Association of Social Workers, 1952.)

TUNNARD, C. *The modern American city*. Princeton, N.J.: D. Van Nostrand Company, 1968.

U. S. DEPARTMENT OF HEALTH, EDUCATION, AND WELFARE. *Closing the gap in social work manpower*. Washington, 1965.

VINCENT, C. *Unmarried mothers*. New York: Free Press, 1961.

VON BERTALANFFY, L. General systems theory and psychiatry. In S. Arieti (ed.), *American handbook of psychiatry*. New York: Basic Books, 1966.

VON BERTALANFFY, L. General systems theory. In N. J. Demerath, & R. A. Peterson (eds.), *System change and conflict*. New York: Free Press, 1967, pp. 119–129.

WALLERSTEIN, R. Psychoanalytic perspectives on the problem of reality. *Journal of the American Psychoanalytic Association*, 1973, *21*, 1.

WEINER, H. J., S. H. AKABES, & J. J. SOMNER. *Mental health care in the world of work*. New York: Association Press, 1973.

WHITE, M. A. Little red school house and little white clinic. *Teachers' College Record*, December 1965.

WHITE, R. W. The concept of healthy personality: What do we really mean? *The Counseling Psychologist*, 1973, *4*, 2.

WHITE, R. W. Ego and reality in psychoanalytic theory. *Psychological Issues*, 1963, *3*, 3.

WHITTAKER, J. K. *Social treatment: An approach to interpersonal treatment*. Chicago: Aldine Publishing Company, 1974.

WILENSKY, H. L., & C. N. LEBEAUX. *Industrial society and social welfare*. New York: Russell Sage Foundation, 1958.

WOODROOFE, K. *From charity to social work*. Toronto: University of Toronto Press, 1962.

WYNNE, L., I. RYCKOFF, J. DAY, & S. HIRSCH. Pseudo-mutuality in the family relations of schizophrenics. *Psychiatry*, 1958, *21*, pp. 205–220.

YARMOLINSKY, A. The service society. *Daedalus*, The Conscience of the City, Fall 1968.

YLVISAKAR, P. Working session on centralization and decentralization. *Daedalus*, Toward the Year 2000, Summer 1967.

YOUNG, L. *Out of wedlock*. New York: McGraw-Hill Book Company, 1954.

Index

Index

Index

Adams, J. E., 158n
Age-specific tasks, individual
 developmental, 72–74t
Arabes, S. H., 196n
Atherton, C., 140n

Balsam, D., 196n
Bandler, B., 157n
Barker, R. L., 212, 227, 230
Barr, S., 232–34
Bartlett, H., 150n
Bateson, G., 134n
Beck, D. F., 31n
Bendix, R., 137
Birnbaum, M. L., 232n
Boulding, K. E., 136
Bowlby, J., 158n
Brager, G., 11n

Brewster-Smith, M., 158n
Briar, S., 25n
Brieland, D., 227n
Briggs, T. L., 212, 227, 230
Brown, C., 53

Cannon, A., 128n
Care, day, 10
Carr, S., 50, 60
Caudhill, W., 185n
Coelho, G. V., 158n
Continuum, educational
 (social work), 207
Council on Social Work Ed-
 ucation, 207, 219
Crises and typical problems,
 expectable transitional,
 72–74t

Cumming, E., 185n
Cumming, J., 185n

Davis, K., 51n
Day, J., 134n
Day care, 10
De Schweinitz, E., 194n
De Schweinitz, K., 194n
Devereaux, G., 155
Diagnosis, 170–75, 180–81
Dilemmas and Directions
     (Chapter 1), 4–38 et
     passim
  ambiguity of society's man-
     date, 5–13
  ambiguous professional
     goals, 30–34, 38–40,
     119–21, 165–67
  cause and function, 34–38
  halting development of
     social services, 13–19
     developmental services, 9,
        18–19, 196–97
     public welfare, 15–18
     voluntary agencies, 13–15
  professional constraints and
     opportunities, 19–29
  social indices, 6–8
  social worker as scapegoat,
     11–12, 32–34
  specialization, 20–29, 199
     fields of practice, 22–23
     methodology, 22–29, 93–
        94, 165
Dolgoff, R., 122n
DuBos, R., 157n
Dumpson, J. R., 32n

Epstein, L., 227n

Erikson, E. H., 70, 122, 131,
     154, 157
Expertise, professional, 62–64,
     167–68

Family, changing, 43–44, 50,
     66–70, 75–76, 79
Federal Bureau of Investiga-
     tion, 8n
Fine, S., 227
Finestone, S., 124n
Fitch, L., 59
Flexner, A., 19
Frameworks and Knowledge
     (Chapter 4), 119–63 et
     passim
  case boundaries, 132–36,
     162–64
  changing knowledge,
     149–57
  ecological perspective, 122,
     157
  eco-systems and manpower,
     208
  eco-systems perspective, 129,
     130, 176–77, 182–84
  ego psychology, 131, 154,
     157–59
  General Systems Theory,
     129, 136–149
  interactional perspective,
     134–35
  life model, 157–61
  linear perspective, 133–34
  medical model, 130
  model of life, 131–32
  personality theories, 151–55
  practice models, 130–32,
     184–89

social theories, 156–57
transactional perspective,
    135–36, 138
unit of attention, 123–38,
    179*t*
using the environment,
    159–61
Freudian theory, 152–54

Germain, C., 27, 97, 122, 129,
    131, 136, 157, 161
Getzel, G., 122*n*
Gladwin, T., 158*n*
Goldstein, H., xv*n*
Goodwin, R., 80
Gordon, W., 176*n*
Gottleib, W., 181*n*
Gray, W., 140*n*
Greenwood, E., 20*n*

Haley, J., 134*n*
Hamburg, D. A., 158*n*
Hamilton, G., 152, 170, 172
Hanrahan, T. E., 113*n*
Hartman, A., 140*n*
Hartmann, H., 122, 131, 154
Heyman, M., 227*n*
Hirsch, S., 134*n*

Individualizing, 167–175,
    188
Institutions providing social
    services, 72–74
Interface, 176
Social Work Intervention
    (Chapter 5), 169–203
    et passim
    assessment, 176–89

history (client's), 173–75
professional relationship
    and skills, 199–202
social work at the crossroads,
    189–96
    hospitals, 198
    labor unions, 191
    pre-natal clinics, 190–92
    schools, 197
    Social Security offices,
        194–96
    waiting rooms, 192
strategy and task, 184–87

Jackson, D., 134*n*
Janchill (Sister) M. P.,
    140*n*
Jenkins, S., 7
Jones, C. H., 232*n*
Jones, O., 196*n*

Kadushin, A., 120*n*
Kahn, A., ix, 11, 22, 196
Kahn, R. L., 140*n*
Kaiser, T., 140*n*
Kamerman, S., 122*n*
Katz, D., 140*n*
Klein, P., 13*n*
Kluckhorn, F., 128*n*
Kogan, L., 7
Kuhn, T., vii*n*

Lebeaux, C. N., 4, 64
Lee, P. R., 34
Leichter, H. J., 75
Lidz, T., 43, 134*n*
Loewe, B., 113*n*
Lubove, R., 13*n*
Lynch, K., 50, 60

The Differential Uses of Social Work Manpower (Chapter 6), 204–51 *et passim*
    accommodations to lack of strategies, 209–11
    approaches to differential use of staff, 227–32
        child welfare, 246–48
        family service and child guidance, 248–50
        hospital social service, 243–45
    career guidelines, 237–38
    causes of manpower gaps, 212–14
    educational categories, 218–24
    extent professional shortage, 211–12
    implications for practice, 214–16
Manpower
    and psychotherapy, 208
    and related disciplines, 224–27
    and social worker unemployment, 204–207
    statistics, 211–12, 219
    strategy through staff development, 246–48
    teams, 239–45
Martindale, D., 49, 56, 63
Mayer, J., 94n
Mencher, S., 13n
Menninger, K., 136, 154, 170, 173
Meyer, C. H., 16, 24, 26, 96, 134, 210, 248n

Meyer, H., 31n
Minahan, A., xvn
Minuchin, S., 128n
Mitchell, S., 140n
Mitchell, W. E., 75
Mullen, E. J., 32n

National Advisory Commission on Civil Disorders, 53
National Association of Social Workers, 22, 207, 219
Nelsen, J., 122n

Parad, H. J., 111n
Pearl, A., 232n
Perlman, H. H., 28, 175n
Pincus, A., xvn
Policy and Program (Chapter 3), 89–118 *et passim*
    accountability, 94–97
    accurate perception of problems, 100–18
    aged, 115–16
    autonomy of thought and action, 99–103
    child placement, 109–14
    epidemiology, 97–99
    limitations of social policy, 90–92
    mentally ill, 114–15
    penal offenders, 117
    role of social workers in policy, 93–118
    unmarried mothers, 105–109
Practice, private, 100

Rabkin, R., 155n
Rapoport, L., 12n

Rapoport, R., 159n
Reductionism, 137
Reid, W. J., 96n
Reissman, F., 232n
Research, 120
Reynolds, B., 78n
Richan, W., 227, 230
Richmond, M. E., 170, 201n
Ripple, L., 212, 219
Rizzo, N., 140n
Roberts, R., 105n
Rothman, S., 10n
Ryckoff, I., 134n

Sample, W. C., 227n
Schein, E., 140n
Scherz, F., 128n
Schlesinger, A., Jr., 15
Schwartz, C. G., 155, 161
Schwartz, E. E.. 227n
Schwartz, M. S., 155, 161
Seabury, B., 159n
Self-help groups, 205
Service, episode of, 231
Services
    decentralization of, 77
    developmental, 70–77, 196–97
    halting development of, 9, 18–19
    preventive, 96
    quantity, 68, 95, 109
    universalization of, 125
Shlakman, V., 108, 191n
Shyne, A., 96n
Siporin, Max, 74n
Skidmore, R. A., 196n
Sobey, F., 227n

Social Darwinism, 9, 10, 30, 36, 46, 91
Social services, institutions providing, 72–74
Social work
    definitions, 1–2
    values, 166
Sommer, J. J., 196n
Specht, H., 11n, 232n
Spiegel, J. P., 128n, 138
Stamm, I., 154n
Stanley, J., 181n
State Communities Aid Association, 32n
Stein, H. D., 156
Studt, E., 22, 184

Taft, J., 175n
Timms, N., 94n
Titmuss, R., 125, 127
Toffler, A., viin
Towle, C., 5
Tunnard, C., 58

U.S. Bureau of the Census, 8n
U.S. Department of Health, Education and Welfare, 8, 211n
U.S. Drug Enforcement Administration, 8n
U.S. Office of Economic Opportunity, 8n
U.S. Public Health Service, 7n

Vincent, C., 105n
Von Bertalanffy, L., 140n

Wallerstein, R., 158n

The Way People Live
(Chapter 2), 42–88 *et
passim*
changing family, 43–44, 50,
66–70, 75–76, 79
facing the fact of money,
55–57
individualization as a social
invention, 64–66
interdependent urbanized
environment, 45–47
location of services, 75–79
participation as a reality,
60–64, 84–88
problems of power relationships, 51–55
promotion of participation,
84–88
redefinition: psycho-social
to ecological thinking,
58–60
special case of cities, 47–49

terms of service, 86–88
urban migrations, 53–55
where individuals and insti-
tutions intersect, 70–74
why people live in cities,
49–51
Weakland, J., 134n
Weiner, H. J., 196n
White, M. A., 189n
White, R. W., 122, 131, 151,
157
Whittaker, J. K., xvn
Wilensky, H. L., 4, 64
Woodroofe, K., 13n
Workers, indigenous, 226,
232–36
Wynne, L., 134n

Yarmolinsky, A., 49, 59, 65
Ylviskar, P., 80
Young, L., 105n

SACRIFICE AND PRIESTHOOD

SACRIFICE AND PRIESTHOOD

JEWISH AND CHRISTIAN

BY

S. C. GAYFORD

FORMERLY VICE-PRINCIPAL OF WILBERFORCE COLLEGE, CUDDESDON,
AND BISHOPS' COLLEGE, CHESHUNT.

WITH A NEW PREFACE BY
THE RT. REV. F. D. V. NARBOROUGH,
BISHOP OF COLCHESTER

METHUEN & CO. LTD., LONDON
36 Essex Street, Strand, W.C.2

First Published July 17th, 1924
Second Edition, 1953

2.1

CATALOGUE NO. 5682/U

PRINTED IN GREAT BRITAIN

2·3 2.4

G 25s2

70955

TO MY BROTHERS

THE OFFICERS AND STUDENTS

AT CUDDESDON AND CHESHUNT
1899–1914

FOREWORD

FROM the days of E. F. Willis at Cuddesdon (he was Vice-Principal, 1870–1880, and afterwards Founder of the Oxford Mission to Calcutta) it became an almost sacrosanct tradition of the College that the Old Testament Lectures should give especial attention to the Sacrifices of the Old Covenant. To that tradition I acknowledge a great debt of gratitude. It launched me on a voyage of discovery which has been for many years an unfailing source of profit and delight. Why should the Christian Doctrine of Sacrifice, a subject second to none in importance and interest, find so inadequate a place in the ordinary University Theological curriculum?

Of the many friends and colleagues to whom I have been indebted for help of various kinds, there are three especially I should like to mention by name: Canon F. C. N. Hicks, Canon Du Buisson, and the Reverend Leslie Owen, who have given invaluable assistance in seeing the book through the Press.

S. C. GAYFORD

THE LICKEY
April 1924

PREFACE TO THE SECOND EDITION

THE republication of this book I believe to be an event of considerable importance in the course of theological development. Its inaccessibility to students through being out of print has been a regrettable handicap.

Nothing that has happened since its first publication in 1924 is likely to be found to have invalidated its thesis. A great deal of the Biblical study of that day carried criticism to irrational and almost morbid extremes of suspicion, aspersion and scepticism, against which neo-fundamentalism has been a natural reaction. Gayford was one of the few to make constructive use of the results of historical research and analysis. His book shows the power of a sane Higher Criticism to bring about an increase of spiritual insight.

He expounds a loftier conception of the theology of the Old Testament sacrifices than those to which we have been accustomed. His own arguments in its favour receive reinforcement when we remember the use of the Psalms in the Jewish Temple, providing, as they did, a deeply spiritual accompaniment to the rather strange proceedings of the ceremonial. The whole argument is gathered up into a doctrine of the Eucharist rich enough to make us exclaim at the manifold wisdom of God.

The lectures out of which this book originated were delivered by Gayford at Cuddesdon and at Bishops' College, Cheshunt. The present Principal of Cheshunt, Canon Lindsay Dewar, has interested himself in the reprinting of this book. As a Cuddesdon man convinced of its value, I welcome the opportunity of reintroducing it.

DUDLEY COLCHESTER

DERBY HOUSE,
COLCHESTER.
July, 1953.

CONTENTS

CHAPTER   PAGE

PREFACE BY THE RT. REV. F. D. V. NARBOROUGH, BISHOP OF COLCHESTER

INTRODUCTION 1
The Sacrifices and Biblical Inspiration—The Prophets and the Sacrifices.

PART I

THE JEWISH SACRIFICES

I. GENERAL : JEWISH IDEAS OF SACRIFICE . 9
Our business with Sacrifice as a working system in the time of Our Lord—Underlying ideas.

II. CLASSIFICATION OF THE SACRIFICES . . 23
Sacrifice (*zebaḥ*) and Offering (*minḥah*)—Different kinds of animal Sacrifices—Bases of division : degree of atonement, order of origin, spiritual sequence—Limitations of purpose.

III. THE CEREMONIAL ACTS OF SACRIFICE . 59
Presentation—Laying on of hands—Slaughtering—Meaning and use of the blood—Disposal of the carcass.

IV. THE DAY OF ATONEMENT . . . 83
Date of origin—Its purpose—Its ceremonial—The "sprinkling" of the blood—The mercy seat—The scapegoat.

V. THE DOCTRINE OF ATONEMENT UNDERLYING THE SACRIFICES 100
Meaning of *kipper*—The *poena vicaria* theory—The facts to be taken into consideration—Conclusions from them—The death and the offering of the blood—The ideas of "cleansing," "consecrating," and "atonement"—Death essential but not central—The element of vicariousness.

PART II

THE SACRIFICE OF THE NEW COVENANT

CHAPTER   PAGE

VI.   COMPARISON OF SACRIFICE UNDER THE OLD
      AND THE NEW COVENANT   .   .   .   123
      Their continuity—" Fulfilment" of the old—
      Differences : imperfections of the old.

VII. THE CHRISTIAN SACRIFICE : CHRIST AND
      THE CHURCH   130
      The unity between the Son of man and all
      mankind—" In Christ "—His Offering and
      ours,—These together make up the fullness
      of the Christian Sacrifice.

VIII. THE CHRISTIAN SACRIFICE : (A) AS FUL-
      FILLED IN JESUS CHRIST   .   .   .   136
      The perfect Sacrifice : meaning and implica-
      tions—Sacrificer, victim, Priest—The acts of
      His Sacrifice : (i) His incarnate life. (ii) His
      death : its relation to the life ; its distinct-
      ness in regard to the atonement. (iii) The
      Resurrection: blood means " risen life."
      (iv) The Ascension : His Priesthood and
      Priestly work : its scene, the Heavenly
      Temple : the perpetual Offering : Meaning
      of " the One Offering "—The Epistle to the
      Hebrews—" Sacrifice and Offering."

IX.   THE CHRISTIAN SACRIFICE : (B) AS FUL-
      FILLED IN THE CHURCH'S LIFE AND
      WORSHIP   158
      Sacrifice in daily life—Its expression in
      worship—The Eucharist linked with
      sacrifice—Its relation to (i) the death of
      Christ, (ii) the Heavenly Offering.

      INDEX   177

INTRODUCTION

THIS book is the outcome of a course of lectures delivered to several generations of students in the Theological Colleges at Cuddesdon and Cheshunt, and now published in book form at their kind request. Its ultimate purpose is religious and practical. I hope and believe it may serve as an eirenicon between the Catholic and Evangelical schools of thought not only within the Anglican Communion but also in other Christian bodies. That God may so bless it, is my earnest prayer. But at the same time it represents an attempt at research in its subject on scientific lines. For anyone educated as a Christian, however slight the Christian training, to approach such a subject with a blank mind is of course an impossibility. I have tried throughout to treat impartially the evidence supplied by the Jewish sacrificial system, to be guided only whither it led, and to follow through into Christianity the lines laid down in the Jewish preparation. The main results do not claim to be original. Theologians who differ widely in other respects have agreed in maintaining that Sacrifice consists not merely in killing something, but in the offering of a life that has passed through death, i.e. a *risen* life. What I have tried to do is to justify this conception of Sacrifice by a detailed study of the Jewish Sacrifices and the Sacrifice of Jesus Christ (chiefly as treated in the Epistle to the

Hebrews), and then to show that it leads to a view of the Eucharistic Sacrifice, which includes all that a faithful Catholic would demand as *essential*, and at the same time nothing which the Evangelical is bound by his principles to reject.

In this as in many other cases a great deal might be done in the way of reconciliation by a more exact definition of terms. Needless controversy is created by using words in different senses. I cannot help thinking that this has been the case with the much-abused word " Sacrifice " itself. This word to many people is, rightly or wrongly, so closely associated with the *death* of a victim that it is doubtful if we shall ever be able to widen its connotation so as to include the thought of offering life rather than death.[1] The New Testament, and especially the Epistle to the Hebrews, gives some support to the popular use of the term. Following this usage we should need two words, " Sacrifice " and " Offering " to cover the complete idea of Sacrifice : the former referring especially to the death, and the latter to the presenting of the blood. We should have to guard in that case against any attempt to separate the two, or to treat them as anything else than inseparable parts of one indivisible whole : " Sacrifice " and " Offering " together making up the act of worship properly called " Sacrifice." In any case, it would be a great step in the direction of peace if we could agree to speak of the " Eucharistic *Offering* " rather than the " Eucharistic *Sacrifice.*"

There are certain preliminary questions we may

[1] See further, p. 24.

anticipate in some degree in our Introduction. Every student of the Jewish Sacrifices is bound to face the questions : Are there spiritual ideas behind the ceremonial acts of the Sacrifices ? If so, are they such ideas as can be accepted by the Christian teaching ? To both questions we shall answer " Yes." [1] It is admitted by all that the ceremonial acts had a spiritual significance ; so much is implied by the interpretation of one of them in Lev. xvii. 11. Whether the ideas which they symbolize are consistent with Christianity we shall have to judge when we see what they are. But the acknowledgment of their permanent religious value leads to a further question : How far was the Jewish Church conscious of the truths embodied in its Sacrifices ? Is it enough for us to show that to those who have first learnt them from Christian teachers these truths are recognizable as the underlying meaning of the old ceremonies ? No doubt in part the symbolism was perceived by the choicer spirits among the Jews ; so much we can gather from the glimpses they give us now and then, e.g. in Pss. xl., l., and li. But we can see in the Sacrifices more than was ever dreamt of by the wisest among them ; and that without any fanciful or arbitrary allegorizing, but simply by the light of a higher revelation. The Sacrifices were pregnant with deeper truth than anyone realized before a new light was thrown on them by the Death and Resurrection and Ascension of our Lord. The more this becomes clear to us the more we realize the claim of the Law to Inspiration. It bids us correct a modern tendency

[1] See Sanday and Headlam, " Romans," p. 92.

almost to confine to the Prophets the title to Inspiration, while the Law is treated as an alien intruder in the sacred writings. With its spiritual value reinstated and vindicated, the Law must be restored to its rightful place among the inspired writings. The very acknowledgment of its *latent* Christianity is a strong argument for its Inspiration. It proves that the Jewish law-makers were moved and guided, like the Prophets, by an inspiring power which implanted in their teaching seeds of deeper truth than they themselves were aware of : seeds, the fruit of which only came to the light of day at a later time. In proportion as our interpretation of the sacrificial ceremonial is natural and unstrained, and its results yield truths of real and abiding worth when valued by the Christian standard, the argument for Inspiration becomes more cogent. Restoring the Sacrifices of the Old Covenant to the full honour which is their rightful due, we are able at the same time to restore to the Christian Apologetic a valuable weapon which it has been in danger of losing.

In the last few sentences we have already anticipated another possible objection. It has been questioned whether the religion of the Jewish Prophets allowed any room for the Sacrifices as a genuine element in the revelation of Jehovah to His people. It is suggested that we should be nearer the mark in regarding the Sacrifices as a heathen intrusion and survival, which the Prophets at the most barely tolerated and sometimes openly repudiated. For some years it has been the fashion to speak of the Old Testament as if it contained two antagonistic religions

—the Priestly and the Prophetic—one of which had necessarily to make way for the other in preparing the way for Christianity.[1] It is easy, indeed, to make a selection of passages which, if they stood alone in the prophetical utterances, might be interpreted in some such sense, e.g. 1 Sam. xv. 22 ; Amos v. 21–25 ; Hosea vi. 6 ; Mic. vi. 6–8 ; Is. i. 11 ; Jer. vi. 20, vii. 21, 22 ; Pss. xl. 6, l. 8, li. 16. But these passages must be balanced by other words and actions of the Prophets. It must be recognized that the Sacrifices formed a regular part of the personal and public religion of Samuel (1 Sam. vii. 9, 17, ix. 12, x. 8, xvi. 2) ; that Isaiah received his call in the Temple, and the very object of the Temple's existence was before all else the offering of Sacrifices ; that even in Amos there are signs that he considered the laws relating to Sacrifices as binding on the people.[2] A still higher estimate of the Temple is seen in Is. ii. 2–4 ; Micah iv. 1–3 ; and with it we may compare Jer. xvii. 26, xxxi. 14. The last references reveal to us that the Prophets, even in their picture of an ideal restored people and worship, include the Temple and its Sacrifices as permanent features of the higher religion of the future. We have to remember that two at least of the Prophets—Jeremiah and Ezekiel— were also Priests, and that any sense of antagonism between Priest and Prophet of the earlier days disappeared entirely after the Exile. Very probably the

---

[1] See e.g. W. Robertson Smith, "Old Testament in the Jewish Church," pp. 293–295 ; G. A. Smith, " Book of the Twelve," vol. I, pp. 102–104 ; and more guardedly Westphal, " The Law and the Prophets " (E.T.), pp. 320–328.

[2] Kirkpatrick, " Doctrine of the Prophets," p. 105.

Sacrifices had their roots in primitive heathenism. The Christian Fathers recognized this long before the modern study of Comparative Religion made it familiar to us.[1] But without doubt the Prophets accepted them as being sanctioned by the God of Israel, and incorporated into His worship. What they condemned was either Sacrifice which was a mockery because it was divorced from religion or morality, or Sacrifice regarded as a mere piece of mechanical ceremonial, i.e. in both cases the survival of heathen ideas in the popular conception of Sacrifice. Perhaps in Oriental fashion they seem sometimes to hold one idea in their heads to the exclusion of its counterbalancing truth (as, for instance, St. Paul seems to do with the two truths of Divine Omnipotence and human responsibility), and to speak as if denouncing Sacrifice *in toto*. But " it is inconceivable that they should wage any war against Sacrifice in itself."[2]

The teaching of the Prophets contains little in the way of direct interpretation of the Sacrifices and their ceremonial. Occasionally, however, as in 2 Sam. xxiv. 24, we see that they got at the heart of the matter, and saw in Sacrifice an expression of religious truth. Isaiah liii. brings the Sacrifices into the direct line of witness to the Messiah. But it is the attitude of our Lord Himself which gives the final sanction to the view that the Sacrifices were meant to have an honoured place in the Divine Revelation. Many instances will occur to every one of the way He obeyed and enjoined on others the fulfilment of the

---

[1] See Chrysostom, " Homily on St. Matthew," vi, 3.
[2] A. B. Davidson, " Old Testament Prophecy," p. 427.

Sacrificial Laws. We need mention only the most significant of them. At the Last Supper He spoke of His coming death as a Sacrifice, the " Blood " of which was to inaugurate the " New Covenant." In fulfilling the word of the Prophet Jeremiah (xxxi. 31), the Founder of the New Covenant vouches for a true continuity between the Jewish Sacrifices and His own. He adopts the sacrificial language of the Old Covenant and applies it with all its associations to the New. The Old Covenant was dedicated with the blood of victims slain as Burnt Offerings and Peace Offerings (Ex. xxiv. 5–8); the New Covenant is dedicated " with the Blood of Christ, Who through the Eternal Spirit offered Himself without blemish unto God " (Heb. ix. 14). After this it is unnecessary to labour further the point that the Jewish Law of Sacrifice was not merely a tolerated survival or a heathen intrusion in the religious development through Judaism to Christianity, but a genuine part of the main stream of that development in its course to the Ocean of Grace and Truth.

SACRIFICE AND PRIESTHOOD

PART I

THE JEWISH SACRIFICES

CHAPTER I

SACRIFICE IN GENERAL AND THE JEWISH IDEAS OF SACRIFICE

THE purpose of these lectures leaves a good deal of the subject of Sacrifice in general outside their scope. We are engaged in the study of the subject as a point of practical Christian religion. We do not need to trace the idea of Sacrifice back to its origins or to follow its various expressions in different religions. We are not directly concerned even with its origin or development in the religion of the Old Testament. It is with the stage at which the Jewish Sacrificial system stood at the birth of Christianity, with the Sacrifices as the Author of Christianity found them, and used them as the basis of His own religion, that we really have to do. And that means the fully developed system of Sacrifice as seen in the Priestly Code of Law—the Levitical Law.

It has often been stated that this Levitical Law of
Sacrifice was never actually carried out, but remained
as an unrealized ideal—a piece of paper legislation.
But at the most this cannot mean more than that the
system was never completely carried out to the letter
in all its details.   That the Priesthood and the faithful
among the people at the opening of the Christian Era
did aim at fulfilling scrupulously the Law of Sacrifice
is indisputable ; further, that they imagined themselves to have succeeded in doing so ; and finally that
the law in question was the *Levitical* Law. How far
the nation as a whole succeeded in carrying out the
Priestly Code in all its details is a question to which
we have hardly sufficient evidence to give an answer
with any certainty.   But so far as the Sacrifices are
concerned we have good reason to suppose that the
law was observed substantially as it stands in the
Priestly Code.   At any rate, this much is certain : that
the points of ceremonial which are of importance in
the relation of the Old Covenant to the New were
familiar features of the Jewish worship and formed a
living part of their religion.   There is a world of
difference in this respect between Ezekiel's vision of
the restored Temple-worship and the regulations of
the Priestly Code. The one admittedly was never
more than an ideal ; the latter for many centuries
actually entered into the religious life of the people,
and formed a part of their training in preparation for
the Gospel. Zacharias, Elizabeth, Simeon, Anna,
Joseph, and Mary,[1] the first of their nation to whom
the Gospel came, are all found diligent in attendance

[1] See St. Luke i. 5-23, ii. 22-42.

at the Temple worship. In the language of the strongly Jewish document on which St. Luke bases his account of the Nativity, they were " righteous before God, walking in all the commandments and ordinances of the Lord blameless " ; and these words from such a source cover the ceremonial as well as the moral law. We have good ground then for taking the Levitical regulations as the working standard of Sacrifice at the time of the birth of Christ. This Levitical Code embraced, and as far as possible harmonized, the earlier legislation found in the Pentateuch. The current ceremonial of the Temple also included certain partially independent features derived from the " Oral Tradition." But these were not very numerous or very significant. They were mostly explanations or amplifications of the Levitical Code.

In enquiring into the significance of many of the ceremonial and other details we shall necessarily be led at times into the history of their origin and development. It is only so that we can keep along the lines of a sound method. But it is occasional excursions into the history of some particular detail or the meaning of some significant word that we shall be called to make rather than a systematic exposition of the whole history of the Jewish Sacrifices. This preliminary defining of boundaries will perhaps anticipate and prevent the criticism of those who otherwise might be disappointed at missing a fuller treatment of this part of the subject. The archæology of the Jewish sacrificial system concerns us only in so far as it throws light on the meaning of this or that feature. *A fortiori* is this the case with the more primitive heathen religions. Sacrifice, we are told, is as universal as prayer in the primitive religions.[1] It is absent from some of the more advanced religions, which have outgrown the primitive and semi-barbarous ceremonies, but in them also the spirit which prompted the earliest forms of Sacrifice is present, only it has found a more refined and perhaps a more spiritual form of expression.[2] This is the case with Christianity too, but the Christian religion is fortunate in having retained much of the terminology of the earlier worship as a witness to its continuity with the past. Other religions, such as Buddhism or Confucianism, have dropped the older terminology and given themselves thereby a more revolutionary aspect. In some cases they represented, perhaps, such a leap forward in spiritual idea that their real continuity with the past has escaped notice, and they are credited with being spontaneous and original discoveries on the part of their founders. But they do not really form exceptions to the general truth that religion in all its forms has for one of its foundation stones the idea or ideas implied in the offering of Sacrifice.

What, then, are we to understand by the underlying idea or ideas of Sacrifice ? Running right through its history from its first appearances to its latest development in Christianity two ideas are found to remain constant. The first is the Gift idea. Sacrifice is a means by which man offers to God a gift. The motive of the gift may be gratitude or desire for a reward, or fear, or penitence. The other idea—generally called

[1] Robertson Smith, " Religion of the Semites," p. 214 ; Jevons, " Comparative Religion " (1913), pp. 21, 22.
[2] Jevons, " Comparative Religion," pp. 142, 143.

the Communion idea—is not so easy to grasp. In its earliest form it rests on the belief that by sharing with their god in a common meal on the sacred flesh and blood of the totem animal the sacrificers were brought into communion with him. This was more clearly the case when the victim, the totem animal, was itself identified with the god. The sacrificial feast was then nothing less than an actual feeding upon the god and receiving his life into themselves. It was more than communion : it was union.

Of these two purposes of Sacrifice, the Gift and the Communion, it is a disputed point which is the more primitive. It is urged on the one hand that before the idea of property arose the Gift idea could not exist, and therefore the Communion idea is the older. But it has been pointed out, on the other hand, that the earliest Sacrifices would not be offered by individuals or even by families. They would be corporate actions of the entire community, the clan, or the tribe. And though the notion of separate individual or family property may be comparatively late, communal property is as old as community life. There is no objection, then, to the primitive character of the Gift idea if the primitive Sacrifices were tribal acts, as it is generally agreed they were. The question is, however, one which for our present purpose we may leave to the anthropologists to decide.[1]

[1] The Gift theory—the older of the two—is represented by Tylor, " Primitive Culture," Lecture XVIII (3rd ed., 1891) and Herbert Spencer, " Principles of Sociology," § 139 (1893). The Communion theory seems to have been first suggested by Sykes, " Nature of Sacrifices," pp. 59–80 (1748) ; but the evidence in its favour was set out fully for the first time by Robertson Smith, " Religion of the Semites," Lecture VIII (2nd ed., 1894). See also Jevons, " Introduction to the History of Religion," Chaps. XI, XII (1896), " Comparative Religion," Chap. II (1913) ; Frazer, " Golden Bough " (1890), Chap. III.

Whether both ideas are equally primitive, or one of them is original and the other later, the fact remains that throughout the historical period of Hebrew religion, from first to last, the Gift idea is by far the more prominent of the two. The common meal, indeed, was always the chief feature in the ceremonial of the Peace Offering, and always signified a fellowship between the offerer and his God. But it would be fair to say that the idea of fellowship between the offerer and his invited guests came to be more prominent than that of communion with God.[1] And every trace of the prehistoric " eating the god " has disappeared from the Old Testament. Grace, in the

[1] The idea of communion with God as being effected by Sacrifice is probably more clearly seen in the *Covenant-making* Sacrifices than in the Peace Offering. In these the blood of the victim is shared between the altar (on which it is " poured " or " put "), as representing God, and those with whom the Covenant is made. So at the inauguration of the Old Covenant (Ex. xxiv. 6–8) the blood was " poured " (not " sprinkled " as in the Revised Version) on altar and people. Similarly at the cleansing of a healed leper (Lev. xiv. 14) and at the consecration of a Priest (Ex. xxix. 20; Lev. viii. 23) the blood was applied to the person concerned as well as to the altar. In each case, moreover, the touch of the blood imparts to him the property of " holiness." By the original Covenant Sacrifice (Ex. xxiv.) Israel, sharing with God in the same life-blood, is made a " holy " people : the touch of the blood both " cleanses " the people from the uncleanness of its previous contact with the " profane " world and also " consecrates " them, sets them apart, as " holy to the Lord." In the case of the leper the blood restored him to the " holiness " from which the " uncleanness " of his disease had excommunicated him. In the case of the Priest the blood gave him a still closer union with the Deity—an intensified " holiness." Perhaps in these instances we may trace a survival from the primitive Sacrifices in which the offerer eating the flesh and drinking the blood of his god became united with him. When blood became forbidden as food its virtues were imparted to men by the contact of touch. It would be of deep interest to know how much of this train of thought is latent in the discourse of St. John vi. (especially 53–56). Undoubtedly some of it survives in the Epistle to the Hebrews (see especially ix. 13, x. 22, xii. 24) and possibly in Revelation i. 5 (if λούσαντι is to be read), vii. 14 ; 1 Peter i. 2, 19.

sense of Divine help to the soul, was not looked for in the Peace Offering, or indeed in any of the Sacrifices of the Old Covenant.[1] Throughout the Old Testament the offering of a gift in the Sacrifices completely overshadows the idea of seeking communion with God. There are, perhaps, indications of a time when the Peace Offering was the only form of Sacrifice ; [2] but, as far as the actual evidence takes us back in the Old Testament, the Burnt Offering always appears side by side with the Peace Offering. And the whole aim and object of the Burnt Offering was the offering of a gift to God. No part of the victim was left either for Priest or for offerer : the whole was surrendered to God. Several other facts show how prominent in the historical period was the idea of the gift. In pre-exilic times the generic name for the thing offered in all Sacrifices was *minhah* (= a tributary gift). After the Exile this word was confined to the offering of the fruits of the field, but the general word for Offering, the familiar *corban* (*qorban*), also meant a gift or present. The ordinary term for offering a Sacrifice (*hiqrib*, from the same root as *corban*) means " to present " (*lit.* " to bring near "). These facts show how strongly the Jews associated the idea of the gift with their Sacrifices, and how completely the idea of communion had retired into the background. But at the same time it was never, perhaps, quite forgotten. It remained, as it were, in suspense until Christianity took it up and brought it to the front again in the Christian Sacrifice. Must we not recognize in this fact one of the many proofs of an overruling Providence

[1] See p. 55.   [2] See p. 32.

guiding the unconscious driftings of the Jewish mind ? All was working towards its predestined fulfilment in the Gospel. And at the same time have we not here, too, an indication that the Jewish Sacrifices were intended by the Holy Spirit to play a leading part among the forerunners of the Messiah ?

Returning to the Gift idea in the Sacrifices, we see further that the Jews came to realize not only the rightfulness of giving in the abstract, but also the peculiar kind of gift that was most acceptable with God. At an early stage the truth was grasped that animal life being of a higher order than plant life the gift of an animal was of more value than the fruits of the field. Abel's offering of the " firstlings of his flock and the fat thereof " was outwardly as well as inwardly better than Cain's gift of the " fruit of the ground." With a true sense of ceremonial fitness the outward was made a proper counterpart to the inward superiority. Corresponding with this, too, is the regulation by which the blood (" which is the life "—the animal life) was not shared by man with God, as in the heathen Semitic Sacrifices ; the " life " of the living thing was given to God exclusively. Nor is it arbitrary to trace the same line of thought a stage further. It is true that human Sacrifice is alien to the Old Testament religion, but at the same time the chosen people are reminded of a deeper principle underlying it. Abraham is prevented from the slaughter of Isaac, but he is shown that the offering of a son reveals a greater Sacrifice than the offering of an animal. It is not only that human life is of a higher order than animal life (some inkling of this is to be seen in the sacrificial slaughter of prisoners of war common in Semitic heathenism) ; but this sacrifice required a surrender of the life that is nearest and dearest to a father's heart—the first-born son, the only son ; it is not merely or principally the value of the gift in itself, but the *cost* of the gift to the giver, that comes into view. He is not asked to offer something which, however intrinsically precious, touches himself in a secondary degree : it is almost, if not more than, his own life which is demanded of him. In other words, the greatest of all Sacrifices is a self-sacrifice. And though the allusions to human Sacrifice in the Old Testament show that it could never have a place in the revealed religion of Israel, the Israelites were reminded that their nearest and dearest belonged of right to God if He chose to claim His due (Exod. xxii. 29). The first-born son has to be " redeemed " in acknowledgment that he is owed to the Lord and that the claim of God, though waived, is not surrendered (Num. xviii. 15, 17). And once more the Christian fulfilment unexpectedly takes us back to the crude original starting-point in its literal form. God Himself on our behalf gives His Only Begotten Son in human flesh to the horrors of a violent form of physical death. And yet that literal form—the horror and savagery of death by crucifixion—is transfigured into a thing of glory, and infused throughout with spiritual significance : " God so loved the world, that He gave His Only Begotten Son." And the Man, Jesus Christ, setting forth the perfect pattern of Sacrifice, offered not another life, but Himself. Self-sacrifice is the only perfect Sacrifice.

Looking back over the Old Covenant in the light of

this revelation of the perfect Sacrifice, we discover other features in the Jewish Sacrifices of significant meaning to those who had eyes to see. Such were three specially significant limitations of the material accepted for Sacrifice :

(1) The thing offered must be the personal property of the sacrificer : " of thy flock," " of the fruit of thy ground " (see, e.g., Exod. xxii. 29, xxiii. 16 ; Lev. i. 2, ii. 14 ; Deut. xii. 6, xxvi. 10, etc.).   David feels it to be an offence against the fundamental principle of Sacrifice to accept Araunah's gift and offer unto the Lord Burnt Offerings which cost him nothing (2 Sam. xxiv. 24). Now this means that it is not the intrinsic value of the gift that God regards but its cost to the giver. By the mouth of the Psalmist He reminds His people that He does not need their gifts, for His " are the cattle upon a thousand hills " (Ps. l. 9, 10.) *It is the degree of self-sacrifice involved in the gift that makes it precious in His eyes* ; in other words, all Sacrifice, so far as it is worth anything in the sight of God, is self-sacrifice. In another Psalm this truth is stated outright : " Burnt offering and Sin-offering hast thou not required : then said I, Lo, I am come . . . to do Thy will, O, Lord " (Ps. xl. 6). The present forms of Sacrifice fade away and are no longer necessary or desired when the spiritual reality which they can only partially express is an accomplished fact.[1]   All lower forms of Sacrifice are gathered

[1] This distinction between the outward and non-essential forms of Sacrifice and its inward permanent essential meaning is clearly grasped by Philo, "De Sacrificantibus," c.3 : "[The righteous] even if they bring nothing else . . . when they bring themselves . . . they are offering the most excellent of all sacrifices."

up and superseded in this perfect Sacrifice ; there at
last the inner devotion finds its full expression.

(2) The offerings chosen were the staple articles of
daily food : oxen, sheep, goats, pigeons;[1] and of
field produce, corn and oil and wine (*cf.* Ps. iv. 7).
The ass, the horse, gold, jewels, and raiment were
more highly treasured possessions, but were not
permissible Offerings for Sacrifice. Why this limitation
to the food Offerings ? In part no doubt it goes back
to Semitic heathenism and to the prehistoric ceremonial
according to which feeding on the part of the god or
the worshipper, or both, was an essential part of
Sacrifice. But in other Semitic nations exceptions to
this rule were frequent : the horse, the swine, the dog,
and the mouse are examples (*cf.* Is. lxv. 4, lxvi. 3, 17) ;
they were sometimes eaten at these heathenish
sacrificial feasts, but forbidden as ordinary food.
The Hebrew Sacrifices are strictly confined to the
articles of daily food, i.e. the support of daily life.
The connexion between food and life was closer to the
Semitic mind than to ours. It rested not only on the
common knowledge that our life depends upon food.
This was reinforced by further ideas. The distinction
between clean and unclean foods was based not only

[1] It has been disputed mainly on the ground of absence of allusion
that the pigeon was one of the staple articles of food among the
Hebrews (Robertson Smith's " Religion of the Semites," p. 219).
If this were established, it might still be noted that the offering
of a pigeon was exceptional. But the pigeon is the commonest of
the birds not excluded as " unclean " (Deut. xiv. 11 ff ; Lev. xi. 13 ff).
And several allusions point to it as a domestic bird : Gen. viii.
8, 9 ; 2 Kings vi. 25 (the reading is only conjecturally disputed) ;
Is. lx. 8. Pigeons were in common use as food in the New Testament
times and are so at the present day. There is no reasonable ground
for supposing that they formed an exception to the general rule
of Sacrifice.

on physical and sanitary grounds, but on the notion
that food has an effect on the man himself. A man's
" soul " is made " abominable " by " unclean " food
(Lev. xx. 25). Again, feeding together (" commensality ") on the same flesh was held to constitute a
real kinship where blood-kinship did not exist.[1] To
share the same food establishes a unity of life between
two men. In giving to God the flesh of the victim
which would otherwise have gone to sustain and even
to constitute his own life the sacrificer was making a
gift which very closely represented himself. It would
otherwise have passed into and constituted his own
life, and the offering of it was in a sense a self-oblation.

(3) There is a third limitation with a like significance.
Not even all kinds of food were offered in the Sacrifices.
Wild game—apparently allowed in primitive times (Gen.
xxvii. 4)—wild birds, fish, and the natural produce
of the land which grew wild, such as wild fruit, milk,
and honey,[2] though used as Offerings by other Semitic
races, were not admitted in the list of Jewish Offerings.
Of animals only those were included which belonged
to the sacrificer himself : oxen, sheep, goats, and (for
the poor) tame doves (see above). Wild animals, as
well as honey, milk, and fruits were common in
heathen sacrifices.[3] But in the Jewish regulations

[1] Robertson Smith, " Religion of the Semites," p. 274 ; " Kinship," p. 149.
[2] Milk and honey (which includes the juices of certain fruits)
were the typical natural products of an uncultivated fertile land,
which was described as " flowing with milk and honey." Robertson
Smith (" Semites," p. 220) thinks that the reason of their prohibition
was that they were generally eaten fermented ; but, if so, why was
wine allowed ?
[3] See " Encycl. Bib.," IV. 4188, 4193 ; Driver " Leviticus,"
note on Chap. I, ver. 2.

the Offering must be " of the herd and of the flocks "
(Ex. xxii. 29, 30 ; Lev. i. 2 ; contrast Deut. xii. 15, 16).
Normally in a pastoral or agricultural community
this would imply the personal labour of the sacrificer
in the rearing of the victim. When the development
of city life made this no longer possible, in every case
the feeling that it must cost the sacrificer something
is still strong (2 Sam. xxiv. 24). If it did not represent
his own personal labour directly, at least he must pay
for it with money he had earned by the sweat of his
brow. And in this we have again the hint that his
Offering is a thing which stands in a close relation to
the sacrificer himself. It represented a self-oblation.

When we come to examine the ceremonial of
Sacrifice we shall see that the idea of an identity
between the victim and the sacrificer is suggested
there also, and especially by the laying on of hands.[1]

If, then, the most prominent underlying idea of
Sacrifice at this stage is the offering of a gift to God,
we may go further and add that the gift which is
shown to be dearest of all to Jehovah is the offering
of self. It is interesting and full of import that a
spiritually minded Jew like Philo should have grasped
this truth without the help of the Christian Revelation.
In speaking of a Sacrifice which would be real and
acceptable even if no animal victim were offered, he
says : " For what is a true offering but the devout
piety of a God-loving soul ? " [2] The sacrificer is like
the Burnt Offering he offers, " because he surrenders
to God not only his first-fruits but also himself." [3]

[1] See pp. 62ff.
[2] " Vita Moysis," II (III), par. 10.
[3] " De Victimis," c. 14.

The righteous worshippers, "even if they bring nothing else, yet bringing themselves, the most complete entirety of goodness, they offer the best of Sacrifices, honouring God their Benefactor and Saviour with hymns and thanksgivings.[1]" The Scripture "regards as the Sacrifice not the victims but the mind and purpose of the sacrificer."[2] Here is another Jew who is not far from the Kingdom of Heaven.

[1] " De Sacrificantibus," par. 3.
[2] *Ibid.*, par. 6.

CHAPTER II

CLASSIFICATION OF THE SACRIFICES

WHEN we consider the different kinds of Sacrifice in the Jewish system, a cardinal distinction at once appears between the " Offerings of the fruit of the land " and " of the herd and the flock," the vegetable and animal Offerings. And to this distinction of kind. is added a further difference of the means by which the Offering is made. The animal victim was given to God by the shedding of its blood, and this became so distinctive a feature of these offerings that their generic name was " the slaughter Offering " (*zebaḥ*). In distinction from these the vegetable Offerings are called the *minḥah* (= a gift, but with the further idea of a gift as an acknowledgment of the inferiority and dependence of the giver's relation to the receiver ; a tributary gift). This word *minḥah* was originally applied to all kinds of Offerings, but afterwards confined to the " meal Offering " as distinct from the " slaughter Offering." In the later Priestly legislation the generic term for all kinds of Offerings is *corban* (= the thing presented to God), but the distinction between *minḥah* and *zebaḥ* is earlier than this. It is found in I Sam. iii. 14 (" The iniquity of Eli's house shall not be expiated with sacrifice [*zebaḥ*] nor offering [*minḥah*] for ever ").

The *locus classicus* for this distinction is Ps. xl. 6, where the whole range of Sacrifices is covered by the two terms " sacrifice and offering Thou hast no delight in." The same terms, in their Greek equivalents, are used to cover the whole field of Sacrifice in Hebrews viii. 3 : " Every High Priest is appointed to offer both gifts [δῶρα = *minḥah*] and sacrifices [θυσία = *zebaḥ*]." In English the word " Sacrifice " is commonly confined to the " slaughter Sacrifices," and this has become so usual that to the popular mind " Sacrifice " is essentially associated with the killing of a victim. We are almost compelled sometimes, however, to use the word in the wider sense, which its derivation [1] suggests, as covering all dedication of Offerings to God. It should be clear from the context whether the word is employed in the wider or the narrower sense, and so we hope that any confusion may be avoided.

Taking, then, this primary distinction let us consider first :

A. The " Offering " (*minḥah*), i.e. the bloodless or vegetable Offerings of the produce of the field. The *minḥah* had a subordinate place in the sacrificial system, and it is not quite certain whether in normal use it was an independent Offering. It might be so used as a substitute for a Sacrifice in case of extreme poverty (Lev. v. 11–13), and possibly also on other occasions, when offered privately. The public *minḥah* seems to have been always an accompaniment or appendage to a Sacrifice. Whether this was the case with the private *minḥah* or not, at any rate its subordinate position had this important effect, that it

---

[1] *Sacrificium*=something made " holy," i.e. by dedication to God.

was quite overshadowed in importance by the *zebaḥ*; when a Jew thought of oblation in general it would be the *zebaḥ* in particular that he had in mind. This dependent position of the *minḥah* was a natural legacy from primitive times when the Sacrifice was regarded as literally the food of the god. " When the Hebrew ate flesh he ate bread with it and drank wine, and when he offered flesh on the table of his God, it was natural that he should add to it the same concomitants which were necessary to make up a comfortable and generous meal." [1]

The ingredients of the *minḥah* were *corn* and *wine*, to which we must add *oil*, *salt*, and *frankincense*. Corn, wine, and oil were the staple vegetarian articles of daily food. The corn was offered parched (Lev. ii. 14), or ground into flour (*ibid.*) or made into a cake (*ibid.* 4). Oil was poured upon it in all these cases as in daily secular use. Salt is commanded in every case (*ibid.* 13), and the symbolism is explained by calling it " the salt of the covenant of thy God." Salt preserves food from corruption. This command is then the correlative of the prohibition against the use of leaven, with its opposite effect of producing fermentation and decay (*ibid.* 11). A covenant between men was cemented by a common meal (Gen. xxxi. 44–46), and the use of salt in this meal symbolized the inviolable nature of the covenant entered into, which was called " a covenant of salt for ever " (Num. xviii. 19; 2 Chronicles xiii. 5). As every Offering both rested upon the original Covenant with God for its acceptance, and also was in a sense a

[1] Robertson Smith, " Religion of the Semites," p. 222. We might add that for the same reason oil would be poured over it.

renewing of the original Covenant Sacrifice with its
accompanying meal (Ex. xxiv. 11), it was fitting that
the inviolable steadfastness of this Covenant (Jer.
xxxiii. 25, 26 ; Is. liv. 10) should be expressed by
the symbol of the salt.[1]

Another accompaniment of the *minḥah* was frankincense (Lev. ii. 15 ; vi. 15), with this difference, however,
that while the oil and salt were thoroughly mixed
with the meal, the frankincense was so placed upon it
that the whole of it was burnt. The whole of the
frankincense was laid upon the portion assigned to
God and burnt upon the altar. The Priest's portion
was free from incense. It is possible, as Robertson
Smith suggests,[2] that in the first instance the function
of cleansing was attached to incense, the gum from a
tree which is still regarded by the Arabs as " very
holy." In the light of this idea the obligation of
offering to God that which was clean may have been
emphasized by sprinkling the incense on the *'Azkarah*

[1] *Cf.* Mark ix. 49, 50 : " Every one shall be salted with fire."
Whatever may be the exact meaning of this passage, certain points
are clear :

(1) The reference to Lev. ii. 13, expressed in the (doubtful)
addition " every sacrifice [θυσία, a regular LXX. equivalent for
minḥah as well as *zebaḥ*] shall be salted with salt," at once gives
the passage a sacrificial connexion. Those who would offer themselves to God must be " salted " to preserve them from rottenness.

(2) The function of salt is transferred to another purifying agency
—the refiner's fire (*cf.* Zech. xiii. 9 ; Mal. iii. 3). This refining
fire is different from the punitive destroying fire of the previous
verses. The sacrificial fire was also regarded as a refining, etherializing agent in contrast with the fire that destroys (see pp. 79–81).

The preserving effect of salt is implied in other passages : " Have
salt in yourselves " (Mark ix. 50) ; " Ye are the salt of the earth "
(Matt. v. 13) ; " Let your speech be . . . seasoned with salt "
(Col. iv. 6), i.e. have in it something to preserve it from degenerating
into corrupt talk. Is it with reference to this thought that in the
parallel passage (Eph. iv. 29) the apostle warns his converts against
language that has " gone rotten " (λόγος σαπρός) for want of salt ?

[2] " The Religion of Semites," p. 427.

only (the portion offered to God). But the idea of purifying in connexion with incense had disappeared (if it ever existed) in the historic times of the Hebrew religion, and its place was taken by another idea so well known that it can hardly have been absent from its symbolic significance in the Sacrifices. Incense is the symbol of prayer (Ps. cxli. 2 ; Rev. v. 8). The reason of the comparison is clear : as the smoke rises from the earthly altar up to Heaven, so the prayer rises from the heart of man to the throne of God : " Let my prayer be set forth as incense before Thee " (Ps. cxli. 2). So while the angelic " Tersanctus " was chanted in the Temple, " at the voice of him who cried," the house was filled with smoke (Is. vi. 4). And while Zacharias burnt the incense on the golden altar within the Holy Place, " the whole multitude were praying without at the hour of incense " (Luke i. 10). Incense is the " etherializer " of the prayers of the saints (Rev. viii. 3, 4). In the light of this we can hardly do otherwise, in this case, than connect the thought of prayer with the use of incense in the *minḥah*. This suggests a further reason why the incense should have been used with the '*Azkarah* only. Men who consume their food by eating it would not use frankincense with it as they used oil or salt : it would serve neither for nourishment nor for flavouring But God consumes His portion of the Offering by means of etherializing fire, to the smoke of which incense adds a special fragrance. From the material point of view there was, then, a reason why only the '*Azkarah* should be sprinkled with incense. But a spiritual reason also lies ready to hand. If incense symbolizes the offering of worship, it is rightly restricted to God alone.

The *minḥah* subdivides naturally into two classes : (*a*) the *occasional* Offerings of individuals, or on behalf of the nation ; (*b*) the *perpetual* public Offerings on behalf of the nation.

I.   THE OCCASIONAL MINḤAH

(See regulations in Lev. ii., vi. 14 ff.)

These Offerings were made on the altar of Burnt Offering in the Court of the Temple (Lev. vi. 14). In the large majority of cases they were presented by private individuals, but they might be made also on behalf of the nation (e.g. Lev. ix. 17). This *minḥah* consisted of two parts, a solid and a liquid, which were probably not always combined. A meal Offering might be made without a drink Offering, but as far as we know a drink Offering never stood by itself. To the solid or cereal part of the *minḥah* (corn or flour or cake) the name *minḥah* is sometimes applied separately, while the liquid part is called the *drink Offering* (*nesek*). The whole Offering is then described as the *minḥah* (meal Offering) and *nesek* (drink Offering), e.g. Numbers vi. 15. But generally the term *minḥah* covers both the corn and the wine, where the Offering of the latter is included.

There are some points in the ceremonial of the cereal Offering which should be noticed. The first is that in no case did the offerer receive any share of the

Offering as he did in one of the slaughter Sacrifices (the Peace Offering). Perhaps it was in accordance with the whole idea of the *minḥah* (= tribute) that he was required to make an entire surrender of his gift to God and expect nothing for himself. Another significant point is the ceremonial connected with the *'Azkarah* mentioned above. The Priest was required (Lev. ii. 2, 9, 16, vi. 15) to separate a handful of the Offering, which was called "the memorial" (*'Azkarah*). The whole of the incense was to be placed upon the "memorial," which was then burnt upon the altar fire. The rest of the Offering was eaten by the Priests. The word *'Azkarah* (LXX, μνημόσυνον; R.V. "memorial") is derived from the causative form of the verb "to remember," and signifies, therefore, that which causes the Lord to remember, i.e. commends the sacrificer to the favourable notice of God. We may compare it with the idea in Isaiah lxii. 6, of the Lord's "remembrancers," who are to give Him no rest till He established Jerusalem ; or, again, the " stones of memorial " upon the Ephod bearing the names of the Children of Israel "before Jehovah for a memorial" (*cf.* also Ex. xxx. 16 ; Numbers x. 10, xxxi. 54). Similarly, in Acts x. 4, Cornelius is told, " Thy prayers and thine alms are gone up for a memorial (μνημόσυνον) before God."

The *drink Offering* (Numbers xv. 1–10) of wine as the name *nesek* implies, was poured on the altar (Hos. ix. 4 ; *cf.* Ex. xxx. 9). The *nesek* is not mentioned in the laws directly relating to the Offerings (Lev. i to vii). Possibly the omission shows that it was regarded with some suspicion, and as a fermented substance we should expect this to be the case. It is noteworthy that outside the Pentateuch the drink Offering is quite as often mentioned in connexion with the worship of heathen gods as of Jehovah.

II. THE PERPETUAL PUBLIC MINHAH

The perpetual public *minḥah* was offered regularly by the Priests on behalf of the nation, and the place of the Offering was the " Holy Place," the first of the two chambers of the Temple proper, in which stood the Table of Shewbread, the Golden Altar of Burnt Incense, and the Seven Branched Candlestick. The material of this *minḥah* was the same as in the private *minḥah*, but the ceremonial differed considerably. The Offering was made in three distinct ways :

(1) *Bread and wine* were set forth on the *Table of Shewbread* and renewed weekly, the old supply being eaten by the Priests alone (Ex. xxv. 23–30 ; Lev. xxiv. 5–9 ; *cf.* 1 Sam. xxi. 6 ; Mark ii. 26). Frankincense was placed upon the bread " for a memorial, even an offering made by fire unto the Lord," the incense alone in this case being the '*Azkarah*, which was probably burnt at first on the Brazen Altar of Burnt Offering, and later (see next page) on the Golden Altar of Burnt Incense.

The word " Shewbread " means literally " Bread of the Face (or the Presence) of God," i.e. bread set out on a table before the Lord. (LXX. ἄρτοι προθέσεως).

The use of wine is inferred from the mention of flagons, bowls, and spoons (Ex. xxv. 29).

(2) Incense offered separately by being burnt on the Altar of Incense every morning and evening as a " perpetual " incense (Ex. xxx. 7, 8 ; *cf.* Luke i. 9). It is probable that the use of incense as a separate Offering was not introduced into worship until the period just before the Exile. The Altar of Incense is not mentioned in Solomon's Temple or in the reformed worship of Ezekiel (Chap. xl. ff.) or until the Levitical legislation.

The use of incense in worship probably arose from its secular use as a way of showing honour to a guest. On the general principle that what is pleasing to man would be also acceptable to a god it was introduced from social life into heathen religion, and from heathen cults it was imported into the worship of Jehovah. But here it came under the influence of a more spiritual atmosphere, which gave it a new and beautiful significance as the symbol of prayer (see above, p. 27).

(3) Oil offered separately by burning in the Seven Branch Candlestick (Ex. xxv. 31–40 ; Ex. xxvii. 20, 21, xxx. 7, 8 ; Lev. xxiv. 1–4 " to cause a lamp to burn continually.") Probably the lamps were only alight by night: this was certainly the case at an earlier time (1 Sam. iii. 3), and seems to be implied in Lev. xxiv. 3 ; Ex. xxvii, 21, xxx. 7, 8, *cf.* 2 Chron. xiii. 11. There is a reference to a seven branch candlestick in Zech. iv. 2.

The perpetual *minḥah* may have been meant as a sort of appendage to the daily public Burnt Offering, similar to the relation between the occasional *minhah* and the private slaughter Sacrifices.

B. The Animal Offerings.—To all of these, in distinction from the *minhah*, the name of " *slaughter Offering* " (*zebah*) was applied. In later times *zebah* was used specifically of the Peace Offering, though occasionally it is found in its wider sense (e.g. Ps. xl. 6). This would be natural if (as is probably the case) the Peace Offering was the most primitive form of Semitic Sacrifice. The name *zebah*, given originally to the Peace Offering when it was the only kind of Sacrifice, naturally stuck to it afterwards, when other forms of Sacrifice had arisen. Ultimately, four forms of slaughter Sacrifice, called in our English Bible the Peace, Burnt, Trespass, and Sin Offerings, were recognized as parts of Jewish worship. The Burnt Offering, so far as we can trace it in the documents, dates from the earliest times ; indeed, if we look at the Old Testament alone, we might regard it as equally primitive with the Peace Offering. It is only from the study of other Semitic religions that the Peace Offering appears as probably being the oldest form of Sacrifice. The Trespass Offering and the Sin Offering are hardly earlier than the Exile (see below).

These four historical kinds of Sacrifice have been arranged and classified in many different ways : in their chronological order (as above), or according to their differences of ceremonial, or according to their spiritual meanings and purposes. The most useful classification, however, will be the one which uses as a basis of division a feature not merely common to all four Sacrifices in different degrees or different ways, but also at the same time of real significance in the Hebrew conception of Sacrifice. It is not of much value to classify them by a common feature which is comparatively unimportant.

This quest leads us ultimately to the all-important question of the spiritual meaning of the Sacrifices. To consider them merely from the point of view of their historical order, or of their ceremonial differences, is not enough by itself, because it only provokes the further questions : Why this order of time ? Why these differences of ceremonial ? And the answer to these questions is to be sought in the spiritual region. Now, there is one spiritual fact which is common to all the Sacrifices : they all express the human desire for fellowship with God. We may perhaps go a step further and say that all of them, even the most confident and joyful, imply some sort of consciousness that the fellowship with God is not a continual unbroken union, but needs to be renewed. To this renewal of fellowship we English have given the very expressive name of " at-one-ment." Now, if this consciousness is a fact, it supplies us with a very fundamental and significant basis of division, viz. the degree of at-one-ment present in the various Sacrifices. Applying this criterion we find we have to put them in the same order as the order of their historical origin, viz. (1) Peace, (2) Burnt, (3) Trespass, (4) Sin Offering. But the historical order has behind it a spiritual reason. Hebrew religion in its earliest form was pre-eminently a religion of joy, of festival and thanksgiving. Men felt gladly confident of the Divine favour, and the Peace Offering, the most joyous of the Sacrifices, particularly expressed

this sense of fellowship with God by the common meal
shared between Him and His worshippers. But very
soon, if not at the first, appeared a consciousness that
the bond might need renewal, and so from quite early
times Sacrifice was regarded as an atoning act, a means
of reconciling, if any estrangement was felt to have
crept in.   Even the Peace Offering was, occasionally
at least, regarded as an atoning Sacrifice. Traces
of this are seen in 1 Sam. iii. 14 (where even the
minhah too has the same aspect ; *cf. ibid.* xxvi. 19,
where however, *minhah* is probably used in the wider
sense to include the *zebah*, and Ezek. xlv. 15, 17).
As time went on the early childlike gladness faded out
of life, and in its place appeared a deepening sense that
God had hidden His Face from them ; they had
forfeited the Divine favour and must needs recover it
again.   The cloud arose at first from the political
troubles and anxieties which cast over the people a
spell of gloom and an uneasy feeling that their God was
not well pleased with them. As time went on it
developed into an increasing conviction of sin and sinfulness, and a growing sense of the need of atonement.
So it came about that new forms of Sacrifice grew up,
expressing a deepened desire for atonement, and also
the desire was read into the older Sacrifices which
had been hitherto comparatively free from it. Of the
class of new Sacrifices were the Trespass Offering and
the Sin Offering ; to the older class belong the Peace
Offering and (probably) the Burnt Offering. In the
Levitical period the atoning aspect of *all* slaughter
Sacrifices was declared emphatically by the canon of
Leviticus xvii. 11 : " I have given it [i.e. the blood]

to you upon the altar to make atonement for your souls." In this passage, no doubt, the Sin and Trespass Offerings are mainly in view, with the Burnt Offering included in a subordinate degree ; but on consideration it would be impossible to exclude the Peace Offering also. The old division into *expiatory* and *non-expiatory* Sacrifices was not strictly correct ; they should be arranged according to the degree of an atoning purpose present in all of them, i.e. (1) Peace Offering, (2) Burnt Offering, (3) Trespass Offering, (4) Sin Offering. This as we have already explained, is also probably the historical order of their origin in the religion of Israel. Let us take them then in this order.

I. THE PEACE OFFERING

As well as the name *zebaḥ*, dating from the time when it was probably the only form of slaughter Sacrifice, this offering was also called the " *zebaḥ-shelamim*," or simply " *shelamim*." It is not necessary here to enter into the vexed question of the original meaning of " *shelamim*." The ordinary English " Peace Offering " is taken from the LXX. translation θυσία εἰρηνική. In adopting this name, however, we must beware of a misconception. This Sacrifice is *not* the Sacrifice to *make peace* with an offended God. If the name were used in this sense the Peace Offering would be beyond all others *the* atoning Sacrifice. The peace to which it refers is a peace *already existing when the Offering is made* ; it is because the offerer *is* at peace with God that he dares to invite Him to eat and drink

with him.   The Peace Offering was forbidden to anyone
who was " unclean," and therefore out of communion
with God (Lev. vii. 20).   When it is compared with
the Christian Communion this must be carefully
borne in mind.

This consciousness of Divine favour made the Peace
Offering the most joyous of all the animal Sacrifices.
There is a note of gladness, of praise and thanksgiving
(Lev. vii. 11 ff.) about it, which is repeatedly echoed
in the Psalter (e.g. Ps. xxii. 25, 29, l. 14, lvi. 12, lxi. 8,
lxv. 1, cvii. 22).   It was peculiarly the Offering for
festal occasions, and especially at the chief of all the
feasts, the Passover.   To eat and drink is the natural
symbol of making merry.   Were it not for the express
statements in the older documents, such as 1 Sam. iii. 14,
we should not have suspected that behind this
gladness there lurked sometimes the thought of sin-
separation from God.   In any case this thought must
have been generally quite in the background and overshadowed by the glad sense of the favour of God.
In this connexion, too, the different kinds of Peace
Offering reveal a further fact of significance.   The
offering of this Sacrifice was always occasioned by
some particular benefit received or expected.   The
general sense of the Divine loving kindness broke out,
as it were, into an act of thanksgiving when some
particular mercy or blessing filled the heart to over-
flowing.   It might be the commemoration of some
great historical deliverance, as at the Passover, or just
the thanksgiving of a humble individual for God's
goodness to him personally.   In any case it referred
to some special occasion.   The three kinds were

(1) the *Thank Offering* or *Sacrifice of Praise* or *Thanks-giving* for some particular benefit already received (Lev. vii. 12 ff.) ; (2) the *Freewill Offering* (Lev. vii. 16 ff.), probably of the nature of a voluntary " thanks in advance," a thank Offering made spon-taneously at the time a thing was prayed for ; (3) the Votive Offering, or vow, distinguished from the Thank Offering in that it was the fulfilment of a vow, and therefore obligatory ; and distinguished from the Freewill Offering by the further fact that it was offered *after* the prayer was answered and the blessing received (see Lev. vii. 16 ff., xxii. 21). Both the Freewill Offering and the vow seem to have taken the form occasionally of a Burnt Offering instead of the usual Peace Offering (see Lev. xxii. 18 ; Ps. lxvi. 13).

The central and distinctive idea of the Peace Offering, a fellowship with God, was expressed by its peculiar ceremonial feature—the common meal. The portion assigned to God consisted of the blood (poured upon the altar) and the fat, which, being commonly regarded as the vital essence of the flesh, was forbidden food to men (Lev. vii. 22). The Priest's portion was the *heave thigh* and the *wave breast* (Lev. vii. 30, 32, 34). The *waving* was a ceremonial act expressive of the Priest's offering this portion to God and receiving it back from Him. The expression " Wave Offering " is used of a thing offered to God and returned by Him (e.g. the Levites offered to the Lord and returned by Him " as a gift to Aaron and his sons " to assist them in the Tabernacle ministry, Num. viii. 11-22). The word " heave " seems to be used of taking a part from a larger whole, e.g. the first-fruits from the whole

crop ; so here the right thigh from the whole carcass.
There would seem to be this distinction, that the breast
was offered to God in acknowledgment that it was His
due, and given back by Him to His Priest, while the
thigh was simply taken from the offerer's portion.
Thus the position of the Priest as mediator and bridge
between God and man was indicated : his portion
was derived partly from " the portion of the Lord "
and partly from the layman's share.[1] The rest of
the flesh was then eaten by the sacrificer and his
friends. It was a meritorious act to invite guests and
especially the poor to share in this banquet with its
associations of sacred and social festivity (I Sam.
ix. 13 ; 2 Sam. vi. 19, xv. 7-11 ; Neh. viii. 10, *cf*.
Ps. xxii. 26).

We have already spoken of the ideas associated by
the Semitic peoples with the act of feeding together
at the same table and from the same food.[2] The
common meal in social life not only cemented an
alliance of friendship, but even constituted a sort
of kinship as valid as blood kinship.[3] The same
life-giving food entered into the lives of those who
shared it and united them by a kind of vital identity.
In prehistoric heathen Sacrifice, when the victim was
identified with the god, the common life which united
the worshippers was the divine life ; their god became
their life within them ; they partook of his being.
When the animal victim was distinguished from the

---

[1] This is especially true of the Levitical legislation, but the
Priest's portion seems to have varied at different periods ; see
I Sam. ii. 13 ff. ; Deut. xviii. 3.

[2] See pp. 19, f.

[3] See Robertson Smith, " Kinship," p. 148 ff. ; " Religion of
the Semites," pp. 274, 313.

god, the union of the worshippers with their god was effected in the kinship established by the common meal. Something of these ideas, no doubt, survived in the Jewish Peace Offering ; but not enough to convey to the worshipper any sense of Divine indwelling through the Sacrifice. There is no hint in the Old Testament that men became partakers of the Divine nature through this sacred banquet. Here again we have to notice a radical distinction between the Peace Offering and the Christian Communion. Indeed the expression " Communion with God " applied to the Peace Offering is liable to this very serious misunderstanding through its Christian association. It would be better to substitute for it " *Fellowship* with God."

A comparison with the ceremonial of the Covenant Sacrifice (Ex. xxiv. 5–11) illustrates further the nature of this fellowship with God. The sacrificial " blood of the Covenant " is there applied to the altar (as representing God) and the people. God and His people are united in a holy bond by " partaking " of the same sacred *life-blood*. The people are " consecrated " by its touch : *cf*. the same use of the blood in the consecration of a Priest (Ex. xxix. 20, 21 ; Lev. viii. 30, 31). This sharing in a common life-blood inaugurated the Covenant relationship between God and His people at the first, and that relationship once established was afterwards continued in the common meal of the Peace Offering. While blood alone can create the vital union, its continuance is sufficiently secured by the sharing of common food. In the most primitive times we know that the " blood " of the victim was drunk by the worshippers. It was later that the sacredness of the " blood," as the life, led to its being forbidden as human food, and its touch was substituted as man's share in the Covenant ceremony by which God and His people were made one. The consecrating efficacy of the touch of blood is evidently to be explained from the most primitive type of Sacrifice in which the tribe and their god were united in one life by feeding together on the same life-blood. Something of the same train of thought most probably lay behind the putting of the blood on the doorpost in the original Passover ceremony. The house and its occupants were united to Jehovah in a sacred bond by the touch of the same life-blood, part of which was given to Him on His altar, and the other part put on the doorpost. Thus was first inaugurated that peculiar tie between Him and the people of Israel, which was afterwards reconstituted (see Ex. xxiv. 5–11) on a more definite Covenant basis, viz. the Law and its observance (this is the significance of the " Book of the Covenant " in Ex. xxiv. 7 ; it contained the terms of the Covenant).

II. THE BURNT OFFERING

This comes next in the ascending degree of atonement. The expression " to make atonement " is very frequently used of the Burnt Offering, and especially during the time before the Exile, when it was the principal atoning Sacrifice (see e.g. 1 Sam. vii. 9 ; Mic. vi. 6, 7). But all through its later history also the idea of atonement clings to the Burnt

Offering (*cf.* Job i. 5, xlii. 8; Lev. i. 4, xvi. 24). There is no doubt that this intention is much stronger here than in the Peace Offering.

The origin of the Burnt Offering is shrouded in mystery. The earliest documents of the Old Testament, such as the early narratives in Genesis, connect it with the most primitive times. The Sacrifices of Abel (Gen. iv. 4), Noah (*ibid.* viii, 20), and the Patriarchs (e.g. Abraham, *ibid.* xxii. 2) invariably take the form of a Burnt Offering. They imply, indeed, that it was the oldest of all the Sacrifices, and, as we saw above, it is only our knowledge of heathen Semitic Sacrifice and the tell-tale fact that *zebaḥ*, the Jewish name for Sacrifice in general, was also the specific name for the Peace Offering in particular, which makes it almost certain that the latter, and not the Burnt Offering, was the oldest form of Sacrifice from which the others were evolved. Where the two are found side by side in the early documents, it is noticeable that the Burnt Offering seems to have been felt to be the more appropriate for times of anxiety (as at the opening of a campaign, Judges vi. 26; 1 Sam. xiii. 10), or of grief and fear (e.g. 1 Sam. vii. 9). The peculiar feature of the Burnt Offering (the burning of the whole carcass on the altar) set forth the worshipper's desire to abstain from the common meal, and to hand over the whole of his Offering to God. From this we readily see how the Burnt Offering came to be associated with the idea of atonement. The feeling that for some reason God might be displeased led to the desire to propitiate Him by making over the whole victim to Him as a gift rather than to assume the relation of fellowship which the common meal of the Peace Offering implied.

The two Hebrew names for the Burnt Offering both refer to the peculiar feature of its ceremonial, viz. the burning of the *whole* body of the victim upon the altar. They are *olah* (= that which goes up, i.e. in smoke, to heaven ; or, possibly, but less probably, that which is brought up to the altar), and *kalil*, " whole," translated in E.V. as " the whole Burnt Offering." Both names, as well as the ceremonial on which they are based, emphasize the fact that in the Burnt Offering the chief idea is the offering of a gift to God as distinct from the sharing of a common possession (as in the Peace Offering). Further, the gift offered is not merely a precious possession, but a possession representing the giver's own self [1] by offering which he made in symbol the Offering of himself, soul and body. This latent meaning of self-oblation is brought out clearly in the New Testament, e.g. Romans xii. i.

Unlike the Peace Offering and the Trespass or Sin Offerings, the making of the Burnt Offering needed no special occasion to call it forth, nor did it have reference to any particular event or experience in the mind of the offerer. It was the only Sacrifice that was general rather than special in its bearing on the sacrificer's relation with his God. While the Peace Offering was made with reference to some particular mercy of God, and the Trespass and Sin Offerings with reference to some particular sin, the Burnt Offering was a general acknowledgment of the

[1] See pp. 16–22.

whole duty of man to God, and especially of Israel to Jehovah. Self-surrender and self-dedication are the keynotes of Israel's relation to God under the Covenant He had made with His people. That Covenant is compared with a marriage contract (e.g. Jer. iii. 14; Hos. i–iii) and as the wife gives herself altogether to her husband, so should Israel present herself to Jehovah. " Thou shalt love the Lord thy God with all thy heart, and with all thy soul, and with all thy might " is the Deuteronomic summary of the Law (Deut. vi. 5), as " Ye shall be holy unto me : for I the Lord am holy and have separated you from the peoples that ye should be mine " is the Levitical (Lev. xx. 26). Both intentions were expressed in the ceremonial of the Burnt Offering. The representative character of the victim and the burning of the entire carcass set forth the completeness of the self-surrender ; and the surrendered self was offered to God upon the altar, which by its sanctifying touch and the etherializing fire made the gift " holy to the Lord "—dedicated it (Exod. xxix. 37 ; cf. Matt. xxiii. 19). It was natural and appropriate, then, that this Sacrifice, expressing the normal duty of Israel to Jehovah, should be chosen for the daily public Offering on behalf of the nation (see Exod. xxix. 38–42 ; Numb. xxviii. 3–8 ; Lev. vi. 8 ff. ; but the custom is earlier than the Priestly Code, e.g. 2 Kings xvi. 15). Originally offered in the morning only, the evening " oblation " being a minḥah (1 Kings xviii. 29, 36), after the Exile it was commanded in the evening as well. It was known as the " continual Burnt Offering " (Numb. xxviii. 3 ; Exod. xxix. 42), bearing its perpetual witness that the people of Jehovah owed themselves and all they possessed to their God. Public Sacrifices were practically always either Burnt or Sin Offerings. If the Sacrifice had for its special purpose the making of atonement, a Sin Offering was offered ; but otherwise a Burnt Offering. The Trespass Offering was always private, and the Peace Offering, which originally in Semitic heathen religion was *always* a corporate tribal act, in course of time became a personal, or at most, a family Sacrifice. The Passover was a domestic as distinct from a national Offering ; every family had its own lamb (Exod. xii. 3). So the only *general* public Sacrifice (i.e. without special intention) was the Burnt Offering.

III.   THE TRESPASS OR GUILT OFFERING

We now come to those Sacrifices in which the sense of sin and the need of atonement were uppermost. In the Peace and Burnt Offerings other ideas and feelings occupied the foreground, sin and atonement being subordinate to them. In the Trespass and Sin Offerings the whole intention is that of penitence and the desire for reconciliation. The order of origin is again the order of ascending degree of atonement and directs us first to the *asam*, the Trespass Offering (to call it by its familiar name—that of the A.V.) or the Guilt Offering (as the R.V. translates the Hebrew). The earliest form of this Offering was a gift counted as a recompense for wrong inflicted on anyone, e.g. the golden mice and tumours sent by the Philistines to the Israelites when the ark was restored (1 Sam. vi. 3–5). Before the Exile there is mention of an *aṣam* as a money payment made to the Priests (2 Kings xii. 16). The *aṣam* first appears as a Sacrifice in Ezekiel's legislation (Ezek. xl. 39, etc.) ; but Ezekiel seems to imply that his readers would be already familiar with it, and we may perhaps date its origin as Sacrifice just before the Exile. Its meaning and purpose are first defined in the Priestly Code (Lev. v. 14ff., vi. 6 ; Numb. v. 6–10.[1] The *Guilt Offering* was for sins for which a reparation in kind was possible. It presupposed a legal compensation (called in Numb. v. 8, the *aṣam*, as if distinct from the Sacrifice, a usage recalling the original meaning of the word), consisting of entire restitution of the loss inflicted, plus a fine of an additional fifth of the loss (Numb. v. 7 ; *cf.* Lev. vi. 5). Together with this compensation the Guilt Offering atoned for the sin in its moral aspect. The ceremonial of the Guilt Offering was the same as that of the Burnt Offering, except that the fat only was burnt on the altar, the rest of the carcass being eaten by the Priests. This point of ceremonial it shared in common with the Sin Offering, from which it differed, however, in the application of the blood ; here it followed the usage of the Peace and Burnt Offerings. One peculiar feature recalls the distinctive character of the Trespass Offering : the victim was valued by the authorities (Lev. v. 15, 18, vi. 6), as if its cost formed part of the compensation made. This

---

[1] Lev. v. 1–13 refers to the Sin Offering in spite of the use of the word *aṣam* in verses 6, 7, which retains its older meaning of a " fine," or " recompense." This is more probable than that the passage confuses the two kinds of Offerings.

was the only trace in the sacrificial system of any idea of paying a recompense to God for sin. It is noteworthy also that, judged by modern ethical standards, the sins for which a Trespass Offering was demanded were more culpable than the merely ceremonial offences (see below) " covered " by the Sin Offering. Conscious theft, fraud, and false swearing are included (Lev. vi. 1–3) as well as " unwitting " offences.

One of the most interesting facts with regard to the Trespass Offering is the use of the word *aşam* in Is. liii. 10. Speaking of the suffering servant of Jehovah, the Prophet says : " When Thou shalt make his soul an *aşam* " (see R.V. margin). This part of Isaiah was probably written just before the close of the Exile, and the Prophet was almost certainly familiar with Ezekiel's legislation, and therefore we may be fairly sure that the *aşam* is here used in the sacrificial sense. The Servant is the victim in a Trespass Offering, and his life-blood (soul) on the altar makes atonement for the sins of his people. His sufferings and death are thus brought into line with the Sacrifices, and particularly the atoning Sacrifices, of the Old Covenant. The mention of the Trespass Offering rather than the Sin Offering, the highest atoning Sacrifice, is explained by the fact that the Sin Offering, which did not exist as a Sacrifice before the Exile, is only used in Ezekiel in connexion with cleansing persons and things for sacred offices, and has not the general atoning aspect it bears in Ezra's legislation. At the time of Isaiah liii. 10 the Trespass Offering was the highest atoning Sacrifice.

IV. THE SIN OFFERING

The Hebrew word *ḥaṭṭath* first of all means "sin" itself. In 2 Kings xii. 16, along with the *aṣam*, it is used of a money payment to the Priests, evidently in compensation for offences. It is not until Ezekiel that *ḥaṭṭath* is used of a Sacrifice.[1] With him the Sin Offering is mainly, if not entirely, connected with consecration and cleansing (Ezek. xliii. 18 ff., xliv. 27, xlv. 18 ff.). It is only in the Priestly Code (that is, with the legislation of Ezra) that it has become a regular Sacrifice for the "covering" of sin; and here it is the chief of the atoning Sacrifices. Its pre-eminence is shown by the fact that it was the Offering appointed on the great Day of Atonement, and also by the peculiar feature of its ceremonial. In all other Sacrifices the blood was "poured" upon the altar; in the Sin Offering alone it was "put" upon the *horns* of the altar.[2]

Comparing the Sin and Trespass Offerings with our modern standards of guilt and responsibility, we should undoubtedly expect the opposite of this. The Sin Offering is in all instances for "unwitting" offences, and with two possible exceptions (Lev. v. 1, 4) offences against the laws of ceremonial cleanness.

The failure to bear witness when called upon and the rash vow are the only cases involving what we should consider moral guilt, and that only in a minor degree. Even these (see above) very possibly belonged to the Trespass Offering.

[1] The reference in Lev. xxiii. 19, belongs almost certainly to the later Priestly redactor and not to the original Law of Holiness.

[2] For discussion of the significance of this act in the Sin Offering, see pp. 74–76.

The Trespass Offering, on the other hand, was intended to meet cases of fraud, i.e. real sins consciously committed, acts which according to our standards would certainly require a higher atoning sacrifice than the others. We have to remember that the Law made no distinction between moral and ceremonial offences : both were equally breaches of the rule of life commanded by God. Even an unwitting offence made the offender " unclean," as physical contact with disease might infect his body. A great part of the Prophets' mission to Israel was to " moralize " the Law, and so prepare the way for its " fulfilment " in the Gospel. But when we remember " it is impossible that the blood of bulls and goats should take away sins," it becomes of deep significance that the highest atoning Sacrifice of the Old Covenant should have been appointed for sins which were not sins. It was a Divine " irony " for those who could understand, and a hint that these things were only " a copy and shadow of the heavenly things." We have to bear in mind also that in the case of the Trespass Offering the Sacrifice was only an adjunct to a recompense already made. Damages had to be paid to the injured person before the wrongdoer might offer his Sacrifice. In this case, therefore, the atonement was divided between the compensation and the Sacrifice, while in the Sin Offering the whole burden fell upon the Sacrifice, and the offender acknowledged his inability to make any restitution for the wrong done. It is intelligible then, even if from a higher standpoint it is indefensible, that the Sin Offering should be the chief atoning Sacrifice.

Moreover this same indefensibility is not without a purpose and a significance ; the author of the Epistle to the Hebrews finds in it his chief argument for the superiority of the Gospel.

The special connexion of the Sin Offering with ceremonial cleanness explains its use in services of dedication. The blood, or even the flesh, of the Sin Offering was " most holy." It " hallowed " everything which it touched ; even a garment or a vessel accidentally touched by it was to be washed or scoured before being used again (Lev. vi. 27, 28). It was by the blood of a Sin Offering that the Tabernacle and the altar were originally consecrated (Exod. xxix. 35–37) and purified from pollution by a reconsecration each year on the Day of Atonement (Lev. xvi. 15–19). In connexion with this it is to be remembered that as a Sacrifice the Sin Offering first appears in Ezekiel's vision as a means of consecrating persons and things (see above). And it is probable that from first to last this was the root idea of the Sin Offering. The offences, for which it was appointed, had the effect of making the offender " unclean," i.e. cut off from relationship with God. The Sin Offering purified him and reconsecrated him. He was restored to membership of the people made " holy to the Lord."[1] Now the act of consecration involves a double process.[2] First, it is the " separation " of a thing or person from among the " profane " things of ordinary everyday life—the things that are " common or unclean." This is a " cleansing " act, purifying the object from previous pollutions. Secondly, it is a separation of a

[1] See further on this, p. 114.
[2] See Robertson Smith, " Religion of the Semites," p. 427.

more positive kind—a separating, a setting apart of the person or thing as " holy," i.e. belonging to God : a hallowing or sanctifying or dedication, a consecration in the more proper sense. These two ideas " cleansing " and " consecrating," each the converse of the other, are constantly associated as the effects produced by contact with Sacrificial Blood ; see e.g. Ezek. xliii. 20, 22, 26 ; Lev. xvi. 19 ; Exod. xxix. 36 ; cf. Heb. ix. 13. In the last passage it is suggestive that the author combines the same two ideas in speaking of the " sprinkling " of the Blood of Jesus : " How much more shall the Blood of Christ . . . cleanse your conscience from dead works to serve the living God." The combination is implied also in Heb. x. 19, 22, where the consecration of the believer is described : " Having therefore boldness to enter into the holy place [a right belonging only to those who had been consecrated to the Priesthood] by the Blood of Jesus . . . let us draw near . . . having our hearts sprinkled from an evil conscience."

Another point of interest is the choice of a victim for this Sacrifice. In contrast with the Burnt Offering, the victim was one single animal, as if to exclude any possible idea of quantitative compensation. For a public Sin Offering (and this includes a Sacrifice offered by a public official, the King or the Priest) the victim was always either a bullock or a goat (Lev. iv. 1–26, xvi.) ; for a private person, a lamb or a goat ; or, in case of poverty, pigeons or even a meal Offering of flour. The victims in the greatest of all Sin Offerings, on the Day of Atonement, were a bullock for the High Priest and a goat for the people ; in reference

to this fact it is with the " blood of bulls and goats "
that the Epistle to the Hebrews contrasts the Blood of
Christ (e.g. Heb. ix. 12, x. 4). The Baptist's description
of Our Redeemer as " the Lamb of God that taketh
away the sin of the world " has been generally adopted
in Christian language (e.g. 1 Pet. i. 19 ; Rev. v. 6)
and Christian art to portray Our Lord as the Sacrificial
Victim. But it must be remembered that the lamb
was not chosen in this connexion as being the traditional victim in the highest Sin Offerings, but for
other reasons : chiefly in reference to Isaiah liii.,
(cf. Acts viii. 32), and also to the Passover Lamb
(Exod. xii. 3 ff. ; cf. 1 Cor. v. 7 and Our Lord's
reference at the Last Supper to His coming death).

It may be useful here to sum up in tabular form the
conclusions we have reached as to the order of these
four Sacrifices, the intention of each, and its ceremonial
expression. In the last column we need only insert
the ceremonial act *peculiar* to each class of Sacrifice :
it is in the ceremonial peculiar to it that each kind
of Offering found expression for its proper intention.
In the next chapter will be found some account of
the *full* ceremonial of all the Sacrifices. Putting them
in the order given above we have the following table :

Offering	Intention	Peculiar Ceremonial
(1) Peace Offering	Expression of fellow-ship with God.	The common meal.
(2) Burnt Offering.	Expression of self-surrender and self-dedication.	The burning of the whole carcass.
(3) Trespass Offering	Recompense for wrong.	No *single* peculiar feature.[1]
(4) Sin Offering.	Atonement for sin.	The blood " put " on horns of altar.

[1] See pp. 59, 60.

We have treated the Sacrifices in their order of origin because, as we saw, their historical order resulted from a natural development in Hebrew religious thought.

But they can be arranged on another principle which will lead to a different order of succession. When the four (or, rather, three, for the Trespass Offering came to be quite overshadowed by the Sin Offering) were already established, a spiritual mind might seek to combine them on some principle of spiritual succession, much as, for instance, a liturgy is built up by the arrangement of prayers in an intelligible spiritual order. Now, when we consider the intentions of the different classes of Offering, a spiritual order of succession at once suggests itself. Before sinful man can draw near to God he needs something to remove the barrier between himself and God, something to " make atonement " for himself. This was provided by the *Sin Offering*. When the sin-caused barrier is removed, he is free to dedicate himself afresh to God, and it his duty to do so ; and this was the " intention " of the Burnt Offering. Finally, in the Peace Offering the sacrificer expressed that sense of fellowship with God, which is the Divine response to self-dedication. Justification, dedication, union constitute the spiritual order ; to the Jewish mind it would express itself as (1) restoration of the Covenant relationship (impaired by sin) ; (2) fulfilment of the normal Covenant obligation, i.e. a self-dedication (see above under *Burnt Offering*) ; (3) enjoyment of Covenant privilege, i.e. fellowship with God. Remembering this, and bearing in mind our general principle (see Preface) of belief in the overruling guidance of the Holy Spirit, it is significant that the three Offerings (Sin, Burnt, Peace) are very frequently found in combination and almost invariably in this very order of succession. (See e.g. Exod. xxix. 14, 18, 28 ; Lev. v. 8, 10, viii. 14, 18, ix. 7, 8, 12, 22, xiv. 19, 20, 22, 31, xv. 15, 30, xvi. 11, 24 ; Numb. vi. 11, 16, 17, viii. 12 ; Ezek. xliii, 19, 27 ; it will be seen that sometimes the Peace Offering is omitted, but the sequence is not disturbed).[1] It would seem to have been the general rule that a Sin Offering should be followed by a Burnt Offering : i.e. the worshipper is not allowed to rest content with the negative removal of past sin, but must proceed to a renewed dedication of life to God. He must be not only " dead unto sin " but also " alive unto God." In the pre-Exilic period before the Sin and Trespass Offerings came into existence, the order (Burnt and Peace Offering) is otherwise carefully observed.[2]

The frequent occurrence of the three Offerings in combination suggests a further thought : viz., that the ideal purpose of Sacrifice is only realized in its

[1] The only exceptions to this order occur in the Book of Numbers (e.g. vii. 27-29 ; xxviii. 11, 15, 19, 22). It is of interest that they should be confined to one book, and if the reason could be discovered it might be found to have some bearing on the problems connected with the authorship of the Pentateuch. But in some at least of the instances the order given is not necessarily the order of sequence, and in any case the exceptions are few enough not to disturb the general rule.

[2] See 1 Sam. vi. 15, x. 8, xiii. 9 ; 2 Sam. vi. 17, xxiv. 25 ; Ex. xviii. 12, xxiv. 5, xxxii. 6 (all J.E. passages) ; Josh. viii. 31 ; Judges xx. 26, xxi. 4 ; 1 Kings iii. 15, viii. 64, ix. 25 ; 2 Kings xvi. 13 ; Ezek. xlv. 15, xlvi. 2 ; Is. lvi. 7 ; 1 Chron. xvi. 2, 3, xxi. 26 ; 2 Chron. vii. 1. The only exceptions to this order are found in 2 Kings x. 24 ; 2 Chron. xxix. 24. But the order in these passages (Peace, Burnt Offering) is not essentially the order of Sacrifice.

5

completeness by the three taken together—Forgiveness, Dedication, Communion. The three cover the whole range of religious devotion, and, by including all three, Sacrifice becomes co-extensive with the entire area of worship and the consecrated daily life which alone gives meaning and reality to worship. So when Our Lord came to "fulfil the Law," His Sacrifice was the fulfilment not of one only but of all four types of Sacrifice under the Old Covenant. He gathered into one Sacrifice the intentions of Sin Offering, Trespass Offering, Burnt Offering, and Peace Offering : atonement, satisfaction for sin, dedication, communion.[1] It is to His perfect Sacrifice that we look for the final revelation of Sacrifice in its ideal perfection. We see there how the four previously distinct Sacrifices are combined and focused in one. Each of them by itself presented but a partial aspect of one complete whole. It was then a wonderful and providential forecast of future perfection that the old Sacrifices should have been so frequently combined, and with such uniformity in their order of succession. Even if it were shown that this order arose in some dim, prehistoric past out of mere matter-of-fact or even sordid circumstances, unconnected with such high and spiritual ideas, we have only to consider what we mean by Providence to see that this would not invalidate our argument. It would only be another instance of the way in which the Allforeseeing God overrules the blind choice of men in one generation to be a vehicle of teaching to a later age. The history of Comparative Religion is seen to be full of such

[1] See pp. 125, 126.

instances, when once we admit the conclusions of a living faith in Divine Providence working through the ages. The very fact of Sacrifice is itself a remarkable case in point. How is it that the Cross of Christ should be foreshadowed away back in the very beginnings of primitive heathen Sacrifice ? That with all their barbaric crudity and grossness they should yet contain within themselves the germs of such high truths ?

Before we leave this subject we should note some significant limitations in the scope and purpose of the Jewish Sacrifices. First, that no one of those Sacrifices had any *grace-giving* power. Either they expressed some *present* feeling of the sacrificer (the Burnt Offering, his desire to offer himself to God ; the Peace Offering, his sense of fellowship with God) or they refer to something in the past (the Peace Offering, as a thanksgiving for a past blessing ; the Sin and Trespass Offerings, to make atonement for some past offence). *No Sacrifice looked forward to the future,* far less contained any promise of grace to meet future temptations. In this respect they stand in strong contrast with the Christian Sacrifice. " The Law was given by Moses ; *grace* and truth came by Jesus Christ " (St. John i. 17). " If there had been a law given which could make alive, verily righteousness would have been of the law " (Gal. iii. 21). In this connexion we may refer the reader to our remarks on the common meal in the Peace Offering.[1] It is immaterial for the present purpose whether God or the sacrificer is to be regarded as the host in the

[1] See p. 39.

sacrificial meal.[1] In either case, the meal is the expression of a fellowship *already existing* ; it did not create or restore the fellowship.

There are other limitations which present the same contrast with the Christian Sacrifice. In one respect only could the Jewish Sacrifices be regarded in the light of a prayer or a means of obtaining a gift from God, i.e. the " making of atonement " for sin. This may be regarded as equivalent to a prayer for cleansing and forgiveness. But it is when we come to the forgiveness of sins that the contrast between the Sacrifices of the Law and the Gospel is most startling. At the outset, the very conception of sin is radically different in the Levitical Law and in the Gospel (or indeed in the Prophets of the Old Testament and to a lesser extent in the Deuteronomic Law). We have seen [2] that the Law made no distinction between moral and merely ceremonial offences in respect of guiltiness. Both alike are violations of the " commandments of the Lord " and bring guilt upon the offender. A breach of the ceremonial regulations (e.g. as to food) involves " iniquity " just as if it were a moral sin. We saw also [3] that the highest atoning Sacrifice, the Sin Offering, was almost solely for ceremonial offences. Except for one or two cases

---

[1] The point is disputed (see references in Kurtz, p. 164), but I cannot help feeling that the ceremonial of the Peace Offering points to the sacrificer as host. The " fat " and " the blood " alone were presented on the altar : the wave-breast and heave-thigh seem to constitute the Priest as sharer in the meal, representing both God and the sacrificer (see p. 37) ; the rest of the carcass remained the sacrificer's property throughout as his portion in the meal. It was not offered to God and returned by Him.

[2] See p. 48.   [3] See p. 47.

of fraud covered by the Trespass Offering,[1] the Law
provided no expiation for the real moral offences
such as theft, adultery, lying. Again, even the ceremonial offences were only forgivable if committed
" unwittingly." This involves a totally different conception of sin. Even unconscious offences were
counted under the Law as sins. The offence was
regarded as residing in the act itself apart from the
agent. From the legalist point of view the Jewish
lawyers saw no inherent contradiction in the repeated
formula of Lev. iv. to vi., " If a man sin unwittingly
and be guilty " (*ibid.* iv. 27), or the downright statement
of v. 17, " If anyone sin . . . . . though he knew
it not, yet is he guilty and shall bear his iniquity."
Whether the " unwittingness " might be stretched
to include sins of infirmity is not certain : in Numb.
xv. 30, the sins contrasted with unwitting offences
(verses 22–29) are acts done " with a high hand "
(*lit.* " with the hand lifted up," i.e. deliberately and
defiantly). The iniquity for these cannot be expiated
by Sacrifice (*cf.* 1 Sam. iii. 14 ; Heb. x. 28) ; the
offender is beyond the reach of sacrificial expiation :
" That soul shall be utterly cut off, his iniquity shall
be upon him " (Numb. xv. 31).[2]

We see then how the Sacrificial Code of the Old

---

[1] See p. 46.

[2] There is a further doubt as to whether the Sin Offerings on
the Day of Atonement provided forgiveness for more real and
serious sins. On the one hand, we have the repeated emphasis
on " *all* the sins," etc., of the people in Lev. xvi. 16, 21, and the
fact that the Day of Atonement was unique in many respects (see
post, p. 85). On the other hand, there is the probability that
" all the sins " means only all offences of the kinds mentioned above
and generally included under the expiating efficacy of Sacrifice.
And this probability comes nearer to a certainty when we find these
sins described in Heb. ix. 7 as " ignorances," (ἀγνοήματα).

Covenant was overruled by the Inspiring Spirit of God to confess its own inability to win forgiveness of sins. The overruling is the more evident because the Jews themselves looked upon these unwitting ceremonial offences as " sins." But the Sacrifices were only shadows and not realities, and the sins were only nominal sins. For real and grave sin the Law provided no atoning Sacrifice : the offender could only seek forgiveness by casting himself in penitence upon the mercy of God. God required no Sacrifice from the sinner—only the broken and contrite heart (Ps. li. 16, 17 ; *cf.* 2 Sam. xii. 13). " It is impossible that the blood of bulls and of goats should take away sin " (Heb. x. 4).

CHAPTER III

THE CEREMONIAL ACTS OF SACRIFICE

THE table shown overleaf will be found useful as a summary of this part of the subject. A few words may be added in explanation. The order in which the Sacrifices are here arranged has no significance : it is adopted merely for the convenience of arranging the vertical lines. The five ceremonial acts are given in their time order. In the vertical lines a broken line means that there is no difference between the Sacrifice in question and its neighbour in regard to that particular act ; a solid line draws attention to a *peculiar* feature of ceremonial. Only the more important and significant ceremonial acts are mentioned. The table shows at a glance that in regard to the first three acts (presentation, laying on of hands, slaughtering) all four Sacrifices were alike ; the peculiarities are to be found in the use of the blood and the body of the victim. The Sin Offering alone shows a peculiar use of the blood ; in the disposal of the victim's carcass the Sin and Trespass Offerings were alike, but the Burnt and Peace Offerings had each its peculiar feature (the holocaust and the common meal). It will be noticed that the Trespass Offering has no one feature peculiar to itself ; its peculiarity lies in its combination of the ceremonial acts.

Burnt Offering.	Peace Offering.	Trespass Offering.	Sin Offering.
I. P r	e s e n t	a t i	o n
II. L a	y i n g o n	o f H a	n d s
III. S L	A U G H	T E R I	N G
IV. Blood	poured on	Altar	Blood put on Horns of Altar.
V. Carcase Burnt	FAT	ONLY	BURNT
	Breast and thigh eaten by Priests. The rest eaten by sacrificer and his friends.	Rest eaten	by Priests only.

Parts of the above ceremonial were probably derived from the primitive Semitic Sacrifices and originally served a different purpose and bore a different meaning from that of the Levitical Code. The latter is true also of their significance in periods of Hebrew history previous to the Exile. In all probability the same ceremonial received different interpretations at different stages of religious growth.[1] For our purpose the archæological questions of the origin and primitive meaning of the ceremonial acts concern us only in so far as they throw light upon their significance in the Levitical Code, out of which emerged the sacrificial ideas of the Christian Church. That the acts had a meaning is plain from Lev. xvii. 11 ;

[1] Robertson Smith, " Religion of the Semites," p. 399.

they were not meaningless but significant ceremonies. The Law seems to imply that their meaning was obvious to the Jews ; where it is not so to us we shall have to try to recover it from our knowledge of Jewish social and religious life.

Before considering the acts in detail we may notice that there are three living agents in all Sacrifice : the offerer, the victim, the Priest. If what we saw above is true, that the ideal perfect Sacrifice must be a self-oblation the first two agents at least will be ultimately merged in one and the same person ; but, even so, it is all important that they should be distinguished in thought. Much has been lost in Christian teaching by obliterating this distinction and losing sight of the person of the offerer as distinct from that of the Priest and victim. It was clearly present to the mind of Our Lord, as we see from such utterances as, " I lay down [My life] of myself : no man taketh it from Me " (St. John x. 18), or " The Son of Man came . . . to give His life a ransom for many " (St. Mark x. 45) ; the words are spoken from the standpoint of the offerer rather than of the Priest. Our understanding of the moral and spiritual grandeur of the Passion suffers a serious loss if we look upon Our Lord solely as the patient Sufferer and forget that it was He Who ordained the Passion, Who was also ordering and arranging its details, the manner, the means, the time of His death. But still more has the doctrine of Sacrifice and its interpretation in the Epistle to the Hebrews suffered from this omission of the person of the offerer. It is this in particular which has led to a serious confusion of thought between the Sacrifice

on the Cross and the Priestly Offering in Heaven.[1]
It is well, then, that attention should be drawn at the
outset to the importance of the person and work of the
offerer in the Jewish Sacrifices.

When we come to the consideration of the ceremonial
acts in detail we notice that the agents in the first
three acts are the offerer and the victim. The Priest
takes up the action with the fourth and fifth acts,
during which the offerer takes no further part except
in the Peace Offering.

(1).   The offerer presented the victim before the Priest
in the Fore-court of the Temple.   The word technically
used for this presentation is *hiqrib* (Lev. i. 3) (*lit.* " to
bring near " ; R.V. " to offer ").   The same word is also
used of the Priest's work in presenting the blood
(e.g. Lev. i. 5) and the flesh (e.g. i. 13) of the victim
upon the altar. The Priest examined the victim to
see that it was free from any blemish.[2]

(2).   The *laying on of hands* was the work of the
offerer. He was required (Lev. i. 4, etc.) to " lay
[better, " lean," " rest," denoting pressure] his hand
on the head " of his victim. For this act the technical
word is *samak* (*lit.*, " to lean upon," e.g. Amos. v. 19,
and " leaned his hand on the wall "). This ceremonial
laying on of hands was not confined in the Old
Testament to the Sacrifices : a complete list of its
various uses is given in a note communicated by
Dr. Driver on the subject to the conference summoned
by Dr. Sanday on " Priesthood and Sacrifice." [3] One
idea which seems common to all of these uses is the

[1] See p. 137.
[2] See Philo, " De Victimis," c. 2.
[3] See pp. 39 and 40 of the Report published by Dr. Sanday.

intention of conferring on another something which either belongs to the person who performs the act or is in his power to bestow. The meaning in the case of the Sacrifices seems to be clearly explained in Num. viii. 10, 16, 18, where the congregation present the Levites before the Lord and lay their hands upon them. Aaron then offers them " before the Lord for a *wave Offering on behalf of the children of Israel.*" The ceremonial follows as far as is possible the ordinary course of Sacrifice. The Levites are to represent the whole nation in the service of the Tabernacle. The people, as sacrificers, " offer " them to the Lord instead of themselves, and the laying on of hands empowers them to stand for their people. So in general the laying on of hands in Sacrifice signifies the sacrificer's bestowing upon the victim the power to represent himself—so, e.g., Lev. i. 4: " He shall lay his hand upon the head of the Burnt Offering and *it shall be accepted for him* to make atonement *for him.*" (This is the more significant following upon the words " that he may be accepted before the Lord.") [1] What the victim does and suffers is then representatively the action and suffering of the sacrificer.

We cannot leave this subject without reference to the ceremony with the scapegoat on the Day of

[1] Dr. Swete (Hastings, D. B., III, 85, " Laying on of Hands ") accepts the same interpretation of this ceremony in the sacrifices : " The offerer solemnly identified himself with the victim." Robertson Smith (" Semites," p. 423) explains the significance by the primitive idea that " physical contact between the parties serves to identify them." If the ceremony dates from primitive Semitic religion it is interesting to connect it with the primitive idea that the victim (the tribal totem animal) is of the same kin as the sacrificer ; the blood relationship gives him the right to make the victim his proxy.

Atonement. Lev. xvi. 21, orders that " Aaron shall lay both his hands upon the head of the live goat and confess over him all the iniquities of the children of Israel . . . and shall put them upon the head of the goat." The action in this case is explained as the means of transferring sins ; and it has been held that this was the significance of the laying on of hands in the Sacrifices. The sins were laid upon the victim, whose death was their punishment. But it must be noted that the scapegoat was *not* a sacrificial victim. Its fellow had already been offered as a Sin Offering with the proper ceremonies.[1]

3. The *slaughtering*. Another technical term is found for the slaying of the victim. Three Hebrew words are used for the English " to kill." The word *harag* is used almost entirely of killing human beings and never of the sacrificial slaughtering. *Zebah*, which in the earliest times gave the name to the class of animal Sacrifices (*zebah*), was always used rather of the whole group of actions included in a Sacrifice in the sense in which we should say " to *offer* a Sacrifice," and never seems really to have been confined in its meaning to the act of killing, which it properly denotes. For the act of slaughtering a Sacrifice the technical word in the Priestly Code is *shahat*, a word occasionally used in earlier times of killing men, but after the Exile confined to the sacrificial slaughter of animals.

The chief point of importance in regard to this act is that it was performed by the sacrificer. In the Priestly Code this is definitely enjoined in the Peace Offering (Lev. iii. 2) and the Sin Offering (Lev. iv. 29,

[1] See p. 96.

33, etc.), and is probably taken for granted in the Burnt Offering (Lev. i. 5) even if the verb here be impersonal,[1] "one shall kill." That this was the normal rule is implied by 2 Chron. xxx. 16, 17, where an exception seems to call for explanation. In the public Offerings for the whole nation the victim might be slain by the Levites (e.g. Ezek. xliv. 11)[2] or the Priests (as, e.g., on the Day of Atonement, Lev. xvi. 15), but clearly as representing the sacrificers, and not *qua* Priests or Levites. It may be taken for certain that the acknowledged rule at all periods was for the sacrificer to slay the victim ; [3] and there was felt to be an appropriateness in this, as the victim was recognized to be in closest relationship with the offerer and even identified with him. The " killing," in this light, appears as a symbol of self-immolation, the voluntary laying down of one's own life, which is essential to the idea of perfect Sacrifice. But more of this later on ; only we may note once more in passing, how the seeming accidents of the early Sacrifices appear in time to have had a significance undreamt of at first. A Mind is at work guiding all things with an eye on the distant future, as a mother guides her child, looking forward to the day when he will be a man and understand what he now does unthinkingly and almost unconsciously.

[1] See Driver, Leviticus (*ad loc.*).

[2] Moore (" Encyc. Bib.," IV, 4199, art. " Sacrifice ") takes this message to refer to private Offerings, but describes it as " a very radical departure from immemorial custom," and adds : " This innovation, however, did not prevail."

[3] The only exceptions (apart from the one mentioned in the text above) I have found are the Sacrifices offered at the consecration of Aaron (Ex. xxix. 11, 20 ; *cf.* Lev. viii. 15, 19), and the Sin Offering of a pigeon (Lev. v. 8). In these cases the special circumstances offer a ready explanation why the sacrificer is not the slaughterer.

Except for the rule just mentioned hardly any regulations are given as to the manner or means of the slaughtering. In the Burnt and Guilt and Sin Offerings the victim was killed "before the Lord" (Lev. i. 5, iv. 4, etc., vi. 25, vii. 2). The same expression in 1 Sam. xv. 33 ; 2 Sam. xxi. 9 is possibly an allusion to the Burnt Offering at an earlier time, if the slaying of Agag and of Saul's sons was semi-sacrificial. This expression may mean no more than the corresponding injunction " at the door of the Tent of Meeting " in the case of the Peace Offering (Lev. iii. 2, 8, 13), but possibly there may be a significance in confining it to the greater atoning Sacrifices, as if in their case the necessity of death satisfied some stern decree of God, Who is called in to witness its execution (*cf.* Heb. ix. 22).

In the primitive Sacrifices it appears that the victim was slaughtered actually upon the altar itself so that the blood should fall directly on the sacred stone or mound of stones or earth (Exod. xx. 24, 25 ; *cf.* 2 Kings v. 17) of which the altar was composed. This ancient custom is implied in the Hebrew name for altar *mizbeah* = " the place of slaughtering." It was in use long afterwards amongst the Arabs [1] and references to it are found in the Old Testament (see especially Gen. xxii. 9, and *cf.* 1 Sam. xiv. 34).[2] But long before the dawn of the Old Testament revelation the victim was slaughtered not upon, but by the side of the altar, which was then used for the application of

[1] Robertson Smith, " Religion of the Semites," p. 338.
[2] The passage in Ps. cxviii. 27, " Bind the Sacrifice with cords even unto the horns of the altar," is very obscure, and probably there is some corruption in the text. It cannot be quoted as a reference to the custom of slaughtering at or upon the altar.

the blood and the burning of the flesh. But the original name *mizbeaḥ* was retained long after its meaning ceased to have any appropriateness ; indeed, so much so, that the name was applied even to the table of Shewbread (Ezek. xli. 22) and the Altar of Incense which had no connexion whatever with the slaughtering.

This comparative absence of regulation is not without its negative importance in the interpretation of the sacrificial symbolism. Coupled with this is the further fact that the different kinds of Sacrifice were not marked by any difference in the ceremonial of the slaughter. Attention was not concentrated upon the death, as such, however necessary it might be, but upon the ceremonial acts following after the death. Up to this point we have seen no differences of any importance between the different classes of Sacrifice. It is in the last two acts that these differences occur, and this fact is significant as showing that in them, and not in the first three acts, lies the centre of gravity in the drama of Sacrifice. Whatever may have been the case in prehistoric Sacrifice—whether the oldest word for Sacrifice, *zebaḥ* (= "slaughtering"), implies, or not, a time when the killing was regarded as the central act—at any rate in the Old Testament this was not so. The ceremonial directed the mind of the worshipper past the death of the victim to something beyond, viz. what was done with its blood and its carcass. Let us turn now to these acts.

(4). *The use made of the blood.* We must first notice certain facts about the meaning and significance of the blood. There is a striking unanimity in this regard amongst primitive races of all countries and ages. The blood is the seed of life ; more than this, to the Semite it was *the actual life itself.* Not only does the " life [soul] of the flesh " reside " in the blood " (Lev. xvii. 11) as a spiritual principle embodied in a material, the blood and the life (soul) are one and the same thing : " The blood is the life " (Deut. xii. 23 ; Gen. ix. 4).[1] It is not too much to say that the Hebrews regarded the life-blood almost as a living thing inside the body which it quickened ; and not only was it the vitalizing life while it pulsated within the body, but it had an independent life of its own, even when taken from the body. That it was still alive when it left the body, and continued to live, was the justification for its use in Sacrifice and the secret of its power and efficacy. " The life of the flesh is in the blood : and I have given it to you *upon the altar* to make atonement for your souls : for it is the blood that maketh atonement by reason of the life." It is because the *blood is still alive* after being drawn from the victim's body that it makes atonement upon the altar.[2] It is not merely a figure of speech when Cain is told, " The voice of thy brother's blood crieth unto Me from the ground," and when we read of the " blood of sprinkling " which " *speaketh* better than [? that of] Abel " (Heb. xii. 24).[3] To us moderns blood, and particularly blood that has been shed, brings up the

---

[1] This belief and its theological consequences are worked out in the well-known excursus of Dr. Westcott in his " Commentary on the Epistles of St. John " (additional note on 1 John i. 7).

[2] See W. Milligan, " Resurrection of Our Lord," pp. 137–138.

[3] The Greek of this passage runs, " speaketh better things than Abel " (speaketh), and the allusion is to Abel's sacrifice, by which " he being dead yet speaketh," not to Abel's blood.

associations of death ; to the Hebrews it meant life that has passed indeed through the experience of death, but has not itself been killed by that experience : it still lives. We can hardly draw attention too emphatically to this radical difference between the modern western mind and the ancient Semitic associations of thought, running down, as they do, through Hebrew and Jewish religion into Christianity and colouring so much of primitive Christian theology and its expression.

Bearing in mind these ideas attached to the sacrificial blood, we may trace the various ways in which it was employed at different times. Perhaps at the earliest stage the victim's blood was all drunk by the worshippers. This would be the case where the victim was identified with the god and men partook in this way of the divine life-blood : they " ate their god." When a distinction was drawn between the god and the victim, the blood was divided—part was drunk by the worshippers and part poured for the god into a pit in the ground or upon a sacred stone ; in this way, by partaking of a common " life," the original kinship between the god and his people was renewed from time to time. At a further stage came the time when men shrank from using " blood " as a food ; this may have been partly due to physical disgust at the idea, but it rested also on some vague spiritual idea of the mystery of life and awe of the life-blood, even of a beast, as a thing too sacred for human food. Blood is an awe-inspiring, even terror-striking thing. It has a mysterious potency and efficacy. Then, when the blood was no longer eaten it

was on occasions poured or sprinkled on persons or
things, and the same idea of consecration by sharing
with God in a common sacred life is preserved. The
very touch of blood makes a thing or person " holy."
This supernatural life, which has come direct from the
creative hand of God and is employed to reunite man
and God, consecrates whatever comes into contact
with it, and the person or thing made " holy " by its
touch is to be separated from profane or common use.
By the double process of consecration[1] he, or it, was
at the same time " purified " from previous uncleanness ; so, e.g., the house and all who dwelt in it, by the
blood on the doorpost (Exod. xii. 23) ; the Tabernacle
and its furniture being polluted by the sins of the people
are cleansed by the blood (Exod. xxix. 36 ; Lev. xvi.
16, 18, 19 ; cf. Heb. ix. 20 : the leper on his recovery is
cleansed by blood (Lev. xiv. 14, 25). In these cases the
prominent thought is the cleansing power of the hallowing blood ; " according to the Law, I may almost say all
things are cleansed with blood " (Heb. ix. 22). It is
with the same association of ideas that by its touch
the " Blood " of Jesus " sprinkled " on the heart
(Heb. x. 22 ; cf. xii. 24) or the conscience (Heb. ix.
14) cleanses the believer from all sin (cf. 1 John i. 7).
The same thought of the " cleansing " power of blood
underlies its use for the consecration of the High
Priest to his office (Exod. xxix. 20) or of a new
altar for Ezekiel's Temple (Ezek. xliii. 20 ; cf.
26), or of the nation of Israel to be the " holy "
people (Exod. xxiv. 8, xix. 6 ; Lev. xx. 26 ; cf. Heb.
ix. 19 ff.).

[1] See p. 49.

In this last instance a " kinship " is created, as if by " commensality," between the altar (representing God), the Covenant-Book and the people by sharing together a common life-blood, and by that " kinship " with God Israel is consecrated to be a people " holy unto the Lord." This brings us back from our digression on the consecrating power of blood to the point from which we set out. If this is the general significance of blood, how are we to interpret its use in the altar transaction of Sacrifice ? On the Day of Atonement one, if not the chief, of its functions was to cleanse and reconsecrate the Tabernacle and the furniture of worship (see p. 94 f.). But it is clear that this was not the case in the ordinary public and private Sacrifices ; there is no hint that every Offering of blood on the altar was in order to reconsecrate it after pollution. Bearing in mind, besides the primary truth that the blood is the soul or the life, two other facts : (1) that by the laying on of hands the victim is identified with the person of the offerer, and (2) that the altar is the " Table of the Lord " on which men present their gifts to God, we arrive at a fairly certain interpretation of this part of the ceremonial. *The presentation of the blood on the altar signifies the offering of the sacrificer's own life to God.* The blood is *offered, presented,* to God (Lev. i. 5, of the Burnt Offering ; Lev. vii. 33, of the Peace Offering ; Heb. ix. 7, of the Sin Offering). This idea of a gift to God is also present in the great Sin Offering of the Day of Atonement (see Heb. ix. 7). Two apparently distinct uses of the blood appear then in the Levitical system : (1) as a means of con-

secration (see above), and (2) as an offering to God.
The Day of Atonement combines the two.

The ceremonial use of the blood did not vary in the
Burnt, Peace, and Trespass Offerings. The blood was
caught in a bowl as it left the victim's body and was
handed at once either by the offerer or by an attendant
Levite (2 Chron. xxx. 16, xxxv. 11) to the officiating
Priest, who " poured " or " dashed " it on the altar.
The technical word for this act is *zaraq*. The verb
means " *to toss or throw in a volume*," [1] and there is
no doubt that it corresponds to our word " pour."
Further proof of this, if necessary, is seen in the
derivative noun *mizroq* (= a " bowl " or " basin "). The
verb should always be translated in English by
" pour " or some equivalent word. The A.V. render-
ing " sprinkle," which is retained in the R.V. (e.g.
Exod. xxiv. 6, 8, to mention one of the most prominent
instances), is a mis-translation, and pregnant also
with serious consequences. There was *one Sacrifice,
and one only, to which the act of " sprinkling " the blood
properly belonged*, i.e., the Sin Offering on the Day
of Atonement. [2] It would follow that in the New
Testament wherever reference is made to " the sprinkling " of the Blood of Jesus (e.g. Heb. xii. 24 ; 1 Pet. i.
2), the allusion is not to the old Sacrifices in general,
but to this particular one. But in the New
Testament, also, the issue is confused to the English
reader, because the revisers have translated the Greek
προσχεῖν, πρόσχυσις (= *zaraq*) by " sprinkling " (Heb.
xi. 28), in reference to the Passover, a Sacrifice belonging
to the class of Peace Offerings. The proper equivalents

---

[1] **Driver-Briggs Hebrew Lexicon**, s.v.   [2] See p. 89.

of " sprinkling " (ῥαντίζειν, ῥαντισμός) are found in
Heb. xii. 24 ; 1 Pet. i. 2. But there is one passage
where the Greek as well fails to observe the distinction,
viz. Heb. ix. 19, 21, which translates the Hebrew *zaraq*
(= "pour") of Exod. xxiv. 6, 8 by ῥαντίζειν, and therefore justifies the English translators in this particular
passage in using the word " sprinkled." The use
of ῥαντίζειν in these two verses is the more striking
because the LXX, which the Epistle generally follows,[1]
observes faithfully the distinctions of the Hebrew
terminology and translates *zaraq* of Exod. xxiv. 6, 8
by προσέχεεν (verse 6) and κατεσκέδασεν (verse 8).
This version consistently translates *zaraq* by προσχεῖν
—the only exceptions being the κατεσκέδασεν of
Exod. xxiv. 8 and the solitary use of ῥαίνειν in
Ezek. xxxvi. 25 (= *Heb. zaraq*). Correspondingly,
for the " sprinkling " proper the word ῥαίνειν and
its compounds are regularly used by the LXX. It is
remarkable then that the Epistle to the Hebrews, in
the face not only of the Hebrew (with which the
author was probably unacquainted),[2] but also of the
LXX (the version of the Old Testament almost
certainly used by him), should change the word to
" sprinkling " in Chap. ix. 19, 21. A little further
study of the passage suggests strongly that the change
was intentional. A remarkable feature of this chapter
is the apparent confusion of the annual Sin Offering
on the Day of Atonement with the original inauguration
Sacrifice described in Exod. xxiv. 1-11. In verses
7-12 and 24, 25 the author is thinking of the Day of
Atonement ; verses 15-21 refer to Exod. 24 ; and in

[1] See Westcott, " Epistle to Hebrews," pp. 476 ff. [2] *Ibid.*, p. 479.

verses 22 and 23 he has both occasions in view. The link between the two Sacrifices is that suggested above —namely the use in both of the blood as a means of cleansing and consecrating. The Day of Atonement was an annual renewal of the inauguration Sacrifice of Exod. xxiv, and it is doubtless this identity which led the Epistle to the Hebrews to alter " pouring " to " sprinkling " in Chapter ix. 19, 21. If this is the true explanation, the "blood of sprinkling" is meant to refer to both events, the inauguration (Exod. xxiv.) and the yearly renewal of the Old Covenant (Day of Atonement, Lev. xvi.), but not to any of the ordinary Offerings (Burnt, Peace, Trespass, or Sin).

In the Sin Offering the ceremonial use of the blood was as follows :—

On receiving the blood in the bowl the Priest dipped his fingers in it and *smeared* (E.V. " put ") the blood on the Horns of the Altar. The word used for this action is *nathan* = " to give " (in its widest sense) or " put." This very ordinary word becomes a technical term in the ceremonial of the Sin Offering, and is consistently used as such (see, for example, Lev. iv. 7, 18, 25, 30, 34). Of course only a very small quantity of the blood could be used in this way, and so the direction continues " All the blood . . . shall he pour out at the base of the altar " (Lev. iv. 7, etc.). We should note that the word for " pour " in this case is not the technical *zaraq* but *shaphak*, a general and non-technical word, which marks the fact that this pouring was not a part of the sacrificial ceremony, but only a means for disposing of the rest of the blood. It is to be noticed also that this pouring was not upon the *altar*, but upon the *ground* beside the altar. The sacrificial and significant ceremony is the " putting " of the blood upon the *Horns* of the Altar. These were the most sacred part of the altar (see 1 Kings i. 50 ; Amos iii. 14). They were made of a piece with the altar (Exod. xxvii. 2), even as the altar itself was originally intended to be of a piece with the earth, being a raised mound either of earth (Exod. xx. 24 ; 2 Kings v. 17), or of unhewn stones (Exod. xx. 25). An artificial altar of hewn stone or of metal, such as Solomon's brazen altar, could only be regarded as placed upon the earth, not as forming a part of it, and therefore Solomon's altar was replaced by one of unhewn stones by Maccabeus (1 Macc. iv. 47). The altar was, in fact, a representation in miniature of a " high place." Naturally, then, the highest part of the altar was the most sacred part. Further, this part was made into the shape of horns. Possibly in its prehistoric origin this may have arisen from a custom of draping the altar stone with the skin of the victim,[1] but in the historical period there is little doubt that quite different ideas were associated with the Horns of the Altar. The word " horn " was used figuratively by the Hebrews in two different but closely related ways. On the living animal, ox or ram, the horns were the seat of its strength—*vim cornibus addit.* So the word is very commonly used for strength, power, confidence : " Lift not up your horn on high " (Ps. lxxv. 5) ; " all the horns of the wicked also will I cut off : but the horns of the righteous shall be lifted up " (*ib.* 10 ; *cf.* Ps. lxxxix. 17, 24, and often).

[1] See Robertson Smith, " Religion of the Semites," p. 436.

The horn of the dead beast was used as an oil flask (e.g. 1 Sam. xvi. 1), and probably (though we have no direct evidence) as a drinking cup, from which came its figurative use of " abundance " (*cf.* " cornucopia "). Both uses suggested the appropriateness of the horn-shape for the most sacred part of the altar, and to these may have been added the use of " horn " for a hill (e.g. Is. v. 2 ; see R.V. margin). It is quite possible that, as with the belief in the sacredness of hilltops and high places, so here, the thought of the horns being the highest part of the altar, and therefore nearest to heaven, had something to do with the special reverence attached to them ; but in any case they represented a closer spiritual nearness to God. The blood is, then, brought nearer to God in the Sin Offering than in the other Offerings.

The same thought is continued in a higher degree in the higher Sin Offerings. For the layman the blood was "put" on the Horns of the Altar of Burnt Offering, which stood in the Court before the Tabernacle (Lev. iv. 18, 25, 30, 34). For the " anointed Priest " the blood was " put " on the Horns of the Golden Altar of Incense in the Holy Place (Lev. iv. 7), to which the Priests were admitted in their daily ministrations (Heb. ix. 6), but the laity were excluded. Lastly, on one occasion in the year, viz. the Day of Atonement, when atonement was made by a Sin Offering for the High Priest, the Priesthood, and the whole nation, the blood was " sprinkled " (for explanation of this term see p. 89) on the Mercy Seat, above which rested the manifested Presence of God himself (Lev. xvi. 2, 14, 15). In each case the sinner was restored to that particular degree of " nearness " to God which belongs to him by right of his rank in the congregation.[1]

(5). *The use of the flesh.* We saw above (p. 66) that in early Semitic heathenism the victim was slaughtered actually upon the sacrificial stone or mound, and this is implied in the very name for altar, *mizbeah* (= " place of slaughtering "). From the first, however, the slaughtering upon the altar was for the sake of convenience rather than an essential feature of Sacrifice. What was essential was that the living blood should fall upon the altar and the easiest way to do this was to kill the victim upon the altar. These early altars were just low mounds. But when the practice arose of burning part or whole of the carcass the altars were made higher and more convenient for this purpose and then the victim was slaughtered by the side of the altar, and the altar itself became solely the place of offering to the god the blood and the flesh which was his portion in the Sacrifice. In primitive heathenism the god may have been supposed to consume his share in human fashion ; such an idea is mentioned and forbidden to the Israelites in Ps. l. 13 : " Will I eat the flesh of bulls or drink the blood of goats ? " But though purged of its grossness the idea still remains that God does receive and use what is offered to Him upon the altar—so the flesh and blood are called His " bread " or His " food " (Ezek. xliv. 7 ; Lev. iii. 11, xxi. 6, 8, etc., xxii. 25 ; Num. xxviii. 2 ; Mal. i. 7, 12). The word for arranging the different pieces of meat upon the altar, *arak*, is the same as

[1] See further, p. 114.

that used for laying and furnishing a table. Lastly, the altar itself is called the " Table of the Lord " (Mal. i. 7, 12) ; and, as showing that the terms are interchangeable, the " Table of Shewbread " is called in Ezek. xli. 22 an " altar." The reader will not need to be reminded that this term, the " Table of the Lord," was taken over into Christian usage (1 Cor. x. 21). But attention may well be drawn to the meaning attaching to the phrase from its Jewish associations. St. Paul has just said that the Israelites " which eat the sacrifices " have " communion with the altar " (1 Cor. x. 18) ; in like manner we who partake of the Body and Blood of Christ partake of the " Table of the Lord," from which, like the Priests under the Old Covenant, we are fed by the " portions " sent by Him to us (cf. 1 Cor. ix. 13). Conversely (Heb. xiii. 10) we are fed from " an altar whereof they have no right to eat which serve the Tabernacle." It is plain that in Christian as in Jewish usage " altar " and " table " are the same, and therefore in both the primary idea attached to the " Table of the Lord " is that of an altar on which man's Offering to the Lord (the body and blood of the victim) is laid, and from which the Lord sends " portions " to His Priests.

It will be seen by the Table of Ceremonial[1] that in the *Burnt Offering* the whole carcass (i.e. all the parts considered fit for food) were given to God on the altar ; in the other three Sacrifices the fat alone was offered. In the Trespass and Sin Offerings the rest of the flesh belonged to the Priests and was eaten by them ; in the Peace Offering the Priest had his portions,

[1] See p. 60.

the *heave-thigh* and the *wave-breast*, and the rest was then eaten by the sacrificer and his friends.[1] Thus in all cases the *fat* at least was reserved as God's portion. The Israelites were forbidden to eat the fat of any sacrificial animal (Lev. vii. 23). The parallel between this prohibition and that of eating blood (Lev. vii. 26) may point to a similar belief connecting the fat with the life of the animal. It is possible that the practice of anointing in consecrating a man to an office may have originated from some such belief ; anointing with the fat, like sprinkling with the blood, may have been regarded as making a person " holy."[2] But this to a great extent is a matter of conjecture, and it is a sufficient explanation that the fat was regarded as the choicest part of the flesh (*cf.* the metaphorical use in Gen. xlv. 18 ; Num. xviii. 12 ; see R.V., margin), and therefore set apart as sacred to God.

The " portion of Jehovah " was conveyed to Him by being burnt in the fire of the altar. The technical word for this action is again full of significance. This word, *hiqtir*, means literally " to cause to go up in sweet smoke " ; so this altar-burning is " for a sweet savour unto the Lord " (Lev. iv. 31). The verb and its kindred noun *qetoreth* (sweet smoke) are used *only* of sacrificial burning and sacrificial smoke (which includes also the smoke of incense).[3] It is evidently meant that the effect of the sacrificial fire upon the Offering was to refine and etherialize what is carnal and earthly ; the gross flesh, changed into the sweet smoke, ascends heavenwards, until it reaches the

[1] See p. 37.
[2] *Cf.* Robertson Smith, " Religion of the Semites," p. 383.
[3] See p. 27.

heavenly realms. It is significant also that while
hiqtir is used only in sacrificial language, the word
saraph (= " to burn up "), the ordinary secular word for
destructive burning, is never used of the portions burnt
upon the altar, although, in pointed contrast with the
sacrificial *hiqtir*, it is used of consuming the portions
which were not burnt on the altar. *Cf.* Lev. xvi. 25
(" The fat . . . he shall burn [*hiqtir*] on the altar ")
with verse 27 (" they shall burn [*saraph*] in the fire,"
i.e. a fire lit " without the camp," their skins, etc.) ;
the same distinction is observed also in Lev. iv. 10, 12,
19, 21, vii. 5, 17, ix. 10, 11. For the use of *saraph*
in connexion with parts of the flesh not burnt on the
altar, see also Lev. vi. 30, x. 16. From these passages
it is clear that the burning upon the altar is to be
interpreted very differently from the destructive
burning of the useless and rejected portions of the
flesh. The fire on the altar was a sacred fire. It
came down from Heaven in the first instance on
Aaron's first sacrifice (Lev. ix. 24), and it was never
allowed to go out (Lev. vi. 12, 13). God signified His
acceptance of Elijah's Offering by sending down fire
from Heaven to burn it (1 Kings xviii. 38). It is
plain, then, that of the two purposes of fire—to refine
and to destroy—the former is its use in Sacrifice. The
fire purifies the gift and makes it an offering of " sweet
savour " (Gen. viii. 21 ; Exod. xxix. 41 ; Lev. i. 9, 13,
17, viii. 21, 28 ; *cf.* Lev. xxvi. 31 ; 1 Sam. xxvi. 19
mg. ; Amos v. 21 mg.), and the burning is a token of
God's pleasure in accepting the gift. This is true not
only of the Peace and Burnt Offerings, but of the Sin
Offering also (Lev. iv. 31), and it quite negatives any

idea of a penal altar fire destroying a sin-bearing
victim. The bearing of this fact on the whole conception of the meaning and purpose of Sacrifice will be
seen later on.   It is interesting to note that the expression " Fire Offering " (= " an offering made by
fire ") became so technical that it could be applied to
Offerings which were not burnt on the fire at all, such
as the Shewbread, which was eaten by the Priests
(Lev. xxiv. 7, 9 ; cf. Deut. xviii. 1 ; Josh. xiii. 14 ;
1 Sam. ii. 28). The figure is carried still further in the
New Testament, where Our Lord's self-oblation is
called " an odour of a sweet smell " (Eph. v. 2 ; cf.
2 Cor. ii. 15), and the gift made to him by his converts
is described by St. Paul as " an odour of a sweet
smell, a sacrifice acceptable, well-pleasing to God "
(Phil. iv. 18). On the expression " salted by fire "
see above, p. 26.

So far we have seen what was done with the parts
of the flesh offered to God and with the refuse or offal.
We have still to treat of the portions assigned to the
Priest and to the offerer.   In the Peace Offering both
Priest and offerer had their portion, and the sacred
tie of hospitality and of commensality (nourishment
by the same food) bound together all three parties—
God and the offerer and the Priest, who represents
each to the other.[1]   In the Sin and Trespass Offerings
the Priest's portion included all except the fat, which
was offered to God (Lev. vi. 26 ff. ; vii. 6 f.) ; the
offerer received no portion.   In these Sacrifices, as
well as in the *minḥah* it is clear from Lev. vi. 17, 18
that the Priest receives his portion as the representative

[1] See above, p. 38.

of God. All that is not kept and eaten by the offerer (i.e. the whole of the flesh except in the Peace Offering) is made over to God, who accepts it in part directly through the altar fire and in part indirectly in the person of His Priest. It follows that when the Sin or Trespass Offering was made by a Priest for himself or on behalf of the whole congregation, including himself, there was no one to eat the rest of the flesh after the fat was burned ; and in this case the remainder was burnt (*saraph*)—not a sacrificial but a destructive burning outside the camp (Lev. iv. 12, 21, viii. 17, ix. 11, xvi. 27). In Lev. x. 16 the Sin Offering of the people (see Lev. ix. 3, 15) is distinct from Aaron's own Sin Offering (Lev. ix. 8–11), and in that case Aaron and his sons should have received their portion and eaten it within the sanctuary ; it is noted as an irregularity that instead it had been burnt without the camp. The meaning of this part of the ceremonial of the Sin and Trespass Offerings seems fairly certain. In these penitential Sacrifices there is a common meal in which God and His Priest share, but the sacrificer, as a mark of penitence and mourning, is required to abstain from the feast. In the Peace Offering the ceremonial indicates that the sacrificer is the host who calls God to be his guest at the feast ; but the "waving " (and possibly also the " heaving ") shows that God returns a part to the Priest, who thus becomes God's guest directly, and indirectly the guest of the sacrificer (Lev. vii. 34 ; see p. 38).

CHAPTER IV

THE DAY OF ATONEMENT

(For the name see Lev. xxiii 27, 28, xxv. 9)

THE regulations for the Day of Atonement are contained in Lev. xvi. Certain other passages (Lev. xxiii. 26–32; Num. xxix. 7–11) add practically nothing to Lev. xvi; but Exod. xxx. 10, incidentally supplies a not unimportant detail omitted in this chapter. The observance of the Day is probably not earlier than the Exile. The first we find of anything like it is in theVision-Legislation of Ezekiel (xlv. 18 ff.). On the first or seventh day of the first month (or as the LXX, perhaps with better authority, reads: " On the first day of the seventh month, i.e. the month Tisri, in which the Levitical Day of Atonement was kept) a Sin Offering is ordered " to cleanse the sanctuary " or " make atonement for the house " (= the Temple) " for every one that erreth and for him that is sinful." The " cleansing " and the making " atonement " for the furniture of worship (the altar, the Temple, etc.) was a feature of the original consecration of the altar (Ezek. xliii. 20, 22, 26), when from being " common or unclean " (i.e. ordinary and secular in use and associations) it was consecrated (i.e. set apart as " holy to the Lord"). From Ezek. xlv. we see that its contact with an erring and sinful people was held to pollute it, so that each year it needed a new consecration. The same Sin Offering which was made for the sins of the people (Ezek. xlv. 20) served also to reconsecrate the sanctuary. This throws a new light on the purpose of the Day of Atonement in the later Priestly Legislation. Here also we see the same connexion between the people and the sanctuary : the people's sins pollute their sacred places, and the making of atonement is needed not only for the people but for sanctuary and altar also as at their original consecration (Exod. xxix. 36 f.). The hallowing of these by the touch of the sacrificial blood (to " cleanse " and " make atonement for " them) is like a new consecration each year. At the same time the blood sprinkled on the holy places as a Sin Offering for the sins of the people and their Priests made atonement for them also. Further, although the blood was not sprinkled on the people or Priests (cf. Exod. xxiv. 8), yet we see from Heb. ix. that the nation as well as its altars and sanctuary was *reconsecrated* each year on the Day of Atonement. This explains the apparent confusion of the references in Heb. ix. to the Day of Atonement (in verses 9–12, 22, 24) and the original consecrating Covenant Sacrifice of Exod. xxiv. in vv. 15–20. Every year the Covenant was in some sort renewed, the sanctuary and its furniture were rededicated with blood, and by its own consecrating touch the altar rededicated the Priesthood and the people who worshipped at it. We have to remember, also, that the blood of these Sin Offerings was identified with the " life " of those who offered them (i.e. Priests and people) ; so that while, *as blood*, it exercised its cleansing effect and rededicated the sanctuary, at the same time, as representing the offerers, it received from the altar its own rededication.

Before describing the ceremonial of the Day two things deserve to be noted about it : First, it was the only penitential Day ordered in the Law. " Ye shall afflict your souls and shall do no manner of work . . . it is a Sabbath of solemn rest unto you " (Lev. xvi. 29). It was " *the* Fast " (Acts xxvii. 9). Secondly, the Sin Offerings of this Day were not merely the highest in importance of all the atoning Sacrifices : they summed up all the atoning power of the others. It is repeated again and again that *all* the sins of the nation are included under the atonement made on this Day (Lev. xvi. 16, 21, 22, 30, 34). It has been thought[1] that this repeated " all " would include the greater moral sins which we saw were not covered by the ordinary Sin Offerings (p. 57). But this is doubtful in itself, since it would be a reversal of the general principle of atonement by Sacrifice ; and the offences are described in Heb. ix. 7 as ἀγνοήματα (" errors," i.e. "sins of ignorance "), which makes it clear that, as generally understood by the Jews, there was no difference in principle between the Sacrifices on the Day of Atonement and other Sin Offerings. The fact remains, however, that these Sacrifices summed up and included all the atonement for sin that could be made by means of Sacrifice under the Old Covenant. It is for this reason that the New Testament generally, and the Epistle to the Hebrews in particular, referring

[1] Dale, " Jewish Temple," p. 287.

to the atoning Sacrifice of Christ, speak of the " sprinkling " of the blood, which was peculiar to the Day of Atonement.[1] It is important to remember that the Day of Atonement is the " type " which is seen by the Christian inspired writers to be fulfilled by the Crucifixion, the Resurrection, and the Ascension.

THE CEREMONIAL OF THE DAY OF ATONEMENT

The occasion given in Lev. xvi. for the institution of this day is important in its bearing upon the meaning and purpose of its Sacrifices. Aaron's sons, Nadab and Abihu, had offered " strange fire " on the Altar of Burnt Incense, and " there came forth fire from before the Lord and devoured them, and they died before the Lord. Then Moses said unto Aaron, This is it which the Lord spake, saying, I will be sanctified in them that come nigh Me " (Lev. x. 2, 3). This is referred to in Lev. xvi.: " The Lord spake unto Moses after the death of the two sons of Aaron, when they drew near before the Lord and died. . . . Speak unto Aaron thy brother that he come not at all times into the Holy Place . . . that he die not." The key to the meaning of the Day of Atonement is to be found in the words, " I will be sanctified in them that come nigh Me." The office and work of the Priests was " to draw near " unto the Lord to offer the Sacrifices (Lev. ix. 7, xxi. 17 ; Num. xvi. 40). This they did every day at the Altar of Burnt Offering in the outer Court, and also at the Altar of Incense in

[1] See pp. 72–76.

the Holy Place (*cf.* Hebrews ix. 6) ; but on one day in the year, one of their order, the High Priest, was privileged to enter into the more immediate presence of God in the innermost shrine, the Holy of Holies. Here was the " Mercy Seat," the " footstool of the throne of God " ; above it rested the " Glory " of the Lord adored by the worshipping Cherubim on either side. This was the most God-filled, most sacred spot on earth : to it even the High Priest might not " draw near " at all times, but only once a year, and then for a very special purpose—to make atonement for all the sins of the nation, to cleanse and hallow both them (especially their Priesthood) and their sanctuary, that they might " draw near " on other occasions as a " sanctified " people. Thus there are two different strands of thought in Lev. xvi. : (1) The warning (drawn from and illustrated by the consequences of Nadab and Abihu's presumption) that the Holy of Holies is not to be entered but upon one day in the year, and (2) the observance of a great culminating act of atonement in the Holy of Holies upon that day. Scholars have found such difficulty in harmonizing the two intentions in this chapter that some have been led to regard them as imperfectly combined from two distinct sources. In any case, however, it is clear from Hebrews ix. that the two were closely united in Jewish thought of the Christian era, for the " entering " as well as the " sprinkling " is there considered as an act of great significance (see verses 7, 11, 24 ; *cf.* Chapters x. 19, 20, vi. 20). The Christian has the Priestly right of entering at all times within the veil without fear of being presumptuous, because by the

Blood of Jesus his heart has been sprinkled from an evil conscience : he is " sanctified." He may with bold- ness " enter into the Holy Place " by the Blood of Jesus by the way which he dedicated for us, a new and living way, through the veil (Hebrews x. 19), and there " draw near " to offer His Sacrifice.

Bearing in mind these two purposes of the Day of Atonement —(1) the ceremonial " entry " into the Holy of Holies, and (2) the making of atonement for the sins of Priests and people, along with the rededica- tion of the sanctuary—let us now review some of the more significant features of the ceremonial. They may be considered in order under five headings :

(A)   The making of atonement for the Priesthood.

(B)   The making of atonement for the people.

(C)   The making of atonement for the sanctuary and its altars.

(D)   The dismissal of the scapegoat.

(E)   Completion of the Sacrifices.

The references below are to Lev. xvi. Of that chapter, verses 1–10 give a summary description, which is repeated with more detail in verses 11–28.

(A) *The atonement for the High Priest and his " house," i.e. the Priesthood.*—Having " bathed his flesh in water," the High Priest put on his plain linen vestments (coat, breeches, girdle, and mitre—verse 4) as a token of penitence, leaving off the Ephod, the robe of the Ephod, the Breastplate, and the Crown upon the Mitre, viz. the holy garments " for glory and for beauty," which he wore in his ordinary ministra- tions (Exod. xxviii). He then took a bullock as a Sin Offering for himself and his house (verses 3 and 6) and two goats, one of which was selected by lot for the people's Sin Offering, and the other for " *Azazel* " (verses 5, 8, 10) ; also two rams as Burnt Offerings for himself and the people (according to the regular rule, by which a Sin Offering was always followed by a Burnt Offering, as the token of renewed self-oblation of the purified reconsecrated life). Being himself the sacrificer, the High Priest killed the bullock (verse 11 ; *cf.* Lev. ix. 8). Taking a censer with live coal from off the Golden Altar of Burnt Incense in the Holy Place, and sprinkling incense upon it, he entered within the veil, holding the censer before him, so that the smoke might rise up between himself and the Mercy Seat " that he die not." Leaving the censer there, he took of the blood of the bullock and " sprinkled " it " with his finger " upon the Mercy Seat on the east, and before the Mercy Seat seven times (verses 12–14), and so made atonement for himself and for his house.

Note :—(1) The incense smoke symbolizes the veil of prayer rising up between the sinner and the presence of God.

(2) The word " sprinkle " is of importance. It denotes a ceremonial act quite distinct from the *putting* or *smearing* of the blood with the finger in the ordinary Sin Offerings or the *pouring* in the other Sacrifices (pp. 72–74). The word here used is *hizzah*, the causative form of the verb " to leap " or " to jump " and meaning therefore " to cause to jump." It is used in Isaiah lii. 15, meaning " to startle, astonish " (see R.V., margin). The A.V. and R.V. translation, " sprinkle many nations," is not justified in this passage, and unfortunately introduces

the thought of sacrificial atonement, which is foreign
to the passage, while the idea of astonishment is in
full agreement with the context : " Many were
astonied at thee . . . kings shall shut their mouths
at him." The simple verb " to start " or " leap "
is used of blood in 2 Kings ix. 33 : " Some of her
blood splashed against the wall " ; and Isaiah lxiii. 3 :
" Their life blood is splashed upon my· garment." In
the *hiphil* (causative) form the sacrificial meaning is " to
make to splash," i.e. " to sprinkle." In the Sacrifices
this was done by dipping the finger in the bowl full
of blood and jerking it so that the blood was sprinkled
on the Mercy Seat (Lev. xvi. 14). Comparing *all* the
passages in which the " sprinkling " (*hizzah*) of blood
is mentioned, we see that except in these great Sin
Offerings on the Day of Atonement there was only
one Sacrifice in which the blood was " sprinkled "
upon the altar, and that a minor form of the Trespass
or Sin Offering (Lev. v. 9), when a pigeon might be
offered by a poor person in place of the more costly
victim. In this instance the direction that the blood
was to be " sprinkled " was probably for convenience'
sake ; in any case it certainly does not mark out this
form of Sin Offering as *more* important than the others.
In all other cases the " sprinkling " of the blood is
either upon persons or things, to hallow them (Exod.
xxix. 21 ; Lev. viii. 30, xiv. 7, 51) ; or towards a *more*
sacred spot in an ordinary Sin Offering—towards the
veil when the blood was put on the Horns of the
Altar of Incense in the Sin Offering for the Priest or
for the whole congregation (Lev. iv. 6, 17) ; or *towards*
the tent of meeting (Num. xix. 4) in the Sin Offering

(verse 9) of the red heifer. These passages include all the instances of " sprinkling " of blood in Sacrifice. In many other places (notably Exod. xxiv. 6, 8) our E.V. has unfortunately used the word " sprinkle " to translate a quite different word in the Hebrew, viz. *zaraq* (p. 72), and has thereby blurred the emphasis which is thrown upon the Day of Atonement and its Sin Offerings, both in the Old Testament and, what is far more important, in the New Testament.[1] It cannot be too strongly emphasized that it is with the Day of Atonement that Calvary, the Resurrection, and the Ascension are compared in their sacrificial aspect as the making of atonement for the sins of the world.

(3) The Mercy Seat was the spiritual centre of the Tabernacle, which was called the " house of the Mercy Seat " (1 Chron. xxviii. 11). The Hebrew *kapporeth* comes from the same root as the verb *kipper*, which is translated in our English Bible " to make atonement." From the belief [2] that the original meaning (now lost) of this root was " to cover," some scholars maintain that the word simply meant " the covering " or " lid " of the Ark, on the top of which it rested. But nothing is certain about the original meaning of *kaphar*, and the " Mercy Seat " was not a part of the Ark, but a distinct thing laid upon it. The description of it is given in Exod. xxv. 17 ff. Our translation " Mercy Seat " is derived from the metaphorical meaning of *kipper* = " to make atonement," and is supported by the sprinkling of the blood upon it on the Day of Atonement

[1] See p. 72.　　　　[2] See p. 100 ff.

" to make atonement " for sin. It is the oldest interpretation of the word that we can trace, appearing in the LXX, ἱλαστήριον, which shows that already in the third century B.C. the Hebrew *kapporeth* was traditionally connected with the cycle of ideas attaching to atonement. The Vulgate has *propitiatorium*. Our English " Mercy Seat " (derived from Luther's *Gnadenstuhl*) is a paraphrase rather than a translation. The proper meaning of *kapporeth* is " that which makes atonement," denoting not the *place*, as implied in the word " Mercy Seat," but the *instrument* of atonement. This is also the proper meaning of the Greek ἱλαστήριον. The Mercy Seat became the means of atonement by virtue of the blood sprinkled upon it, as was the case with the altar in the ordinary Sin Offerings (Lev. xvii. 11). It was, however, a still greater means of atonement—in fact, the greatest of all—because above it and between the wings of the overshadowing Cherubim was the Presence of God (Exod. xxv. 22, xxx. 6 ; Lev. xvi. 2 ; Num. vii. 89). It was the offering of the Sacrificial Blood on this, the most sacred spot in the whole earth, where God came nearer than anywhere else to his people, that made the most complete atonement which the Sacrifices of the Old Covenant were able to provide. In the Epistle to the Hebrews (ix. 24, 25) the anti-type to this is the entry of Christ " into Heaven itself " now to appear *before the face of God* for us, and this " appearing " is described in the next verse as " offering Himself " upon this Heavenly Mercy Seat as the Jewish High Priest offered " blood not his own " in the Tabernacle (*cf.* verse 7).

For references in the earlier books to the Mercy Seat and its peculiar sanctity as the dwelling-place of God, see 1 Sam. iv. 4 ; 2 Sam. vi. 2. The Mercy Seat was probably lost along with the Ark at the time of the Exile, but the blood was still sprinkled on the spot where the Ark and Mercy Seat would have stood. This was the practice in Our Lord's time (see Josephus " Antiquities " III, x, 3 and the Mishna tract " Yoma "). In this way the original idea was kept alive down to Christian times.

(B) *The atonement for the people.*—After sprinkling the blood of the bullock on the Mercy Seat the High Priest came back to the Court of the Temple, and taking the " goat of the Sin Offering," i.e. the one " on which the lot fell for the Lord " (Lev. xvi. 9), he killed it himself. The proper ceremonial required that this victim, which was the people's Sin Offering, should be killed by someone representing the offerer—the whole nation ; and in this capacity once more and not in his capacity as Priest, the High Priest slaughtered the goat. He then " sprinkled " the blood as before on the Mercy Seat and before it. In this way atonement was made for the people.

(C) *The atonement for the Holy Places.*—The " sprinkling " of the Blood by which atonement was made for the sins of the Priesthood and the people at the same time made atonement for the Holy Place (i.e. the Holy of Holies). A word of explanation seems called for here to answer the very natural question : How could it be needful to make atonement for an altar or any inanimate object ? Does not the very idea of atonement imply responsibility and guilt,

which can attach only to persons? Yet in Lev.
xvi. 16 the same sprinkling of the blood, by which
the High Priest makes atonement "for himself and
his house and all the assembly of Israel," is said to
make atonement for the Holy Place. In Exod.
xxix. 36 (*cf.* Lev. viii. 15) three effects are mentioned
as proceeding from the use of the blood in the Sin
Offering at the consecration of an altar—purging
(or cleansing or purifying), making atonement, and
sanctifying. We have seen that purifying (from
previous uncleanness) and hallowing (or sanctifying)
were the two complementary processes of consecration.
Now Exod. xxix. 36, " Thou shalt cleanse the altar by
thy making atonement for it " (R.V., margin), practically identifies the making of atonement with purging
(see further, Chapter V on the meaning of " Atonement ").[1]   The same expressions are combined in our
present chapter also (Lev. xvi. 18, 19). The sanctuary
has been defiled by the uncleanness of the people and
therefore needs cleansing ; but also—and here the
inanimate altar is almost personified as if it were a
responsible being whose guilt incurs Divine disfavour
—atonement must be made for it, to restore it to
Divine favour. The blood of the Sin Offering effects
a change not only in the altar itself (from uncleanness
to " holiness ") but in the attitude of God towards
it (from disfavour to favour). The former is called
to cleanse, purge, purify, or hallow ; the latter is
called making atonement for it. In the same way,
but as a separate action, atonement was made for the
" tent of meeting," i.e. the first chamber of the Taber-

[1] Esp. p. 113.

nacle (see Lev. xvi. 17, 20), and the Holy Place in particular (verse 16). How this was done is not defined in Lev. xvi., but is mentioned incidentally in Exod. xxx. 10 : " And Aaron shall make atonement [i.e. for the Golden Altar of Incense in the Holy Place] upon the horns of it once in the year ; with the blood of the Sin Offering of atonement once in the year shall he make atonement for it throughout your generations : it is most holy unto the Lord." The last words are interesting as showing again the close connexion between consecration and atonement. The " holy " altar desecrated by the sins of the Priesthood and people is reconsecrated by the blood of the Sin Offering, which makes atonement for it. . . . Finally, atonement was made for the " altar that is before the Lord," i.e. the great altar of Burnt Offering in the Fore-Court (verse 18), by " putting " of the blood of the bullock and the goat upon its horns and by " sprinkling " (verse 19 : the same word *hizzah* as in verse 14, 15) upon it seven times. Note again that the " cleansing " with blood is also a " hallowing " and a " making atonement."

(D) *The dismissal of the scapegoat.*—The only parallel to this in the Levitical Ceremonial Law was in the " law of the leper on the day of his cleansing," and the cleansing of a leprous house (Lev. xiv). In that case one of two birds was killed, and the other, the live one, after being dipped in the blood of the first, was " let go . . . into the open field." So on the Day of Atonement two goats were taken " for a Sin Offering " (xvi. 5) ; one was chosen by lot for the Lord " and the other " for *Azazel*." This second goat, the " Goat for *Azazel*," is familiar to us from the A.V.

as the " scapegoat " (= the " escape-goat," the goat that was " let go in the wilderness "). An odd feature in the history of the English term " scapegoat " is the way in which its original meaning has been exactly reversed. In common usage it has come to mean not the one who escapes a punishment, but the innocent party who is substituted for the guilty and bears the penalty of another's crime. This description would apply to the goat that was offered for a Sin Offering rather than the " scapegoat." The meaning of the latter, and his rôle in the ceremonial of the Day, is clear. Atonement has already been made for the sins of Priests and people by the sprinkling of the blood upon the Mercy Seat (verse 17) before the scapegoat enters on his part of the ceremony. The sins are already forgiven for which Aaron laying his hands upon the head of the " Goat for *Azazel* " confesses " all the iniquities of the children of Israel and all their transgressions, even all their sins," " putting them upon the head of the goat." (The laying on of hands in this connexion undoubtedly signifies the transferring of sin, although its meaning in the ceremonial of ordinary Sacrifices was a different one.[1] Bearing the sins of the people, the scapegoat was led into the wilderness (by the hand of a man that is in readiness), and there in " a solitary land " he was set free (verse 21, 22). The spiritual meaning is very beautiful and is often found in the Old Testament. Man needs not only that his sin should be forgiven, but also that the sin itself and its entail—the trammelling consequences, the shameful and paralysing remem-

[1] See page 64.

brance of it[1]—should be taken away out of his life.
The removal of forgiven sin, sending it right away
where it can no longer lay its hand upon us again, but
is excommunicated, banished to a solitary land where
no man dwells—that is the truth symbolized by this
part of the ceremony. The same thought with regard
to the physical uncleanness of leprosy is set forth by
the dipping of the live bird in the blood of the other
and letting him go into the open field." The
leprosy from which the leper is cleansed by the blood
of the first bird is carried by the living bird far away
where it can do no more harm. Parallels may be
found in Ps. ciii. 12 : " As far as the east is from the
west, so far hath He removed our transgressions from
us ; " in Mic. vii. 19 : " Thou wilt cast all their sins
into the depths of the sea " ; and most vividly in the
vision of Zech. v. 5–12, where the woman called
" Wickedness " is carried away from God's people
into the " land of Shinar," to be set there " in her
own place." So on the Day of Atonement the sins
of Israel were taken away from their midst and
banished from human society into the wilderness
where no man dwells. . The wilderness *is* inhabited—
not by men, however, but by evil spirits. It was
into the wilderness that Our Lord was led to be
"tempted of the devil" (Matt. iv. 1) ; " the unclean
spirit when he is gone out of the man passeth through
waterless places " (Matt. xii. 43). It is to one of these
evil spirits, *Azazel*, that this goat with its load of sin

[1] *Cf*. Dante's " Purgatorio " (Canto 33, ll. 91–99) ; when sin is forgiven and penance completed, its very remembrance is blotted out
by the waters of Lethe.
[2] See an article by A. Smythe Palmer in the "Guardian,"
January 27, 1909, " The Spirit-land in Hebrew Folk-lore."

was sent. *Azazel* is mentioned in the Book of Enoch (viii. 1, x. 4–8) as a fallen angel, one of the "sons of God" mentioned in Gen. vi. 1, who for a punishment was bound hand and foot in the desert. Lev. xvi. does not say what *Azazel* will do with the goat, and there is no hint that it was doomed to a cruel fate : it was only to be "let go." Later Jewish ritual, as described in the Mishna tractate "Yoma" (= "The Day"), ordered that it should be cast down a precipice, but no Biblical support can be found for the idea that this goat was made to suffer, still less to be killed, in expiation for the sins of others. Nor do the translations of the Greek and Latin versions give any countenance to the idea of vicarious punishment. In all the various forms of the Greek versions, as also in the Vulgate *caper emissarius,* from which came our English "scape [= "escape"] goat" (first found in the Great Bible of 1539), the original idea is preserved. It was probably under the influence of Calvinism that this original idea was lost and a meaning attached to the scapegoat very different from its etymological significance.[1]

(E) *Completion of the sacrifices.*—In accordance with the invariable rule [2] the two Sin Offerings of this Day were followed by Burnt Offerings of two rams (verses 3, 5)—one for the Priests and one for the people (verse 24). For this purpose, and also to mark that the penitential side of the Day was over, Aaron is directed at this point to put off the linen garments

---

[1] It is significant that the scapegoat is never mentioned in the New Testament as a type of Our Lord. The reference in the words "that taketh away [or "beareth"—R.V., margin] the sin of the world" (John i. 29 ; *cf.* 1 John iii. 5 ; Heb. x. 4–11) is to the Sacrificial Lamb. Holman Hunt's picture certainly represents present-day popular ideas rather than the original Biblical teaching.

[2] See p. 53.

and to put on his proper Priestly vestments (verses 23, 24). The instruction to burn the fat of the Sin Offering (verse 25) is perhaps misplaced ; at any rate, we should expect this to take place and the Sin Offerings to be completed before the High Priest changed his vestments. Since the whole of the Priesthood (including the High Priest himself) was included among the offerers in both Sin Offerings, there was no sacrificing Priest as distinct from the offerers to whom the rest of the flesh could be assigned, and therefore, in accordance with the rule laid down in Leviticus vi. 30 (*cf.* x. 18) the whole carcass of both Sin Offerings (except the fat) was burnt (verse 27—*saraph*, not *hiqtir*[1]) *without the camp.*[2]

So the ceremonies of the great Day were concluded. Before we leave this description of them, attention may be drawn to a point which illustrates one of the great principles of the atoning Sacrifices. Although it was the sins of the whole people for a whole year for which atonement was to be made on this Day, yet the victim was only one goat. We should have expected hecatombs of victims if any idea of compensation entered into the question of atonement. The difference between the Sacrifices on the Day of Atonement and the ordinary Sin Offering for an individual layman was not in the number of victims or the cost they represented—it lay only in the bringing of the blood into the nearer Presence of God.

---

[1] See p. 80.
[2] *Cf.* Heb. xiii. 11, 12, a passage which shows once more how exclusively the author looks to the Day of Atonement as the type of the Christian Sacrifice.

CHAPTER V

THE DOCTRINE OF ATONEMENT UNDER-LYING THE SACRIFICES

THE Hebrew *kipper*, translated "to make atonement," is the intensive form of a verb which in its primitive simple form, "*kaphar*," was obsolete probably before even the earliest part of the Hebrew Bible was written. Modern scholars are divided as to the original meaning of "*kaphar*." Some think it meant "to cover"; others—and these are probably in the majority—"to wipe."[1] The question is further complicated by the fact that the object of *kipper* is sometimes the *sin* (e.g. Ps. lxv. 3: "As for our transgressions, Thou shalt purge them away"; or in the passage Is. vi. 7: "Thy sin is purged"); sometimes *the face of the person sinned against*, as in Gen. xxxii. 20: "I will appease him [*lit.* "*kipper*" his face] with the present"; and sometimes, even the sinner himself (e.g. Deut. xxxii. 43; *cf.* Lev. xvi. 20, 33). Thus there are at least four possible suggestions as to the literal meaning underlying the use of *kipper* in connexion with the forgiveness of sin:

[1] E.g. Wellhausen, Deissman, and Brown-Driver-Briggs (Hebrew Lexicon, s.v.) favour "to cover"; Robertson Smith, Burney, Kennedy, "to wipe." The last (Hastings D. B. IV, 665) says "The most recent research seems to point in favour of the meaning 'to wipe off.'"

(1) To wipe away the sin. This is a very common idea in the Old Testament under various figures of speech, such as " to blot out," " wash away," " take away " sins (e.g. Ps. li. 9, lxxix. 9, cix. 14; Is. i. 18, xxvii. 9, xliv. 22; Neh. iv. 5; Jer. xviii. 23; Mic. vii. 19; John i. 29; Acts iii. 19, xxii. 16; Heb. ix. 26, x. 4; and akin to these are the many references to the cleansing of the sinner from his sin, e.g. Ps. li. 2; 1 John i. 7).

(2) To wipe the face of the offended person, i.e. to remove his anger, make his face shine with glad favour (cf. Num. vi. 25; Ps. xxxi. 16, lxvii. 1, lxxx. 3).

(3) To cover the sin so that it no more appears (see, e.g., Job xxxi, 33; Ps. xxxii. 1, lxxxv, 2; Jas. v. 20; 1 Pet. iv. 8); this meaning often works out very nearly the same as (1).

(4) To cover the face of a person so that he no longer sees the offence (cf. Job ix. 24; 1 Sam. xii. 3; Ps. x. 11, li. 9).

The uncertainty is increased when we find that the subject of *kipper* is sometimes God Himself (e.g. Deut. xxi. 8, xxxii. 43; 2 Chron. xxx. 18; Ps. lxv. 3), in which case if any trace of the original meaning lingers the thing covered or wiped must be the sin, i.e. meanings (1) or (3). In the terminology of the Priestly Code, however, the agent who " makes atonement " is always the Priest, and the verb *kipper*, with one or two exceptions, is intransitive or at any rate the object is unexpressed. The Priest " makes atonement " " for " or " on behalf of " the sacrificer " because of " or " on account of " his sin. Lev. xvii. 11 (" it is the blood . . . that makes atonement ") is not inconsistent with this, since it is understood in all Sacrifices that the Priest makes atonement by means of the blood. When used transitively, *kipper* is followed by an accusative of the thing " covered " or " wiped," which is in this case not the sin, but the offender, e.g. the Holy Place, the Tent of Meeting, the altar, etc. (Lev. xvi. 20, 33 ; Ezek. xliii. 20, 26, xlv. 20), or the land and the people (Deut. xxxii. 43).

If we may set aside as exceptional the instances just mentioned where a place or a person is the object of " *kipper*," we can reduce the possible meanings to two groups of ideas. The first group describes the effect as regards God the Holy One, and includes the ideas connected with *propitiation*. The Greek Bible consistently translates *kipper* by ἐξιλάόκεσθαι (= to propitiate, to appease), and this seems to have been the thought most prominently associated with the Hebrew word at about the third century B.C. Closely akin to this is the idea of *reconciliation*. *Kipper* implies a reconciling of estranged parties, without necessarily stating on which side the estrangement has existed, i.e. whether it is man who is to be reconciled with God, or God with man. Reconciliation is therefore a wider idea than propitiation, which implies an offended God. The second group describes the effect upon the sin, and the ideas then suggested are the *forgiveness*, the *removal*, or the *annulment* of the sin. In the case of either group the English translation " to make atonement " is misleading at the present day. In the sixteenth century it was used in its literal sense to make an " at-one-ment," i.e. to reconcile, and this would fit the first group of ideas (to propitiate). But nowadays "atonement" has come to imply the idea of reparation : we speak of an offender "atoning" for his faults. This is quite foreign to the Hebrew word. Further, the translation "to make atonement" overlooks entirely the second group of ideas (the forgiveness and annulment of the sin). It seems impossible, indeed, to find any one English equivalent which combines both senses, in which case it is perhaps best to leave the present E.V. translation "to make atonement" in possession, always remembering that both ideas (the reconciliation of the sinner and the undoing of the sin) must be included in the connotation of the phrase.

Up to this point we have been trying to get at the meaning of *kipper* in the general usage of the Old Testament. When we confine ourselves, as we may now do, to its particular use as a technical term in the Laws of Sacrifice, the matter becomes simpler in many ways.[1] In the first place, these Laws contain practically no idea of the Sacrifice being a means to appease the wrath of God. The Covenant relationship, although impaired, is not destroyed by the sins for which Sacrifices were provided. The sins, as we have seen, were almost entirely "unwitting" offences of a ceremonial nature. This being the case, such words as "propitiate" are misleading as applied to the sacrificial atonement, and we are left with the second meaning, to "purge" away the sin. Perhaps the best

[1] In one case incense is said to "make atonement" for the people (Numb. xvi. 46) when wrath had "gone out from the Lord." But it is not clear whether this was an *Offering* of incense any more than in Lev. xvi. 13, which is not an Offering, but, as it were, a veil between sinful man and God.

translation would be " to make a purging "—the
unexpressed object being the sin, and in a few cases
(see above) the thing or person polluted by the sin.
This does not mean that the idea of reconciliation is
entirely absent. The primary associations, however,
are those of " covering " or " wiping away " the sin,
" reconciliation " being a secondary and derivative idea.

How, then, was this " purging " effected by the
Sacrifice ? If we can find the answer to this question
we shall get at the root of the doctrine of Atonement
expressed in the Sacrifices of the Old Covenant. Let
us consider, first, the once common theory of a *substitu-
tionary* or *vicarious punishment*. The theory itself
was straightforward and simple enough. The penalty
of sin is death. " The soul that sinneth, it shall die."
In the sacrifice an animal victim was substituted for
the sinner, and its death accepted by God as a satisfaction for the sin.[1] With these assumptions the acts
of Sacrifice were interpreted as follows : By the laying
on of hands the sacrificer transferred his sin to the
victim, which was then put to death in his place. Its
blood was poured on the altar as a proof before God
that it had been slain ; its body was burnt as a polluted thing, or (some said) as a type of the everlasting
fire of Hell (*cf.* Is. lxvi. 24).

For the most part this conception of atonement was
based on an *a priori* view of punishment and forgiveness. In human society the offender is punished for
his misdeed and is then forgiven. The penalty is paid

[1] This theory has been so widely held that Kurtz in his " Sacrificial
Worship of the Old Testament " (written in 1862) speaks of it as
" the orthodox traditional view," and traces it back to the Jewish
Rabbis and the Early Christian Fathers (p. 123, English Translation).

and justice is satisfied.   But if the penalty is death
the offender is beyond the reach of forgiveness that
follows.   So the mercy of God provided as a substitute
for the sinner an animal victim on which the guilt and
the punishment were laid.   Did not God provide just
such a substitute in the ram which was offered instead
of Isaac ?   Again, in the only place where a meaning
is assigned to the laying on of hands in the Sacrifices,
viz. the case of the scapegoat (Lev. xvi. 21), is it not
clear that this ceremony symbolized the transferring
of the offence from the sinner to the victim ?   " Aaron
shall lay both his hands upon the head of the live
goat and confess over him all the iniquities of the
children of Israel . . . and he shall put them upon
the head of the goat."   To the first of these instances
we should reply that in the case of Isaac there was no
question of sin or punishment.   And to the second,
that the " scapegoat " was not offered in a Sacrifice
at all : the " atonement " for the sins of the people
had already been made *before* the " scapegoat " came
upon the scene.[1]

The evidence for this theory is doubtful ; the
objections to it are almost overwhelming.   (*a*) No
Sacrifice could make atonement for a sin that was
punishable by death.[2]   The very character of the
" sins " for which the Sin Offering was provided seems
decisive against the *poena vicaria*.   (*b*) There is nothing
in the regulations of the Sacrifices which gives any
support to the idea of propitiating an angry God.

[1] Robertson Smith, " Semites," pp. 422–443.   For a consideration
of Is. liii. 10, sometimes urged in favour of the *poena vicaria*, see
p. 102.
[2] See pp. 57 f.

(*c*) It may be taken as a sure guide in explaining the Sacrifices that it is to the peculiar ceremonial of each Offering we must look for an explanation of its special object and purpose. Now, in the Sin Offering, where the making of atonement is the chief object in view, the peculiar feature of the ceremonial appears not in the slaughtering of the victim, but in what was afterwards done with the blood. The slaughtering was the same in the Sin Offering as in the other Sacrifices. It is not in the death of the victim, but in the " putting " of the blood on the Horns of the Altar that we shall find the explanation of the means of atonement. This is borne out by Lev. xvii. 11 : " I have given it [i.e. the blood] to you *upon the altar* [i.e. as presented after the victim's death] to make atonement for your souls." The theory of a *poena vicaria* throws the whole emphasis on the act of slaughtering, since it makes the death the central feature of the Sacrifice. But as this part of the ceremonial was precisely the same in all the Sacrifices, we should expect them all to be alike in their atoning purpose and power : which, of course, was not the case. Again, if the killing of the victim occupied such a central position in the ceremonial of Sacrifice, we should expect to find the ceremonial rubrics of the Law laying particular stress upon this act. But, on the contrary, there is less detail prescribed in regard to this than to any of the other acts. It simply says the sacrificer shall kill it " before the Lord," " on the side of the altar northward," or " at the door of the Tent of Meeting " (Lev. i. 5, 11, iii. 2). The brevity of the instructions seems designed to pass by the killing as a feature necessary indeed, but only as a preliminary to the later and culminating acts, viz. the disposal of the carcass in the Burnt and Peace Offerings, and the presentation of the blood in the Sin Offering. Later Jewish thought also recognized the truth that " the sprinkling of the blood is the main point in sacrifice."[1] (d) Other features of the ceremonial also tell against this theory. If the laying on of hands signified the transferring of the sin, the body of the sin-bearing victim would be regarded as polluted and accursed. But, on the contrary, even in the Sin Offering it is a " most holy thing." Its touch " consecrates " anyone who comes in contact with it, so that he must wash before he goes back to secular life (Lev. vi. 27, 28). As being " most holy " it could be eaten by the Priests alone. The burning of the fat, so far from being destructive or penal, was the means of sending it up " in sweet smoke " to Jehovah, for whom it makes a " sweet savour of acceptance " (Lev. iv. 31). The use of the technical word *hiqtir* as distinct from *saraph* is itself enough to dispose of the idea that the burning denoted a penal destruction. Lastly, if the killing represented Divine punishment for sin, the true expression of this idea in the ceremonial would be for the Priest, as the representative of God, to kill the victim. But there is no evidence that the Priest *qua* Priest ever slew the animal : where he did so, it was either as sacrificer or as representing and included among the sacrificers, e.g. on the Day of Atonement.

[1] Maimonides (a Spanish Jew born at Cordova in A.D. 1135), " De Sacrificantibus," i, 2, § 6 ; quoted in Westcott, " Hebrews," p. 269.

The victim was always killed either by the sacrificer himself, or by someone representing him.[1]

These facts are decisive as against any view of the transference of guilt and punishment from the sinner to the victim. But what are we to put in its place ?

Let us first review the facts to be taken into consideration in answering this question.

We shall naturally take as our starting point the only passage in the Law which suggests an interpretation of the ceremonial and points to the means by which the atonement was made : " The life [= "soul," R.V., margin] of the flesh is in the blood : and *I have given it to you upon the altar to make atonement for your souls : for it is the blood that maketh atonement by reason of the life*" (Lev. xvii. 11). It should be noted that this interpretation is not given on purpose to explain the ceremonial. The Law gives no explanation of the meaning of its regulations. They were symbolic and had a meaning of their own, the knowledge of which is taken for granted. The immediate purpose of these words is to give a reason why blood was a forbidden food. The " soul " of the flesh is in the blood ; for that reason the blood upon the altar makes atonement for your souls (the same word— *nephesh*—is used in both places in the Hebrew) ; and therefore blood may not be used as a food. This is a great departure from those heathen Semitic Sacrifices in which the drinking of the blood was an essential feature. In this passage the blood, as the *living life that has passed through death* (for that is what is meant by the " blood "[2]) is said to make atonement.

[1] See p. 64.   [2] See p. 68.

Now, let us take up another point in this verse.
What is involved in the words : " upon the altar " ?
We saw (p. 71) that there were two distinct purposes
for which the blood was applied to the altar : to
consecrate or reconsecrate the altar itself and to
present the blood to God. We speak of these as
distinct purposes, but possibly there was once some
unifying idea, now lost to us, which linked them
together. In the great Sin Offerings of the Day of
Atonement both purposes were included in the
" sprinkling " of the blood : the High Priest " offered "
the blood (Heb. ix. 7 ; cf. 25. ; and ? Lev. xvi. 6, 11),
and the blood " cleansed " the Tabernacle (Heb. ix.
23 ; cf. Lev. xvi. 16, 17, 19). If, however, the latter
purpose was ever attached to the ordinary Sin Offering,
all trace of it has completely disappeared in the
regulations for its ceremonial and in the descriptions
of it in the history of worship.   The blood was certainly
" presented on the altar in the Burnt " Offering (Lev. i. 5 ;
cf. Ps. l. 13) and the Peace Offering (Lev. vii. 33),
and Heb. ix. 7 shows that, in the Sin Offering also, the
" sprinkling " or " putting " of the blood, signified
the offering of it to God.   This point is of such importance that it is well to draw attention to it, although
it has been generally taken for granted.   It would be
possible, however, to make out a case for the contention that on the Day of Atonement (and by inference
in the ordinary Sin Offerings) the " cleansing " of the
holy places and of the worshippers was the only object in
view in the ceremonial use of the blood, and that no
Godward intention of Offering attached to it.   This
contention, if made good, would have a most important

bearing on the doctrine of Atonement. It would affect the New Testament as well, for the sprinkling of the blood on the Day of Atonement is made the type of the self-oblation of Jesus Christ in the Heavenly Sanctuary (Heb. ix.). There is a cleansing of the " heavenly things themselves " by the Blood of Christ as well as of their earthly copies on the Day of Atonement. But, also, as the High Priest offered the blood of others year by year in the Holy Place, so Christ offers Himself in the Heavenly Sanctuary (Heb. ix. 25). In both Covenants there is an " Offering " of the blood to make atonement.

We have now reached a second stage in our investigation. In the atoning Sacrifices the blood—the life that has been laid down in death but still lives—is offered to God upon the altar, and as so offered cleanses the altar and the worshipper. A third fact emerges from the answer to the question : Whose life is represented by the blood ? The blood of bulls and goats ? Yes ; but was that all ? What was implied in the relation of the sacrificer to his victim? What was symbolized by the laying on of hands ? We have seen (pp. 18–21, 63) that the connexion between offerer and victim was so close that it could in no unreal sense be called an identity, and that the laying on of hands symbolically represented the identification. In symbol the worshipper laid down his own life ; in symbol it was the worshipper's own " blood " which the Priest " put " on the Horns of the Altar or " sprinkled " on the Mercy Seat. The goat or bullock was not a victim entirely " other " to the man who offered it ; the Offering was not merely " vicarious " in the sense

of being made instead of, in the place of (*vice*), another.
The victim was not a substitute but a representative,
a deputy, for that other, and in symbol identified with
him : " He shall lay his hand upon the head of the
victim, and it shall be accepted *for* [ל the *dativus com-
modi*] him, and *make atonement for* [על " on behalf of "]
him " (Lev. i. 4).   It was *the sacrificer's own life*
which first was laid down in death, and then " upon
the altar " made atonement for him ; *his own " soul "
in a further and higher stage of spiritual development
makes atonement for itself—himself—in his present
sin-laden, sin-polluted state.*   The perfected " risen "
self redeems the sinful self ; his own repentance carried
to its completion through a death unto self, self-will,
sin, earns his forgiveness.

The Christian will say, Who is sufficient unto these
things ? Do not we also need someone other and
better than ourselves yet wholly one with us, to be
the victim we offer ? Such for each one and all
mankind is the Lamb of God that taketh away the
sin of the world.   And that other yet one and the
same with ourselves who is perfectly represented in
the Son of Man, was partially and typically represented
by the animal victim in the old Sacrifices.

The blood signifies, therefore, the sacrificer's own
life seen in its ideal perfection in that other yet the
same life which has gone through death.   The sacrificer must perforce be represented by another for
(1) the atonement could only be effected through a
dying, a life wholly surrendered with nothing kept
back, and (2) the life was to be " presented " to God ;
but who would dare present his own life in its *actual*

sin-defiled state to the Holy God ? Sin is repeatedly compared by the Prophets to adultery : it is unfaithfulness to One to Whom man owes himself altogether soul and body. If the wife commits adultery with another, it is not enough for her simply to return to her true allegiance. She dare not bring back and offer to her husband a polluted self. So the sinner, after his sin, dare not offer to God a polluted life ; yet it is only by offering himself again to God that he can cleanse and reconsecrate his life. This was the dilemma to meet which the Sacrifices were provided by God under the Old Covenant as the type to be fulfilled in the New. All speaks of Divine Love and Mercy. The desire of God is that the sinner may be restored to the Covenant Sonship from which he has fallen. The system of atoning Sacrifices was a provision of God for bringing back the Prodigal to the Father's Home. " *I have given you* the blood . . . to make atonement for your souls." God will provide Himself a Lamb.

There remains yet one more stage in our reconstruction of the ideas of atonement underlying the atoning Sacrifices, viz. to bring together our third fact (that the blood is the sacrificer's own life), and the second (the nature and meaning of the altar transaction). What was done with the blood and what did it mean ? We saw that the " putting " of the blood upon the Horns of the Altar in an ordinary Sin Offering signified the " presenting " of it to God, and that the " sprinkling " on the Mercy Seat and the " putting " on the Horns of the Altar of Incense and the Altar of Burnt Offering on the Day of Atonement signified, in addition to this, the cleansing touch of the blood upon the Holy Places and upon the people whose Offering it was ; further, that perhaps (though unexpressed) the same cleansing of altar and people was meant to be effected by the ordinary Sin Offerings. Can we get beyond this ? We hinted above at a possible link—known perhaps to the Jews of old, but since forgotten—which might connect the two apparently distinct and separate ideas. I will venture tentatively to suggest such a link. We have repeatedly been reminded of the fact that to the Jewish Law " cleansing " and " consecrating " were not two but one thing, the obverse and reverse of one single act by which a thing or person is withdrawn from the general secular world of things " common or unclean " into the circle of " holy " things, hallowed and consecrated to God. Every " cleansing " is *ipso facto* a " hallowing " or consecrating ; and, vice versa, every " consecrating " is *ipso facto* a " cleansing." Now, what is meant by " consecrating " a thing to God ? Is it not just handing it over to Him—" dedicating " in the etymological sense of " making over " to God : in other words, " presenting," " offering " to Him ? The very act of presenting a thing to God consecrates it and therefore " cleanses " it. Presenting, consecrating, cleansing are, after all, just one and the same thing viewed from different angles, and to " make atonement " covers all three intentions. So it is the blood upon the altar that makes atonement because, being presented to God and dedicated to Him, it is thereby hallowed, cleansed from all impurities contracted in the world and consecrated to be a possession of God. Remembering that this " blood " was (in symbol) the sacrificer's own life : that he belonged to a people called out from among the common " Gentile " herd to be a nation " holy unto the Lord," a peculiar treasure unto Him from among all peoples (Exod. xix. 5), which had been once and for all cleansed and consecrated by the " blood of the Covenant " (Exod. xxiv. 8 ; *cf.* Heb. ix. 18–22) : and that the effect of sin is to pollute and desecrate the sinner : we see that to " make atonement " means in effect to restore to his proper " nearness " to Jehovah one who has lost it by an offence. He was " far off," but he is now brought " near " again. It is of interest to notice that the very word translated " to present " (*hiqrib*) means literally " to bring near." The difference of ceremonial between the different Sin Offerings acquires a fresh interest in this light. " Holiness " admitted of degrees : there were degrees of spiritual " nearness " to Jehovah which were symbolized by degrees of physical nearness. The individual lay Israelite was admitted into the Fore-Court of the Tabernacle, from which the heathen was excluded. In the Sin Offering the Horns of the Great Altar of Burnt Offering " before the Lord " at the door of the Tabernacle represented the limit of his approach to God ; and it was to that degree of " Holiness " he was restored by the blood of the Sin Offering " put " on the Horns of this Altar. The " anointed Priest " and the Priestly nation as a community (which included, of course, the Priesthood as well as the laity) were admitted within the " first Tabernacle " (i.e. the Holy Place), and for them the blood was " put " on the Horns of the Altar of Burnt

Incense, which stood " before the veil " and was the link between the Holy Place and the Holy of Holies.[1] Lastly, on the Day of Atonement, which was a sort of annual renewal of the first dedication of the people (the inaugural Covenant Sacrifice of Exod. xxiv. 1–8), Priesthood and people were restored to the closest approach to God permitted to earthly men— the Holy of Holies and the Presence above the Mercy Seat.

It will be seen that in this light the sacrificial atonement is brought back to something like its original and etymological sense (" at-one-ment "), and also into close relation with the idea of " reconciliation " (cf. Eph. ii. 13, 18 ; 1 Pet. iii. 18). An estrangement has intervened between God and man and they are brought together again. But it is man who has estranged himself from God. The estrangement is not on God's side. It is God Who seeks for reconciliation and provides the means for an at-one-ment. There is no propitiating or pacifying of God in the Sin Offering. There is no thought of a " satisfaction " or " recompense " made by man ; far less of a quantitative satisfaction proportioned to the number or enormity of the offences.

At the risk of some repetition it will repay us to go over the ceremonial of the Sin Offering again in the light of these ideas. Of the laying on of hands enough

---

[1] So closely in fact was it connected with the Holy of Holies that some passages (e.g. Ex. xxx. 6, xl. 5 ; 1 Kings vi. 22) gave the impression that it was actually inside the veil. This accounts for the descriptions in Rev. viii. 3, ix. 13, xi. 1, and the apparent mistake of Heb. ix. 3. I say " apparent " because in any case the verse reveals an extremely intimate knowledge of the Jewish worship.

has been said. We have touched also upon the slaughtering as expressing self-renunciation in its extremest form. He who would be dedicated to God must *first* die to self. The self-regarding life can never be the dedicated life. Self-love is innate and inbred in fallen human nature. Sin is the following of self-love ; and the only salvation, the only redemption, from sin—the only undoing of sin—lies in its complete opposite, an absolute self-surrender, a self-sacrifice, so entire that no self-regarding element is left in it, i.e. in a death unto self. So the sacrificer in symbol dies to himself. *This death is essential for the undoing of sin*. It has been the fashion sometimes, in reaction from the theory of Sacrifice described at the opening of this chapter, to run to the opposite extreme of treating the killing of the victim as a mere incident of no great intrinsic importance. This is a great mistake. " Apart from shedding of blood there is no remission." The offering of the blood still within the body of the victim would represent a life unsurrendered ; to offer some only of the blood drawn from its body would typify the surrender of but a part of the life. The *entire* surrender of the *whole* life is essential before it can be given over to God, and therefore nothing less than the death of the victim is required, though but a little of its blood was needed to " put " on the Horns of the Altar. But as soon as it has been laid down in death the life acquires a new power and a new value. It is in the Pauline spiritual sense a " risen life." The blood " speaketh " of penitence and surrender to God (Heb. xii. 24).

But, when the death is accomplished, the atonement

is not yet made.   It is not effected by the death of
the sinner, necessary though that death may be, as
a prior condition.   It is *through* a death unto sin and
by a life unto God that atonement is made ; and it is
to the latter—the dedication of the surrendered life—
that we now turn.   We notice that in the symbolic
acts of the Sacrifice this was the work not of the
sacrificer but of the Priest.   The sacrificer has done
all that is even ideally possible for him to do : he has
loved not his life unto death.   But the atonement is
not yet wrought—the sinner cannot restore *himself* to
" holiness."   For this he needs a mediator, and therefore at this point the Priest comes in to make the
penitence effectual by offering to God the surrendered
life and so to consecrate and cleanse it.[1]

Before concluding this chapter we may briefly
compare the idea of atonement above described with
the *poena vicaria*.   Perhaps the chief point of difference
will be found in the shifting of the centre of gravity
from the death of the victim (in the *poena vicaria*
theory) to the presenting of the blood.   But while it
is true to say that we regard the presenting of the
blood (the reconsecration of the cleansed life) as the
culmination of the Sin Offering, and the victim's
death as a preliminary condition, we must again
emphasize the fact that the latter is an *indispensable*
condition.   The two theories have been described as
follows :   while the *poena vicaria* theory may be compared to a circle having for its centre the death, our view
likens the Sin Offering to an ellipse having for its

---

[1] With the whole of this paragraph *cf.* W. Milligan, " Resurrection
of Our Lord," pp. 274–280.

two foci the death and the presenting of the blood. The latter comparison perhaps over-emphasizes the slaughtering, but it has the merit of recognizing it as an essential element in the Sacrifices. It safeguards the double side of atonement in the same way as St. Paul does in regard to the Christian fulfilment of the Sin Offering, when he says of Christ, the Sacrificer, Priest, and Victim, that we are reconciled by His " death " and " saved by His [risen] Life " (Romans v. 8) ; with which we may compare *ib*. vi. i--ii, where Christians are described as so identified with Christ by Baptism that, united with His Sacrificial Death and Risen Life (= Blood), they also are " dead indeed unto sin " but " alive unto God " (i.e. reconsecrated). The fact that St. Paul is not speaking in sacrificial terms, or indeed with the Jewish Sacrifices before his mind, makes all the more impressive the close agreement between his line of thought and this interpretation of the Sin Offering and of atonement in general.

There is another point in reference to which we may compare the two theories of atonement, viz. the *vicariousness* of the Sacrifices. No interpretation of the Jewish Sacrifices can get rid of this element. The fact is indisputable that the animal suffered death and *its* blood was presented ; this, and not anything done or suffered by the sacrificer, constituted the Sacrifice on its " outward and visible " side. But there is a great difference between the idea of *mere substitution* —the one of two quite unrelated lives being arbitrarily substituted for the other—and the idea of *representation*, in which a close union existing between the two

gives the one a kind of right to represent the other,
as e.g., one brother might stand for another. And such
a union we have seen to exist between sacrificer and
victim. It was his property, it represented his labour,
it had been bred and brought up by him, it would
have supplied his life-sustaining food, and as such it
received from him, by the laying on of hands, the
right to stand for him. Subject to this reservation
the Sacrifice *was* vicarious. But, as we have seen, it
was vicarious as the *vicarious offering of a risen life*,
rather than the *vicarious suffering of a penal death*.
What does this amount to when we come to think it
out further ? It must be a risen life that is offered and
there must be a death before there can be a risen life :
the risen life is only risen because it has first died.
That " *must* " is the Divine decree because of sin.
Does not this give back to the death of the victim
something of the penal character we have taken from
it ? Undeniably it does : *suffering unto death is a
penal condition for the sinner's reunion with the Holy
God* ; and, where this suffering is undergone by one
on behalf of another, that is a vicarious enduring of
punishment. What we have gained over the theory
of the *poena vicaria* is that we have found the suffering
to be a means, *a preliminary condition*, to that which constituted the atonement (viz. the rededication of new life
to God) rather than the end. The death is not regarded
in itself as a satisfaction, a propitiation, an atonement.
From the moral standpoint this makes an immeasurable
difference between the two theories of atonement.

It is in the light of such thoughts as these
that we must regard the idea of vicarious suffering

and its redemptive value, especially as it appears in Is. liii.: "He was wounded for our transgressions . . . The Lord hath laid on Him the iniquity of us all." His soul (= life = blood) was made a "*Trespass Offering*" (see R.V. margin); not a "*Sin Offering*" (as in the text of R.V.) for the simple reason that the Sin Offering did not exist at the time this chapter was written. It is also possible that the word *aṣam* in this passage is not used in its sacrificial sense at all, but with its earlier non-sacrificial meaning of a payment made in compensation for an offence.[1] But although "he was cut off out of the land of the living," there is a risen life and a glorious future for Him beyond His suffering and death. "He shall see his seed, he shall prolong his days, and the pleasure of the Lord shall prosper in his hand. He shall see of the travail of his soul and shall be satisfied."

.   .   .   .   .

Before we pass from the Jewish to the Christian Sacrifice we may briefly trace the development of the pre-Christian idea of atonement in the Hebrew and Jewish Sacrifices. Four stages are seen to emerge:

(1) The earliest form in which the idea seems to exist and express itself is in Semitic heathenism. In very early times, yet late enough, however, for the childlike gladness of primitive Semitic worship to have been troubled by sorrow and suffering, the feeling crept into men's minds that something had caused an estrangement between their god and themselves.

See p. 45.

The sharing of the victim's blood, which was the common life-bond between them, was then held to have obliterated *ipso facto* any strained relations. Feeding together proved the friendship to have been re-established and the union restored. In this light communion presupposed and implied atonement (in the sense of reconciliation) rather than effected it. Whatever quarrel may have existed, both parties desired its removal; they were already friends at heart before the common meal cemented the reunion.

(2) With the entry of the *Gift idea* into Hebrew Sacrifice, and the deepening sense of Divine disfavour, undoubtedly at first there arose the picture of an angry God to be propitiated by a gift just as a subject might try to appease an offended monarch by a present. So David says : " If it be the Lord that hath stirred thee up against me, let Him accept an offering "— *lit. " smell a minḥah "* (1 Sam. xxvi. 19) *cf.* Gen. viii. 21 " The Lord smelt the sweet savour " (of Noah's Burnt Offerings) " and said, I will not curse the ground any more for man's sake." The gift might be the fruit of the field (*minḥah* : see 1 Sam. xxvi. 19, quoted above ; also *ibid.* iii. 14) or the flesh of a Burnt Offering (Gen. viii. 21).

(3) But gradually the supreme sanctity of the life-containing and life-conveying blood brought about the recognition that the highest gift of all was the " blood "; and as nothing less than the highest would suffice, so it was especially in the presenting of the blood that atonement was effected after the estrangement caused by sin. The appearance of the " Gift idea " created entirely different associations in connexion with the

blood of the Sacrifices. The original purpose of the blood as the bond of union between the God and His worshippers remained as a survival in the Sacrifices for inaugurating a " Covenant " (Exod. xxiv.) and for the " cleansing " of the Tabernacle by blood on the Day of Atonement. It appeared also in the power of the blood to " make holy " the thing or person it touched, e.g. in the restoration of a leper and the consecration of a Priest. But the later idea of the "life-blood " as the most precious gift to be presented to the Lord quite overshadowed the older, just as the " Gift idea " came to be the most prominent intention of Jewish Sacrifice in general.

(4) Lastly, so far as the victim was in some sort identified with the sacrificer emerges the thought that this life presented in propitiation for a sin is the sinner's own life, which by the very act of presentation is " brought near " to God, reconciled, reunited, and restored to the Priest's or the layman's degree of nearness to God. The sinner's life, as represented by the victim's blood, is touched by the sanctifying altar or Mercy Seat, and so is reunited to God—reconse-crated. And, conversely, on the Day of Atonement, the " Blood " as being a risen life dead to sin but alive unto God, reconsecrates the sacred spot which has been desecrated by contact with sin. So, while the offering of the best a man has to give (his own life) satisfies Divine justice and holiness—the only sense in which a " propitiation " can be understood in the highest development of the Jewish Sacrifices—the mode of presentation (i.e. the ceremonial use of the blood) reconsecrates the life, reconciles, reunites it to God.

PART II

THE SACRIFICE OF THE NEW COVENANT

CHAPTER VI

COMPARISON OF THE OLD AND THE NEW

MOST of us, I suppose, if told to compare the Jewish Sacrifices with the Christian Sacrifice would at once think of the points of contrast familiar to us from the Epistle to the Hebrews. But the same Epistle, it is to be noted, in the very act of contrasting the two, implies and draws out points of likeness. Modern controversies have drawn attention, disproportionately perhaps, to the contrasts, and left the spiritual side of the old Sacrifices too much in the background. A study of the opening part of the Sermon on the Mount should correct this one-sided valuation. The New Covenant is not a reversal but a fulfilment of the Old. There is a true line of continuity between them. The same truth is embodied in both : perfectly and fully in the New, but present, or at least foreshadowed, in the Old. It is to this side of the comparison we will first address ourselves.

We have already had occasion in the previous chapters to anticipate some of these points of likeness.

At the outset, in Chapter I,[1] the primitive notion of communion with God through the drinking of blood was seen to be present, though dormant, all through the historical period of the Jewish religion to revive in a " heavenly and spiritual manner " in Christianity. Then we saw how the Gift idea developed until some at least of the higher spirits among the Jewish saints realized that the only perfect gift is the gift of ourselves, and that in true Sacrifice the offerer must offer *himself*, i.e. sacrificer and victim, the giver and the thing given, must be personally identical.[2] Again this self-oblation was expressed under two forms in the Old Covenant, and in either case the latent spiritual meaning becomes explicit in the New. In the Burnt Offering it was characteristically expressed by the burning of the carcass, which went up in " sweet smoke " to Jehovah. In the New Testament the thought and the phraseology are taken over in the description of the God-dedicated life and its virtues as an " odour of a sweet smell " (Phil. iv. 18 ; *cf.* Eph. v. 2 ; 2 Cor. ii. 15). In all the Sacrifices, but particularly in the Sin Offering, the self-oblation was expressed in the offering of blood as a life first surrendered in death, then received back by a Resurrection and rededicated as a Risen Life. And this, too, is expressed in the Christian religion by the symbolism of immersion in Baptism, signifying the death unto sin and the new birth unto Righteousness, and in the continued stress on the need of self-mortification before a man can dedicate his life to God. In several of the details also we have seen in the Old an anticipation

1 See pp. 13, 14.   2 See, e.g. pp. 16–22.

of the New; e.g. the order of the Sacrifices (Sin, Burnt, Peace Offering),[1] the relative importance of the death and the oblation as set forth in the ceremonial acts (p. 67), the meaning of the " Table of the Lord " (p. 78). The very use of the word " blood " in the New Testament at once links up the New Covenant with the Sacrificial System of the Old. We do well then to remind ourselves first of the essential unity or continuity between the Jewish and the Christian Sacrifice. Here also Jesus Christ came not to destroy but to fulfil the Law—to take up and carry on to their complete perfection the spiritual ideas contained, though partially, and expressed, though imperfectly, under the older forms. We shall see that Hebrews ix. is quite as much imbued with the identity as with the contrast between the Day of Atonement and the Death and Priesthood of Jesus. Sacrifice is inherent in the New Covenant as in the Old, and in both the same lines of truth are discerned by eyes open to the vision revealed by Him.

There are one or two points with regard to this continuity which call for further notice. The most familiar of all contrasts between the Old and the New is the many Sacrifices of the former and the one Sacrifice of the latter. The comparison is applied generally to the endless repetition of the Old Sacrifices, as against the " one oblation of Himself once offered." But it applies also to the many different kinds of Offering in the Old, the meal Offering, Burnt, Peace, Sin, and Trespass Offerings. The one Sacrifice of Christ gathers up and embraces all the different

[1] See pp. 52 f.

meanings and purposes of the former many. But this is an advance in the line of continuity rather than a reversal of the old. And to a certain extent it was foreshadowed by the frequent combination of Sin, Burnt, and Peace Offerings on the same occasion ; as if to acknowledge that the meaning of Sacrifice was only partly expressed in any one of the three by itself, and for the whole meaning we must look to one complex offering combining all of them.[1] Every aspect and every intention of Sacrifice is included in the One Sacrifice of the New Covenant : the self-oblation for the purpose of making atonement (corresponding to the offering of the blood in the Old Sacrifices, Lev. xvii. 11); the self-oblation with the simple intention of self-dedication[2] (answering to the burning of the carcass) ; the common meal shared by the sacrificer, his friends, the Priest, and God Himself. So the characteristic intentions of the Sin and Burnt and Peace Offerings are here combined in one single Sacrifice. There is another point of likeness and continuity which I must ask the reader to take for granted until it comes up for fuller discussion :[3] the acts which make up the complete drama of Sacrifice follow the same order in the Old and New Covenants. We shall see how the ceremonial acts described in Chapter III are repeated in the same order, no longer as ceremonial symbols, but as actual realities, in the Life, Death, Resurrection, and Ascension of Jesus Christ and through the Eucharist in His Body, the Church.

[1] See p. 54.
[2] Heb. x. 5 describes the offering of " a perfect life irrespective of any thought of sin " (Westcott's " Commentary," *ad loc.*, p. 310).
[3] See Chapter VIII.

Let us turn now to the *differences* between the two Sacrifices, i.e. the points in regard to which the first was so inadequate that it had to be " taken away " in order for the second to be " established." At once we think of the complete change in all the outward and visible side, the " ceremonial " expression. The Christian Church has entirely discarded animal Sacrifice. And while there is some outward as well as inner spiritual likeness between the victim's death in the Jewish Temple and on Calvary, there was this paramount contrast. In the Death on Calvary there was something which made its repetition unnecessary and therefore impossible. Equally also there was something in the Jewish Sacrifices which made it not only possible but essential that the Offering must be repeated again and again. The underlying difference is, of course, that Calvary was the Perfect Sacrifice —perfect in itself as a Sacrifice, but perfect also as securing finally and for ever the objects for which it was made on our behalf. The old Sacrifices, on the other hand, were imperfect in themselves, and therefore necessarily unable to " make perfect them that draw nigh " (Heb. x. 1).

The perfect Sacrifice must be perfect in all the elements which go to make it up. Its agents, the Sacrificer, the Victim, and the Priest, must be fitted each to carry out his part : inwardly in heart with the right intention in the right degree, and also in outward qualification duly authorized to fulfil his office. The Sacrificer must be within the Covenant, the Victim worthy of its offerer, the Priest properly called and appointed. Lastly, the external setting of the Sacrifice, the " ceremonial acts," must be such as are worthy and adequate to express in its fullness the inner intention. This is an important consideration. The moralizing of Sacrifice does not lie in " dropping the outward expression and accentuating solely the inward act of will . . . it is essential to Sacrifice that it should be the outward act by which the inward intention is realized."[1] Consider now how the Old Sacrifices fell short of these requirements.

(1) " Self-surrender, self-dedication " : these we saw to be the inward intentions of true Sacrifice. But the Jewish sacrificer at his best was but dimly conscious that this was what God asked of him ; and even so far as he understood it, the best he could give was a very far from a perfect surrender.

(2) The Priest must be a true Priest. The Aaronic Priest was himself a sinful man and needed such a Priest to be his own mediator (Heb. v. 3). His Priesthood was divinely authorized indeed (Heb. v. 4) but only until such time as it should be merged in a Priest of a higher order (Heb. vii. 11–18).

(3) The victim must be not merely perfect of its kind but also of a kind spiritually equivalent to the sacrificer. But an animal life, however perfect of its kind, could never be sufficient to represent a human life : it is of a lower order. Again, the victim must actually and entirely represent the offerer's own self —not partly represent it, nor even fully represent just a part of himself and not the whole. Does it not follow from these requirements that the Perfect Sacrifice cannot be a vicarious Offering ? But with the Jews

[1] Scott Holland in " Sanday Priesthood and Sacrifice," p. 85.

the life laid down was not only something else's life instead of the sacrificer's. It was not even voluntarily surrendered, but forcibly and brutally taken. How could such an action be an adequate outward expression of the voluntary surrender of one's own life ? At the best it was but an acted parable of Sacrifice, not the real thing itself. It was inevitable, therefore, that when the true meaning of Sacrifice was revealed, not merely in vision or in word, but in the object-lesson of realized fact, the offering of animal victims should cease to have any longer a place in the worship of God. The Sacrifices of the Old Covenant continually reminded the worshippers of sins : in them was an " ἀνάμνησις ἁμαρτιῶν " (Heb. x. 3), because they never really made atonement for them. But when we share in the Sacrifice of the Covenant we are reminded (" this do εἰς τὴν ἐμὴν ἀνάμνησιν "—1 Cor. xi. 24, 25) of the Lamb of God which *taketh away* the sin of the world. So, in common with the Covenant to which they belonged, the old Sacrifices suggested needs and aroused desires which they could not fulfil or satisfy, and by that very fact they pointed forward to the better Sacrifice of the " Lamb of God."

CHAPTER VII

THE CHRISTIAN SACRIFICE: CHRIST AND HIS CHURCH

WHEN we speak of the Sacrifice of the New Covenant our thoughts turn to One Person, Jesus Christ, and to one place and moment, Golgotha and the Crucifixion. But, right though it is, this does not in itself contain the whole of the truth. Questions at once arise and demand an answer. Is there no place for the Resurrection and the Ascension in the Christian Sacrifice? In what sense, if any, may we speak of a Sacrifice in the Holy Eucharist? Again, in what sense and by what means does the Sacrifice offered by Jesus Christ become to each one of us " *my* Sacrifice " and to all of us corporately " the Church's Sacrifice " ? Have we not seen that no true Sacrifice can be vicarious ? The offering of Himself by Jesus Christ may truly be for *Him* a Perfect Sacrifice, but how can it be such for *me* ? The answer to the last three questions takes us right into the heart of deep mysteries—the Incarnation and the Atonement. What is meant by the union betwixt Christ and the Church which is His Body ? In what sense have we each a personal distinctness apart from the common humanity, which is all " summed up " in Him ? We have only to put

together the two truths—(1) that He offered a Sacrifice
for sins, (2) that He was sinless and did not need to
offer such a Sacrifice for Himself—to see that He and
His Sacrifice are representative of mankind. He is
not isolated from us, and merely setting before us an
object-lesson of Perfect Sacrifice. We are in Him,
and that Sacrifice is ours in being His. But does this
mean that, after all, we share in it vicariously, by
some sort of more or less unreal " imputation " ? Is
there nothing corresponding to it that has to be
fulfilled in *our* lives before that Sacrifice can be said
to be in the true sense completely ours ? Without
following out in detail this line of thought, may I
summarize what seems to be the issue of it ? Such
a summary statement is necessary here as a postulate
to certain sides of our view of the Christian Sacrifice.

In the Manhood of Jesus Christ is summed up the
whole human race. He is not just one among many,
a son of man, but One in Whom all others are represented, *the* Son of Man. When, therefore, He offers
His Sacrifice to the Father, He does so not in our
stead, but on our behalf.[1] We may perhaps compare
Him with the minister in public worship who offers
the prayer of spoken words not *instead of* but on *behalf
of* the congregation. If he were acting instead of the
people, all that would matter would be his personal
sincerity and faith. But because he speaks on their
behalf their co-operation is demanded : each and all
must pray with him, must be filled with the spirit of
the prayer he utters. So if Jesus Christ offers the

---

[1] The reader will remember that the regular preposition in the
New Testament in this connexion is not ἀντί (instead of) but ὑπέρ
(on behalf of).

Sacrifice on our behalf we too must do what He does.
. . . But we cannot. The vision of the ideal is
beyond our ken, the intention beyond our reach ; still
less possible is its fulfilment in act and suffering. And
yet when God sees within us, at the very bottom of
our personality, a tiny seed-germ of Faith, accepting
this Sacrifice as our own, and therefore desiring to
make it *actually* our own, He is ready here and now
to account it ours and to respond to it with His gifts
of Forgiveness, Reconsecration, and Reunion—the
fruits of the Sin, the Burnt, and the Peace Offering.
So shall we be ever strengthened until, our manhood
made perfect even as His, we can ourselves offer
the Perfect Sacrifice.

But there is something more than a difference of
time between the fulfilment of Sacrifice in Christ and
in us. We are sinners, He is sinless ; and the *sinner
can never make atonement for his own sin*. Even could
he live the life of perfect dedication, what would that
be but simply what he would have owed to his Maker
if he had never sinned ? It is the Sinless One, living
the life of perfect dedication *at the utmost cost*, of
suffering even unto death, who pays the price of sin.
The Sacrifice of Christ alone can be called in the true
sense the Sin Offering. Even were our Sacrifice like
His in outward form it could not bear this fruit : it
would not be a " propitiation for sin." Ours is the
Burnt Offering of dedicated life which follows upon
and is made possible and acceptable only through the
preceding Sin Offering. The spiritual order is the
same as in the Old Covenant,[1] and again, as of old,

[1] See p. 52.

the response to Sin and Burnt Offering comes in the Peace Offering with the call to fellowship with God, with the Priest and with one another in Christ Jesus. He it is Who offers the Peace-Offering and bids God and man to join with Him in the Feast.

So we reach a wider view of the Christian Sacrifice : it is the Sacrifice of Jesus Christ taken up and carried on by His Body, the Church, as her Burnt Offering of dedicated life and her Peace Offering of the Eucharistic Feast. All three types of Offering are fulfilled in Him : the Sin Offering by His Death and Priestly entrance to the Heavenly Holy of Holies to offer the Blood upon the Mercy Seat (Heb. ix. 11, 12, 23–26) ; the Burnt Offering by the " Offering of His Body." Heb. x. 5–10 (see Westcott's note *ad loc.*) in lifelong dedication, " to do the Will of Him that sent Me " ; the Peace Offering (in its characteristic feature the Fellowship with God) through the Ascension and taking of His Manhood to sit at the right hand of the Father on the Throne of His Glory. As the glorified Son returns to the Fellowship with the Father, which He had before the world was, He brings with Him His Manhood, uniting it into the same Fellowship with God.

In *all* this the Church, which is His Body, has a share in virtue of Her Union with Her Lord. This Union, effected in the Incarnation, whereby the Son of God took Humanity into Unity with His Divinity, and renewed in every Eucharist, whereby we take unto ourselves again His Sacred Humanity, for ever unites His Sacrifice to ours. Whatever He does, the Church, His Body, the organ of His sacrificial work and suffering, does in and through Him. Whatever His Church does, He does in and through Her. We cannot separate, except in thought, the Sacrifice of Christ and that of His Church ; they are not two but one Sacrifice. It is true that this contemplates the Ideal Church—the Church that is to be at the end of the ages ; a very different Church from the actual Church as we see Her now, while the tares are still growing with the wheat. Yet the Eye of God, as it were, looks through the long ages to the end and sees Her only as She is *now* found in Jesus Christ, and will be actually in Herself at the last.

The Christian Sacrifice is not therefore to be confined to one single act in the life of Jesus Christ. It is a drama including a long and complex series of acts in which Christ and His Church are concerned, beginning with the Incarnation,[1] continued by the life of perfect obedience, by Calvary, the Resurrection, the Ascension, and the Perpetual Work of the great High Priest in the Heavenly Temple, " ever living to make intercession for us " : taken up on earth by His Body, the Church, from the moment of Her Birth and carried on by Her dedicated life of act and suffering as She

[1] " Beginning with the Incarnation," did we say ? Can we take Sacrifice still further back into the Eternity of the Inner Life of the Blessed Trinity ? There from Eternity is Love, and the essence of Love is Self-giving. Is not self-giving in turn the Essence of Sacrifice ? Some, e.g. H. B. Jeaffreson (essay on the " Priesthood of Melchizedek," in the volume " The Doctrine of the Trinity ") speak of Sacrifice within the Bosom of the Godhead, each Person giving Himself to each in mutual Love. But as a matter of language, we use the word " Sacrifice" of a self-giving which involves suffering, self-denial, death, that is, self-giving as conditioned by sin (see R. C. Moberly, " Ministerial Priesthood," pp. 246–249 ; also " Atonement," pp. 245–248). It is best to confine the word " Sacrifice " to this form of self-giving ; otherwise it leads to confusion and needless controversy (see below, pp. 141–143.)

dies with Him to sin, rises again to righteousness,
ascends to sit with Him on His Throne: including every
single Offering made by each of Her members to God :
beginning with the Incarnation and completed only
with the end of time—one single indivisible Sacrifice :
at once Sin Offering, Burnt Offering, Peace Offering
fulfilled : nothing short of that is the Christian
Sacrifice in its fullness.

NOTE

THERE is one statement in this chapter which needs considerable
qualification. On page 138 Gayford writes about Christ " In His
case even the ordinary words ' Into Thy hands I *commend* my
spirit ', ' He *gave up* the Ghost ' have an *active* significance, which
could not be attached to any other human death ". Such a statement must not be allowed to obscure the fact that Christ calls us
to follow Him in this respect. Christ could say " My meat is to
do the will of Him that sent me and to finish His work." Yet
nothing in the Gospels is more obviously clear than the reality of
Christ's agony of temptation in the Garden of Gethsemane. His
" Thy will be done " was a victory after a very hard-fought battle.
He continued to the end to will the way which led to the Cross.
Is not this one of the vital ways in which, by virtue of His achievement, He calls us to follow Him ?

Even when Christians are not called to a voluntary death, a death
of self-sacrifice, they are called to will their death when it is
inevitable, when it comes in the ordinary way of old age or of illness.
It will make all the difference to our spiritual condition at the last
whether we will death or rebel against it. The crux of a Christian
life is death to self and living unto God (see page 111) : and for us to
will death, when the time for it comes, and to commend our spirits
to God, in entire dependence on God and utter trust in Him, is the
one completely searching, as well as the final, test of our death to
self and our living unto God. A man approaching his end might
say to himself, " Here by *accepting* death I prove the reality of
my Baptism as a burial together with Him and of every Communion
as my fellowship with Him both in His sufferings and in His
Resurrection."

It would be deplorable if Gayford's words on page 138 had the
unintentional effect of obscuring the fact that Christ calls us in
life and death to follow Him in commending our spirits to the
Father. No such argument or implication is necessary to safeguard
the voluntariness of Christ's action as the Offerer or Sacrificer.

D. C.

CHAPTER VIII

THE CHRISTIAN SACRIFICE

(A) AS FULFILLED IN JESUS CHRIST

WE are now for a time to isolate in thought the Sacrifice of Christ from the Christian Sacrifice in the fullest sense as it appeared in the last chapter, and to contemplate the perfect ideal of Sacrifice as fulfilled by Him.

His is the Perfect Sacrifice. It is well to remind ourselves at the outset of one consequence of this. His Sacrifice is the norm, the measure, the standard for all other Sacrifices ; the degree of truth and value in all other forms of Sacrifice can only be gauged by comparison with His. They are to be explained by reference to His, not His by reference to them. Postulating as we did from the outset (pp. 3, 4) a belief in the guidance of the Holy Spirit in the historical development of Sacrifice, we have seen in all its forms things which pointed forward to the Lamb of God. Consciously or unconsciously we have all along anticipated this chapter : His Sacrifice has been our standard of judgment throughout. We shall now turn to that Sacrifice and try to see wherein its perfection consists.

A Perfect Sacrifice must be perfect in all the elements which constitute a Sacrifice. There must be the three agents—Sacrificer, Victim, Priest. Three, not two only as some seem to think when they leave out of sight the person of the Sacrificer, and with what loss and confusion, as we shall see, to their whole conception of Sacrifice. Then, each of the three agents must be perfect of his kind—inwardly, in the heart and its intentions ; outwardly, in the life of act and suffering ; and lastly, by true commission from God, authorizing him for the office he fulfils. Finally, the " ceremonial " of Sacrifice, its " outward and visible sign," the acts by which the inward intention is expressed, must be worthy and adequate to express the great inward spiritual realities. Let us consider the Sacrifice of Jesus Christ in the light of these requirements.

(1) He combines in His own Person the three offices of Sacrificer, Victim, and Priest. The passages which reveal Him as Sacrificer are those which dwell on the voluntariness of His Sacrificial Death, and particularly such a passage as St. John x. 17, 18 : " I lay down My life . . . . No one taketh it away from Me, but I lay it down of Myself. I have power to lay it down and I have power to take it up again." It will be noticed that here is something more than the passive willingness to allow His life to be taken away from Him, such as we see, e.g., in the " not as I will but as thou wilt " of Gethsemane, or the " obedience unto death " of Phil. ii. 8. His Dying and even His Resurrection are described as the results of a deliberate *act of will* on His part : He *wills* to lay down His life and He *wills* to take it up again. It is His own deliberate act ; the outcome of His perfect obedience to the Father, but nevertheless His own act and not

another's. In His case, even the ordinary words " Into Thy Hands I *commend* My Spirit," " He *gave up* the Ghost " have an *active* significance, which could not be attached to any other human death.

The office of Victim is so frequently expressed or implied of Jesus Christ in the New Testament as hardly to need particular mention. It is contained in the title " Lamb of God " ; it is implied wherever the thought is expressed that it was *Himself* that He offered and not another (e.g. Mark x. 45 ; Heb. ix. 12, 25, *et passim*). We may say, indeed, that while the passages describing His Death as actively the result of His own Will reveal Him especially as Sacrificer, in those which dwell on the aspect of passive self-surrender we see Him regarded as the Victim. But equally to the active and to the passive side of His Death belongs the *completeness of the obedience*, and it is that which makes Him both Perfect Sacrificer and Perfect Victim (*cf.* Heb. x. 8 ff). What a contrast is here between the calm deliberate resolve of Calvary and the scene presented—try to imagine it, Reader— at the slaughtering of the Victim in the Jewish Sacrifices ; its wild terror, its unwillingness to die, the cruel force and violence with which its desperate struggles were overcome. But besides the willingness of the Victim there is another point of contrast to be noted. The life of an animal is no equivalent for the life of a man. But here the life which the human Sacrificer offers is not only a human life—it is human life in its ideal perfection. And, to crown all, the surrender of self is not only complete—it is made also at the greatest possible cost to the giver. It is no costless obedience but the climax of uttermost self-sacrifice that we see wrought out in Gethsemane and on Calvary.

For the truth of Our Lord's Priesthood we need only refer to the Epistle of the Hebrews (see especially Heb. ii. 17—iii. 6, iv. 14—v. 10, vi. 20—x. 25). Divinely appointed to this office He was trained by suffering in the sympathy towards man (Heb. ii. 18, iv. 15 to v. 2) and obedience towards God (Heb. v. 8–10), which are the inward marks of a perfect Priest ; towards God, a Son (Heb. vii. 28) ; towards His fellow-man, a man and a brother (Heb. ii. 11–14). Lastly, by Divine dispensation, the Priesthood conferred on Him " after the order of Melchizedek " is a greater than the Aaronic Priesthood of the Old Dispensation. Not only is His Offering a better one, but His Tenure of Office is eternal and immutable : He has no successor (Heb. vii. 23 ff). And His Priestly office is executed not in an earthly Tabernacle " made with hands " but in the " true Tabernacle, which the Lord pitched and not man," " eternal in the Heavens."

(2) In regard to the outward expression, the acts, of the Sacrifice of Jesus Christ, there is another essential difference to be noted from the Sacrifices of the Law. So long as Sacrificer and Victim were personally distinct there was an unbridged gap between the outward expression of Sacrifice and its inward intention. The two were accomplished within distinct and imperfectly related planes of consciousness. The feelings and desires of the heart belonged to the human sacrificer, but the doings and sufferings were those of the animal victim. Two lives, two " per-

sonalities," we might almost say—certainly two wills disunited and at variance—were involved. But now the Sacrificer and His Victim are one and the same. A breach of harmony is repaired. The outward expression is not merely ceremonial and symbolical ; it stands in real and vital relation to the inward intention.

In every way His is therefore the Perfect Sacrifice ; and for this reason it is one only, and once only offered. It is all-sufficient and therefore *needs not* to be repeated. It is Heaven's last word, God's last offer to man, and therefore it *cannot* be repeated : " By one offering He hath perfected for ever them that are sanctified " (Heb. x. 14).

It remains for us now to consider the acts by which this intention of the Perfect Sacrifice found true and worthy expression in act and suffering.

1. The whole Life of Jesus Christ from its earliest conscious moment was throughout its course a living Sacrifice. Like the Burnt Offering of old it was the offering of a dedicated life to fulfil the will of God. That was His " meat and drink." It was the fulfilment of the Burnt Offering. But this obedience was not a will-less or painless Offering. He was tempted in all points like as we are. He " learned obedience," and the self-surrender involved was a foreshadowing of His Death and its fulfilment of the Sin Offering. Or, looking at it from the point of view of the Sin Offering, we may regard the earthly life as the preparation for the Sacrifice, and compare it to the rearing of the victim for the Old Sacrifices.

2. *Calvary.* In one sense the Death of Jesus Christ was the culminating expression of that spirit of surrender and obedience which marked His whole life. His death was the supreme test of that self-surrender, but the difference between it and the rest of His life from this standpoint was one of degree, not of kind. Some writers on the Atonement[1] insist strongly that this is the whole of the truth : the Cross is the proof of an obedience " unto Death " ; it is not to be isolated in any way from the life of which it is the climax. But if due weight is given to all the references in the New Testament to the significance of the Cross, and to the " Blood " of Jesus, this view of His Death cannot be accepted as sufficient. It is a Christian, not a Jew, who quotes and applies to the Christian Sacrifice the words, " Apart from the shedding of blood there is no remission." There is a real danger, in our reaction from Calvinism, that we should underestimate the essential and central place of the Death in our Lord's Sacrifice. It is quite true that in the offering of the Blood, i.e. after the Death, we are to see the moment of the making of Atonement. But we must not forget that the Death was an essential condition for this Offering. Death and the offering of the Blood are both essential, and equally central in the Sacrifice of Christ.

His Death was essential ; " it behoved the Christ to suffer " ; but *why* this Divinely decreed necessity ? The answer is—because of sin (see, e.g., Rom. iv. 25 ; Gal. iii. 13 ; Heb. ix. 28 ; 1 Pet. iii. 18). It was sin

---

[1] E.g. Sabatier, " The Atonement in Modern Religious Thought," p. 220.

which made it necessary that the suffering of death should have a place in the Offering made by Jesus to the Father. But there are two ways of looking at this truth : (a) It was the hatred of sinful men that nailed Him to the tree. The more faithfully He carried out His mission the more inevitable became the hostile opposition of human sinfulness. Priest and Pharisee embody for the moment the permanent sinfulness of the whole race in opposition to the Will of God. We may justly say that so it was the sins of the world that crucified Christ. But, in this light, how would His Death differ from that of any other martyr ? Their sufferings were also the natural result of a faithful witness for God in a sinful world. The connexion between sin and the Cross goes deeper than this. (b) " It *behoved* the Christ to suffer," " apart from shedding of blood there is no remission." The forgiveness of sin demanded the Death of the Christ ; nothing short of that could be sufficient. Continually in the New Testament " the Cross " or " the Death " or " the Blood " of Jesus are mentioned as the means by which we are delivered from our sins ; for a few instances see, e.g., Rom. v. 10 ; Eph. ii. 16 ; 1 Pet. iii. 18 ; Col. i. 20–22. It is by His Death that we are justified. His Sacrifice was a " Sacrifice for sin " (Heb. x. 12), and therefore Death had a unique place in it. We have to remember again that the ultimate cause of His Death was Himself : " I lay down My life of Myself : no man taketh it from Me." The laws of cause and effect might be the instruments and wicked men the agents, but the first cause was the Will of God. It was the Divine decree that the Son of God must suffer Death before the sins of men could be forgiven. The teaching of the Bible from beginning to end emphasizes the connexion between Death (i.e. the bitterness of Death, the " sting of Death ") and sin (see, e.g., Gen. ii. 17, iii. 3, 19 ; 1 Cor. xv. 56 ; Rev. xx. 14). It was divinely ordained under the Old Covenant that Death must have a place in all atoning Sacrifices, and we cannot make the Death a mere incident in that of the New. Nor is the meaning of Death in this connexion far to seek. It is the expression of a contrition which reaches to the utmost limit of self-renunciation. Sacrifice offered under the condition of a nature rooted in selfishness (i.e. under the conditions of sin) must involve a *mortifying* of the natural man ; only so can the offering of self to God be fulfilled. And to lay down one's life, to submit to physical death, has always been felt to be the highest expression of such a self-renunciation. We can understand that such an entire self-forgetting, so complete a self-sacrifice, would be the only adequate recompense that man could make for sin, the only real atonement between himself and God. So it is that " apart from shedding of blood there is no remission." The root of all sin is self-seeking ; the undoing of sin must therefore be accomplished by self-renunciation, i.e. death.

It must be observed, however, that this " laying down of life " is essentially distinct from that involuntary death, which is the *penalty* of sin (Gen. ii. 17 ; 1 Cor. xv. 56 ; Rev. xx. 14). Such a Death as this is the absolute opposite of the separation from God, which is the essence of the penal death.[1] This is the

[1] See F. W. Robertson, " Sermons " (People's Ed.), 2nd series, p. 92.

voluntary self-separation from sin in order to live nearer to God. The fruit of it is not death-bringing, but life-giving, both for Christ Himself and for others as well. The Crucifixion has for its necessary sequel the Resurrection, and the Risen Lord quickens others also. We pass on then from the Death to :

3. The Resurrection. From the analogy of the Old Covenant, in which the offering of the Blood was so vital a feature in Sacrifice, we should expect that the Christian Sacrifice would not close with the Crucifixion but be continued in the Risen Life of the Saviour. This expectation is justified, when we examine the New Testament teaching. Professor W. Milligan[1] has collected and examined the passages treating of the Blood of Jesus Christ, its meaning and efficacy, and compared with them the corresponding sayings in reference to His Death. The conclusion which he draws is that when the Apostolic writers wished to describe the full effects of the atoning work of Christ they almost invariably prefer to speak of His Blood, rather than His Death, as the means by which He won salvation for us. We need not remind our readers that the word " Blood " in itself involves the idea of Sacrifice. It was by a Sin Offering that Atonement was made under the New Covenant as under the Old. But further, " Blood," in its sacrificial associations, refers particularly to something which took place after the victim's death, i.e. to the altar-transaction, the " pouring " or " putting " or " sprinkling " of the Blood. Also the blood itself was the

---

[1] " Resurrection of Our Lord," Appendix to note 56, pp. 290–304.

symbol of the life that *had been through death*, i.e. the risen life. So, the " Blood of Christ " refers us to a *sacrificial* work belonging to the *Resurrection-life*. His offering of the blood is fulfilled by something which he does in his Resurrection-state and with His Risen Life. What that action is we must enquire when we come to speak of the Ascension. Meanwhile, it is enough to have established this very significant fact that the " Blood of Jesus " implies a reference to His Risen Life and a place for the Resurrection in the Sacrifice which He offered for the sins of the world.[1] This explains St. Paul's insistence on the Resurrection as an integral part of the atonement (e.g. Romans iv. 25, v. 10 ; 1 Cor. xv. 17).

4. The Ascension. We pass now to the work of the Ascended Lord in Heaven and the questions which arise in connexion with it. Does it form part of His Sacrifice ? What is its relation to His Death ? Closely connected with these questions is the doctrine of Our Lord's Priesthood. When did He enter upon this Priesthood ? Where is the scene, and what is the time of its exercise ? The answer to these questions is to be found chiefly in the Epistle to the Hebrews, and the evidence of that Epistle has been interpreted in three different ways :

(1) The first view is that Our Lord was already the High Priest during His earthly life, and that the sacrificial part of His Priestly work was completed with His Death. The Priestly work in the Ascended Life is confined to pleading by a Sacrifice finished

----

[1] See further, Sanday and Headlam, " Romans," note on Chap. III, verse 25, and excursus on pp. 91 f.

" once and for all " on Calvary. This is the ordinary " Evangelical " or " Protestant " view of the Sacrifice of Christ, but it may also be fairly called the ordinary " Roman " view as well, in so far as it is implied in the common expression (as old as St. Ambrose), " the altar of the Cross." The *ara crucis* is mentioned in the definition of the Sacrifice of the Mass in the Council of Trent, and Our Lord is described as the Melchizedekian High Priest, there and then offering Himself in bloodywise to the Father. Any continuation of this Sacrifice is to be seen in the Eucharist, and the idea of a Priestly Offering in Heaven does not appear in the utterances of the Council. But Roman writers often speak of a Priestly Offering in Heaven as belonging to Our Lord's Sacrifice.[1] The ordinary " Roman " position does not deny—it merely overlooks the sacrificial work of the Heavenly High Priest. The keystone of the " Protestant " position, however, is the conviction that the Sacrifice offered by Our Lord was completed by His Death, and therefore to speak of the work of the Heavenly High Priest as sacrificial is to depreciate the unique value of the Cross. (A well-known book on the " Catholic " side, Mortimer's " Eucharistic Sacrifice," on the same grounds denies the reality of the Heavenly Sacrifice, but this part of his argument is vitiated by many inaccuracies and confusions). For an exposition of the " Protestant " position see Tait, " Heavenly Session of Our Lord."

There are two passages in the Epistle to the Hebrews

[1] E.g. Manning, " Eternal Priesthood," p. 4; De Condren, " Eternal Sacrifice," pp. 59–61.

which are constantly quoted as conclusive proof of
this position, viz., (1) " Who . . . when He had made
purification of sins, sat down . . . " (Heb. i. 3) ; and (2)
when He had offered one sacrifice for sins, for ever sat
down. . . ." (Heb. x. 12). Taken by themselves,
apart from the Epistle as a whole, these words might
well seem conclusive, and it must be granted that in
any case it is not easy to fit them into the framework
of thought to which we have been led by our study
of the Old Testament Sacrifices and of Our Lord's
Death and Resurrection. They remain, I frankly own,
a difficulty. But to take the general Protestant
interpretation of them and to make them dominate
the whole Epistle raises other and by far greater
difficulties. In particular it stultifies the comparison
in Chapter IX between the Jewish High Priest's work
in the Holy of Holies on the Day of Atonement and
Our Lord's work in the Heavenly Tabernacle. If the
former is not merely Priestly but also Sacrificial (i.e.
forming an integral part of the Sacrifice), how can it
be contended that the same is not true of the latter as
well ? The evidence of the Epistle to the effect that the
Melchizedekian Priesthood belongs to Our Lord's
Ascended and Heavenly Life, and that He was
appointed to this Priestly Office at the Ascension or
the Resurrection, is so clear and strong that nearly
all commentators are agreed on the point. Some of
them, nevertheless, feeling compelled to claim for
Our Lord the Priestly Office and the Priestly work
during His earthly life, have conceived the strange
idea of a double Priesthood, or two Priesthoods—an
earthly Aaronic and a Heavenly Melchizedekian Office.

This is the second line of interpretation which we will now consider.

(2) *The double Priesthood.*—The motive for this idea, as we have just seen, is the supposed necessity that the Death upon the Cross must be regarded as a *Priestly* work. The idea of a Double Priesthood is not by any means new in Christian Theology. It dates back to the fourth century.[1] The attempt to see in the earthly Priesthood an anti-type to the Aaronic is comparatively modern. It is familiar to English readers chiefly through two books—Professor Bruce's " Humiliation of Christ " and Bishop Westcott's " Commentary on the Epistle to the Hebrews." How far does the Epistle countenance such an idea ? It says nothing, of course, about a " Priesthood after the Order of Aaron " being held by Our Lord. It says a good deal, on the other hand, which seems inconsistent with such a Priesthood. The whole burden of the Epistle is the *contrast* between His Priesthood and the Aaronic, in regard to its nature, its tenure, its work, and its power. Melchizedek, not Aaron, was the Old Testament type of this great High Priest. Such a passage as Heb. vii. 11-14 seems quite plainly to rule out the idea of an Aaronic Priesthood. The earthly Jesus was of the Tribe of Judah, " from which no man hath given attendance at the altar " : " As to which Tribe Moses spake nothing concerning Priests." Jesus is described as " another Priest . . . after the Order of Melchizedek, and not . . . reckoned after the order of Aaron." And the whole idea of an earthly Priesthood is excluded by

[1] See Bruce, " Humiliation of Christ," pp. 279-283.

the words of Heb. viii. 4 : " If He were on earth, He would not be a Priest at all, seeing there are those who offer the gifts according to the law." Two Priesthoods cannot exist side by side at the same time. The one has superseded the other and that other has no longer any validity or reality.

At the bottom of this misunderstanding is the supposed necessity of maintaining that the Death on the Cross must be a Priestly act if the Cross was a Sacrifice.[1] But to a Christian Jew of the first century, A.D.—and to such the Epistle was addressed —no such necessity would exist. He was perfectly familiar with the fact that in the old Sacrifices the Priest's part began with the offering of the blood, and that the slaying of the Victim was the work of the *Sacrificer* ; also that even if in a public Sacrifice the Priest slew the Victim, he did so as representing the Offerer and not *qua* Priest. It would be quite in accord with the Jewish view of Sacrifice that Our Lord should enter on the Priestly part of His Sacrificial Work after His Death. It is difficult to avoid the conclusion that the whole of this unfortunate confusion has sprung from our overlooking the person and work of the sacrificer in a Sacrifice. That Our Lord's Death was sacrificial we should vehemently assert ; but because it was His work as Sacrificer laying down His life of Himself, and not because it was a Priestly act. The exercise of the Priestly office is to be seen in those acts which correspond to the presenting of

---

[1] Even Professor G. Milligan (" Theology of the Epistle to the Hebrews," p. 129), while contending against the Doctrine of the Double Priesthood, calls it " satisfactory as enabling us to bring Our Lord's Death . . . under His High Priestly service."

the Victim's blood and its body, and these acts pre-
suppose the Death as an accomplished fact ; indeed,
without the Death that has gone before, they would
be valueless and even impossible. That Heaven
should be the scene, and the Risen and Ascended Life
the time, of the Priestly work is the only condition
that satisfies the truth of the Sacrifice.

(3) *The heavenly Priesthood.*—Let us turn now to
the evidence of the Epistle that Our Lord entered
upon His Priestly Office—or at any rate, upon the
exercise of that office, on His Priestly Work—at the
Ascension. We have already dealt with the teaching
of Heb. vii. 11–14 and viii. 4, 5, and found it conclusive
against any other view but this.[1] The chief passages
on the positive side are Heb. v. 1–10, viii. 1–3,
ix. 11, 12, 24–26. In the former, especially in verses
7–10, is described the preparation of Our Lord for
His Priesthood—a preparation of human sympathy
and obedience to God ; then, the struggle over and
the victory won, " having been made perfect," He
was " named [or " proclaimed "] of God a High Priest."
With this we may compare Heb. vi. 20 : " Whither [i.e.
" within the veil " into Heaven] as a forerunner Jesus
entered for us, having become a High Priest." The
second passage (Heb. viii. 1–3) shows us Our Lord,
like Melchizedek, as King sitting upon His Throne
(verse 1) and also as ministering Priest in the Heavenly
Sanctuary (verse 2), engaged in offering both " Gifts
and Sacrifices " (i.e. the *minhah* and the *zebahim*,
verse 3). In Heb. ix. an elaborate parallel is drawn
between the duties of the Aaronic High Priest on the

[1] See pp. 148 f.

Day of Atonement (verses 1-8) and those of our High
Priest in Heaven (verses 11, 12, 24, 25). [For the
significance of the apparent confusion between the
Day of Atonement (verses 1-8) and the Inaugural
Covenant Sacrifice of Exod. xxiv. (verses 15-21), see
pp. 78-79]. The full significance of the parallel appears
most clearly when presented in the following tabular
form. Each column should be read downwards :—

Old.	*New.*
The Aaronic Priest (v. 7) ..	The true Priest (v. 11).
Once each year (v. 7) ..	once for all (v. 12).
entered the Holy of Holies (v. 7)	entered the true Holy Place, i.e. Heaven itself (v. 24 ; *cf.* v. 11, if παραγενόμενος means the same as the "appearing" of v. 24).
and offered the blood of another (vv. 7, 12)	to appear before the Face of God for us (v. 24), which is explained in v. 25 as " to offer Himself " (*cf.* v. 14)

It will be seen that in both cases *the Death of the
Victim* is presupposed as an already accomplished fact

before *the Priestly work is begun*. The Heavenly
Sanctuary with the Heavenly *Shechinah* (verse 24) is
the scene of the Priestly Ministry ; the entry into that
Sanctuary marks the time of His Ascension into
Heaven, where He will abide until His Second Coming
(verses 25–28 ; *cf.* Acts i. 11).

It will be noticed that Our Lord is said outright
in verse 25 to " offer Himself " in the Heavenly
Sanctuary, and the same phrase is used in verse 14,
where it may, however, and perhaps does, refer to the
Sacrificer's offering of self (i.e. the Death on the Cross).
In verse 12 the writer seems to be on the verge of
saying, " Christ offered [not the blood of goats and
calves, as the Aaronic High Priest did, but] His Own
Blood." It is evident that He avoided the actual
words as being liable at the time to a physical, materialistic misconstruction.[1] But the expression, though
not actually found in the Epistle, is completely
justified by its teaching. In verse 24 this offering of
Himself is called " to appear before the Face of God."
The word ἐμφανισθῆναι, an unexpected word, means
" to be made clearly visible," so that he could not be
overlooked, i.e. to be a " Lord's Remembrancer "
a " memorial " before God of the Passion and Death,
the marks of which He bears. The underlying thought
is the same as that of Rev. v. 6 : " I saw in the midst
of the throne and of the four living creatures and of
the elders [i.e. as Mediator between God and man] a
Lamb standing [i.e. alive] as though it had been slain "
(with the marks of His Passion upon Him). The
sacrificial association is present, though latent, in the

[1] See Moberly, " Ministerial Priesthood," pp. 264–266.

Priest-Victim's " appearing." But also He is said " to appear before the Face of God *for us*," on our behalf. It is a mediatorial Offering of Himself. The words link this Sacrificial Offering with the Heavenly intercession of Heb. vii. 25 ; Rom. viii 34, and in turn we are reminded that the word " intercession " (ἐντυγχάνειν) is wide enough to include the thought of a sacrificial Offering for others.[1]

From the foregoing discussion it is clear that the general teaching of the Epistle is as follows :—

(1) Our Lord has but one Priesthood—after the order of Melchizedek.

(2) He entered upon the exercise of that Priesthood (if not upon the office itself, as Heb. v. 5 and 10 seems to imply) *after* His Death.

(3) The scene of His Ministry is the Heavenly Temple.

(4) He offers Himself, His Blood ; and this Priestly Offering is the anti-type to the offering of the Blood in the Holy of Holies on the Day of Atonement.

This Offering is the true, complete, and final making of atonement for the sins of men ; therefore it is one only Offering and can never be repeated. But there is opened out before us here a far wider conception of the One Sacrifice than the common view which would confine it to the Death on the Cross. The Sacrifice of Christ is One *in so far as He is Sacrificer and Victim*, as a completed act of past time, accomplished at the moment of His Death. That is the significance of

---

[1] See Westcott, Note on Heb. vii. 25 (p. 191), and W. Milligan, " The Ascension," p. 152.

the saying from the Cross, " It is finished." The source of the atoning power of His Sacrifice is the Cross, and the Cross alone. He " made there by His One Oblation of Himself once offered, a full, perfect, and sufficient Sacrifice, Oblation, and satisfaction for the sins of the whole world." The all-sufficiency of the Cross is the keystone of His Sacrifice. But it is also One Sacrifice in so far as He is the Priest, in that He entered " once for all " (Heb. ix. 12) into the Heavenly Holy of Holies, there to offer Himself for us. There can be but one Priestly entry just as there can be but one Death of the Victim.

It is often said that Our Lord's " appearing " for us, His " intercession," represents Him as pleading by a Sacrifice which was past and over with the Crucifixion. But against this we have to urge (a) this pleading is integral to the Sacrifice, and, as in the Jewish worship, it represents the Priest's function in a Sacrifice ; (b) the " appearing " is identified with the offering of Himself, which, like the offering of the Blood on the Mercy Seat, is sacrificial. If, however, those who hold this position would allow that there is this Heavenly Offering (as surely they must do) the difference between us and them would become merely a verbal difference in the definition and use of terms. It might well happen that a long controversy should be concluded by a mutual agreement to speak of *Sacrifice* (referring to the Death) and *Offering* (in reference to the Priestly Work), provided it were understood that these were two parts of one undivided act. It is because the word *Sacrifice* is generally used to cover the whole act that I should prefer to retain it in this wider sense ; [1] but that is not essential.[2]

One final point remains to be discussed with reference to the Heavenly Offering. Does the Epistle to the Hebrews regard that Offering as a completed act of past time or as a continued action, such as is implied in the phrase, " the perpetual offering " ? The answer really turns upon the meaning of the passages, Heb. i. 3, vii. 27, x. 12–14. It is not possible to regard the last passage at least as a reference to the Sacrificer's part in the Sacrifice which was completed with the Death. Heb. x. 12–14, and possibly the other two passages, refer to the Priest's work, and, if so must be taken to imply that the Offering made at the moment of the entry was then completed, and followed by the Session on the Throne. The Priest Who stood to make His Offering, sat on His Throne as King when that Offering was finished. If so, there is a verbal inconsistency with other passages which regard the Offering as perpetually being made in the Sanctuary. Such, as we have seen, is Heb. viii. 1–3, where the two ideas—the Session as King and the Ministry as Priest—are regarded as *present* facts ; and the justification for this, as to the Priestly Ministry, is that " it is necessary that this High Priest also have somewhat to offer " (the aorist as usual in the subjunctive is timeless).[3] The same truth is involved in

---

[1] See above, pp. 2, 24.

[2] Professor Swete in a private letter suggests the value of retaining the two terms with distinction as above : " Sacrifice " representing the Biblical θυσία and " Offering " προσφορα

[3] See J. H. Moulton, "Greek Grammar" (1906), p. 134; G. Milligan, "Theology of the Epistle to the Hebrews," p. 142.

the words " Eternal Spirit " in Heb. ix. 14, and in the emphatic "*now* [i.e. "at this present moment"] to appear for us " in Heb. ix. 24.   Both passages imply " a manifestation which is both one and unceasing."[1] With this agrees, too, the vision of the Lamb in Rev. v. 6, and the perpetual Intercession of Hebrews vii. 25, Romans viii. 34.

After all, either of these conceptions expresses a truth.   At the first moment of the entry into Heaven the Sacrifice was completed and the atonement made ; it needed neither reinforcement nor renewal.   Yet, on the other hand, in Him Humanity for ever makes before God its Offering of self.   Probably, to the author of our Epistle, sometimes the one and sometimes the other truth was present in his mind, and not being aware of long subsequent controversies, he expressed himself according to the thought of the moment without noting any inconsistency.   It is going too far to say that he regards all the acts of the Sacrifice, the Cross, and the Priestly Work as eternal and therefore timeless.   This idea is too philosophical for him, and it is certain that he does conceive of a time-sequence in the order of the Sacrifice, corresponding to the sequence in the Sacrifices of the Old Covenant. The One Sacrifice is presented before our eyes in the form of a drama beginning with the Incarnation and continuing until the end of time : one, not in the sense of one action within certain circumscribed limits of past time, but in the sense of one continuous act— never repeated, because always going on till the end of the world.   Christ " is a Priest for ever, not by

[1] Moulton, "Commentary on the Epistle to the Hebrews," *ad loc.*

a perpetual series of acts of memory, not by multiplied and ever-remoter acts of commemoration of a death that is past, but by the eternal presentation of a life which is eternally the ' life that died.' "[1]

---

[1] Moberly, " Ministerial Priesthood," p. 246. The New Testament describes Our Lord as engaged *after His Death* in doing three things with His Blood : (1) By it He " cleanses," " washes," " looses," us from our sins (1 John i. 7 ; Heb. ix. 14 ; Titus ii. 14 ; Rev. vii. 14, i. 5). (2) He gives It to us in the Sacrament. (3) He offers It upon the Heavenly Altar. No one doubts that the first two of these describe actually present facts—they are perpetual actions. Is there any reason why the same should not be true of the third as well ? The Blood is the Life : It is the Living Christ Himself, Who by His touch cleanses, washes us, and gives Himself to be our Food. It is the same Christ Who, *because* He is Living with a Human Life, must ever be doing that which is essential to the creature's relation to the Creator, i.e. offering Himself to Him. But for the fact that the Epistle to the Hebrews in view of temporary conditions refrains from using direct sacrificial language the truth of the Perpetual Offering would not have been overlooked or disputed.

CHAPTER IX

THE CHRISTIAN SACRIFICE

(B) AS FULFILLED IN THE CHURCH'S LIFE AND WORSHIP

I MUST remind the reader, at this stage, of the subject-matter of Chapter VII. We spoke there of the dedicated Life of the Church as Her Burnt Offering, Her share in the Christian Sacrifice in dependence upon and union with the One Sacrifice of Her Lord. The dedication of the whole life (Rom. xii. 1; *cf. ibid.* vi. 13; Hebrews xiii. 15; 2 Cor. ii. 14, 15), every single good deed and every exercise of virtue (e.g. acts of charity [Heb. xiii. 16; Phil. iv. 18]), on the part of the Church corporately and of Her individual members separately, make up Her Burnt Offering, which rises unceasingly from Earth to Heaven; but always in union with the One Offering of Her Lord—acceptable only in Him, possible only through Him (1 Pet. ii. 5). "This [i.e. the life of good works] is the Sacrifice of Christians: we being many are one Body in Christ; and this also is the Sacrifice which the Church continually celebrates in the Sacrament of the Altar . . . in which She teaches that She Herself is offered in the Offering She makes to God." [1] St. Paul speaking of his apostolic ministry depicts himself

[1] St. Augustine, "De Civitate Dei," X, vi.

as a sacrificing Priest (ἱερουργοῦντα) presenting to God as his Offering the Gentile Church in its sanctified life (Rom. xv. 16 ; the same thought is latent in 2 Cor. xi. 2). Very instructive, too, in this connexion is the train of thought in Heb. x. 19–25. There we have a picture which embraces the whole Christian Sacrifice throughout the ages. The Church is admitted through the veil into the Heavenly Sanctuary (verses 19, 20) ; there She beholds Her Great High Priest engaged in His Work of offering Himself (verse 21) ; She is bidden to " draw near," i.e. to join with Him in that Offering, in Her Baptismal Robe of Faith and Purity (verse 22) ; and Her share in the Offering is the exercise of Faith, Hope, Love, Good Works, and Worship (verses 23–25).

In that passage, as perhaps nowhere else,[1] there is set forth the Christian Sacrifice in its fullness : the Sacrifice of the Lord Himself through His Incarnate Life and Death, His Ascended Life and Heavenly Priesthood, taken up and made Her own by His Church in dedicated life and worship ; Sin and Burnt and Peace Offering perfected ; the Law not destroyed but " fulfilled."

It remains for us to speak of that Sacrifice as expressed in Christian Worship. The function of worship is to gather up and focus in one intense moment the whole Godward side, in all its parts, of the daily life. And if Sacrifice be co-extensive with life—as it must be, if the definition of Sacrifice as

---

[1] Another interesting passage is Heb. xiii. 10–16, where, again, we have the Sacrifice of Christ and the Church linked together as making up the fullness of the Christian Sacrifice : its aspects as Sin Offering, Burnt Offering, Peace Offering : and the relation of dedicated life to worship.

" the exercise of love within the atmosphere of sin "
(p. 143) be a true description—then it must be co-
extensive with worship also.   Every side of worship—
prayer, praise, thanksgiving, confession of sin, confession of faith, adoration—is an Offering of the soul
to God ; the " lifting-up of the hands" is a " Sacrifice "
(Ps. cxli. 2).   For this reason, if for no other, the one
distinctive and Divinely ordained act of Christian
worship, which incorporates all the elements of
worship—the Eucharist—must be a Sacrifice.

But the sacrificial action in the Eucharist is more
particular and special than this, because it is linked
very closely and very definitely with Calvary and the
Heavenly Priesthood.   It is in the nature of that link
that the true conception of the Eucharistic Sacrifice
is to be found.   Let us consider first the *fact* of that
link and then enquire into its nature.

I.   Let us recall the scene of the Institution.   At the
Last Supper Our Lord anticipated two events which
had not yet happened.[1] He spoke of His coming
Death as a *present* fact : " My Body which *is being
given*." " My Blood which *is being shed*." The
present participles (διδόμενον and ἐκχυνόμενον) are
emphatic by their very unexpectedness.   Also, He
stood there in the rôle, not only of Sacrificer and
Victim, but also of Priest to His Church ; He anticipated the Heavenly Priesthood as well as Calvary.
The moment at which he places Himself, so to speak,
is after the Ascension ; the Communion proper, like
the meal in the Peace Offering, follows after the Death
and the Presenting of the Blood.

[1] See Gore, " Body of Christ," note 19, p. 315.

But in saying this we are assuming the sacrificial character of the Eucharist. Let us proceed to justify this by pointing to the various sacrificial features in its institution.

(1) First, there is its *connexion with the Passover*. Whether the Last Supper was actually the Passover meal or not, there is no doubt that Our Lord intended to connect the two together in the Disciples' minds. Passover night or not, it was to be *their* Passover Supper. The Passover was a primitive Sacrifice of the nature of a Peace Offering. The meal was a part of the Sacrifice. The expression "a feast upon a Sacrifice" is misleading if by it a separation is implied between this and the other acts which made up the Sacrifice of a Peace Offering. At the back of the expression lies no doubt the false and mischievous identification of Sacrifice with death and death alone.

(2) Our Lord's acts and words would remind the Jewish Disciples that they were being called upon to take part in a Sacrifice. He took Bread and Wine, the materials of the *minḥah*; He spoke of them in terms of Body and Blood, the objects of Offering in the animal Sacrifices (*zebaḥim*); He called them His own Body and Blood, identifying Himself with the Victim in the Sacrifice. Leaving aside the question whether the word "given" (Luke xxii. 20; *cf.* 1 Cor. xi. 24) was actually used by Him,[1] He spoke of His Blood as "outpoured" (ἐκχυνόμενον). The mention of "Blood" and (in lesser degree) of "Body" would in

---

[1] In any case it expresses the exact truth and is strongly supported by John vi. 51.

itself show the Disciples that it was a Sacrifice He was thinking of. To speak to a Jew of " blood " in a religious connexion would at once suggest this. The idea would be clinched by the " shed " or " outpoured," recalling the moment of the slaughtering of the Victim.[1] It is something to do with the Blood now being shed and made available for further use, i.e. to the Blood *after* the Victim's Death which is pictured as taking place at the very moment of the Speaker's words.[2]

The mention of the " *New Covenant* " adds further particulars relating to Sacrifice. It is " the Blood of a Covenant Sacrifice," i.e. by which a Covenant is to be inaugurated. The " New Covenant " fulfils the promise of Jeremiah xxxi. 31 ff ; the Blood of the Covenant is a direct reference to the Sacrifices by which the Old Covenant was established (Exod. xxiv. 5–11). Moses took the Blood of the Burnt and Peace Offerings and poured (not " sprinkled ") it on the book containing the terms of the Covenant, on the altar and on the people. Jesus takes the Blood of the New Covenant and bids His people drink of it, receive into themselves its life-giving power. This takes us back to the primitive drinking of blood, which was afterwards succeeded by the pouring (as in Exod. xxiv).[3]

[1] It is fairly certain that the Greek ἐκχυνόμενον does not refer to the presentation of the blood upon the altar. If so, we should expect either " sprinkled " or " put " as in the Sin Offering. Also the word for " pouring" on the Altar is προσχύνειν ; ἐκχεῖν is only used for a *non-sacrificial* pouring out of the blood at the base of the altar, as a reverent means of disposing of it (see p. 74).

[2] It should be remembered that the word " Blood " in itself denotes a life that *has passed* through death ; the present participle does not mean that it is the Blood before or in the moment of death that Our Lord bade the Disciples to drink.

[3] The New Testament parallel with the " pouring " of the blood upon the people is found in other contexts, e.g. Heb. ix. 14 ; 1 John i. 7 ; Rev. vii. 14.

When we remember that it is the same blood of the same Sacrifice which is presented on the Heavenly Altar, we see there is the closest connexion implied between the Holy Communion and the Heavenly Offering, i.e. a sacrificial act.

Finally, we have to consider the sacrificial associations gathered around the words " *do* this " and " in memory of Me." The Hebrew *asâh* (= "do ") and its Greek equivalent ποιεῖν (the word used here) in a sacrificial context often mean " to offer." It is almost certain that this is the meaning in St. Luke ii. 27, " to do [i.e. " offer "] concerning Him after the custom of the Law." The context in this case also is sufficiently sacrificial to make it a probable though not a certain conclusion that here too it bears the sacrificial meaning. If so, however, the point was lost to the Early Church, which almost universally interpreted the word in the simple sense " to do." But this is not conclusive against the other interpretation.[1] On the whole, the balance of probability is in favour of rather than against the meaning " to offer," but there is no certainty.

The words " in remembrance of Me " (εἰς τὴν ἐμὴν ἀνάμνησιν) occur only in the earliest account of the Institution (1 Cor. xi. 24, 25 ; in St. Luke xxii. 19 they probably do not belong to the original text). The word ἀνάμνησιν is once only found in the LXX as a translation of the sacrificial *'Azkarah*,[2] for which the regular equivalent elsewhere is the kindred μνημόσυνον. It is used certainly once, and probably in two other

---

[1] As, e.g., Bishop Gore seems to think; "Body of Christ," note 20.

[2] See p. 29.

places, of a memorial before God, but its connexion with this idea cannot be called particularly strong. The same may be said of St. Paul's explanatory words, " Ye do *proclaim* " [καταγγέλλετε] the Lord's Death." The word καταγγέλλειν is used elsewhere in the New Testament always of preaching the Gospel to men, and that is the readiest sense in which to take it here. The Eucharist is the Church's witness to the Lord's Death, its meaning, and its power. In it She " remembers " Him and preaches Him to others. The " remembrance " before God is by no means excluded, but it is not primarily suggested, far less asserted, by the choice of such a word as καταγγέλλετε.

(3) The Communion itself, as we have seen (p. 37ff) must be regarded as a part of the Sacrifice—a fact sometimes obscured by the implied distinction between "Communion" and "Sacrifice" or "Offering." This fact was the more emphasized at the Last Supper by the very startling difference between the Peace Offering meal and the Christian Communion in the command, " This is My Blood : drink ye all of this." The Old Testament prohibition of Blood as a food was so emphatic and repeated, the Jewish abhorence of such an act so deep seated, that these words must have left the Disciples thunderstruck (*cf.* John vi. 52–60). But the very reason for which it was previously forbidden is the ground on which it is now commanded : " the blood is the *life* thereof." *Grace* and truth came by Jesus Christ : we have now a Grace-giving, a Life-giving Sacrifice.[1]

[1] Are we justified in supposing a distinction in the two gifts of the Body and the Blood ? The separation and the interval which separated the two at the Institution seem to suggest a difference

(4) There are one or two passages outside the Gospels which must not be overlooked in this connexion. The Epistle to the Hebrews contains very little direct mention of the Sacraments.[1] The clearest reference to the Eucharist is in Heb. xiii. 10 ff. We (i.e. the Priestly Church as a whole) have an altar from which the Jewish Priesthood (" they that serve the Tabernacle ") have no right to be fed. They are debarred, not only because they are not Christians, but also by the terms of their own Law. When the Sin Offering was made for another the sacrificing Priest received the flesh (except the fat) as his portion ; but if the blood was brought into the Holy Place (i.e. if the Sin Offering was for himself or for the whole congregation, and therefore including himself) he was not allowed to eat of it, and the whole of the flesh except the fat was burnt outside the camp (Lev. vii. 11–14).[2] This, of course, was the case with the Sin Offerings on the Day of Atonement (Lev. xvi. 27), to which our passage directly refers as the Type of Our Lord's Sin Offering. But the Christian Sin Offering, unlike the Jewish, invites its Priesthood to feed upon

---

between them. The blessing of the Cup would hardly be separated from that of the Bread, if both were meant to convey precisely the same gift. The Jewish sacrificial distinction of *Body* and *Blood* points in the same direction. In the gift of the Sacred Body we receive His Perfected Sinless Human Nature and all that belongs to it, its attributes and virtues ; in the Sacred Blood, the perfected quickened Risen Life which vivifies His Body. The two together make the complete gift of His Living Humanity ; not a catalogue of virtues but a living Life, which embodies and expresses them. Regarded in this light, the withholding of the Chalice from the laity is seen to have a special gravity (see W. Milligan, " Resurrection of Our Lord," p. 288 (1st ed. 278) and Miss A. E. Peacock, " The Life Thereof."

[1] For the reasons, see G. Milligan, " Theology of the Epistle to the Hebrews," pp. 219 ff.   [2] See p. 82.

the Flesh of the Victim, not in a carnal, but after a
" heavenly and spiritual " manner (*cf.* verse 9).   The
reference to the Priesthood and to the Day of Atonement and its Sin Offering confirm the interpretation
which the word " altar " itself suggests.   The purpose
of an " altar " is that the Priest may offer upon it ;
this altar is in the Heavenly Sanctuary, on it our High
Priest offers Himself, His Body, and His Blood, and
from it we, the Christian Priesthood, receive our
Priestly " portion " of the Body and the Blood.   But
if it is *our* altar, the implication is that *we* also in
common with Him "draw near " to make an Offering
there.   Our earthly " altars " are but the visible
counterpart of that One Altar in the Heavens.

In this passage Communion and Sacrifice are
inextricably interwoven.   It is also a precious Biblical
witness to the " glorious interchange " of Heaven and
earth in the Eucharist.   All this is lost when the altar
is regarded as the place of slaughter and identified
with the Cross.   It was probably from this passage
so interpreted that the expression " *ara crucis* " arose.
A truer conception and a richer vein of teaching are
found in Irenæus,[1] and Origen [2] who place this
Christian altar in the Heavenly Sanctuary.   Origen,
in particular,[3] identifies it with the " heavenly altar "
of Revelation vi. 9.   If (as is of course true) in Heb. x.
19-25 the prime reason for the " assembling of
ourselves together " is the Breaking of the Bread, we
have in that passage also the same interchange of
Earth and Heaven and the same interweaving of
Communion and Sacrifice as in Heb. xiii. 10 ff.

[1] IV., xviii. 6.   [2] " Exhort. ad Martyrium," 30.   [3] *Loc. cit.*

A passage closely linked with Heb. xiii. 10 and presenting the same association of Communion with Sacrifice is 1 Cor. x. 14–21. The Apostle is warning his converts of the danger of idolatry in eating meats that have been offered on idol altars, taken thence by heathen priests as their altar portion, and sold by them in the markets for common use. His argument is this : " Being fed from the Table of the Lord, you have Communion with the Lord. What is it if knowingly you get your food from heathen altars ? Gentile beliefs and Jewish law should be a reminder and a warning to you " (verses 18–20). This is the context in which St. Paul speaks of the " Table of the Lord." The phrase, as we have seen (p. 78), comes from the Old Testament, where it means the " altar," and the idea associated with it is that of *Offering*. It is the " Table " on which man offers to God the " Bread of the Lord." From that " Lord's Table " the Priest received a portion for himself, and so he had communion with the altar " (verse 18). From the Christian " altar " on which the Great High Priest makes the Offering of His Body and Blood we, the Christian Priesthood, are fed. This " Table of the Lord " is the Heavenly Altar on which is made the Heavenly Offering, and it is with this train of ideas that the Holy Communion is linked. In that Sacrament there is an Offering made to God as well as a gift received from Him.

THE NATURE OF THE EUCHARISTIC SACRIFICE

Our examination of passages expressing the *fact* of

a Eucharistic Sacrifice has already advanced us considerably on the way to a conception of its nature. We have at least reached the following conclusions :—

(1) The Sacrament is not merely a *present* Feast following upon a *past* Sacrifice, for the meal is an integral part of the Sacrifice.

(2) Further, the Eucharistic Sacrifice is not merely the Feast regarded as part of a Sacrifice ; it includes an Offering on our part as well as a Receiving.

(3) That which we offer is something more than the " Sacrifice of Praise and Thanksgiving," if by that is meant " the fruit of lips which make confession to His Name." It includes that, of course ; but if that were all, the Eucharist would not differ from any other worship in its sacrificial aspect.

(4) Nor is it merely the offering of " ourselves, our souls, and bodies." The Evangelical will be the first to acknowledge that the offering of self can never be separated from the One Offering of Himself made by Our Lord ; that we are one with Him and He with us ; that in Him alone, as bound up with His Self-Oblation, can our Offering of self be acceptable to God. We pray that God will " only look on us as found in Him." This is true to all that is best in the Evangelical doctrine of Justification by Faith ; nay, we may go further and say that it is demanded by a consistent acceptance of that doctrine. But, when once this is granted, what momentous issues follow ! For it unites inseparably this our earthly offering of ourselves with the Heavenly Offering made by the Heavenly Priest on the Heavenly Altar in the Heavenly Sanctuary. The Church's myriad altars in all the world are one

with that Heavenly Altar, Her Priesthood is One with His. In offering Himself to God upon that Altar He offers His Church, the redeemed human race, for He is the "Son of Man." In offering ourselves to God we, the Priestly Church, cannot but be offering Him in Whom we all are gathered up. The reality of the Sacrifice is in Heaven, of which the Earthly is an image. The Sacrifice of the Mass is the same as that offered by Our Lord in Heaven.[1]

(5) It follows from this that the Eucharistic Sacrifice does not consist in the pleading of a Sacrifice which was completed at some past time (i.e. with the Death on the Cross). We have seen that the view which reduces the Heavenly Offering to this "pleading" is not true to the New Testament teaching. That Offering is a real Offering. So, too, the Eucharistic Offering, which is parallel, or rather identical, with this Heavenly Offering, is also a real Offering. It is not merely the pleading by a past and completed Sacrifice, but forms an integral part of that Sacrifice.

So much for the negative conclusions. But positively, also, we have arrived at this. In the Eucharist we are joined with Our Lord as He offers Himself upon the Heavenly Altar, and He unites Himself with us in our Offering. From time to time as the Sacrament is celebrated we enter through the veil into the Heavenly Temple and join in its unceasing Offering (Heb. x. 19 ff.). Earth is merged in Heaven, Time in Eternity, the Finite in the Infinite. This

[1] De Condren, "The Eternal Sacrifice," pp. 34, 101. *Cf.* St. Augustine, "De Civitate Dei," X, 6 (quoted above, p. 158), and other passages from St. Augustine quoted in Gore, "Body of Christ," pp. 204-209.

Heavenly interchange " is witnessed in the Liturgies by the *Sursum Corda* bidding us enter the Heavenly Sanctuary, and the *Sanctus*, in which we take our place in the " whole company of Heaven " and our part in the Angelic Worship. In regard particularly to the Eucharistic Offering the interchange is expressed in two ways :

(*a*) By the prayer that the earthly gifts may be borne by the hand of angels to the Heavenly Altar (so in the Roman Canon of the Mass).

(*b*) In the thought of the Christ coming down to be the Priest at the Earthly Altar : (*cf.* Dr. Bright's hymn, " And having with us Him that pleads above," and the striking words of Dr. Moule in the " Fulham Conference on Communion," p. 91, conveying the same idea, although with reference to the Communion and not to the Sacrifice).

We can now gather up the various expressions of sacrificial Offering in our Liturgy. Most of them are common to all the Liturgies and inherent in the most primitive type of Eucharistic Prayer.

(*a*) We take bread and wine—natural gifts—and offer them to God as a symbol that all we have is His and owed by us to Him.

(*b*) He accepts and blesses them and gives them back to us as the *Risen* Body and Blood of Christ. (N.B.— " Blood " in sacrificial sense always means a " Risen " life, one that has passed through death, but is alive).[1]

(*c*) Receiving them, we are made one with Our Lord, and also one with all the Faithful (i.e. we act

[1] See pp. 68, 144.

corporately as a Church, not singly as individuals or as congregations ; in every Eucharist it is the Church Catholic of all ages and all nations which offers the Sacrifice). So united, (1) we join with Him in His Perpetual Self-Oblation. This is represented in our Liturgy by the words " By the merits and death of Thy Son . . . and through Faith in His Blood " ; it is much to be desired, however, that a more direct recognition of this side of the Eucharistic Offering should be included in our Communion Service, bringing it back into line with the other Catholic Liturgies. Could an Evangelical, reading what we have said above (p. 168), object to such an inclusion ? (2) In Him and through Him we make our own Offering, laying it, as it were, upon His on the Heavenly Altar and uniting it with His.[1] As He in offering Himself to the Father offers us as well, so we in offering ourselves offer Him.

(d) This joint-offering of ours includes (1) the offering of Prayer ; hence the beautiful significance of the all-inclusive pattern of Prayer, the *Paternoster*, in the position it occupies in the Canon. (2) The " Sacrifice of praise and thanksgiving " ; hence the name " Eucharist," itself a sacrificial term. (3) the offering of the dedicated life, " ourselves, our souls, and bodies." In this Offering we gather up the whole of life on all its sides—work and play and sleep, home and friendships, everything is here laid on the Heavenly Altar as our Eucharistic Gift. It is another of the

---

[1] A beautiful parallel has been noted in the Old Testament. The *Perpetual* public Burnt Offering lay on the Altar day and night so that the Offerings of individuals were laid upon it (Ex. xxix. 38–42 ; Lev. vi. 8–13).

glorious interchanges, a precious linking of worship to the everyday life.

.   .   .   .   .

We may conclude this review of the Eucharistic Sacrifice with a few disconnected notes.

(A) This conception of the Eucharistic Sacrifice makes it the earthly parallel of Our Lord's Priestly Offering in Heaven. It is impossible here to review even in barest outline the history of the doctrine of the Eucharistic Sacrifice.[1] But this conception to which we have arrived, besides being based on the New Testament, has been represented continuously in the teaching of the Christian Doctors from the earliest times down to the present day. In the Roman Church it has come to be largely overshadowed by the view which sees in the Eucharistic Sacrifice a parallel to the Death upon the Cross. This conception, also an ancient one, seems to rest on two assumptions : (1) The Eucharist represents in itself the whole of a Sacrifice in all its parts, and therefore must include a parallel with the Lord's Dying. Our view, on the other hand, makes it represent one phase or stage of the drama of Sacrifice, viz. that which corresponds to the offering of the Body and the Blood upon the Altar. If we take this view we cannot with strict correctness speak of " the Eucharistic Sacrifice." The Eucharist is *sacrificial*, but not a whole Sacrifice. The term " Eucharistic Offering " expresses the exact truth and is in every way to be preferred to the other.

[1] For this see Darwell Stone, " History of the Doctrine of the Holy Eucharist."

(2) Sacrifice implies "destruction."[1] We have endeavoured to show that both the killing of the victim and the burning of the body in the Jewish Sacrifices were associated with the idea of "more abundant life" rather than with the negative idea of destruction. By the killing, the blood became not less but more living ; the altar fire was not a destroying but a purifying, etherializing agency.

Under the influence, conscious or unconscious, of these two ideas the Eucharist was thought to represent mainly the Death of Christ. There must be something in it which "should congruously represent the blow of the sacrificial knife," [2] and this was found in the *separate* consecration of Bread and Wine, whereby "with bloodless cutting thou dividest the Body and Blood of the Lord, using thy voice as a sword." [3] "Thus we have the picture of the Cross of Calvary, and the very act that makes the picture constitutes the reality of the Sacrifice." [4] But apart from the question of what was intended by the interval between the blessing of the Bread and of the Cup at the Last Supper—whether it was merely occasioned by the ceremonial order of the Passover, or implied a difference in the underlying gifts [5] or a "bloodless cutting" (but what evidence can be offered for this last ?)—it is

---

[1] Bishop Hedley (Roman Catholic Bishop of Newport) describes this as a part of the definition of Sacrifice accepted by Catholic theologians ("The Holy Eucharist," p. 151). He says, however (p. 160), "Some modern theologians have entirely discarded from the notion of Sacrifice all idea of destruction."

[2] Hedley, p. 164.

[3] Gregory Nazianzen, Epistle 171, addressed to Amphilochius, Bishop of Iconium.

[4] Hedley, p. 165.

[5] See p. 164 note.

difficult to see how this view can really escape the charge of attempting to " repeat " (to " *re*-present " rather than " represent ") the Death on the Cross. To speak of it as " mystical " or " sacramental " does not remove the difficulty. The other conception seems not only truer to the Gospel teaching but free from this difficulty. The Heavenly presentation and its counterpart, the Eucharistic Offering, both alike look back to Calvary, and rely entirely on the Cross for their reality and their saving power. This view is also represented—although not nearly so generally as the other—in modern Roman Catholic theology.[1]

(*B*) Our interpretation puts aside entirely any possibility of competition between the Cross and the Eucharistic Sacrifice. They are in no sense rivals— both belong to the One Sacrifice. To distinguish between the Cross as the propitiation for original sin and the Eucharist for actual sins becomes impossible. In what sense then, if any, can we say the Eucharist is a " propitiatory Offering " ? The Council of Trent (Session XXII, Chapter 2) speaks of it as " *vere propitiatorium.*" Our Prayer of Humble Access says of the *Communion* " that our bodies may be made clean by His Body and our souls washed through His most Precious Blood." In the Prayer of Oblation the same thought is closely linked with the Sacrifice : " accept this our Sacrifice of praise and thanksgiving ; that by the merits and death of Thy Son Our Lord Jesus Christ, and through faith in His Blood, we and all Thy Whole Church may obtain remission of our sins and all other benefits of His Passion." The

---

[1] Hedley, p. 166.

Sacrifice of our Lord's Death and His Heavenly Offering is alone truly propitiatory. If the only Sacrifice in the Eucharist were that of " ourselves, our souls and bodies " it could at most be a dedicatory Burnt Offering resting upon the Lord's Sin Offering. But there is no offering of ourselves apart from Him and His Offering ; and in this way the Eucharist is bound up with Calvary and the Heavenly High Priest's work, and we may therefore, without any separation of the two, and consequently without any disparagement of the Cross, look upon the Eucharistic Offering as " propitiatory." It is, of course, in no sense our share in it which makes it such, but only the fact that it enters into and belongs to the One Offering. By it we have " communion with the Atonement." [1]

.   .   .   .   .

Our vision of the One Sacrifice now lies spread before us. At its root is the Eternal Divine Love of the Son to the Father before the foundation of the world. By the Incarnation that Love sought and found its expression in the dedicated will of Man to God. " Lo, I come to do Thy Will." Worked out under the conditions brought into the world by Sin, the fulfilment of this obedience involved for the Sinless Son of Man the necessity of Sacrifice, Suffering, and Death. This was completed on Calvary. There the Offerer accomplished the perfect offering of Himself by laying down His Life in Death, by shedding His Blood. Then that Life rose again from Death, and the Priest in the Heavenly Temple offers it upon the

[1] See R. C. Moberly, " Journal of Theological Studies," April, 1901.

Heavenly Altar and "makes atonement" for the sins of men. But also, He Who already as Victim and as Offerer and as Priest represents the redeemed mankind, draws His Church into still closer Union with Himself by the Sacrament of His Body and His Blood, so that She dwelling in Him and He in Her may grow up into the fullness of His Manhood and form His congregation in the Heavenly Temple to offer Him and Herself in Him to God. The Life and Death of Jesus, His Heavenly Offering and its earthly parallel the Eucharistic Offering of Him and of ourselves, mankind and man's High Priest made one in all this—there the long history of Sacrifice all over the world and all down the ages is brought to its climax and perfection. Oh, the depth of the riches both of the wisdom and the knowledge of God ! how unsearchable are His judgments and His ways past tracing out . . . To Him be the glory for ever. Amen.

INDEX

(See also Index of Contents)

Aaronic Priesthood (of our Lord), 148ff.
Altar of Incense, 31, 115
(the Heavenly), 166.
Amos *v. 21–25*, 5
Anamnesis, 129, 163f.
Ara Crucis, 146, 166
arak, 77
Asam, 44
Atonement, 33, 115
and cleansing, 94
Augustine, St., 158, 169
Azazel, 95f.
azkarah, 26f., 29, 163

Blood :
as food, 14, 39, 69, 124, 164
meaning of, 68f., 108
of Jesus, 144ff.
use of, 67ff., 109
Burning, symbolism of, 80

Chrysostom, St., 6
Cleansing by blood, 70
Commensality, 20, 38, 69
Communion theory of Sacrifice, 13
Comparative Religion, 6, 54
Consecration, 39, 49f., 65
by blood, 71
I Cor. *x. 14–21*, 167 ; *xv. 17*, 145
Corban, 15, 23
Covenant Sacrifice, 14, 26, 39
73f.
and the Day of Atonement, 73, 84

Day of Atonement, 71
Death essential to Sacrifice, 116f., 141–143

" Do this," meaning of, 163
Drink Offerings, 28f.

Enoch, Book of, 98
Exodus *xxiv. 1–11*, 14, 162
Ezekiel, legislation of, 10, 45
47, 77, 83

Fat, as food, 79
Fire, symbolism of, 80
Fire-Offering, 81
Freewill Offering, 37

Gift theory of Sacrifice, 12f.
16ff.
Gregory Nazianzen, St., 173

Heathen Sacrifices, 12, 19, 69, 120
Heave-thigh, 37
Hebrews, Epistle to the, *i. 3*,
155 ; *v. 1–10*, 150, 153 ;
vi. 20, 150 ; *vii. 11–14*, 148 ;
vii. 25, 156 ; *vii. 27*, 155 ;
viii. 1–3, 150 ; *ix.*, 133,
151ff. ; *ix. 13, 14* ; *ix. 19–21*,
73 ; *ix. 22*, 141 ; *ix. 24*, 152,
156 ; *ix. 25*, 152 ; *x. 5–10*,
133 ; *x. 6*, 126 ; *x. 12–14*,
155 ; *x. 22*, 14 ; *x. 19–25*,
159 ; *xii. 24*, 14, 68 ; *xiii.
10*, 78 ; *xiii. 10–16*, 158,
159, 165
High Place, 75
hiqrib, 62, 114
hiqtir, 79
Horns of Altar, 75f.
human sacrifice, 17, 138

Incense, 26f., 31, 89
Inspiration of the Law, 3f.
Intercession and Offering, 153

177

Irenæus, St., 166
Isaiah *i. 11.* 5 ; *ii. 2–4,* 5 ; *liii.,* 120 ; *liii. 10,* 46.

Jeremiah *vi. 20,* 5 ; *vii. 21–22,* 5 ; *xvii. 36,* 5 ; *xxxi. 14,* 5
Jesus Christ : attitude to the Sacrifices, 6f.
John, St., *vi.,* 14 ; *x. 17, 18,* 137f.
Josephus, 93
Justification by faith, 168f.

kalil, 42
kipper, 91, 100ff.

Leviticus *xvii. 11,* 3, 108f.

Maimonides, 107
Melchizedekian Priesthood, 139, 147, 150
Mercy Seat (*kapporeth*), 76, 87, 91f.
Micah *iv. 1–3,* 5 ; *vi. 6–8,* 5
minḥah, 15, 23ff.
Mishna, 93, 98
mizbeaḥ, 66f., 77

New Covenant 162

Odour of a sweet smell, 80f., 124
Offerer, importance of, 61, 137, 149
Offering, cleansing, and consecration, 113
olah, 42
One Offering, the, 125, 134f., 153f., 168f.
Origen, 166

Passover, 40, 161
Philippians, *ii. 8,* 137
Philo, 18, 21f.
poena vicaria, theory of, 104ff.
" pouring " (of the blood), 70, 72
Priesthood of our Lord, 139, 145ff.

Prophets and the Sacrifices, 4–6, 48
Psalm *xl.,* 3, 5, 6, 18 ; *l.,* 3, 5, 18 ; *li.,* 5 ; *cxviii. 27,* 66
" Putting " (of the blood), 74

qetoreth, 79

Revelation *i. 5,* 14 ; *v. 6,* 152, 156 ; *vii. 14,* 14
Romans *xii. 1,* 42

Sacrifice :
  and Offering, 2, 154f.
  definition of, 2
  of praise and thanksgiving, 37, 168
  within the Godhead, 134
Salt, symbolism of, 25f.
samak, 62
1 Samuel *xvi. 2,* 5
2 Samuel *xxiv. 24,* 21
saraph, 80, 82
Scapegoat, 63f., 95–98, 105
shaḥat, 64
Shechinah, 76, 87, 91f., 152
" Shedding " of blood, 162
Shelamim, 35ff.
Shewbread, 30
Sin, idea of, in the Law, 56f.
" Sprinkling " of blood, 70, 72, 74, 86, 89ff., 110

Table of the Lord, 71, 78, 167
  of Shewbread, 67, 78
Thank-Offering, 37
Trent, Council of, 174

Union with Christ, 133ff.

Vicariousness in Sacrifice, 118ff., 131ff., 139ff.
Votive Offering, 37

Wave-breast, 37

zaraq, 72
zebaḥ, 23, 32ff., 64

Printed in Great Britain by
Butler & Tanner Ltd.,
Frome and London